Criminal Incapacitation

THE PLENUM SERIES IN CRIME AND JUSTICE

Series Editors:
James Alan Fox, *Northeastern University, Boston, Massachusetts*
Joseph Weis, *University of Washington, Seattle, Washington*

CRIMINAL INCAPACITATION
William Spelman

DELINQUENCY CAREERS IN TWO BIRTH COHORTS
Paul E. Tracy, Marvin E. Wolfgang, and Robert M. Figlio

RACE AND THE JURY: Racial Disenfranchisement and the Search for Justice
Hiroshi Fukurai, Edgar W. Butler, and Richard Krooth

RAPE LAW REFORM: A Grassroots Revolution and Its Impact
Cassia Spohn and Julie Horney

Criminal Incapacitation

William Spelman
Lyndon B. Johnson School of Public Affairs
University of Texas
Austin, Texas

Plenum Press • *New York and London*

Library of Congress Cataloging-in-Publication Data

Spelman, William.
    Criminal incapacitation / William Spelman.
        p.   cm. -- (The Plenum series in crime and justice)
    Includes bibliographical references and index.
    ISBN 0-306-44383-X
    1. Imprisonment. 2. Recidivism. 3. Criminal behavior.
I. Title. II. Series.
HV9275.S58 1993
364.3--dc20   93-37217
                                                                    CIP

ISBN 0-306-44383-X

© 1994 Plenum Press, New York
A Division of Plenum Publishing Corporation
233 Spring Street, New York, N.Y. 10013

Printed in the United States of America

Preface

There is nothing uglier than a catfish. With its scaleless, eel-like body, flat, semicircular head, and cartilaginous whiskers, it looks almost entirely unlike a cat. The toothless, sluggish beasts can be found on the bottom of warm streams and lakes, living on scum and detritus. Such a diet is healthier than it sounds: divers in the Ohio River regularly report sighting catfish the size of small whales, and cats in the Mekong River in Southeast Asia often weigh nearly 700 pounds.

Ugly or not, the catfish is good to eat. Deep-fried catfish is a Southern staple; more ambitious recipes add Parmesan cheese, bacon drippings and paprika, or Amontillado. Catfish is also good for you. One pound of channel catfish provides nearly all the protein but only half the calories and fat of 1 pound of solid white albacore tuna. Catfish is a particularly good source of alpha-tocopherol and B vitamins. Because they are both nutritious and tasty, cats are America's biggest aquaculture product.

Incapacitation is the channel catfish of crime policy. In a world in which we value elegant solutions to thorny problems, mere imprisonment stands out as ill-bred and underdressed. And when incapacitation is combined with prediction, even the heartiest eaters scan the menu for an alternative. Some observers have made a cottage industry out of identifying the internal inconsistencies, potential injustices, and sheer gaucherie of selective activities. Predictive scales are of "low validity" and bring with them "unjustified risks of abuse." A review of the criminological literature (but not of estimates of the utility or equity of selective policies) finds that

> the evidence is clear that the career criminal idea is not sufficiently substantial to command more than a small portion of the time and effort of the criminal justice practitioner or academic community. (Gottfredson & Hirschi, 1986, p. 231)

Such terms as *low validity*, *unjustified risks*, and *sufficient substance* are rarely defined.

No one wants to eat ugly food. But when there are limited sources of nutrition, appearances seem less important. Can a steady diet of prison construction be toxic? What is the nutritional value of predicting criminality? That's what this book is all about.

This is a complex issue. As I show in the text, many of the potential costs and benefits are difficult to measure or even to describe. So this work is at best a partial analysis of some of the easier questions. But it all proceeds from the position that utility is the most appropriate guide to public decision making, and careful examination of consequences has been noticeably absent where this issue is concerned.

No one writes so many pages without help, and I am grateful to my friends and colleagues for assisting me whenever they could. John Eck was always available to apply good sense to the wildest of ideas and to contribute other ideas even wilder. William Bieck, William Gay, Kai Martensen, Susan Martin, Edward Spurlock, Stephen Pilkington, and Thomas Sweeney all contributed greatly to my thinking on the effectiveness and structure of selective police programs; Brian Forst, Peter Hoffman, and Joan Jacoby provided equally valuable contributions to my thinking on selective prosecution and sentencing programs. I am embarrassed to note that it took 3 years of intermittent haranguing before I took seriously Mark Kleiman's comments on the importance of deterrence; he and Philip Cook showed me that deterrence could be reasonably included in the effectiveness estimates, and their suggestions have improved this document considerably.

Alfred Blumstein, Jan and Marcia Chaiken, Kim English, Andrew von Hirsch, Julie Horney, Albert J. Reiss, Jr., and Barbara Salert all provided valuable data or pointed me to sources of information that proved vital to my understanding. David Geiger provided computational assistance at a time when it was badly needed. Barbara Jann typed the tables, and Jon Hockenyos and Glen Hartnett produced fine graphs on deadline. The primary data set analyzed in this report was collected by the Rand Corporation, under the supervision of Mark Peterson, Jan Chaiken, and Patricia Ebener. Their data were made available by the Inter-university Consortium for Political and Social Research.

This work was funded in part by grants from the National Institute of Justice, U.S. Department of Justice, and the Elspeth Rostow Centennial Fellowship, University of Texas at Austin.

Much of the substance and most of the thinking processes in this book result from Mark H. Moore's end of our discussions over the last 10 years. Had he not exhibited good sense, humor, and patience in the face of my wildest flights—some of fancy, others in airplanes—this work could simply not have been completed. James Q. Wilson, in urging me to completely rethink the policy implications, gave me the best single piece of advice I received in 4 years of writing. Herman B. Leonard simplified my sometimes Byzantine logic. Were Joel Garner, my project monitor at the National Institute of Justice, any more patient and helpful, he would be eligible for canonization. But perhaps I sell him short.

My wife, Nancy La Vigne, was by turns whip, wheedler, and safe harbor during the last stages of writing. Without her good counsel and support, I would doubtless still be making marginal "improvements" well beyond the limits of cognition.

As always, none of the good people or fine organizations cited above may be blamed for the remaining faults and errors of analysis and interpretation. These are all mine. If experience is the name one gives to one's mistakes, in writing this I have no doubt become rich in experience beyond my imagination!

Contents

1. *Introduction* *1*

An Economic Model of Incapacitation 2
The Importance of Effectiveness 10
Estimating the Effectiveness of Incapacitation Policies 12

2. *Validity* *21*

Weighting the Rand Sample 22
The Validity of Offense Rate Estimates 42

3. *The Offense Rate* *55*

Defining the Offense Rate 56
The Average Value of λ 69
The Distribution of λ 79
Offender Specialization 100
Mathematical Models of Offense Rates 109

4. *The Criminal Career* *125*

Defining the Criminal Career 126
The Length of the Average Criminal Career 129
The Distribution of *T* among Offenders 141

5. *Production of Arrests* *167*

Average Probability of Arrest 167
Differences among Offenders 172

6. *Collective Incapacitation* *197*

Modeling the Effectiveness of the Present System 198
Limitations of the Effectiveness of Incapacitation 211
Effectiveness of the Current System 216

7.   *Selective Incapacitation* 229

   Defining Selective Policies 230
   The Effectiveness of Selective Policies 248
   Changing the Length of Jail and Prison Sentences 248
   Changing the Risks of Incarceration 265
   Changing both Risks and Sentences 286

8.   *Conclusions* 289

   Heterogeneous Criminal Justice System 290
   Effect on Offender Population Characteristics 292
   Intermediate Sanctions and Partial Incapacitation 304
   Policy Prescription 311

References *313*

Index *325*

1

Introduction

SPRINGFIELD, MASSACHUSETTS—When Hampden County ran out of jail space, Sheriff Michael J. Ashe, Jr. seized the local National Guard armory to handle the overflow. Nine months later, the state turned down his request for $450,000 to continue the operation, and the inmates were released.

ALBANY, NEW YORK—At their graduation from the New York Correctional Academy, 154 rookie prison guards were informed that they would be laid off in six weeks. Due to the state's budget deficit, almost 3,000 guards lost their jobs—even though the number of prisoners increased by 7 percent.

AUSTIN, TEXAS—Despite a $4.8 billion deficit, the Texas State Senate voted to spend $1.1 billion more to build 30,000 new prison beds. A move to create additional alternatives to prison was dismissed as "a public relations disaster." Meanwhile, fear of crime and sales of burglar alarms and guns rose sharply in Houston after the Harris County Sheriff released 150 inmates to relieve jail overcrowding.

The number of Americans in prison more than doubled in the 1980s, and continues to expand today. Some 740,000 Americans are in prisons, and another 200,000 are in county jails serving felony sentences (Beck, 1991; Cohen, 1991). Often the use of imprisonment has exceeded the capacity: According to 1990 Department of Justice statistics, 32 of the 50 states were imprisoning more offenders than their prisons were designed to hold. The federal system was 51 percent above designed capacity. Still, legislators face considerable public pressure to expand the use of imprisonment. According to public opinion polls, 84 percent of Americans felt the courts were too lenient with convicted offenders; only 3 percent felt the courts were too harsh. Identical figures were reported in 1977—460,000 prison cells ago (Flanagan & Maguire, 1990, pp. 160–161, 583).

Many members of the criminal justice community feel the same pressures. Efforts to rehabilitate and deter offenders, and to reform the society that produces them, have come and gone without apparent effect. But incapacitation—putting criminals behind bars, where they cannot get at the rest of us—seems certain to work, at least temporarily. Will incapacitation strategies be effective enough to merit the costs?

In part as a means of cutting costs, some states have experimented with selective approaches. Criminal justice professionals have long known that a few, especially frequent and serious offenders commit a lot of crimes; by reserving scarce jail and prison space for the most dangerous—and perhaps devoting extra police and prosecution attention to them, as well—some believed we could cut the crime rate at no extra charge. On the other hand, research showed that the frequent and serious offenders looked a lot like the others, and predictions of future dangerousness were often wrong. This ethical dilemma had a practical corollary: If the predictions were wrong often enough, selective incapacitation could do more harm than good. Are selective incapacitation policies a practical solution or a mistake?

To answer these questions, quantitative information about the careers of criminals and the operation of the criminal justice system is needed. In this book, I examine what is known about criminal careers—how long they last, how often offenders commit crimes, how often they get caught—and use the available information to estimate the likely effectiveness of prison expansion and of selective police, prosecution, and judicial policies. Because much of this information is uncertain (after all, offenders go to some trouble to keep their activities a secret), the focus is on setting reasonable limits on the effectiveness of these policies, rather than on making single point estimates.

Criminal careers and incapacitation policies are examined in detail in Chapters 2 through 7. Before turning to the details, however, let us first step back and consider the question of selective criminal justice policies from a broader perspective. In the next section, an economic model of crime control through incapacitation is developed. This model provides the basic framework for considering the benefits and costs of competing policies.

An Economic Model of Incapacitation

The social tradeoff between crime and crime control, like many such tradeoffs, can be considered to consist of two parts: a utility or cost function and a production function. Simply put, the production function tells us what is available, and the cost function tells us how to choose among available alternatives. Consider the cost function first.

The Costs of Crime and Crime Control

Crime is bad news. Victims are sometimes injured. They often suffer financial losses. When they attempt to cooperate with the authorities, they are often inconvenienced. Many crimes involve the use or threat of force, and the victims are understandably anxious about what happened, what could have happened, and what their experience tells them about what may happen in the future. Perhaps most important, bad news travels fast—through the news media, in popular fiction, and most devastatingly, through word of mouth. Many Americans, whether victims or not, are uneasy about their prospects of surviving attacks on their person and property, to the point that crime is usually ranked in public opinion polls as one of the most serious social problems with which the government must deal (Farah & Vale, 1985; Ladd, 1988). To calm our fears, we spend millions of dollars each year on insurance and self-protection devices and organizations; many of us avoid activities we enjoy because we are afraid of victimization.

The primary governmental response to crime—the criminal justice system—is also bad in an important sense. Police, prosecutors, courts, jails, and prisons all cost enormous amounts of money. Some $50 billion is spent on the system each year; this is about 3 percent of all government expenditures, and about 8 percent of state and local government expenditures (Lindgren, 1988). Add in the construction costs of jails, prisons, and office buildings, the loss to society of the (perhaps scant and sporadic) positive contributions of incarcerated offenders, and the economic and psychological costs of incarceration on the dependents of offenders and the communities in which they live, and the costs of crime control grow even larger.

Of course, there are good reasons for spending so much money on the criminal justice system. By providing for police, judges, prisons, and the like, we may buy ourselves a measure of security. Providing the money is well spent, it is reasonable to suspect that the more we spend on crime control, the lower the incidence of crime. And expenditures on crime control make us feel better, too: The thought that justice is done, if less swiftly and efficiently than we might like, salves the wounds created by criminal acts.

Schematically, the tradeoff between crime and the criminal justice system might be portrayed as in Figure 1.1. The costs of crime and the expenses of the

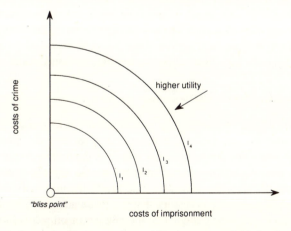

FIGURE 1.1. The best tradeoff between crime and imprisonment probably involves some of each.

criminal justice system are both economic *bads*, and the best situation—the "bliss point"—is the case where there is no crime, and no need for crime control. In making decisions as to how much to spend on crime control and justice, society must trade off between these two *bads*. The social utility of any given tradeoff may be represented by a series of indifference curves, designated I_1, I_2, and so on (Hicks, 1946). The highest valued curves are those closest to the bliss point.

This tradeoff is constrained by what it is possible for the criminal justice system to produce. Consider next how the system reduces the incidence and seriousness of crime.

The Production of Crime Control

The criminal justice system controls crime in several ways. By maintaining a threat of punishment for those who commit crimes, it may deter potential offenders from committing criminal acts in the first place. Alternatively, offenders who have been punished may be deterred by the threat of being punished again. If deterrence is unsuccessful, the system may rehabilitate offenders once they have been caught. And if rehabilitation is unsuccessful, the system can put convicted offenders in jails and prisons where they are unable to harm the rest of us. That is, incarcerated offenders are incapacitated.

Assume for the moment that offenders are only incapacitated while they are serving terms in jail or prison. More dramatic or innovative methods—electrocution or electronic monitoring, for instance—will be put aside for now. The more offenders who are serving time in jails or prisons, the fewer there will be out on the street, and the lower will be the crime rate. Thus the criminal justice system produces crime control according to a schedule—a "production possibilities frontier"—similar in form to that shown in Figure 1.2. Society may trade off between the number of offenders in jail or prison on the one hand, and the number of crimes committed by those at large on the other. A rational society with perfect information will choose Point A, corresponding to that available tradeoff between the two that puts it on its highest valued indifference curve.

Production under Perfect Information

What should this production function look like? It will surely be downward sloping, because the criminal justice system rarely incarcerates innocent people, and guilty offenders are likely to commit crimes in the future. So the more money spent on incarceration, the less crime there should be. Of course, there are infinitely many possible downward-sloping functions; to specify the production function more exactly, it is necessary that we make additional assumptions.

One convenient assumption is that the number of offenders in jail or prison

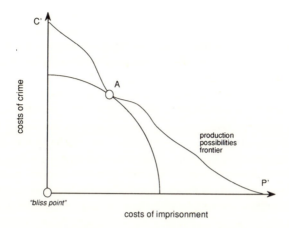

FIGURE 1.2. The production possibilities frontier is the best available set of crime/prison tradeoffs.

does not affect the total number of active offenders, including both those in jail and prison and those out on the street. That is, the size of the criminal population is set by circumstances beyond the control of the criminal justice system; we may choose to keep some criminals in jail or leave them out on the street, but in so doing we do not cause noncriminals to enter the criminal population, and we do not cause these or any other criminals to leave the population. A second convenient assumption is a corollary to the first: By incapacitating or failing to incapacitate any given offender, we do not affect the number and serious-ness of the crimes that offender would have committed, had he or she been free. More simply, the criminal justice system is deterring and rehabilitating no one.

If this were true, then it would be possible in theory to spend nothing on crime control and suffer a given, maximum number of crimes. It would also be possible to spend some finite amount on crime control, lock up all active of-fenders, and suffer no crimes at all. Thus our production possibilities frontier may be anchored on both the vertical and horizontal axes. The anchors are marked C' and P' on Figure 1.2.

This assumption is obviously untenable at the extremes. For example, if there were no punishment at all, many would be tempted to lie, cheat, and steal; if the likelihood of punishment were nearly certain, it is probable that few would remain criminals for long. More generally, it is very likely that some offenders are deterred by current threats of punishment, and that others are rehabilitated as a result of diversion, pretrial intervention, and similar programs (Cook, 1980; Gendreau & Ross, 1979). Nevertheless, the effectiveness of these strategies is in dispute, and at the margin it does not seem unreasonable to suppose that the effects of deterrence and rehabilitation will be small enough to discount. We will consider deterrence and rehabilitation in more detail in Chapter 8.

Between these two anchors there are still an endless variety of feasible production frontiers. To help specify the shape of the correct frontier, let us consider the notion of the benefit/cost ratio.

From the standpoint of the criminal justice system, the costs of incapacitating offenders are those associated with maintaining the jail or prison in which they are held—guards, food, utilities, administration, and so on. We may wish to hold some offenders in more expensive cells than others: Dangerous offenders merit higher security, for example. Still, let us assume for simplicity that the costs of incarcerating each offender per unit of time are about the same.

Not so for the benefits of incarceration. The benefit is the number of crimes that are not committed because the offender is in jail or prison and thus prevented from committing them. All offenders are not alike: Some commit crimes in which the victims are hurt particularly severely; some commit crimes that inspire particularly oppressive fears among the general population; some just commit crimes more often than others. And incapacitation of the most serious, fear-provoking, and frequent offenders will reduce the costs of crime by more than incapacitation of offenders chosen at random from the offending population. So the benefit/cost ratios associated with incarceration of each offender will differ; if we can identify the most dangerous offenders—those with the largest ratios—we would naturally like to be certain they were the first to be jailed.

In a world of perfect information, the optimal policy might work something like this. A central decision maker collects all the information about the future activities of criminal offenders. The decision maker then assigns a numerical benefit/cost ratio to each offender, corresponding to the frequency and severity of the criminal acts this offender will commit over the next decision period—say, 6 months. He or she then rearranges the list, ordering the offenders from most dangerous to least dangerous. The most dangerous offenders—those for whom the benefit/cost ratio is sufficiently large to merit incarceration—go to jail or prison. The others are left free, presumably to continue their criminal careers. By only incapacitating the most frequent and dangerous on the list, the decision maker can get to a point on the highest valued indifference curve.

The optimal policy resulting from such a utopian policy can be summarized in Figure 1.3. Note that the production possibilities frontier is concave, or "inward sloping." Due to heterogeneity in benefit/cost ratios among offenders, the number of crimes has been reduced substantially (here, 50 percent) by incarcerating only a small proportion of the offenders (here, 10 percent). It is easy to see that, the more heterogeneity in benefit/cost ratios among offenders, the more beneficial incapacitative actions of the criminal justice system are liable to be: The frontier will be more concave, and the points on it will lie closer to the bliss point.

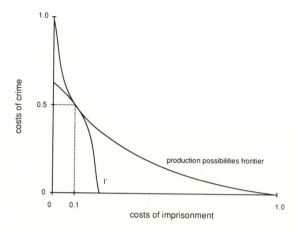

FIGURE 1.3. Optimal incapacitation policy given perfect information.

Production under Imperfect Information

The perfect information allocation sets a standard by which we may compare true allocations. But it is obviously impossible, because the information available is by no means perfect. There are several sources of uncertainty.

First, it is uncertain who the most dangerous offenders have been, much less who the most dangerous offenders will be. Arrest and conviction records, drug and employment histories, and informant reports all provide valuable clues as to the dangerousness of active criminals. But these data are themselves often unreliable, and the picture they give of any given offender's past activities may well be incorrect.

Even if our data as to the recent criminal activities of individuals were perfect, the crime control effectiveness of incapacitation depends upon future, not past activities. It seems reasonable to suspect that the recent past will be highly correlated with the short-term future; but unless the correlation is perfect, some information will be lost. And our reasonable suspicion is little more than that: Little is known about changes in an individual's degree of dangerousness over time.

Third, note that we can only collect information about the present or future activities of individuals by keeping them out of jail for a time, and observing their activities. Now changes in dangerousness become particularly critical: If the typical frequent offender is only very frequent for a short section of his or her criminal career, or if criminal careers are themselves short, then it may be that we are unable to gather enough information about the frequency of offenders until they are no longer committing serious crimes at high rates. In the limiting case, it is conceivable that dangerous offenders stop being dangerous at just about the point that we recognize who they are. Thus selectively incapacitating those offenders who appear to have been most dangerous may be even less beneficial than incapacitating offenders at random.

No matter how good our information as to past, present, or future criminal activities, as a practical matter we cannot imprison people just because we have a moral certainty that they are prisonworthy. Perhaps in part because our information is unreliable, each offender must be implicated in one or more past offenses, charged with committing them, and convicted before being sentenced to jail or prison. Many crimes are not solved, many solved cases will not stand up in court, and the adjudication process is slow. So even if it takes little time to establish that a given offender is dangerous, it will typically be months or years before we can do something about it. Even when we have grounds for imprisoning offenders, we may not have grounds for imprisoning them for very long if the crime is minor.

These are sources of uncertainty about the criminal population. There is also considerable uncertainty as to the indifference function. The cost of any crime is the harm done to the victims, plus the harm to nonvictims who insure, avoid, self-protect, or merely worry as a result. If we could predict all the crimes an offender would commit, we could probably estimate the direct costs of incarcerating that offender (Cavanagh, 1990), and the direct benefits of preventing these crimes (Cohen, 1988). But the indirect benefits and costs are difficult to estimate. It is uncertain the degree to which insurance, avoidance, and other reactions to crime depend on objective crime rates and subjective factors that would not be affected by reductions in crime (DuBow, McCabe, & Kaplan, 1979). And little is known about the effects on the economic and social life of a community of incarcerating a large proportion of its members, even though many urban neighborhoods fit this description (Silberman, 1977). So we cannot even be sure as to the slope of the indifference curve.

All this means that the production possibilities frontier facing the real criminal justice system is less favorable than it would be, were perfect information available: We lose benefits in direct proportion to our inability to collect and use the data we need. Similarly, our inability to evaluate the benefits and costs of different points on the frontier reduces our ability to choose intelligently among different levels of crime control. In the limiting case, it may be that the data are so unreliable, the benefit/cost ratios are so mutable, the opportunities to use what little information is available are so infrequent, and the indirect effects of incapacitation so uncertain, that it is hardly worth the trouble to use this information at all.

This seems to be the (implicit) position of the present criminal justice system. Some police departments have adopted programs aimed at increasing the risks of apprehension to the most dangerous offenders; some prosecutors have adopted procedures that increase the likelihood of conviction and the seriousness of the conviction charge for dangerous offenders; some courts and correctional systems have instituted changes in incarceration policies aimed at holding the worst offenders for longer periods. Some have advocated that prison-construction decisions be made on the basis of benefit/cost calculations, rather than (sometimes slippery) philosophical arguments. But, by and large, the present system makes decisions on the basis of justice (and politics) rather than economics. Characteristics of the offense in question are far more important to the present system than the apparent characteristics of the offender (see, for example, Eck & Spelman, 1987; Green, 1961; Institute for Law and Social Research, 1977). Politicians cite a few, egregious cases when they argue for additional prison beds (e.g., Abell, 1989). So the present criminal justice system is probably not working on the highest-valued production possibilities frontier. For example, by using offender information more effectively, we could obtain any point in the shaded region of Figure 1.4.

If the criminal justice system systematically took benefits and costs into account in decision making, it could presumably achieve a better tradeoff. That is, it could either reduce the number of people in jail, or reduce the number of crimes committed, or both. In attempting to do this, two classes of policy handles are available:

> *Resource levels.* How many jail and prison beds are enough? What proportion of offenders should be imprisoned for their actions? Proposals to reduce crime by increasing the number of jail and prison beds are often referred to as *collective incapacitation.*

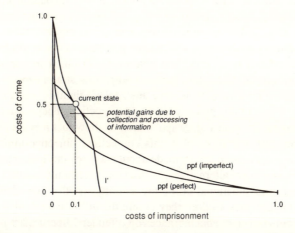

FIGURE 1.4. Better information allows reductions in crime and prison costs.

Resource allocation. No matter how many jail and prison beds are available, they are a scarce resource that may be allocated among the stock of convicted offenders in a variety of ways. Which ways are the most effective in reducing crime? Should a few offenders get very long prison sentences, or should many offenders get short sentences, or what? Does the nature of the most effective policy depend upon the nature of the criminal population? Because crime control strategies that focus on resource allocation involve selecting some offenders for special attention, this class of policy handles is usually referred to as *selective incapacitation.*

The effectiveness of collective and selective incapacitation policies is considered in Chapters 6 and 7. The analysis shows that, for most states and for the nation as a whole, substantial changes in current policies will produce consistently better tradeoffs between crime rates and criminal justice resources.

The Importance of Effectiveness

Should they prove more effective at reducing crime, there are few political or legal hurdles to incapacitation policies. There is much public support for "perpetrator-oriented police patrols" and "career criminal prosecution programs," and for increases in both the likelihood and length of prison sentences ("Public Backs," 1982; "Gallup Crime Audit," 1982; Gallup, 1989). Increases in the number of jail and prison beds are well within the authority of state and local legislatures, and new jail and prison cells are quickly filled: In 1990, only 2 of the 50 states were at less than 90 percent of designed prison capacity (Cohen, 1991). The strict legality of selective police, prosecution, and judicial actions is beyond dispute (Moore, 1986).

Still, the question of effectiveness seems less important than the moral and social questions posed by incapacitative policies. Many civil libertarians agree that crime control is an important goal of the criminal justice system—in the language of constitutional law, it is a "compelling state interest"—but maintain that the system's activities to achieve this goal are tightly constrained by constitutional guarantees of due process and equal protection. They would put the burden of proof on the advocates of incapacitation to show that it is the "least restrictive alternative" that will accomplish this compelling objective (*Shelton v. Tucker,* 1960). Thus no decision can be made about (say) selective incapacitation policies unless less-restrictive alternatives, such as categorical incapacitation, community corrections, and situational crime prevention, are also considered. In the language of the previous section, they accept the utilitarian calculus of cost/benefit analysis, but argue that encumbrances on offenders' liberties are important costs, and that an assessment of the alternatives is critical to making an ethical choice.

Incapacitation policies have also been attacked by desert theorists, or retributivists, who take issue with the utilitarian calculus itself. They maintain that the principal goal of the criminal justice system is to do justice in individual cases, to right the wrong created by each crime (Fletcher, 1982; von Hirsch, 1985). When abstract notions such as crime control guide the operations of the criminal justice system, we treat individual offenders as means toward an end, rather than as ends in themselves—and this is fundamentally wrong (von Hirsch, 1985). One might expect that for such critics as these, the effectiveness of incapacitation policies would be unpersuasive, if not irrelevant. Why examine crime control at all in the face of these ethical objections?

One answer, only partly flippant, is that the civil libertarians and desert theorists are simply outnumbered. For most criminal justice policymakers—and for the vast majority of citizens—crime control is the fundamental issue. If utilitarian decisions are to be made, at least they should be made on the basis of the best available information.

A second answer is that crime control effectiveness is a necessary but not sufficient condition for adoption of incapacitation policies. For example, if selective sentencing can reduce the crime rate by 20 percent, or if each dollar spent on prisons prevents $17 in costs to victims and others, then these policies may be appropriate. Depending upon the importance of the ethical objections, they may not. But if incapacitation policies simply do not work, there is no justification for them whatever, and we need not even consider the ethical arguments. Starting with effectiveness may save us time.

Thoroughgoing retributivists, such as Andrew von Hirsch (1976, 1985) or George Fletcher (1982), will remain unpersuaded by the selective sentencing analysis (Chapter 7). But even the strictest of retributivists leave some room for utilitarian decision making in setting the total amount of punishment delivered (e.g., von Hirsch, 1985, pp. 92–101), and selective criminal justice policies are not limited to selective punishment decisions. Courts, prosecutors, police, and even agencies outside the traditional criminal justice system may all allocate their resources on a selective basis. Most of the actions taken by these agencies do not (at least directly) result in punishment of the offender. Instead, they amount to application of more surveillance, better case development, or a more strenuous prosecution, all of which would presumably be applied to all offenders, if more resources were available. As Moore and others (1984) have put it, "there is no constitutional right . . . to the relatively superficial prosecutions typical of today's overwhelmed criminal justice system" (p. 142).

Finally, an incomplete analysis is better than no analysis at all. The civil libertarian may argue that it is not enough to show that (for example) we may reduce the crime rate by 1.0 percent by spending an additional $1.2 billion per year in prison construction and operations. The human costs of imprisonment and the alternatives must be considered, as well. Still, our benefit/cost calculations will be persuasive as far as they go. If they do not go far enough, that is only because another book needs to be written.

Estimating the Effectiveness of Incapacitation Policies

There are several methods available to estimate the effects of incapacitation policies on crime. The most celebrated of these is the analytical model developed by Avi-Itzhak and Shinnar (1973), but other analytical models (Van Dine, Conrad, & Dinitz, 1979) and simulation models (Spelman, 1983) have been used. The models rely on different assumptions, and each is useful for different purposes. But all rely on a common base of data, and the data available are not precise enough at present to estimate the effects of incapacitation policies with any accuracy. To see why, let us examine two of the best-known applications of the Avi-Itzhak and Shinnar model—Edwin Zedlewski's *Making Confinement Decisions* (1987) and Peter Greenwood's *Selective Incapacitation* (1982).

The Need for Reanalysis

As with all analytical models, the Avi-Itzhak and Shinnar model requires that some assumptions be made about the characteristics of the system modeled. Because relatively little is known about the nature of the offending population, these assumptions are especially critical; small and plausible changes in a few basic parameters can dramatically affect the final result. To illustrate, let us consider two parameters that are particularly important: the average frequency of crime commission among active offenders and the length of the typical criminal "career."

Previous researchers have obtained very different estimates of the average offense rate among active offenders, usually termed *lambda*, or λ. Once the assumptions underlying the estimates have been examined, however, the estimates can be reconciled rather nicely. As described in Chapter 3, for the population of offenders who have been arrested one or more times for index crimes, estimates of average λ cluster around 6 or 8 index crimes per year; for the population of offenders who have been arrested twice or more, average λ is around 10 or 15 index crimes per year. The estimates are roughly the same, whether taken from offender self-reports or official criminal justice records.

In estimating the effectiveness of additional prison construction, Zedlewski relied on the results of the Rand Corporation's 1978 survey of jail and prison inmates in California, Michigan, and Texas. The average value of λ for this sample—187 serious crimes per year—was several times higher than the highest estimate derived from analysis of arrest records. (For our purposes, "serious crimes" include the FBI index crimes, plus forgery and fraud.) As described in

Chapter 2, many self-reported offense rates are inflated, and frequent and dangerous offenders are more likely to be included in inmate samples. Further, the marginal offender—the next criminal in line for a prison cell, should one become available—is liable to be much less dangerous than the average offender already in prison (Zimring & Hawkins, 1988). Half the offenders included in the Rand survey reported committing fewer than 15 serious crimes per year (Chaiken & Chaiken, 1982). On the other hand, we are very uncertain as to the offense rate of any individual sentenced to prison, and it is conceivable that there are many offenders sentenced to probation who are as frequent and dangerous as those in prison (Zedlewski, 1989). So 187—although almost certainly too high—may be closer to the true value for the marginal offender than the official records estimates.

The differences among these estimates are policy relevant. Figure 1.5 shows the benefit/cost ratio associated with each additional prison cell, for values of λ up to 200. If λ is really as high as 187, each additional cell provides $17.20 in benefits for every $1.00 in costs—a phenomenal bargain. The benefit/cost ratio stays above 1.0, so long as the number of crimes prevented by incarcerating the marginal offender is larger than 10.87. This suggests that, if everything else is right, we need more prison cells; 10.87 is much less than 187. Nevertheless, our returns will diminish by an uncertain amount, so the case is not proven.

One way to avoid the problem of diminishing returns is to change the policy: Instead of using the additional prison cells to put more convicted offenders in

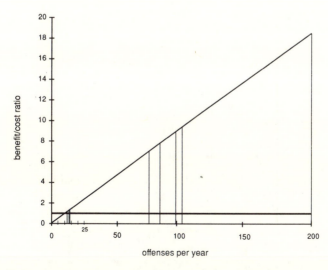

FIGURE 1.5. The lower the marginal offense rate, the smaller the benefits of prison expansion.

prison, we increase the length of the sentences of the offenders already in prison. Because this extends the incapacitation effects to all prisoners—but keeps the marginal offender out on the street—one might argue that 187 is the right number to use to measure the crime reduction benefits (Cavanagh, 1990).

But this creates a new problem: 187 may have been the number of crimes committed during the year before the typical offender was incarcerated; but how many would this offender commit over the next year, were he or she to be released today? The answer depends in part on how long this offender has spent in jail or prison. If most offenders serve short sentences—a year or two—it seems reasonable to believe that most of them will still be active upon release. But some offenders receive sentences of 20 years or more, and most estimate that the average adult offender only commits crimes over a 5- to 10-year period (see, for example, Blumstein, Cohen, & Hsieh, 1982; Shinnar & Shinnar, 1975). One cannot help but think that some of these 20-year sentences have already been wasted on no-longer-dangerous offenders, and that at least some of them can be released without harming the public.

If incarceration does nothing to extend the length of the criminal career and if the average sentence served is now 1.4 years (see Chapter 6), then the benefit/cost ratio of adding a prison cell is moderately sensitive to changes in the length of the average adult criminal career (see Figure 1.6). If most careers are very long—20 years—the benefits change little. But for more reasonable values of 5 to 10 years, the benefit/cost ratio is reduced 20 to 40 percent. It still makes

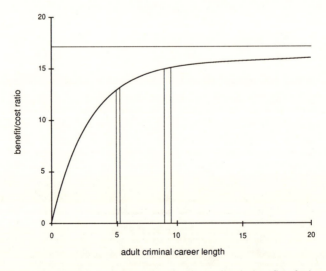

FIGURE 1.6. The shorter the average criminal career, the smaller the benefits of prison expansion.

sense to increase the number of prison beds, but our margin of comfort has been visibly reduced. If there are other flaws in the analysis, our conclusion might change.

Peter Greenwood's selective sentencing proposals are even more sensitive to small changes in these basic parameters. In California in the late 1970s, high-rate robbers tended to get slightly longer sentences than others; if the system were changed so that predicted high-rate offenders got much longer sentences and predicted low- and medium-rate offenders got short jail terms, Greenwood estimated that the robbery rate could be decreased by 23 percent, or the number of robbers in prison could be reduced by 15 percent, or any combination of the two.

Greenwood assumed that the average robber committed 10 robberies per year—about three times the highest estimate derived from arrest records. As shown in Figure 1.7, the maximum reduction in the robbery rate that can be obtained without increasing the number of offenders in prison drops from 23 percent when λ is 10, to 16.3 percent for a λ of 5.0, and to only 8.0 percent for λ of 2.0. Given what is known about the offense rate, a 23 percent reduction seems too high.

Another assumption—that criminal careers are very long, relative to the jail and prison terms served—is even more critical. To reduce the crime rate by 20 percent through Greenwood's selective incapacitation plan, it would be necessary to sentence predicted high-rate offenders to prison terms of 10 to 20 years or more (Spelman, 1986). Because the typical criminal career lasts only 5 to 10 years, there is good reason to suspect that much of the time served by these predicted frequent offenders would be simply wasted.

The sensitivity of crime control estimates to changes in expected career length is shown in Figure 1.8. Even if the typical career lasts as long as 20

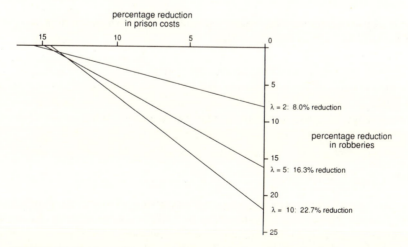

FIGURE 1.7. The lower the average offense rate, the less effective is selective sentencing.

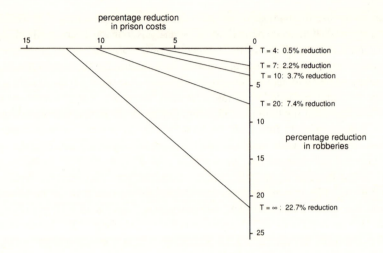

FIGURE 1.8. The shorter the average criminal career, the less effective is selective sentencing.

years—a very unlikely figure that is unsupported by any data—the largest possible reduction in the robbery rate from using this sentencing policy drops to 7.4 percent. For more reasonable average careers of 4 to 10 years, the maximum possible gains are only between 0.5 and 3.7 percent (Spelman, 1986; Visher, 1986).

Clearly, criminal justice officials hoping to rely on selective sentencing as a means of crime control should be cautious; certainly they should not expect miraculous no-cost crime reductions of 20 percent or benefit/cost ratios of 17. More important for our purposes, they should be wary of single-point predictions of the effect of selective policies: There is simply too much uncertainty as to the nature of criminal offending to permit precise estimates.

Still, the theory of incapacitation seems sound. If it is possible to identify a reasonable range of assumptions as to the offending population, the effectiveness of predictive measures, and the justice system's ability to use the predictions, then a range of possible outcomes may be estimated. What might such an analysis look like, and how might it be useful?

Sources of Uncertainty

Consider first the principal sources of uncertainty as to the effects of selective policies. These may be categorized into two types: uncertainty about the criminal population, and uncertainty about the response of the criminal justice system. Of the two, the second group presents by far the easier problem. Much research has been conducted, and government reports and agency records are readily available to help identify how offenders are caught, prosecuted, convicted, and sentenced.

The offending population presents another problem entirely. Some of the most important findings (and speculations) about the structure of offending are shown in Table 1.1. Note that the range of parameters is often very wide; in order to obtain a single-point estimate of the effectiveness of a selective policy, it would be necessary to (more or less arbitrarily) select one figure or assumption from each of these wide ranges. Clearly, single-point estimates are falsely precise, given the enormous uncertainty.

However, it is likely that careful reanalysis and meta-analysis can help shrink these ranges. In particular, the Rand inmate surveys could be reworked to reduce the uncertainty as to these critical parameters:

- The average offense rate, and the distribution of offense rates among offenders
- The degree of specialization among offenders with different aggregate offense rates
- Change in career patterns over time
- Differences in the likelihood of arrest between high- and low-rate offenders, and for offenders at different stages in their career
- Social characteristics of offenders with different offense rates and career lengths, including race, age, drug use, and employment status
- Differences among states as to all of these characteristics.

TABLE 1.1

Range of Estimates for Critical Parameters

Parameter	Range
Lambda (violent)	0.4 to 16.9 crimes per year
Lambda (property)	0.7 to 125.4 crimes per year
Corr (λ_V, λ_P)	Low level of specialization; or much specialization, except for most frequent offenders
Skew (λ)	Most frequent 10 percent of offenders would commit 25 to 80 percent of crimes, if left free to do so
Average career length	4 to 15 years; speculation that it is exponentially distributed
Probability of arrest	Experienced offenders learn to evade police; or police learn to catch frequent offenders
Career patterns	Frequent offenders start early, develop; infrequent offenders start late and drop out
Social characteristics	Little correlation with rates of offending; or highly correlated
Specific deterrence	Prison deters and rehabilitates offenders; or prison is criminogenic

Although information bearing on all of these parameters is directly available from the Rand inmate studies and other criminology research reports, some reanalysis will be required before the results can be used to help structure selective policies. For example, Jan and Marcia Chaiken, the initial analysts of Rand's 1978 survey, provided much data regarding both the specialization of offenders and changes in career patterns. But their results are very complicated: Values of λ are broken down by eight statutory crime types, and so 256 different combinations of offender types could have been identified (Chaiken & Chaiken, 1982, pp. 19–26). As the Chaikens showed, this comprehensive breakdown was useful for identifying patterns in criminal behavior; but for the purpose of making (necessarily crude) estimates of the effect of different public policies, it may be enough to distinguish between violent crimes (robbery and assault) and property crimes (burglary, larceny, forgery, and fraud).

To answer other questions, it will be necessary to build in additional complexity. For example, the Rand 1976 inmate survey indicated that high-rate offenders were less likely to be arrested for each crime they commited than were low-rate offenders (Peterson, Braiker, & Polich, 1980). This suggests that experienced criminals learn to evade capture, perhaps by attacking easier targets or by leaving fewer clues. But the situation may be more complicated than that: Property specialists may face better odds than offenders who also commit violent crimes; even experienced offenders may be likely to be caught if they have many prior arrests to their credit. And race, age, and other social characteristics may be associated with the likelihood of arrest. If we are interested in estimating the effect of police repeat offender programs that change the chances of arrest, the analysis should take all of these factors into account.

Structure of the Book

The remainder of this book details the results of just such a reanalysis of the Rand 1978 inmate survey. The analysis has been designed to identify more precise and more accurate estimates of the fundamental parameters mentioned above. The remainder of the book consists of seven chapters.

In Chapter 2, *Validity*, the results of an exploration into the validity of the survey data are presented. Particular attention is paid to the inmates's estimates of λ, their offense rate. In addition, weights for each case in the Rand survey are developed. Weighting the sample offsets biases in the data resulting from the data collection methods employed by Rand.

In Chapter 3, *The Offense Rate* from the weighted sample are examined in detail. The average value of λ, the distribution of λ among offenders, and the relationship among λs of various offense types are all described. A mathematical model that allows computer generation of random λ consistent with these results is also presented.

Chapter 4, *The Criminal Career*, contains an explanation of the average length of the criminal career and its distribution among offenders. The likelihood that an offender's career will end at any time is shown to depend on the offender's age and offense rate.

In Chapter 5, *Production of Arrests*, it is shown that some offenders are particularly liable to be arrested for each crime they commit, whereas others are adept at avoiding arrest. The implications of this heterogeneity, and some indicators of high- and low-arrest probabilities, are described.

In Chapter 6, *Collective Incapacitation*, the changes made in the Avi-Itzhak and Shinnar model are described, and the parameters developed in Chapters 2 through 5 are included in an analysis of the crime control effectiveness of current incarceration practice. Particular attention is given to the cost-effectiveness of prison construction.

Chapter 7, *Selective Incapacitation*, contains an analysis of selective police, prosecution, and sentencing policies. Implications for the structure of selective criminal justice system policies and programs are detailed.

In Chapter 8, *Conclusions*, the limitations of the analytic model, and the probable effects of these limitations on the findings, are considered.

Two final points. The order of Chapters 2 through 5 is largely arbitrary, and each chapter relies in part on the results of the others. Thus each of these chapters includes extensive cross-references. Although this makes the results difficult to read, the alternative—organizing the presentation so that it paralleled the analysis—would have been far worse. Second, note that "he or she" is used throughout the book to avoid sexism. This is awkward but accurate: women account for almost 20 percent of arrests for serious crimes (Federal Bureau of Investigation, 1990), and about 13 percent of violent crimes (Bureau of Justice Statistics, 1990). On the other hand, all participants in the 1978 Rand survey were men, so "he" is used alone when appropriate.

First things first. How valid are the data collected in the Rand inmate survey? As it happens, the data are of dubious validity in some ways; through careful analysis, however, the effects of these validity problems may be held to a minimum.

2

Validity

Criminals are understandably anxious to avoid publicizing their activities. The secrecy inherent in the criminal profession makes it very difficult to characterize criminal activity: We are forced to rely either on sketchy official records or on the questionably valid confessions of admitted offenders. The threats to validity of official records are well known.

- Most crimes do not result in arrest or conviction, so any measurements of the frequency of offending, the degree of change in frequency over a career, or the length of a career based on official records will all be too low. Of course, if we can estimate the likelihood that a crime will result in the capture of an offender, then we may adjust these measurements and account for the bias.
- High-rate offenders may be more or less prone to arrest and conviction than other offenders. Again, if we can estimate how much more or less prone they are, we may account for it and obtain unbiased results.

The first problem turns out to be fairly easy (Blumstein & Cohen, 1979). The second problem is another story. In fact, the difficulty in deciding whether frequent offenders are more or less likely to be caught provided a telling argument in favor of conducting self-report surveys (Wilson & Boland, 1976).

If official records are sketchy and possibly misleading, offender confessions are fraught with difficulties. Among the most important are the following:

- Offenders may lie. Despite the researcher's assurance that they have nothing to lose by telling the truth, they may understate their criminal activity (to look good to the researcher and perhaps avoid legal harassment), or overstate it (in defiance, or in an attempt to impress the researcher with their wickedness).
- Offenders may forget. They may remember themselves as more active than they really were, or they may involuntarily forget to mention crimes that they did commit.
- The sample may be biased. Here we encounter problems of sampling efficiency: It would be cheap and easy to draw a sample of criminals on Death Row, for example, but it is likely to give a distorted picture of the

activity of the average street offender. A survey of the general population would provide an unbiased cross-section of the offending population, but very few of those sampled would commit street crimes on anything like a regular basis.

Like the threats to validity of official records, all of these problems may be measured and to some degree accounted for or even corrected. Liars and forgetters are apt to be inconsistent in their responses; we may be able to identify particularly inconsistent respondents and delete them from the sample. Alternatively, the respondents's claims may be compared to official records; offenders whose responses deviate consistently from their rap sheets may be deleted from the sample, or their responses "corrected" to look more like the official record. And biased samples may be "corrected" as well, by weighting each case.

In this chapter, all three of these possible threats to validity are evaluated, and methods of correcting validity problems are developed. Consider first the problem of biased samples. Although prisoners are, on the whole, more serious criminals than the typical street crook, it is possible to weight the Rand inmate sample so that it mimics a random sample of active offenders. The methods necessary are fairly straightforward, and adequate data are readily available. And correction of the sampling bias affects the survey results in important ways.

Weighting the Rand Sample

The Importance of the Sample Frame

In any discussion of criminal justice policy, at least four different groups of offenders are potentially important. Which group needs to be considered depends on the kind of policy we are analyzing (Chaiken, 1981, pp. 226–227). For some policies, we care about the group of offenders who are *incarcerated* at any given time. The incarcerated group is appropriate if we are interested in the nature or effects of offenders' jail or prison experiences. Thus studies of the effectiveness of rehabilitation or the special deterrent value of imprisonment, the likelihood of prison violence, or the effects of imprisonment on offenders' knowledge of criminal techniques should all rely primarily on the incarcerated group. The 1975 and 1976 Rand inmate surveys were conducted among incarcerated offenders.

For other purposes, we may be concerned with an *incoming cohort*—the group of offenders who all enter jail or prison at the same time. The incoming cohort is useful if we are concerned with intermediate sanctions, judicial decision making, or other aspects of the allocation of punishment among convicted offenders. An incoming cohort was the sample frame for the 1978 Rand inmate survey.

We may also be concerned with the population of *active offenders*—those people who are actively seeking opportunities to commit crimes. The active offender population includes not only criminals who are free to commit crimes, but also those who are in jail or prison, but would be actively seeking opportunities were they free to do so. Thus the active offender population includes both the incoming cohort and the in-prison group. We should be concerned with active offenders if we are interested in the behavior of criminals in the street, including the distribution of offense rates, the nature and length of criminal careers, and the likelihood of arrest. Most important, if we care about the effects of incapacitation on the crime rate, we need to consider active offenders.

Not all crimes are committed by people who would ordinarily be considered as "criminals," however. Many people admit to committing a few minor crimes, especially in their youth (Visher & Roth, 1986), and if there are enough of these low-rate, impersistent offenders, they may conceivably account for most of the crimes committed. Thus the *entire criminal population* is the appropriate group if we are considering crime control measures that affect everyone—deterrence, drug abuse prevention, or situational crime prevention, for example. We may also need to know how large this group is and how many crimes they commit relative to the others before we can estimate the effectiveness of incapacitation. But because the crimes committed by many members of this group are too trivial to merit incarceration, this group is of less interest for our purposes.

It is easy to identify and sample the population of incarcerated offenders or an incoming cohort—jails and prisons are full of them. And it is reasonable to believe they would provide useful data. Incarcerated offenders have little to lose by telling the truth; with few exceptions, they would be quite right in believing that the authorities have little interest in leveling additional charges against them.

Obtaining valid information about active offenders is much more difficult. Part of the problem is the ambiguity of the term. Serial murderers and big-time cocaine dealers clearly fit the bill; kids who shoplift once on a dare clearly do not. For nearly anyone in between, however, an argument could be made for or against their "actively seeking opportunities" to commit crime. Second, no matter how we define "active offenders," they do not make up a large proportion of the general population. For example, only 16 percent of adults are arrested before their 30th birthday (Tillman, 1987), and not all of them meet our qualifications. Thus any sample of the general population would have to be enormous if a substantial number of frequent offenders were to be included. Finally, active offenders understandably try to remain inconspicuous. Sophisticated crooks might realize that nothing they say could be used in court, but they may still be quite reasonably concerned that their confessions may lead to increased police or community surveillance, or (at least) to the disapproval of the interviewer. All economic classes and races and both genders are well represented among the people who admit to (or boast of) juvenile delinquency. But very few claim to have committed serious offenses at any time, and fewer claim to have committed them recently (Hirschi, Hindelang, & Weis, 1980).

So valid results and reasonably large sample sizes are only possible for surveys of incarcerated offenders or incoming cohorts, whereas our real aim is to measure the activities of active offenders (and, to a lesser extent, everyone else). Since our primary concern is with incapacitation, however, we might reasonably define "active offenders" as those who stand a chance of going to jail or prison. If we can calculate the probability that a given active offender will go to jail, we can use this information to weight an incoming cohort or in-prison sample so that it resembles a sample of active offenders. The 1976 Rand inmate survey was weighted; the method of determining the weights was developed, and the data collected, by Jan Chaiken (1981). His method is adapted and applied to the 1978 inmate sample below. Although the data used are not so good as Chaiken's, they are much better than nothing.

Modeling the Active Offenders

Correcting for sampling bias is mathematically complex but conceptually simple. Consider the following example.

Suppose there are two kinds of offenders on the street, Crips and Brims. All Crips are alike, all Brims are alike, but Crips and Brims differ from one another. There are relatively few Crips, but they commit crimes at high rates and are relatively likely to be caught: The chances are 1 in 4 that a randomly selected Crip will be in prison at any given time. There are many more Brims, but they commit crimes less frequently and are less likely to be caught: The chances are 1 in 10 that a randomly selected Brim will be in prison at any given time.

Now suppose that we took a survey of all offenders in prison and found that half of the prisoners were Crips, and half Brims. From this information, we could derive the total number of offenders belonging to each group.

- Because one fourth of all Crips are in prison, for each incarcerated Crip there are three on the street. Thus each Crip in the prison sample represents four offenders in total.
- For each Brim in prison there are nine on the street, so each imprisoned Brim represents ten offenders in total.

If we wanted our in-prison sample to represent the total population of offenders, we could count each Crip 4 times and each Brim 10 times. Because the weighted sample would now be $(4 \times .5) + (10 \times .5) = 7$ times as large as the original sample, any statistical analysis results would appear more precise than they really were. To maintain the correct level of precision while keeping the sample representative of the entire population, we multiply each of the sample weights by 1/7, the proportion of all offenders who are in prison. Thus each Crip in the prison sample would be weighted as 4/7 of a case, and each Brim in the sample would be weighted as 10/7. Though it seems odd to count a person as only 4/7 of a case, for most statistical procedures such an adjustment poses no problems (Moser & Kalton, 1972, pp. 79–117).

Of course, there are no homogeneous groups of offenders like these fictional Crips and Brims. Nevertheless, we can apply the same logic to each case in the sample, if the likelihood that each case would have been included can be calculated.

A Formula for Weighting an Incoming Cohort Sample

The Rand researchers chose their sample for the 1978 inmate survey in such a way that the result would be representative of an incoming cohort to incarceration. Thus weighting this sample requires that we estimate the probability that any given active offender would be included in an incoming cohort. Let us begin the task by defining our terms in greater detail.

The incoming cohort is the set of all offenders who enter jail or prison in a given year. Some will leave jail or prison before the year is out; some will be rearrested and incarcerated again within a few months. So an offender may be a member of an incoming cohort two or more times. For convenience, let us count offenders only once in our sample. Either they enter incarceration in the year in question, or they do not; whatever happens after they enter jail or prison is of no consequence. This makes the algebra simpler without changing the final weights. And it is what the Rand researchers had in mind when they created the incoming cohort sample of their survey (Peterson, Chaiken, Ebener, & Honig, 1981).

Active offenders are all those who commit offenses serious enough and often enough that they stand a chance of being sent to jail or prison. Clearly, this includes a few low-level offenders (even sporadic shoplifters are occasionally jailed), and even a few one-time offenders (people who commit only one crime may be sentenced to incarceration, if they are caught and the crime is serious enough). But it probably will not include one-time shoplifters or joyriders, since it is very unlikely that a judge would sentence a minor offender with no previous record to jail or prison. Thus the population of active offenders probably accounts for most crimes (Moore et al., 1984), but certainly does not account for all of them. As a result, this group is less appropriate for analysis of deterrence and rehabilitation policies.

Now consider the case of Joe, a typical street offender. What is the likelihood that Joe will enter prison this year? It makes sense to consider two cases:

- Joe may begin the year in jail or prison. Thus he can only enter prison if he is released sometime in the next 12 months, commits crimes after his release but before the year is out, and is arrested, convicted, and sentenced to incarceration before 31 December.

- Alternatively, Joe may be on the street on New Year's Day. Then he will become a member of the incoming cohort if he commits crimes, and is arrested, convicted, and sentenced to incarceration before 31 December.

To make the algebra simpler, let us assume that arrest, conviction, and sentencing happen immediately upon commission of a crime, if they are ever going to happen. Although this biases the probabilities of inclusion in the incoming cohort (all probabilities are too high), they are all biased by proportionately the same amount. Thus the relative weights among different offenders will be the same. Note that this is not true if offenders who have been recently released from prison are arrested, convicted, and sentenced with more (or less) delay than other offenders, or if the arrest and adjudication delay differs for different crime types. Though trial delays are longer for some crimes than for others (Boland, Brady, Tyson, & Bassler, 1983; Brosi, 1979; Church, Carlson, Lee, & Tan, 1978), the differences are probably not large enough to affect the results much.

Now suppose that Joe is free on 1 January. Let λ be the average number of crimes that he will commit this year, given that he is free to commit them all year; let q be the average probability of arrest for each crime he commits; let J be the average probability of incarceration, given an arrest. Assume that crimes, arrests given crimes, and incarcerations given arrests all occur according to a Poisson process. Although this is a fairly restrictive assumption if one is interested in modeling the total number of crimes, arrests, or incarcerations in a given year or over an offending career, it is not unreasonable for measurement of the probability of one incarceration or more.

Then the expected number of incarcerations may be modeled by a Poisson distribution, where λ represents the number of trials (that is, opportunities to incarcerate Joe), and qJ represents the probability of success (incarceration) for each trial. Thus the probability of no successes is

$$
\begin{aligned}
f(0) &= [(\lambda q J)^0 \, e^{-\lambda q J}]/0! \\
&= e^{-\lambda q J}
\end{aligned}
\tag{2.1}
$$

and the probability of one or more successes is just

$$
1 - f(0) = 1 - e^{-\lambda q J}.
\tag{2.2}
$$

If we know that Joe began the year outside of prison, and know the values of λ, q, and J, we can estimate the chances that he will enter jail or prison this year.

Now suppose Joe is imprisoned on 1 January. What is the probability that he will be released by the end of the year? If he was originally sentenced to a term of

5 years, then the probability that he will be released to offend again is 1/5; he stands a 4/5 chance of staying in prison for the remainder of the year. If he stays in prison for the rest of the year, there is no chance of his becoming a member of an incoming cohort. So, if he is serving a sentence of S years, the probability that he enters prison, p(IC), is

$$p(IC) = 1/S \, p(IC|release) + [(S - 1)/S] \, (0). \tag{2.3}$$

The second term simply states that, if he is not released this year, he stands no chance of entering prison this year. Now, what is the probability that Joe will return to prison, if he is released?

If Joe is released on 1 January, he stands the same chance as he would if he spent New Year's Eve on the street:

$$p(IC|release) = 1 - e^{-\lambda qJ}. \tag{2.4}$$

If he is released on 31 December, he stands no chance at all. In general,

$$p(IC|release \ at \ z) = 1 - e^{-\lambda qJ(1-z)}, \tag{2.5}$$

where z is the proportion of the year that has passed, at the point that Joe is released. If Joe is equally likely to be released at any time during the year, z is uniformly distributed between 0 and 1, and the average value of p(IC|release at z) may be defined as

$$p(IC|release) = \int_0^1 (1 - e^{-\lambda qJz}) \, dz. \tag{2.6}$$

This reduces easily to

$$p(IC|release) = (\lambda qJ - 1 + e^{-\lambda qJ})/\lambda qJ. \tag{2.7}$$

Combining Equation (2.2) and Equation (2.7), we find that

$$p(IC) = P[(\lambda qJ - 1 + e^{-\lambda qJ})/\lambda qJ] + (1 - P)(1 - e^{-\lambda qJ}), \tag{2.8}$$

where P is the probability that Joe begins the year in prison, and $1 - P$ is the probability he doesn't. Since 1 January is no different than any other day for our purposes, Joe's p(IC) depends on the chance that he will be in jail or prison at any given time.

This is a problem that may be answered in several different ways, depending on the assumptions we are willing to make and the variables we want to control for. The simplest case makes the fewest assumptions. Suppose that incarcerations occur at the (Poisson) rate of λqJ; that is, Joe would be incarcerated λqJ times each year, if incarceration did not itself prevent him from continuing to commit crimes. Of course, Joe is prevented from committing street crimes while in jail or prison, so any crimes he would have committed, had he been free (and any resulting incarcerations he would have suffered), are "lost." Thus Joe's imprisonment history resembles a queueing problem: Each incarceration represents an "arrival" to a "service" lasting the length of his jail or prison sentence. In fact, if Joe's average sentence lasts S years, then the likelihood that he is in prison at any given time is given by *Erlang's Loss Formula* (Larson & Odoni, 1981, pp. 209–211), which is generally equal to

$$P_n = [A^n/n!]/\Sigma_i \, A^i/i! \tag{2.9}$$

where A represents the ratio of arrivals to services per unit of time, i is the capacity of the system—the number of offenders who may be "served" at any one time (for our purposes, just one), and n is the number of arrivals that are turned away (again, just one). In the case of incapacitation, the number of arrivals per unit time is directly proportional to λqJ, whereas the number of services per unit time is directly proportional to $1/S$. Hence the ratio of arrivals to services is λqJS, and Erlang's loss formula for the case of one server reduces to

$$P = \lambda qJS/(1 + \lambda qJS). \tag{2.10}$$

As it happens, Erlang's formula holds true, no matter what the distribution of S (Takacs, 1969).

Although this result is true on average, it fails to account for the fact that young offenders—those who have recently entered the street offender population—are less likely to begin the year in prison than others. The probability of beginning the year in prison increases asymptotically if the offender remains in the street offending population for a long time. Thus, for young offenders, P will be an overestimate; our estimate of p(IC) will weigh too heavily the chances of entering prison, given that the offender started the year in prison; because p(IC) is higher for offenders who started the year outside prison, combining equations (2.10) and (2.8) would underestimate the probability that a young offender will enter prison this year, and (relatively) overestimate the probability for an older offender. That is, the incoming cohort will have a relatively large proportion of younger offenders in it, because many of the older offenders were in jail all year.

This would be of little consequence if the age of offenders were not a pressing concern of this study. However, much of the analysis that follows concerns the length of criminal careers and the trajectory of offense and arrest rates over an offender's career. Thus it is important to account for and correct this bias.

Chaiken (1981, pp. 230–233), in deriving weights to convert a survey of prison inmates to represent a population of active offenders, has suggested that a reasonable estimate of P, taking career length-to-date into account, is

$$P' = P\,(1 - e^{-t/S - \lambda qJt}), \tag{2.11}$$

where t is career length-to-date in years. A full derivation of this estimate requires a couple of (rather cavalier) assumptions. The average sentence served and the average total career length must both be exponentially distributed; and the average career must be very much longer than the average sentence, and effectively infinite in length. However, as Chaiken (1981) notes:

> The basic justification for adopting [this function] as an approximation is that it has the right value when t is large and makes a reasonably sensible correction for small values of t. (p. 233)

Chaiken goes on to state that the data required to estimate P and P' are themselves so uncertain that it is probably fruitless to quibble over details. In view of the fact that, in some ways, the data available for estimating weights for the 1978 Rand inmate survey are worse than for the 1976 Rand survey, this seems doubly sensible.

Using P' to correct for oversampling of young offenders and combining with equation (2.8) produces a complicated mess, but the effects of weighting are fairly simple. As shown in Figure 2.1, the probability of inclusion in the incom-

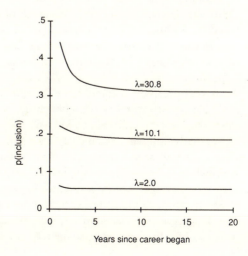

FIGURE 2.1. Sample probabilities decrease over time, especially for frequent offenders.

ing cohort decreases asyptotically as t and S tend to infinity; it increases as λ, q, and J increase. So an incoming cohort sample will be unrepresentative of active street offenders in three ways:

- The incoming cohort will include a larger proportion of young offenders than are in the active offending population.
- The cohort will include a higher proportion of serious, frequent offenders than the active population.
- If the probability of arrest given a crime differs from one offender to the next, the cohort will include a disproportionate number of offenders with high probabilities of arrest.

In order to weight cases in the 1978 Rand sample, it will be necessary to collect information on each offender's λ (average offense rate per year), q (average probability of arrest per offense committed), J (average probability of incarceration given arrest), S (average sentence served per incarceration), and t (career length-to-date). All the necessary values may be reasonably estimated from a combination of official records and the Rand sample itself.

Data for Weighting the Sample

Chaiken's (1981) weighting of the 1976 Rand inmate survey ("Rand 1") was based on information collected from two kinds of sources. For data on each individual's offense rate, probability of arrest, and career length, he turned to the sample survey itself. For data on parameters less likely to differ from one offender to the next—the chances of incarceration and the sentence served per incarceration—he relied on copious official records maintained by the State of California. Greenwood's (1982) reanalysis of the 1978 inmate survey ("Rand 2") relied on information from the same set of sources.

Because offenders provided similar information in Rand 1 as in Rand 2, offense rates, arrest probabilities, and career lengths are readily available in the same form as that used in weighting Rand 1. Unfortunately, neither Michigan nor Texas keeps records as complete as California's; thus less reliable information is available about incarceration probabilities and sentences served in these two states. Nevertheless, there are good reasons to believe that an incoming cohort is substantially different from the population of active offenders and that weighting the sample will have a substantial effect on the results. As a result, it is probably worthwhile to base sample weights on less-than-perfectly reliable information; each case's weight will be a little bit wrong, but on the whole the results will probably be much more correct than if the cases were not weighted at all.

To prevent the weights from introducing biases of their own, ambiguities were resolved in such a way that the respondents would appear to be more similar than they really were. For example, most missing data were replaced by the median values reported by other respondents. Thus the weight each offender received lay somewhere between the "true" weight, reflecting that offender's true probability of inclusion in the sample, and 1.0, the weight each case would receive in an unweighted sample. Even so, a comparison of key results both before and after weighting demonstrates the impact even partial weights can have on the results.

Even when the data available in Rand 2 were identical to those available to the analysts of Rand 1, it was necessary to make some technical decisions about how to measure each of the parameters that make up each case weight. The decisions made, and the reasons for making them, are detailed below.

Offense Rate, λ

Like any rate, λ consists of two elements—a numerator (here, the number of offenses committed during some period of time) and a denominator (the period of time itself). The Rand researchers only asked their respondents to supply information about crimes committed during the 2 calendar years just prior to their most recent incarceration (a period they called "Window 3"), prudently supposing that memory lapses would make estimates for earlier "windows" far too unreliable. Because the bounds of Window 3 were based on calendar years, offenders entered jail or prison at different times of the year. Thus for some respondents Window 3 was larger than for others, and offenders were asked to recall the month in which they entered jail or prison. Moreover, many offenders spent earlier portions of window 3 incapacitated in jails, prisons, or hospitals, and were thus physically restrained from committing crimes against the general population. The offense rate should represent the number of crimes each offender would commit per unit of time, if he or she were not so restrained; thus respondents were required to estimate the number of months they were incapacitated, so that this time could be subtracted from the total window period as well. So calculation of λ requires that several separate pieces of information be drawn together.

Of course, most of this is simple algebra, and for the most part calculation of offense rates from the Rand survey data is straightforward. Most respondents seemed to have little trouble estimating any of the information needed. However, some offenders failed to provide some of the required data, and others provided ambiguous or conflicting responses. As a result, some decisions had to be made as to the best method of handling missing responses. The procedures used in the reanalysis differed slightly from those employed by the original Rand researchers, and so are detailed here.

The first problem was to identify reasonable estimates for the number of "street months" available to offenders in which they could commit crimes. When a respondent provided conflicting or ambiguous estimates, survey editors at Rand examined all of the information the respondent provided and calculated a reasonable estimate of their own. In general, this estimate represented an average of the minimum and maximum number of street months consistent with the responses provided. As Christy Visher (1986) noted in her reanalysis of Rand 2, this could have resulted in incorrectly high values of λ. But use of an alternative procedure did not affect the distribution of street months by much. In this reanalysis, the respondent's estimates were taken as correct except when they were ambiguous; then the calculation provided by the Rand editors was used, and if this was missing, the second response given by the respondent was assumed to be correct. With a few exceptions, this method resulted in the same distribution of street months as that detailed by Visher.

A more complicated problem was to identify the number of crimes committed by the respondent in Window 3. Respondents were to estimate this figure for each of 10 crime types, according to a complex procedure.

- First, they were asked if they committed any crimes of each type during the 2-year period.
- If they reported committing any crimes of a given type, they were asked whether they had committed 10 or fewer of these crimes, or 11 or more of these crimes during Window 3.
- If they committed 10 or fewer crimes of a particular type, they were asked to provide the exact number.
- If they committed 11 or more of these crimes, respondents were asked to make a progressive series of estimates through which they "zeroed in" on the correct figure.

Asked to go through so complex a procedure 10 times, it is little wonder that some respondents got confused and provided inconsistent or incomplete answers. Most missing data were replaced with reasonable estimates based on a combination of the information the respondent did provide and information provided by others who reported committing crimes of each type. More specifically, missing values were replaced as follows.

Offenders who did not specify whether they committed crimes of a given type were assumed to have committed no crimes of that type. Offenders who reported committing crimes of some type but reported no other information were assigned the median value of lambda reported by all other offenders who committed crimes of that type. Although the mean is more often used for replacement of missing values, use of the mean would have increased the number of very frequent offenders, due to the highly skewed distribution of lambda.

When a respondent reported committing 10 or fewer crimes of some type but failed to specify just how many, he was assumed to have committed the mean number of crimes reported by others who committed ten or fewer crimes of that type. This differs from the Rand procedure, where the offender was assumed to have committed 5.5 crimes (the midpoint between the lowest possible value of 1 and the highest value of 10); it also differs from the procedure adopted by Visher in her reanalysis, where the offender was randomly assigned a number between 1 and 10 in such a way that the distribution of random assignments was identical to the distribution of responses provided by offenders who answered the question (Visher, 1986, pp. 42, 99). Although Visher's procedure probably results in a more accurate estimate of the distribution of λ, it introduces an additional source of error into each offender's estimate. As a result, it is less appropriate for the disaggregate analysis detailed later in this report. Offenders who specified a range (e.g., "4 to 6") were assigned the midpoint of that range.

For respondents who committed more than 10 crimes of a given type, the missing data replacement procedures were even more Byzantine. When respondents provided a range, the midpoint of the range was used. When they provided multiple partial responses, the response that was complete (or most nearly complete) was used. When respondents provided multiple complete responses, they were averaged. And if any response was left blank, the mean of the respondents who answered that question was substituted.

It was necessary to make two exceptions to this last rule. First, when respondents failed to provide the number of months they committed crimes of a certain type, the mean percentage of months provided by other respondents who answered the question (that is, the average of the "months-did" responses divided by the "total-street-months" estimates) was applied to the respondent's own "street months" estimate. Had this not been done, some offenders could have been assigned "months did" estimates that were greater than the total number of months they were capable of committing crimes. Second, respondents who reported committing 10 or more crimes of a given type but provided no more information were assigned the median (not the mean) number of crimes reported by offenders who committed more than 10 of these crimes. Again, the mean would have been a poor guess at the number of crimes committed by the "average" offender.

How does this plethora of ad hoc rules and regulations affect the final results? Not by much. Table 2.1 compares selected percentiles of the λ distributions calculated by Rand and by Visher with those used here. For both robbery and burglary, the distributions are very similar at all points. In general, means are very sensitive to changes in a few very large values; the somewhat lower means used here probably result from a small number of differences in coding and calculation.

Probability of Arrest, q

As with λ, information was available on each respondent's recent arrest and offense history. This provided enough information to estimate the probability that

TABLE 2.1

Estimates of λ Are Not Very Sensitive to Differences in Coding Procedures

Robbery

	Rand			
	Minimum	Maximum	Visher	Reanalysis
25th percentile	1.8	2.3	1.5	1.7
50th	3.6	6.0	3.8	4.3
75th	12.0	21.5	12.4	11.4
90th percentile	68.0	100.5	71.6	94.4
Mean	40.6	62.2	43.4	45.2

Burglary

	Rand			
	Minimum	Maximum	Visher	Reanalysis
25th percentile	2.4	2.8	2.0	2.4
50th	4.8	6.0	4.7	6.0
75th	27.3	35.0	23.4	33.2
90th percentile	196.0	265.0	195.9	173.3
Mean	75.8	118.6	79.0	66.1

Sources. Columns 1 and 2: *Varieties of Criminal Behavior,* by J. M. Chaiken & M. R. Chaiken, (1982, Santa Monica: Rand. Column 3: "The Rand Second Inmate Survey: A Reanalysis," by C. A. Visher, 1986, in *Criminal Careers and "Career Criminals,"* edited by A. Blumstein et al., Washington, DC: National Academy of Sciences.

each individual would be arrested per crime committed, for each of the nine crime types under study. This probability was simply the number of times the respondent was arrested for a particular crime type in Window 3 (the 2 years prior to the current incarceration), divided by the number of crimes of each type committed. The same procedure was followed in the 1976 Rand inmate survey (Chaiken, 1981, pp. 236–237). However, because this procedure occasionally produced ridiculous or difficult-to-interpret results, a few adjustments were made.

A few respondents claimed to have been convicted of a particular offense but reported that they had never been arrested for that offense. This is certainly possible; for example, an offender arrested for attempted rape may plead guilty to an assault; alternatively, the offender may have been convicted in Window 3 after being arrested in Window 1 or 2 (2 to 6 years prior to his most recent incarceration). Although it would have been possible to correct for such contingencies as these, it seemed simpler to assume that the respondent had simply neglected to record his arrest. Similarly, offenders who claimed to have committed no crimes of a particular type were assumed to have committed one, if official records or their self-reports show that they were arrested or convicted for an offense of that type.

Many offenders reported that they had never been arrested for some crimes; a few reported that they had committed many such crimes, without a single arrest. Unless the official record indicated that the offender was simply lying, the number of arrests were assumed to be .50. That is, it was assumed that these offenders would probably be arrested at least once, should they attempt to commit the same number of crimes again. This is hardly a scientific assumption, but it does keep the probability of arrest above zero (where it belongs), while reflecting the offender's self-reported likelihood of capture.

The mean probabilities of arrest for each crime are shown in Table 2.2. The means were obtained by weighting each offender's reported likelihood of arrest by the number of crimes of that type he reported committing. Thus the mean reflects the average probability of arrest for each crime across all offenders, rather than the appropriate value for the "typical" offender. This mean value was assigned to offenders who failed to specify either the number of crimes they committed or the number of arrests made of them.

Probability of Incarceration, J

One of the reasons that the Rand researchers failed to weight their sample was that reliable information as to the probability of incarceration given arrest was not collected by two of the three states included in their survey (Chaiken,

TABLE 2.2
Mean Probabilities of Arrest Are Similar among States

Crime type	California	Michigan	Texas
Business robbery	.091	.093	.145
Street robbery	.056	.029	.069
Assault	.180	.161	.190
Burglary	.033	.032	.021
Theft	.014	.019	.012
Auto theft	.031	.024	.095
Forgery	.016	.031	.025
Fraud	.007	.013	.021
Drug sales	.001	.001	.002

1984). This information is still unavailable. And no information is available from the Rand survey as to each individual's likelihood of conviction and incarceration, given arrest. So the best sources of data for one of the vital parameters are unable to provide us with the information needed.

Certainly it would be difficult to weight the sample if no information were available as to values of one of the vital parameters. However, there is good reason to believe that any differences among offenders as to the probability of conviction or incarceration are mainly due to chance. For example, a careful analysis of convictions in Jacksonville, Florida, and San Diego, California (Feeney, Dill, & Weir, 1983), showed that

> individual defendant characteristics such as age, race, and prior record do not appear to be consistently related to the likelihood of conviction in the jurisdictions studied. (p. 244)

Thus an average value will probably suffice quite well. And information gleaned from other official sources is sufficient to justify reasonable estimates of these average probabilities.

California records provide much better than adequate estimates of the average probability of incarceration given arrest. Average values are shown in the first column of Table 2.3. Values reflect the collected records of all county prosecutors in California for the year 1982, so it is necessary to assume these values had changed little since 1978. Although the distribution of sentences passed and served probably changed greatly between 1978 and 1982 due to the implementation of determinate sentencing, there is little reason to suppose that the likelihood of incarceration changed much.

TABLE 2.3

Mean Probabilities of Incarceration
Are Also Similar among States

Crime type	California	Michigan and Texas
Robbery	.461	.46
Assault	.375	.28
Burglary	.570	.42
Larceny	.424	.37
Auto theft	.362	.29
Forgery and fraud	.488	.40
Drug sales	.290	.25

Sources. California: *Adult Felony Arrest Dispositions in California* (p. 42), Sacramento, CA: California Department of Justice. Michigan and Texas: *The Prosecution of Felony Arrests* (pp. 34–49), by B. Boland, E. Brady, H. Tyson, & J. Bassler, 1983, Washington, DC: U.S. Bureau of Justice Statistics; *A Cross-City Comparison of Felony Case Processing* (pp. 114–180), by K. B. Brosi, 1979, Washington, DC: Institute for Law and Social Research.

Such statewide information is unavailable for Michigan and Texas, but information is available for a dozen cities that had implemented the PROMIS recordkeeping system in 1979. If these cities were roughly representative of the nation as a whole, then the average probability of incarceration across PROMIS cities may be used as a reasonable estimate of the true value for Michigan and Texas. These average figures are shown in the second column of Table 2.3; the fact that they are quite similar to the California probabilities suggests that they represent reasonably good guesses.

Sentence Served, S

Although the Rand sample includes no information on prior sentences, respondents were asked about the length of the sentence they were serving at the time of the survey. The data are subject to the usual caveats of offender self-reported data; however, there is little reason for offenders to lie overtly about the length of their sentences, and less reason to believe that they will forget the length of time remaining in their sentences. (One indication of this is that only 6.1 percent of offenders responded that they did not know the time remaining in their sentence.) As a result, it is possible not only to identify the average sentence passed for each of the nine crime types; it is also possible to examine differences among offenders as to the expected sentence.

There is good reason to suspect that, in most jurisdictions, the sentence a convicted offender can expect depends on the offender's prior record, the conviction charge, and the jurisdiction (Eisenstein & Jacob, 1977; Green, 1961; Johnston, Miller, Schoenberg, & Weatherly, 1973). As previous studies have suggested, these are not the only characteristics that matter, and any attempt to identify all the important indicators of the sentence passed is likely to be complex and involved (Gottfredson, Hoffman, Sigler, & Wilkins, 1975). The aim here is much more limited, however; rather than identify all the indicators, it is only necessary to account for relationships among the other parameters included in the weighting equation and the expected sentence, S. That is, the independent variables of interest are limited to (a) the crime for which the offender was convicted, (b) the state in which the offender was arrested and convicted, and (c) the offender's prior criminal history, as reflected in λ, q, J, and t. Although other variables may affect the sentence, including them in the equation will not affect the weight given to each offender.

Should all three groups of variables turn out to affect the expected sentence, it would not be difficult to account for their effects in estimating sample weights. But it would be more pleasant if fewer variables mattered. So a stagewise regression procedure was adopted: It was assumed that the sentence passed would differ from one crime to the next; there would probably be differences among jurisdictions, so this effect was tested next; to identify the effects of prior record on the sentence, the expected number of prior convictions—the product of λ, q, J, and t—was examined in the next stage; finally, interactions between the jurisdiction and prior conviction variables were examined.

Results of this stagewise procedure, shown in Table 2.4, indicate that state differences alone accounted for much of the variation in sentences passed. Prior convictions—as estimated by parameters included in the weight equations—had a substantial effect for only one crime type, burglary, and the effect was about the same in all states. Table 2.5 shows the final equations used to predict the expected sentence for each offender.

TABLE 2.4
Sentences Differ among Crime Types and States,
but Prior Record Is of Little Importance

Crime type	State differences ($n_1 = 2$)	Plus λqJt ($n_1 = 1$)	Plus λqJt by state ($n_1 = 3$)
Robbery ($n = 197$)			
R^2	.033	.035	.040
F	3.354	0.235	0.457
$p(F)$	$p = .037$	$p = .63$	$p = .71$
Assault ($n = 178$)			
R^2	.049	.053	.059
F	4.531	0.707	0.575
$p(F)$	$p = .012$	$p = .40$	$p = .63$
Burglary ($n = 263$)			
R^2	.168	.193	.197
F	26.163	8.161	0.618
$p(F)$	$p < .001$	$p = .004$	$p = .60$
Larceny ($n = 114$)			
R^2	.147	.152	.153
F	9.533	0.745	0.264
$p(F)$	$p < .001$	$p = .39$	$p = .85$
Auto theft ($n = 79$)			
R^2	.156	.156	.174
F	7.006	0.016	0.539
$p(F)$	$p = .002$	$p = .90$	$p = .66$
Forgery and fraud ($n = 69$)			
R^2	.271	.273	.296
F	12.245	0.176	0.758
$p(F)$	$p < .001$	$p = .68$	$p = .52$
Drug sales ($n = 57$)			
R^2	.162	.191	.272
F	5.230	1.907	2.553
$p(F)$	$p = .008$	$p = .17$	$p = .07$

TABLE 2.5
Equations Used to Estimate Logarithm of Sentence Length

Crime type	Intercept	Texas	California	λqJt	Std error
Robbery	3.686	.284	−.096		.815
	(.102)	(.157)	(.135)		
Assault	3.534	.380	−.260		1.084
	(.142)	(.228)	(.186)		
Burglary	1.938	.546	−.267	.204	.184
	(.395)	(.120)	(.128)	(.072)	
Larceny	2.472	.885	.109		.880
	(.134)	(.214)	(.190)		
Auto theft	3.232	.060	−.726		.873
	(.160)	(.264)	(.222)		
Forgery and fraud	2.942	.700	−.366		.815
	(.226)	(.272)	(.275)		
Drug sales	3.039	.779	−.168		.968
	(.216)	(.306)	(.319)		

Career Length

Information about each offender's career—the time between first offense and participation in the Rand survey—was available from the offender's self-reports. Because only inmates of adult prisons and jails were included in the Rand survey, no juvenile offenders were eligible for inclusion in the sample. (A negligible number of juveniles sentenced to adult facilities were sampled but were not included in this analysis.) Thus the appropriate criminal "career" length should exclude time spent as an active juvenile offender. This is the same definition used by the Rand researchers.

The distribution of adult career lengths-to-date among the unweighted sample of offenders was similar among the states; in Chapter 4, it will be shown that the rate of dropout from the offending population was virtually identical among the three states. A few offenders failed to specify their age, the time of their first offense, or some other variable necessary to identify the length of their adult criminal career; these offenders were assigned the median career length for offenders in their state: California, 5.0 years; Michigan, 4.9 years; and Texas, 3.6 years.

Sample Weights

The probability that each respondent in the sample would have been included in an incoming cohort was estimated, using Equations (2.8) and (2.11) and the data defined above. Probabilities were roughly symmetrically distributed about the value .40, indicating that roughly 40 percent of the adult offenders like those in jail or prison enter incarceration each year. The probabilities range from nearly zero to slightly above 1.0. These last figures resulted from the age adjustment factor, Equation (2.11). Although inelegant, these impossible probabilities have no adverse effect on the sample weighting.

The distribution of sample weights is illustrated by Figure 2.2; the average weight has been multiplied through by a constant, so that the apparent number of offenders in the weighted sample will be identical to the actual number of respondents in the unweighted sample. In addition, the weights have been constrained to be less than 10.0. Without this constraint, a few offenders with very low sampling probabilities would have received very large weights, and effectively swamped the rest of the sample.

Was This Trip Necessary?

Deriving and calculating sample weights for the Rand survey was a time-consuming, if straightforward process. Was it really worth the trouble? A before/after comparison of two key results suggests that it was.

Figure 2.3 compares the distribution of offense rates for the unweighted and weighted samples, for each of the three states. Figure 2.4 compares the distribution of adult career lengths for the two samples. Close inspection of these graphs reveals two important benefits of the sample weights used here.

First, note that virtually every part of the distribution changed when the

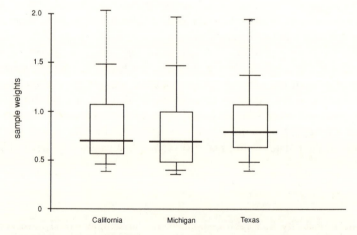

FIGURE 2.2. The distribution of sample weights is slightly upwardly skewed.

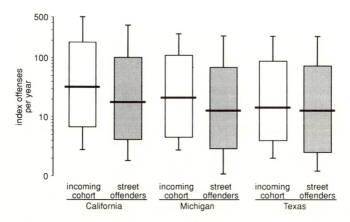

FIGURE 2.3. Effects of weighting on distribution of offense rates (logarithmic scale).

sample was weighted. Some of the changes were very large: in California, for example, the median member of an incoming cohort committed some 33 index crimes per year, whereas the median active offender committed slightly more than half as many. As one would suspect, the more frequent and less persistent offenders among the population of active offenders are more likely to be included in the prison sample. Failure to weight the sample would result in overestimates of the frequency of offending, and underestimates of the average criminal career length.

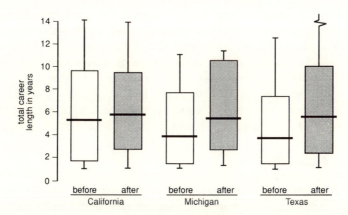

FIGURE 2.4. Effects of weighting on distribution of adult career lengths.

Second, note that the distributions for each state are more alike after weighting than before. For example, the median member of California's incoming cohort committed more than twice as many index crimes each year as the median member of the Texas cohort; but the difference between the median active offenders is only about 30 percent. Had the sample not been weighted, we would have concluded that offenders differed greatly from state to state. Such a conclusion was drawn by the Rand researchers (Chaiken & Chaiken, 1982, pp. 48–49). In fact, most of the differences appear to have been caused by differing patterns of imprisonment. Note also that there is considerable error in the weights assigned each offender; it is possible that weights based on better information would have eliminated the differences entirely.

The 1978 Rand sample, drawn to resemble a typical incoming cohort to jail and prison, includes more high-rate and young offenders, and more offenders who run high risks of arrest, conviction, and incarceration than would a sample of active offenders. Case weighting reduces these biases, changing the analysis results considerably.

The Validity of Offense Rate Estimates

Several parameters must be estimated to identify the selective incapacitation effects of criminal justice policies. All can affect the final result, but there are good reasons to be particularly concerned with the distribution of λ. One reason was demonstrated in the introduction: Relatively small differences in the distribution of offense rates may have a large impact on the effectiveness of selective activities. Another reason is illustrated in the next chapter: The differences among the various available estimates are anything but small.

What is even more important for our purposes, the average Rand 2 offender reported committing crimes far more frequently than anyone had ever estimated before, even after weighting the sample. Because weighting the sample should have brought the Rand 2 offense rates in line with those obtained by previous researchers, it is necessary to consider whether the most important data collected in the Rand survey are simply wrong. This, in turn, casts a shadow on all the reanalysis results presented here. Clearly it is worthwhile to examine the validity and reliability of the offense rates reported in the Rand 2 survey.

Sources of Discrepancy

The discrepancies between prior research and the Rand 2 results may stem from biases inherent in estimation of λ from self-reports or from the unique self-report method employed by the Rand researchers.

Prior research suggests that self-reports are biased, but in prior studies the biases have worked the other way: People tend to deny or minimize their previous involvement in crime (Hirschi, Hindelang, & Weis, 1980). Despite the assurances of confidentiality customarily given to survey respondents, many may be concerned that their responses will leak out to their neighbors (Kahn & Cannell, 1957). Even if the respondents believe the assurances of anonymity, they may be concerned that the interviewer will think less of them (Clark & Tifft, 1966; Farrington, 1973). And respondents may even deny or minimize their criminal activities so that they think better of themselves (Bradburn, 1974; Stocking, 1978). The common ground among these explanations is that people are concerned with deviations from community norms, and their responses are systematically biased to minimize these deviations.

Of course, these are surveys of people who are free. A different dynamic may well be at work in a survey of jail and prison inmates. Inmates have little to lose by admitting their criminal activity in full: the experience of incarceration is itself enough to remind their "neighbors," the interviewer, and themselves that they have done bad things. In fact, they may have something to gain by exaggerating their criminality, since status in prison is tied to dangerousness and slickness outside of it (Silberman, 1977, pp. 386–387). This suggests a "dual bias" hypothesis: Inmates who associate mostly with other offenders when not in prison or who define themselves by their criminal activity may be more prone to exaggeration; those who consider themselves to be "straights," or "working people," associate with noncriminals, and still feel important ties to straight values may deny or minimize their crimes much like members of the general population. On the other hand, as detailed in Chapter 3, the 1975 and 1976 Rand surveys produced self-reports of average λ very similar to those produced through other means. And when a version of the 1978 survey was administered to Colorado prisoners under a wide variety of conditions (including full anonymity, administration in hostile locations, and use of a short questionnaire that prevented the interviewer from establishing a rapport with the offender), the offense rates hardly changed at all (English, 1990). These results suggests that the method of self-reporting may be less responsible for the differences than the specific design of the 1978 questionnaire.

It is easy to see why. In the 1975 and 1976 Rand inmate surveys, respondents were asked directly about the number of crimes they had committed over some period and about the amount of time they had spent on the street during that period, able to commit crimes. Researchers then simply divided the number of crimes by the amount of time available. In the 1978 survey, however, Rand experimented with another method that promised to give more reliable results. The offense rate of each respondent for each crime type was to be calculated from the answer to two questions:

- Respondents were asked to supply a rough estimate for the frequency with which they committed crimes of a given type. For example, they indicated whether they committed burglaries about every month, every week, or every day.

- Respondents were then asked to use this rough estimate to help zero in on the exact frequency of crime commission. Burglars who claimed to commit burglaries every week were asked how many burglaries they usually committed each week; if they claimed to commit burglaries every day, they were asked how many they usually committed each day; and so on.

The researchers then extrapolated from the offender's second, fine-tuned estimate to find the number of crimes that offender committed per year of "street time."

There were indications that this method of obtaining offense rate information is more reliable than other methods. First, because the number of prior crimes is less important than the frequency of crime commission, it is clearly more straightforward to ask direct questions about frequency. In Rand 1, many high-rate offenders probably used a method similar to that used in Rand 2 to estimate the total number of crimes they committed, so this method probably eliminated some mental arithmetic, as well. Replications of the Rand technique on other in-prison samples have provided very similar results (DiIulio, 1990; Horney & Marshall, 1991b; Mande & English, 1988). Finally, the Rand researchers tried out a variety of methods on a sample of police officers. The frequency extrapolation approach provided the most accurate estimates of the number of arrests made and citations written (Peterson et al., 1981, pp. 103–122).

Still, an approach that is more accurate for most offenders may produce badly biased results. Due to purely mechanical reasons, the potential for large errors is highest among the most frequent offenders. For example, a high-rate burglar who in truth breaks into 2.5 houses each week might reasonably state that he committed three break-ins in a typical week. His true offense rate would thus be 130 burglaries per year, but his recorded rate would be 156. Although his estimate is only 20 percent too high, a difference of 26 crimes is important when the median offender reports committing only 2 or 3 burglaries per year. If frequent offenders are equally likely to overestimate as underestimate, and if overestimates are the same proportionate size as underestimates, the errors will of course cancel out. But if there are even small estimation biases among the worst offenders, these errors may swamp the rest of the sample.

Several researchers have examined these and similar questions. By combining their findings with reanalysis results, speculative but useful measures of the reliability and validity of the survey results may be obtained. These measures, in turn, have implications for how analysis of the Rand data set should be conducted and interpreted.

Prior Work

Prior work on the reliability and validity of inmate survey data focused on two kinds of issues:

- *Internal quality* questions focused on how well the respondents were able to follow the skip patterns, crime-type descriptions, and other instructions given in the questionnaire. If a large proportion of respondents seemed confused or gave clearly inconsistent answers, then any results would clearly be suspect from the beginning.
- *External reliability* questions focused on the consistency of respondents' self-reports of arrests and convictions with their official record. If the self-reports and official records were consistent, then respondents would presumably report their offenses accurately, as well.

Although the results were generally favorable, these analyses did not answer all the important validity questions. To see why, let us consider their findings in some detail.

Internal Quality

A large majority of the respondents appeared to follow the sometimes-complicated questionnaire with little difficulty. Ninety-five percent followed the skip patterns without a hitch; 85 percent filled out the calendar correctly to the month. Jan and Marcia Chaiken (1982) concluded that "83 percent of respondents tracked the questionnaire with a high degree of accuracy and completeness, and were very consistent in their answers" (pp. 224–225). Better-educated respondents followed the skips better and left fewer blanks than poorly educated respondents; blacks were more confused and inconsistent; convicted drug dealers and offenders who described themselves as "thieves," "players," and "alcoholics" were significantly less consistent than others (Chaiken & Chaiken, 1982, pp. 242–243). Similar results were obtained when Rand's methods were applied to Colorado prison inmates (Mande & English, 1988).

One recurring problem deserves note. Many respondents had difficulty identifying the time spanned by Windows 1 and 2. As a result, answers to questions about the nature of their criminal activity and general lifestyle during these periods are probably less accurate than similar answers for Window 3 (Chaiken & Chaiken, 1982, p. 224). It will be important to keep this in mind later, since some of the findings of Chapters 3 and 4 rely on comparisons of criminal activity and lifestyle among the three windows.

A few of the respondents seemed to have been considerably more confused than the average, and Chaiken and Chaiken suspected that they may have given systematically different answers to questions about offense rates and criminal activity. As it happened, this was generally not the case. For both Rand 2 and the Colorado study, correlations between measures of internal quality and offense rates were mostly small and insignificant. And when the respondents with the worst internal quality scores were removed, the distribution of λ for each of the crimes surveyed remained largely unchanged (Chaiken & Chaiken, 1982, pp. 247–251; Mande & English, 1988, pp. 114–134).

However, Chaiken and Chaiken did note an interesting pattern in the offense rates among those offenders with poor internal quality: They were abnormally concentrated at the upper and lower tails of the offense rate distribution (Chaiken & Chaiken, 1982, p. 226). A partial explanation for this may have been an artifact of the coding procedures: Some respondents had poor internal quality because they left many items blank, and these offenders were assigned the lowest λ consistent with what they did put down (cf. Chaiken & Chaiken, 1982, p. 226; Visher, 1986, p. 46). Nevertheless, this may not account entirely for the disproportionate number of low-λ responses, and it does not account at all for the greater proportion of inconsistent respondents at the high end of the λ distribution. This result suggests that the highest and lowest reported offense rates are probably less reliable than those in the middle.

A second internal quality problem concerns the effects of intermittent criminality on the results. Rand's frequency extrapolation technique required offenders to estimate their offense rates for a *usual* day, week, or month, and the offenders may have understood this term differently than the researchers did. One problem concerns definition. As used in the calculation of offense rates, *usual* meant *arithmetic average*. Nevertheless, a reasonable offender might easily have understood the word to mean *median* or *modal*. Depending on whether an offender commits crimes in spurts or steadily over time, an offender with a perfect memory and due good faith could have responded in such a way that a researcher would greatly overestimate or underestimate the true offense rate. Reanalysis of the Rand results suggested that intermittent offending was the rule, not the exception (Rolph, Chaiken, & Houchens, 1981). And a study of Nebraska inmates (Horney & Marshall, 1991b) confirmed that only 10 to 25 percent of offenders committed crimes at a steady rate throughout the year. When asked, most offenders reported committing crimes at two or three rates, even when they were active. So most offenders faced such a dilemma.

Even if they define "usual" as expected, offenders may be unable to recall what a usual day, week, or month was like. Although no hard data on offenders' perceptions are available, one might reasonably suppose that many criminals will incorrectly recall as usual those periods in their career in which they are especially active (Cohen, 1986; Visher, 1986). Evidence from the Nebraska inmate study suggests that, if this were true, the mean offense rate would be exaggerated by about 75 percent (Horney & Marshall, 1991b). If high-rate offenders are especially likely to make these errors (Spelman, 1983, pp. 64–65), the skewness of the λ distribution would be exaggerated as well.

As it happens, there is reason to believe that jail and prison inmates carried out this task rather well. In a second study of Nebraska inmates, Horney and Marshall (1991a) compared two methods of frequency extrapolation: A control group of 250 inmates answered essentially the same questions as the Rand inmates; another group of 250 filled out an experimental survey, specifying the number of months they committed particular crimes at (for them) low, medium, and high rates. The experimental group then estimated the rate at which they committed crimes during their low-, medium-, and high-rate months. Surprisingly, the distribution of offense rates did not differ between experimentals and controls, suggesting that offenders did a good job of balancing their various offense rates. This study also suggests that another potential problem with the Rand survey—that it focuses on the period just before arrest when an offender is almost certain to be active—is probably unimportant. For most offenders, periods of high activity came and went so quickly that the bias was minimal.

External Reliability

There are good reasons to compare self-reported arrests and convictions with officially recorded arrest and conviction data: It allows a direct assessment of reliability and validity, the correlation of internal quality measures to reporting errors of demonstrable size and direction, and so on. And offenders may make the same kinds of systematic mistakes in reporting crimes as they do in reporting arrests and convictions. But the analogy should not be taken too far.

One problem is that arrests and convictions were measured the same way in Rand 2 as offense rates were measured in Rand 1—offenders were asked about the number of total arrests and convictions, rather than about the frequency per day, week, or month. This was a perfectly reasonable thing to do; most offenders are not arrested or convicted very often. But we cannot use these results to check the frequency extrapolation method of estimating λ.

Another problem is that self-reports of arrests and convictions may be biased differently from self-reports of offense rates. Because arrests are more salient in an offender's career than serious crimes (and because there are usually fewer of them), they are less likely to be forgotten. In addition, because arrest is in a sense a mark of failure, offenders ready and willing to boast about their wickedness may tell the truth or minimize their official record when asked. Certainly there is less to be gained by boasting about a long rap sheet, especially when offenders know their responses can be checked against the real thing. Despite these difficulties, analysis of errors in arrest and conviction self-reports is cetainly better than nothing. What are the results?

The self-reports of most offenders squared with their official records with few or no disparities. But in most cases of disparity, the inmates reported arrests and convictions that were not found in their official records. As a result, the average number of self-reported arrests was considerably larger than the number reflected in the criminal histories (Mande & English, 1988, pp. 99–100; Marquis, 1981, p. 77).

Some of these cases can be accounted for by inadequacies of criminal records. For example, many respondents claimed unrecorded juvenile arrests and incarcerations. Given the limited availability of juvenile records, it is very likely that these self-reports were more accurate than the records.

Other disparities are more likely to result from offender errors, however, and the pattern of these errors supports the dual bias hypothesis described above. In general, the longer the record, the greater the size of the disparity. And two kinds of inmates systematically exaggerated the length of their arrest records— younger respondents, and those with many felony convictions (Marquis, 1981, pp. 75–76). This fits the hypothesis nicely: Younger respondents are less likely to have developed ties to the conventional social order (Hirschi, 1969), whereas offenders with many convictions are more likely to think of themselves as criminals than their comrades who have been labeled as criminal less often, and who have probably committed fewer crimes (Becker, 1963; Lemert, 1967).

A less direct test also supports the hypothesis: As stated, when offenders are asked exactly how many arrests they have rung up, the self-report total tends to be larger than the officially recorded total; but when they are only asked to state whether or not they have ever been arrested for a particular crime, the proportion who report arrests is consistently lower than the proportion who really were arrested for each crime type, according to official records. Marquis (1981) concludes that

> on balance, the prisoners tend slightly toward denying committing and being arrested for the selected crimes, but if they do not deny, they tend to overstate how often they have been arrested for the offenses they committed. (p. 65)

If this hypothesis held up under further analysis, the practical significance would be substantial. The combination of deniers at the low end and exaggerators at the high end of the arrest distribution (and, perhaps, of the offense rate distribution, as well) means that the mean of the self-report distribution will be larger than the true mean; and the self-report distribution will be more upwardly skewed than the true distribution, because the lower tail will be pushed toward zero, whereas the upper tail is stretched upward. If offense rates are biased in the same ways as the arrest distributions seem to be biased, then policy analyses based on the 1978 inmate data will systematically favor both collective and selective incapacitation. This is because incapacitation works best when the average offender commits crimes often and when the offense rate distribution is very skewed. Given the potential importance of this systematic bias, prudence suggests that this hypothesis be examined more carefully.

Reanalysis

The examination of the dual-bias hypothesis proceeds in two steps. First, it is important to confirm that the self-reported distribution of arrests is more skewed and that the average values are higher than the distribution of officially recorded arrests. If so, then the final result of the system of biases is consistent with that predicted by the dual-bias hypothesis. To answer this question, descriptive statistics of the two distributions are compared. Second, it is important to confirm that the disparities between self-reports and official records are greatest among the offenders with the most arrests and those with the fewest arrests. To answer this question, the disparities between self-reports and official records are calculated for each case in the sample, and broken down by each value of self-reported arrests.

Marquis (1981, pp. 85–86) suggests that reanalysts combine crime types to reduce the effects of random error. Aggregating conceptually similar crimes also has the advantage of simplifying the analysis. Thus each offender's arrests for burglaries, larcenies, auto thefts, frauds, and forgeries—the property crimes considered in the Rand survey—will all be combined; similarly, arrests for personal and commercial robberies and for assaults—the personal crimes considered—will also be combined.

If our working hypothesis is true, then the average offender will report more arrests than will be found in the official records. As shown in Table 2.6, this turns out to be true for both personal and property crimes. The self-reported mean for personal crimes is some 60 percent higher than the officially recorded mean; the self-reported mean for property crimes is 43 percent higher. If the same pattern holds for self-reported offense rates, we would expect mean λ to be about 50 percent higher than that found by previous researchers using different methods.

If this exaggerated mean is due mostly to overestimates among those offenders who have been arrested most often, and particularly if offenders who have been arrested only a few times tend to underestimate their arrests, then the self-reported arrest distribution should be considerably more skewed than the officially recorded distribution. The bottom half of Table 2.6 confirms that this, too, is the case.

It may be that the system producing these consistent biases is different from that hypothesized; but the results of the system (whatever it is) are identical to those predicted.

Systematically higher means and larger skews could be produced by a number of "bias systems" besides the one hypothesized here. For example, it

TABLE 2.6
*The Average Offender Reports More Arrests
than the Official Record*

Crime type	Self-reported	Recorded	*t* (difference)
Personal	.897	.569	10.76
	(.399)	(.335)	($p \ll .001$)
Property	1.102	.769	10.85
	(.357)	(.386)	($p \ll .001$)

Note. Figures shown are the mean and (in parentheses) the sample standard deviation of each distribution.

*And the Self-Report Distribution Is Much More Skewed
than the Official Record Distribution*

Crime type	Self-reported	Recorded	*t* (difference)
Personal	1.337	.752	4.78
	(.086)	(.087)	($p \ll .001$)
Property	1.425	.465	8.26
	(.077)	(.087)	($p \ll .001$)

Note. Figures shown are skewness coefficients and (in parentheses) their standard errors, for each distribution.

may be that all offenders overestimate their arrest record by an amount proportional to their arrest record. Alternatively, it may be that the criminal justice system consistently loses or fails to record some fixed proportion of arrests made. To test the hypothesis more directly, let us consider five quintiles of the self-reported arrest distribution—the first quintile includes the 20 percent of offenders who reported the fewest prior arrests, the second quintile includes the 20 percent who reported the next fewest, and so on. Then we should expect that offenders in the lowest quintile or two would underreport, and that those in the highest quintile or so—the offenders with the most arrests—would overreport their arrests rather dramatically. As shown in Figure 2.5, this is exactly what happens. Note that the degree of exaggeration seems to increase exponentially.

The self-reported arrest records of the most frequently arrested offenders are not only positively biased; the absolute value of the bias is much greater than that of any other group of offenders. In fact, the median discrepancy for offenders in the top quintile is greater than the 90th percentile discrepancy for any other group of offenders. It is no wonder that the mean and skewness statistics are so much greater for the self-reported distribution; the right tail is pulled far out of line by a group of what seem to be shameless braggarts.

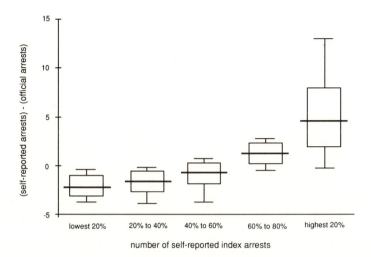

FIGURE 2.5. The absolute discrepancy between self-reports and official records is greatest for the frequent arrestees.

This result seems to be in line with Marquis's hypothesis that random measurement errors are proportional to the value of the variable being measured (Marquis, 1981, p. 85). If this were true, then frequent arrestees would err by much larger absolute amounts than others—as in fact they do. But proportional random error also implies that frequent and infrequent arrestees both err by about the same proportion, on average. By converting all values to a logarithmic (proportional) scale, the discrepancy between the frequently arrested and the infrequently arrested offenders may be removed.

As shown in Figure 2.6, the proportionate random error hypothesis is not strictly true. Instead of being constant across all offenders, the percentage error for arrest self-reports is U-shaped: The most frequently and least frequently arrested criminals make the largest percentage mistakes in measurement. Note in particular the large percentage error recorded by the median offender in the lowest quintile. The median lowest-quintile offender errs by 100 percent in reporting prior arrests, compared to a median error of 25 percent for offenders in the next quintile, and of 50 to 60 percent for other offenders.

On the whole, the dual-bias hypothesis—that infrequent arrestees deny and minimize, whereas frequent arrestees overestimate—describes the pattern of errors very cleanly. The largest and most important biases are concentrated among the highest- and lowest-ranking offenders in the sample; the middle 60 percent or so of offenders seem to be estimating their arrests more accurately than the others. For the reasons noted above, it is by no means certain that these results can be extended directly to self-reported offense rates. But these results do

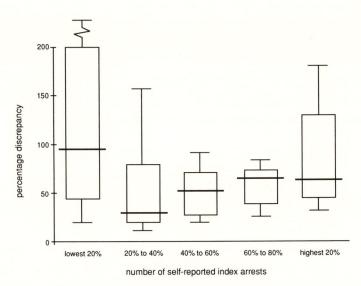

FIGURE 2.6. The percentage discrepancy is greatest for the most frequent and least frequent arrestees.

increase the likelihood that the same dual biases hold for the distribution of reported offense rates.

Implications for Analysis

These results suggest that analysts bent on describing the distribution of offense rates would do well to concentrate their efforts on the respondents in the middle ranges of the distribution, because the self-reports of these offenders are probably more accurate than those on the tails. In particular, the moments of the distribution—the mean, variance, skewness coefficient, and so on—are very likely to be wrong, because they depend so greatly on the highest and lowest values. If one is attempting to fit a Normal, gamma, or other functional form to the empirical distribution of arrests or offense rates, the frequently used method of "matching moments" is likely to yield very unreliable results.

One way around these difficulties is to rely on so-called robust measures. For example, instead of using the (unreliable) mean to characterize the center of the offense rate distribution, the analyst could use the median, or (better) a Winsorized or trimmed mean. Unfortunately, medians, Winsorized means, or trimmed means are downwardly biased descriptions of the center of a skewed distribution; that is, they would consistently underestimate the offense rate of the average (mean) offender. If this underestimate is large, it would have a substantial impact on estimates of the effectiveness of general or selective incapacitation.

Luckily, there is an unbiased solution that is incidentally elegant. For most known functional forms (such as gammas, Normals, and the like) it is possible to identify distribution parameters on the basis of sample quantiles (Johnson & Kotz, 1967). These methods are usually less powerful than moment-matching or maximum likelihood methods, but they are unbiased and resistant to the kind of tail-concentrated error shown here. Thus if theory can help identify the functional form of the offense rate or other distribution, we may be able to use the method of quantiles to estimate the mean, standard deviation, and other descriptive statistics, without the undue influence of the underreporters or overreporters in the top and bottom 20 percent of the distribution.

These results have implications for prediction of offense rates, as well. Even after taking the logarithm of the arrest or offense rate distribution, errors in measurement are likely to be heteroskedastic. Because it is the offenders with the highest and lowest reported offense rates who make the largest errors, regression coefficients are likely to be less accurate than they seem (Kmenta, 1972, p. 256). The distribution of percentage errors is considerably "flatter" than the distribution of absolute errors, however, so taking the logarithm of the dependent variable before running the regression will alleviate the problem.

We can ill afford to throw away estimating power if our estimates are full of random errors, and Marquis's (1981) extensive analysis of the reliability of arrest frequency self-reports (and, by inference, offense rate self-reports) indicates that the estimates for each of the crime types considered are woefully unreliable (pp. 78–81). One solution adopted above is to dispense with a crime-by-crime analysis, and instead consider aggregates such as "property" and "personal" crimes. Another solution is to consider differences among states carefully and combine samples from different states when appropriate. Both of these solutions have been adopted throughout the reanalysis that follows.

Analysis of reported arrests indicates that self-reports are biased in two ways. Offenders with few arrests systematically underestimate the number of times they are arrested. Offenders with many arrests systematically overestimate. Those in the middle are about right.

If self-reports of offense rates are biased in the same ways, then (1) the mean and variance of self-reported offense rates will be larger than the real mean and variance, and (2) the distribution of self-reported offense rates will be more skewed than the real distribution. These biases may be controlled by trimming observations from the tails, using sample quantiles to fit the data to distributional forms, using the logarithm of offense and arrest rates in analysis, and combining crime types and (when appropriate) states to reduce random errors.

3

The Offense Rate

We begin our description of the offending population with what is probably the most important parameter of all—the offense rate. Certainly the offense rate, λ, has received more attention than any other descriptor. There are a variety of reasons for this. For one, the offense rate is critical to estimates of the effects of collective incapacitation strategies. If the average value of λ for all active offenders were known, it would not be difficult to establish a minimum value for the effects of changes in the likelihood and length of incarceration on the crime rate (Cohen, 1978). And the distribution of offense rates among offenders is critical to estimates of the effects of selective incapacitation. In fact, most current selective proposals resulted more or less directly from the Philadelphia cohort study, which verified that a few offenders commit a lot of crimes (Wolfgang, Figlio, & Sellin, 1972).

But the crime-control benefits of incapacitation are not the whole picture. Incapacitation involves costs, as well: The direct expenses of building and maintaining jails and prisons are the most obvious, but removing convicted offenders from the community will also eliminate whatever social benefits they create while they are free. And the offense rate can help us get a handle on the importance of these benefits. For example, if the average rate is high—more than two or three crimes a week, for instance—we would tend to think of crime as a full-time job, and the typical criminal as full-time operator. As a result, most of us would agree that there are relatively few costs of incapacitating the average crook besides the direct costs of imprisonment: The offender is putting little into society but steadily taking a lot out. On the other hand, if the typical crooks commit only a few crimes each year, they must get most of their income from noncriminal sources. So they seem less wicked; we may even find that they put more into society through their legitimate activities than they take out in crime. Given the high costs of imprisonment, incapacitating the typical low-rate criminal might cost us more than it would benefit. Deterrence, retribution, and rehabilitation may all still provide sufficient justification for removing the average offender from the community. But the practical value of incapacitation strategies depends greatly on the average value of the offense rate.

In this section, empirical estimates of the rate of offending among active offenders are examined in detail. The discussion is in four parts. First, the average value of the offense rate is considered. The results of previous research and reanalysis of the Rand survey are integrated, with an eye to identifying a consensus as to the frequency of the typical offender. Second, the distribution of offense rates about this average is considered, with particular attention to the skewness of the distribution. Third, the relationship between offense rates for two distinct types of offenses—property and personal crimes—is measured. Finally, methods for using these results in analytical and simulation models are developed.

Before turning to empirical estimates, however, let us first take a harder look at what we mean by the offense rate—how it may be defined and estimated.

Defining the Offense Rate

Before attempting to define what we mean by the offense rate, it is a good idea to ask what we are going to use it for. λ fulfills two roles in our analysis. First, the offense rate is our basic measure of the benefits of incapacitation. We will use the offense rate to tell us how much society will benefit by incapacitating an individual. Second, λ is an important component in calculating the likelihood that an individual will in fact be incapacitated. Although the innocent are sometimes wrongly punished, generally speaking, one must commit a crime before one can be sent to jail or prison. All else equal, the more crimes one commits, the greater the likelihood of imprisonment; the more crimes one commits per unit time, the greater the proportion of time one must spend behind bars. Let us examine how the offense rate may best be defined, for each of these two definitions.

The Offense Rate as Benefit/Cost Ratio

To see how the offense rate may be used as a benefits measure, let us put it in the context of the criminal history of a hypothetical offender.

Call him Ishmael. He is 40 years old, and has been committing serious crimes intermittently since the age of 14. We have gathered extensive (and conclusive) evidence on Ishmael's illegal activities, from his own reports, from official records, and from friends, colleagues, and other witnesses. Thus we can plot Ishmael's offenses from birth to the present, something like this:

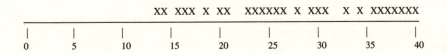

Each "X" represents an index crime. As shown, Ishmael committed his first serious crime at age 14, and has committed crimes in fits and starts ever since. All told, he committed 27 crimes over his 26-year career.

Now suppose that Ishmael had been caught for one of these offenses and received a prison term in punishment. Because he would have been unable to commit crimes against society as a whole while in prison, those crimes that he in fact committed during these years would not have happened at all:

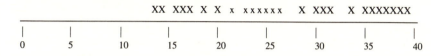

By incapacitating Ishmael for five years in his early twenties, society could presumably have prevented seven crimes. For each year of incarceration, society would have reduced the number of index offenses by 1.4. We might say that the benefit/cost ratio of incapacitating Ishmael for each of these years was 1.4 index offenses per year of prison time.

There are two reasons this figure may fail to correctly measure the true benefit/cost ratio of incapacitating Ishmael. For one thing, the number of crimes Ishmael committed is hardly an exact measure of the full social benefits of stopping his illegal activities; the time he spent in jail is not a complete measure of the full social costs of incarcerating him. More on this in a moment. The more important problem is the second: Use of the offense rate as a benefit/cost measure assumes implicitly that incapacitating an offender will prevent all the crimes he would have committed. This is almost certainly not true.

It seems reasonable on its face: "Jail a criminal, stop his crimes" has a commonsense value that is hard to dispute. But it is also true that imprisonment of some offenders, particularly imprisonment of the most active, will affect the behavior of those still on the street. Because the criminals who have been imprisoned are role models and teachers for some offenders, particularly the young, incarcerating them may prevent their followers and students from committing crimes (Sutherland, 1947), or at least inhibit development of their criminal activities (Elliott, Huizinga, & Ageton, 1985). On the other hand, some imprisoned offenders were parts of ongoing criminal organizations, such as drug distribution rings, juvenile gangs, and less formal offending networks. As a result, they may be replaced by others, recruited to take their place.

Most analysts have considered only the second of these, concluding that "recruitment" is unlikely for street crimes such as robbery and burglary. James Q. Wilson's (1984) description of the effect is probably the most complete:

> For certain crimes organized along business lines—such as gambling, white-collar crime, narcotics trafficking, and perhaps prostitution—it is likely that replacements are recruited or that offenders have the ability to keep competition off the streets. But it

seems unlikely that this process operates with ordinary street crime and familial
violence. For [street crimes] there are no barriers to entry and no scarcity of criminal
opportunities. The supply of robbers is not, at present crime rates, affected by the
"demand" for robbery—that is, by the number of persons acting in ways that invite
robbery. (p. 146)

Recruitment is characteristic of "businesslike" ventures; street crime is not businesslike; hence recruitment is not characteristic of the demand for street crimes.

One problem with this argument is that the syllogism isn't valid. Recruitment is certainly characteristic of ventures that are obviously businesslike, such as prostitution and drug trafficking; yet it is conceivable that less clearly corporate-style offenders would recruit accomplices and helpers as well. Another problem is even more basic: Recruitment is beside the point, because our concern is with the number of crimes actually committed, not with the number of offenders committing them. The two are only equivalent if each offender commits crimes alone, without the help, tacit cooperation, or even knowledge of any other offenders. To make these points more clearly, let us consider a not untypical robbery:

Alan, Bob, and Craig, young men in their late teens and early 20s, are friends and
neighbors in a public housing project. One evening they all get drunk and smoke dope;
Craig suggests that they rob a nearby liquor store. Weeks before, Bob had stolen a
handgun on a burglary; the three decide that Bob will use his weapon. Alan plans the
robbery and drives the getaway car. The crime goes off without a hitch, and the
robbers split their $300 take equally.

Now suppose that Alan, Bob, and Craig find that the robbery was so easy to commit that they decide to rob more liquor stores, at the rate of about twice a month, or 24 per year. Eventually, an eyewitness identifies Bob as the gunman but is unsure of Craig and never sees Alan outside in the car. Bob is arrested, convicted, and sentenced to a 2-year term. What happens to the other two during Bob's period of incapacitation?

If we accept the "recruitment/replacement" hypothesis as it is usually posed, we are forced to assume that they stop committing robberies entirely. And this assumption is not implausible: Without Bob's weapon, the other two robbers may find that robberies are too difficult to commit. Because their association relied much on their previous friendship, and not on the kind of "businesslike" arrangement characteristic of organized crimes, it may be that Bob is irreplaceable. And Bob's incarceration may have a special deterrent effect on the other two. Such close-hand experience of the bitter fruits of crimes could conceivably cause them to go entirely straight. Thus jailing Bob would prevent 24 crimes for each year he was incarcerated.

On the other hand, jailing Bob may have no effect whatever on the efforts of Alan and Craig. Presumably they chose to rob liquor stores because it was among the best available means of getting money; although Bob's arrest may have hammered home to them the risks of their choice, nothing fundamental has changed. Their enthusiasm for armed robbery may even be buoyed by their own narrow escape from prison. So it is easily conceivable that they could continue to commit liquor store robberies in exactly the way they have. They may even recruit their friend Bruce to help out. Under this scenario, jailing Bob would prevent no crimes at all.

Now suppose that our witness had been particularly observant. Not only did she pick out Bob, but she successfully identified Craig and got the license number of the getaway car, leading to the capture of Alan, as well. All three go to jail. How many crimes have been prevented? In reality, about 24 per year. But had we used the offense rate to measure the crime reduction benefits, we would have assumed that the jailing of each offender would prevent all the crimes in which that offender participated. By jailing Bob, 24 crimes per year were prevented; by jailing Craig, another 24 crimes per year were prevented; by jailing Alan, still another 24 crimes were never committed. This triple-counts the actual number of crimes prevented, which is simply wrong.

If faced with the task of making individual sentencing decisions, we might require additional information about convicted offenders: whether they committed most of their crimes alone or in groups, how large the groups were, whether they were leaders or followers. Each individual's offense rate would be adjusted to reflect the probable effects of incarceration on other people's actions. For our purposes, the most reasonable adjustment is to divide (a) the number of crimes in which an offender participated by (b) the size of the group in which the offender typically worked. This is a natural compromise between the lowest reasonable estimate of the benefit/cost ratio (zero) and the highest reasonable estimate (the unadjusted offense rate). In addition, this method has the advantage of providing the correct answer when all members of an offending group are incarcerated at once.

The best available estimates of the number of offenders involved in reported crimes were compiled by Albert J. Reiss, Jr. (1980), in a reanalysis of the National Crime Survey. Reiss's results are shown in Table 3.1. Two offenders are involved in the average personal crime, whereas 1.6 offenders commit the typical property crime. Although these figures are over 10 years old, there is evidence that they still apply today. The 1979 National Crime Survey showed that 73.5 percent of all violent crimes were committed by only one offender (Bureau of Justice Statistics, 1981, pp. 47, 49). In 1988, the figure was 75.0 percent (Bureau of Justice Statistics, 1990, pp. 46, 50). Even when broken down by crime type, the proportion of multiple offender crimes changed hardly at all throughout the decade.

Although the victims had (understandable) difficulty distinguishing between juvenile and adult offenders, limited evidence suggests that group offending is less frequent among adults than among juveniles. Victim reports from the 1988

TABLE 3.1
*The Average Crime Is Committed by More
than One Offender*

Personal crimes	2.10
Rape	1.56
Robbery	2.27
Assault	2.09
Property crimes	1.58
Burglary	1.55
Larceny/contact	1.55
Larceny/noncontact	1.60
Auto theft	1.72

Source. "Understanding Changes in Crime Rates," by A. J. Reiss, Jr., 1980, in *Indicators of Crime and Criminal Justice: Quantitative Studies,* edited by S. E. Fienberg & A. J. Reiss, Jr., Washington, DC: U.S. Government Printing Office.

National Crime Survey suggest that adults were 2.6 times as likely to commit assault by themselves as juveniles, and 2.1 times as likely to commit robbery without assistance (Bureau of Justice Statistics, 1990). Similar results were obtained in studies of juvenile and adult arrestees (Wilson & Herrnstein, 1985, pp. 292–293). So there is reason to believe that the number of adults who participate in the average crime is considerably less than the figures provided by Reiss.

If adults are in fact twice as likely to work by themselves in all crimes, it must be true that the typical adult offender works with about two-thirds the number of accomplices implied by the National Crime Survey figures. Thus we suppose that 1.73 offenders are involved in the average personal crime perpetrated by a group that includes one or more adults; 1.39 offenders are involved in the typical adult property crime. These adjustments reduce the benefit/cost ratio of incarceration by about 42 percent for personal crimes, and by about 28 percent for property crimes. Given the limited information available, however, careful analysis of the sensitivity of the results to small changes in group offending will clearly be prudent.

So, although the problem of multiple offending implies that the benefit/cost ratio will not in general be identical to the offense rate, the two can be reasonably reconciled by dividing by some estimable figure. The other problem with using offense rate as a measure of the benefit/cost ratio—that it is inaccurate—is probably less important, but harder to control. There are really two problems here. First, if we are to allocate social resources effectively, we will need to express this benefit/cost ratio in terms that are not idiosyncratic to crime control—dollars, for example. Second, the ratio is needlessly crude: All Ishmael's crimes are assumed to be equally harmful to society. The best solution to these two problems would be to weight each crime by the degree of harm it causes. We might consider the seriousness of harm done to the victims, the levels and side effects of fear and anxiety provoked among the victims's friends and neighbors, and the marginal effect of the crime on the levels of fear, crime prevention, avoidance, and insurance among everyone else. If rough data on the seriousness of each crime committed were available, they could be used to weight the offense rate and better approximate the benefits of incarceration. We may even be able to put a dollar value on the benefits of preventing Ishmael's crimes (Cavanagh, 1990; Cohen, 1988).

The costs of incapacitating Ishmael are likely to be easier to measure than the benefits. The most obvious of these costs are direct: It takes money to build and maintain prisons, and each additional inmate contributes to the costs. In addition, virtually all individuals benefit society (however slightly) while they are free; incapacitating them eliminates these benefits. Employment is an obvious example: Most criminals (and certainly most who are so intermittent as Ishmael) cannot live on the money they make from stealing, but must supplement it with legitimate employment; incapacitating Ishmael will prevent him from doing his legitimate work and perhaps throw his family on welfare; thus society will suffer the costs of losing a (perhaps marginally) valued member of the labor force (Larsen, 1983; Zedlewski, 1987). Finally, just as we termed *beneficial* the reductions in public fear and anxiety due to reductions in crime, so must we term *costly* the pain and suffering caused by incarcerating Ishmael—to Ishmael himself, and to friends, relatives, and dependents (Zimring & Hawkins, 1988). Although these costs are not linearly related to the time spent in jail, they will increase as jail time increases. So, in a pinch, time incarcerated can stand as a proxy for all of the costs society must bear in order to put one of its members away.

As this formulation makes clear, time is only appropriate as a cost measure when temporary means of incapacitating offenders are chosen—such as jail, prison, house arrest, or hospitalization. If society adopted a permanent method of incapacitating Ishmael—say, by executing him or cutting off his hands—then the appropriate measure of the benefits would be the full social cost of all Ishmael's crimes throughout the rest of his career (perhaps discounted at some reasonable interest rate). Here, the costs could be represented by the marginal addition to social pain, fear, and feelings of inhumanity associated with Ishmael's humiliatingly public loss, or else by the marginal loss of economic productivity that would be a necessary side-effect of any permanent incapacitation method. The point is, we would still want some form of benefit/cost ratio to help allocate punishments among offenders, but the benefits and the costs would both be different.

We may conclude that a full accounting of the costs and benefits of incapacitating any given individual for any given period of time is liable to be very

complicated, even when all the information needed to construct a reliable estimate is available. And, of course, this information will be available only rarely.
There is no substitute for policymakers who must decide among competing
demands at the highest level—say, more prison cells versus better job
programs—so we will return to this problem in Chapters 6 and 7. But if our only
interest is in making resource allocation decisions within the criminal justice
system, the benefit/cost ratios need not be expressed in dollar terms. We can
probably do quite well by using the offense rate, adjusted to account for multiple-
offender crimes and weighted to reflect the seriousness of each crime, as a
measure of this ratio.

The Offense Rate as a Measure of Risk

If the offense rate can be considered the benefit/cost ratio for incarceration
from society's point of view, it can also be considered a measure of risk from the
offender's point of view. For every crime committed, the offender stands a
chance of getting caught. Whether an offender is caught or not is due partly to
luck, partly to his or her own ability. By making intelligent choices among
targets, methods, and partners, criminals may be able to minimize the risks they
run for each crime they commit. (In Chapter 5, it will be shown that offenders
appear to run greatly differing risks, and that they appear to become more skillful
at avoiding risks as they commit more crimes. That is, they learn through experience.) A thorough measure of risk would take all of the factors an offender could
manipulate into account: whether the offender chooses to attack property rather
than people, whether he conceals his identity through masks, rubber gloves, and
the like, or whether she commits crimes at places and times where she is unlikely
to be seen or heard would all be included in the risk measure. Enough is known
about the methods by which the criminal justice system produces arrests, convictions, and sentences that we could probably weight each offender's offenses to
reflect these risks. But, as above, most of the data needed are liable to be difficult
to collect. It is probably sufficient to consider crimes of different types separately
(because the data are likely to be easy to collect, and because the risks differ
considerably from one crime type to the next), and to assume that the risks are
identical for all crimes of a given type. Of course, this measure will systematically underestimate the differences among offenders.

So the offense rate is a useful statistic for at least two different purposes.
Note, however, that for both purposes it represents a compromise. The true
measure of the benefit/cost ratio of incapacitation or of the risks an offender runs
per unit of time requires much data that would be tedious and difficult to collect;
but for both purposes, we converge on the offense rate as tolerably accurate and
tolerably easy to estimate.

Measuring the Offense Rate

The offense rate consists of two elements: a numerator (the offender's crimes) and a denominator (a time scaling factor). In addition, it must be applied to some group of individuals (the offending population). Let us examine each of these components more carefully.

The Offender's Crimes

Totaling up the full social costs of one's existence, or even of one's criminal acts, is bound to be a tall order. Were Jeremy Bentham to make up a wish list, he'd likely ask for information on acts ranging from the incredibly depraved (chainsaw massacres and reservoir poisonings) to the merely naughty (casual threats to murder small dogs or overthrow the government). But for the sake of practicality (if for no other reason), we must restrict our search somewhat. The most common solution is to include only serious crimes, most often the seven index crimes recorded by the Federal Bureau of Investigation (1990). This eliminates consideration of some very serious forms of misconduct, including transgressions that often go unreported (fraud, forgery), those that may be trivial or serious (vandalism), and those that are sometimes considered to be "victimless" (pimping, drug dealing). Nevertheless, use of the FBI index crimes has the advantages of simplicity and ease of data collection.

Until recently, there was a stronger argument in favor of examining only index crimes: they accounted for the vast majority of sentences to jail and prison (Greenfeld & Minor-Harper, 1984). In the last decade, however, the number of offenders incarcerated on drug charges has climbed dramatically. By 1990, over 30 percent of offenders entering state prisons were drug offenders (Snell & Morton, 1992); in big cities, 38 percent of the incoming cohort to incarceration were drug offenders (Reaves, 1992).

Accounting for drug crimes complicates the analysis, for several reasons. Official records are of no help, because a vanishingly small proportion of drug deals are ever recorded. The number of drug transactions made by the typical street dealer is too large to expect self-reports to be very accurate. And, unlike crimes of injury, intimidation, and theft, where the harm done to victims is tangible, the harm caused by drug dealing is for the most part indirect, intangible, and very difficult to measure. In fact, there may be little relation between the number of deals made and the seriousness of harm done.

On the other hand, it is unlikely that incapacitation strategies can reduce drug dealing very effectively. Barriers to entry are minimal, and in big cities there are more willing participants than jobs to fill (Caulkins, 1990; Kleiman,

1992). So long as deterrent effects are small and the stock of willing "wannabes" is large, incapacitation will prevent few drug crimes.

Recruitment of dealers may also be one reason for the failure of the prison boom of the 1980s to reduce the crime rate. If replacement is in fact nearly complete, and if newly recruited drug dealers are more likely to commit crimes of violence and theft, jailing dealers will indirectly increase the number of index criminals. Such an effect is entirely speculative, and no attempt will be made to account for it in the analysis that follows. But it may be worthy of further study.

We may conclude that drug offenders are not amenable to incapacitation strategies, and need not be accounted for in our analysis. The FBI index crimes, plus fraud and forgery, account for almost 90 percent of nondrug incarcerations, and information on offense rates for all these is available from the Rand inmate surveys and other self-report studies. So this is a reasonably accurate and convenient place to stop.

All index crimes are not alike, at least in terms of the harm done to society. To take this into account in our estimation of the benefits of incapacitation, it is necessary to weight offenders' crimes according to the harm they cause society. At one level, this is relatively easy. For example, we could use the Sellin-Wolfgang seriousness index to measure the physical, economic, and psychic harm done to the victim (Wolfgang et al., 1985); or we could obtain a monetary estimate by combining victim reports of time and money lost with civil court award data that approximate the monetary value of pain and suffering (Cohen, 1988). But these only account for direct costs to victims, and indirect costs may be even more important. For example, homicides and rapes provoke grief and stress among friends and relatives, and fear and anxiety among the rest of us. This, in turn, stimulates us to buy insurance, burglar alarms, and additional police officers, or to avoid enjoyable activities because we believe they are risky. These costs may be as high as or higher than the harm done to the victims themselves (Conklin, 1975; Greer, 1984).

The indirect costs of a crime are not necessarily related to the direct costs. For example, the coldbloodedness of the offense, the mental state of the offender, the method chosen for doing harm, may all affect the levels of fear resulting from a crime (DuBow, McCabe, & Kaplan, 1979). Similarly, a pattern of crimes committed by a singular offender may stimulate a wave of fear and anxiety all its own, out of all proportion to the number of crimes in the series (e.g., Capote, 1965). None of this information is included in the Sellin-Wolfgang index or its monetary competitors.

The upshot is that it is very difficult to measure the social costs of an offender's crimes, even when the best available methods are used. Simply too little is known about how and how much crime hurts society. So even if we could gather perfect data as to the activities of individual offenders, we would be hard-pressed to make unequivocal judgments as to the utility of incarcerating them.

We will not be able to identify with any precision how many jail and prison cells need to be constructed, for example. (Some admittedly imprecise estimates are provided in Chapters 6 and 7.)

If we are willing to make the simplifying assumption that the costs of crime to nonvictims are closely related to the harm done to victims, we can make judgments as to the relative merits of incarcerating individual offenders. That is, we can rank criminals from most wicked (thus first in line for incapacitation) to least (and last). Similarly, if the data are available, we may be able to indicate the tradeoff between the two direct costs of crime—criminal justice system costs (in particular, jail and prison costs) and index crime rates.

All this assumes, of course, that we can identify the number and type of crimes an offender has committed. There are two methods of estimating this figure—self-reports and official records. Self-reports involve no more and no less than asking a sample of individuals how many crimes they have committed. Even assuming they would tell us the truth, there would be problems due to forgetting, misunderstanding the questions posed, and so on. This, of course, is the method employed in the Rand research. Some potential validity problems have been examined in the previous chapter.

Alternatively, we may rely on official records to indicate the number and seriousness of the offenses each individual has committed. Because a relatively small fraction of crimes can be attributed to the offenders responsible for them, this introduces a whole new set of errors. A method for constructing the number of crimes an offender has committed from his arrest and conviction records will be examined in the next section. For now, suffice it to say that the data required for the numerator of the offense rate are likely to be very uncertain.

The Time Scale

Our aim in constructing the denominator of the offense rate is to account for the length of time available to the offender to commit the crimes he committed. So it is clearly necessary to exclude periods of offenders' careers when they have been incapacitated by jail or prison: Not only are they not at risk of arrest and conviction during these periods, but including this period would cause us to double-count the benefits of incapacitation.

It is less obvious what should be done about time spent incapacitated in other ways—in a hospital or asylum, or in the military, for instance. Here, our reasons for estimating the offense rate diverge. Offenders run a low risk of committing crimes during these periods; so it seems reasonable to think of them as "temporarily inactive." If we eliminated such periods, however, we would be forced to account for this inactive time explicitly when modeling individual offense patterns; this is liable to be complicated. Moreover, eliminating temporarily inactive periods would cause us to overstate systematically the benefits of incapacitation, because one of the risks we run when we incarcerate offenders is that they might have been incapacitated in some other way, had we simply left them on the street. On balance, it makes most sense to ignore these periods of low offending risk, and only remove from the time at risk those periods in which the offender was incapacitated through incarceration.

The problem of temporary inactivity brings up a more basic problem. When do we start the clock, and how long do we let it run? One could argue that the clock should start when offenders commit their first crime and continue until they commit their last (or most recent). Although this is certainly simple, it fails to account for the fact that some offenders may have begun running a significant risk of committing crimes earlier in their lives, but by chance did not do so until some later time. Consider the case of a 14-year-old who begins hanging around with older kids who have already begun to shoplift and steal cars. We might suppose that it is just a matter of time before he begins to participate in their criminal activities; but by chance or design, it may be months before the older youths recruit him for his first offense. At what point did our 14-year-old begin to seek opportunities to commit crime?

For the moment, let us (a bit grudgingly) assume that a criminal career begins with the first crime and continues unabated throughout the period in which an offender commits crimes. Then let us move on to a related problem that is even more basic: To what population do we apply this definition of offense rate?

The Offending Population

For most people, most of the time, the risks of committing a crime will be very nearly zero. The exceptional 9-year-old might break into a house and steal a friend's belongings, and further have sufficient knowledge of the wrongness of his actions to make it a criminal offense. Similarly, an exceptional 90-year-old may rob a bank. But very few of even the most highly motivated and dangerous offenders commit crimes at age 9 or 90; for the rest of us, the risks are (thankfully) negligible. One might argue that our estimates of the offense rate should exclude individuals who run such low risks; this makes it easier to collect data and results in more accurate estimates. The argument may be logically extended to include the entire lifetime of those of us who consistently run extremely low risks of committing serious crimes. Restricting the sample of interest to "real criminals" who run risks of committing crimes at higher than some arbitrarily determined level would make it much easier to collect good data.

But some crimes are committed by the very young, the very old, and the very innocent. Arbitrarily excluding crimes committed by these individuals would prevent estimates of offense rates from accounting for all crimes.

In itself, this is not particularly a problem. Our goal is to measure the benefits of incapacitation, not to assign all offenses to the offenders responsible. But—if rarely—some of these offenders who run very low risks are incapacitated. Juvenile probation camps occasionally house offenders who are 12 or younger; some 60-year-olds (at least) are sent to prison; even first-time offenders are jailed and imprisoned if their crimes are egregious enough. So not only can we not account for all crimes if we exclude very low-risk offenders; we cannot even account for all jail and prison terms.

All this means that we have two alternatives open to us when choosing the sample of individuals and time periods for which to estimate offense rates. We may attempt to estimate offense rates for (what amounts to) the entire population, confident that we have accounted for all crimes, incapacitation costs, and resulting crime-reduction benefits. In so doing, however, we multiply our data collection and validity problems by an order of magnitude. Alternatively, we may restrict the population of interest to some subset of particularly criminally inclined individuals, confident that the population is sufficiently well defined that we can collect reasonably reliable data as to their activities. In so doing, we bias our estimates of the crime-control benefits and costs of incapacitation by examining them only for that group for which the benefit/cost ratio (that is, the offense rate) is likely to be highest.

Most of the tension between these two choices can be eliminated if we can estimate the proportion of crimes that can be accounted for by the low-risk group. Some guidance as to these proportions can be gleaned from the longitudinal cohort studies of delinquency that have been conducted in recent years. Two studies were conducted in Philadelphia, of the juvenile and young adult careers of people born in 1945 and in 1958 (Wolfgang, Figlio, & Sellin, 1972; Wolfgang & Tracy, 1983). A series of similar studies were conducted in Racine, Wisconsin (Shannon, 1982), and in London, England (Farrington, 1983).

The procedure works like this. For each member of the population, we find the number of serious index crimes committed and the number of times incarcerated over the entire follow-up period. We then divide the offenders into two groups: a low-risk group of offenders who were arrested only once during the course of their career; and a high-risk group of offenders who were arrested two or more times over their criminal "lifetime." The results, shown in Table 3.2, indicate considerable agreement among the four studies. In each study, the high-risk group accounted for about 90 percent of all crimes committed.

This finding is lent credence by some results obtained by the initial analysts of the Rand 1978 survey. There, they found that 90 percent of serious crimes committed in the State of California could be accounted for by the group of offenders who were like those in jail or prison. To put it differently, only 10 percent of California's crimes were committed by offenders who did not run a substantial risk of going to jail (Greenwood, 1982). Because the benefits and

TABLE 3.2

Recidivists Account for Ninety Percent
of Juvenile and Young Adult Arrests

Location of study	Percentage of arrests
Philadelphia—1	84.5
Philadelphia—2	88.0
London	90.3
Racine	93.8

Sources. Philadelphia—1: *Delinquency in a Birth Cohort,*
by M. E. Wolfgang, R. M. Figlio, & T. Sellin, 1972, Chicago: University of Chicago Press. Philadelphia—2: "The
1945 and 1958 Birth Cohorts: A Comparison of the Prevalence, Incidence, and Severity of Delinquent Behavior," by
M. E. Wolfgang & P. E. Tracy, 1983, in *Dealing with
Dangerous Offenders: Selected Papers* (Vol. 2), final report
to the National Institute of Justice, edited by D. McGillis,
M. H. Moore, S. R. Estrich, & W. Spelman, Cambridge:
Harvard University, John F. Kennedy School of Govern-
ment. London: "Offending from 10 to 25 Years of Age," by
D. P. Farrington, 1983, in *Prospective Studies of Crime and
Delinquency,* edited by K. T. Van Dusen & S. A. Mednick,
Hingham, MA: Kluwer-Nijhoff. Racine: "Predicting Adult
Criminal Careers from Juvenile Careers," by Lyle W. Shan-
non, cited in "Delinquency Careers: Innocents, Amateurs,
and Persisters," by A. Blumstein, D. P. Farrington, &
S. Moitra, 1985, in *Crime and Justice: An Annual Review of
Research,* edited by M. Tonry & N. Morris, Chicago: Uni-
versity of Chicago Press.

costs of incapacitation only apply to that sample for which we can seriously contemplate incarceration, it can be argued that we should restrict our analysis of offense rates to the high-risk, twice-arrested group. When assessing the potential crime-reduction benefits of selective policies, however, we must be careful to note that incapacitation strategies are only likely to act on the 90 percent of crimes that are committed by offenders likely to go to jail.

The offense rate may be defined as the number of crimes committed by an offender, divided by the time required in which to commit them, excluding time spent in jail and prison. For purposes of estimating the effects of incapacitation policies, the appropriate population includes two-time arrestees, and more gen- erally anyone who stands a reasonable chance of going to jail or prison. These estimates may be used to assess the risks of incarceration for each offender and (after accounting for multiple-offender crimes, seriousness of offenses, and crimes committed by those who are never incarcerated) to obtain a benefit/cost ratio of incapacitation.

The Average Value of λ

Much effort has been put into estimating the rate of offending of the average street criminal. If this number were known, the number of street offenders could be estimated and compared to the prison population. In this way a baseline for the incapacitative effects of present policies could be determined. A reliable estimate of the average offense rate could also be used to identify the probable effects of prison expansion on the crime rate; several have attempted to do this (Cavanagh, 1990; Cohen, 1983; Zedlewski, 1987).

Knowing the average offense rate would also help indicate the skewness of the distribution of offense rates among offenders. Because there is plenty of anecdotal evidence that at least some criminals commit serious crimes at high rates—once a day or more often—a very low average rate would suggest that these high-rate offenders are an important part of the crime problem. Most criminals would be part-time, sporadic offenders, but most crimes would be committed by highly motivated career criminals. Similarly, a high average rate would indicate a more homogeneous offending population and a lesser impact for selective policies.

Despite the attention given to the offense rate, there is little consensus as to the average value. One review of five studies, conducted in 1978 by Jacqueline Cohen, reconciled five disparate estimates somewhat by accounting for differences in the assumptions made. But Cohen was able to narrow the range only to between 2 and 10 index offenses per year (Cohen, 1978). Blumstein and Cohen (1979) estimated that the average offender committed about 14 index crimes per year. More recent studies—including the first analysis of the 1978 Rand survey—found offense rates an order of magnitude higher. Relying on these estimates, Zedlewski (1987) used a figure of 187 crimes per year to estimate the benefits of increased prison capacity.

Although none of these estimates are exactly wrong, some are more useful for our purposes than others. Sorting through the assumptions underlying each estimate reveals that they are each applicable to a different population, and further that they fit together nicely.

The Critical Importance of Population

At first glance, the population problem is simple. Our concern is with that subset of the American population that commits crimes. Only criminals go to prison, and the effectiveness of prison depends on how often criminals commit crimes.

Closer examination reveals that this commonsense population would be very awkward to study. Perhaps 30 percent of Americans commit crime at some point in their adult lives (Visher & Roth, 1986), but only about 16 percent are ever arrested (Tillman, 1987), and only 5 percent go to prison (Langan, 1985). We can expect that λ would be higher for the people who are arrested one or more times (they are arrested in part because they take repeated chances of getting caught), and higher still for people who go to prison (they also take repeated chances of getting sent to prison). Even if the criminal justice system is not explicitly selecting the worst offenders for more stringent treatment, then, mere chance dictates that the most frequent offenders will filter through to jail or prison (Moore et al., 1984).

As a result, estimates of λ will differ from one population to the next, and will (probably) increase as the offenders become more and more involved with the criminal justice system. Some of these populations are more useful to us in estimating incapacitation benefits than others. For example, suppose we build one prison cell and want to know the crime reduction associated with filling it. We could base this estimate on average λ for the arrestee population (probably too low, because most arrestees do not go to prison), or for an incoming cohort to incarceration (probably too high, because the marginal convict probably commits crime less frequently than the average convict), or on the population of offenders who are ever incarcerated (probably in the ballpark, but with uncertain biases). And these differences are clearly policy relevant: Cohen (1983) used λ for the arrestee population and found that prison construction would not be cost-effective; Zedlewski (1987) used λ for an incoming cohort, and found that it would. As shown in Chapter 6, the population considered is the principal difference between these two findings.

Another reason for differentiating among populations is that the methods used to estimate offense rates for each are likely to produce different biases. These biases are difficult to correct, but by taking them into consideration they may at least help us to reconcile the varying estimates.

A variety of estimates of λ for each population is presented below. The biases associated with each set of estimates, and a rough consensus figure for each population, are also provided.

Estimates of λ for Different Populations

Estimates of λ have been derived from two principal data sources: official arrest records and offender self-reports. Official records estimates are only available for the arrestee population; estimates are also available for the population of recidivists—offenders arrested two or more times. Offender self-report estimates are available for a wider variety of populations, but we need consider here only three populations: the offenders who are in jail or prison at any given time; the offenders who enter jail or prison at any given time (an incoming cohort); and the offenders who have spent some time in jail or prison, whether they are there currently or not.

Arrestees

This population includes everyone who is ever arrested for a serious crime while an adult. It probably accounts for the vast majority of crimes, since it is very unlikely that there exists a cadre of chronic offenders sufficiently skilled to avoid arrest (Silberman, 1977, pp. 77–78). And it accounts for all but a negligible fraction of incarcerations in adult jails and prisons. As such, it is a reasonable proxy for the entire criminal population. But most arrestees are never arrested again for a serious crime, and few first offenders go to prison for their acts, so this population includes a lot of people we would not consider "real criminals."

Several estimates of λ for this population are shown in Table 3.3. They range from 4 to 11 index crimes per year, with a most likely value of about 6. In a similar exercise, Cohen (1978) compared two of these estimates to three others, and concluded that λ for this population ranged from 2 to 10, with a best single guess of about 5.

Although this seems reasonable, there are reasons to believe λ may in fact be a bit higher than this. One reason is that it is difficult to compile comprehensive arrest records on individuals. Some jurisdictions simply do not take good care of their arrest files, resulting in incomplete rap sheets. Some crafty offenders give pseudonyms when they are arrested, making it difficult to link them to all of their arrests. And most offenders commit crimes in more than one jurisdiction, and a sizable proportion commit crimes in more than one state. Most states did

TABLE 3.3
Mean Offense Rates for Arrestees

	Violent	Property	Total
Philadelphia, 1963	0.8	4.8	5.6
Washington, DC, 1965	—	—	5.4
New York, NY, 1970	—	—	11.0
Washington, DC, 1977	1.0	3.4	4.4

Sources. Philadelphia: *Delinquency in a Birth Cohort*, by M. E. Wolfgang, R. M. Figlio, & T. Sellin, 1972, Chicago: University of Chicago Press. Washington, 1965: "The Incapacitative Effect of Punishment," by D. Greenberg, 1975, *Law and Society Review, 2,* 541–580. New York: "The Effects of the Criminal Justice System on the Control of Crime: A Quantitative Approach," by S. Shinnar & R. Shinnar, 1975, *Law and Society Review, 9,* 581–611. Washington, 1977: *The Scope and Prediction of Recidivism* (PROMIS Research Project publication 10), by K. M. Williams, 1979, Washington, DC: Institute for Law and Social Research.

not report arrest records for the FBI's Washington, DC arrestee study (from which two of these studies drew their data), and it seems likely that even the comprehensive records check mounted by researchers in the third study (Wolfgang, Figlio, & Sellin, 1972) failed to uncover all of the jurisdictions responsible for arresting the individuals under study. So we might suspect these offense rates to be a bit too low, perhaps by as much as 25 percent.

A more subtle problem has to do with the relationship between an offender's arrests (which are recorded, if unreliably) and crimes (which are not recorded at all). These studies estimate offense rates by first estimating the number of arrests per year and dividing by the probability of arrest, given a crime. This probability corrects for the fact that many crimes are not reported to the police and that several offenders are involved in many crimes (Blumstein & Cohen, 1979), and is defined as

$$q_i = A_i \, r_i \, / \, (C_i \, G_i), \tag{3.1}$$

where A_i is the number of arrests made for crime type i, r_i is the rate at which crimes of type i are reported to the police, C_i is the number of crimes of type i reported, and G_i is the number of offenders participating in the average i-type crime. Averaging over all types of serious crime, the average offender stands a .045 chance of arrest every time he or she commits a crime. Thus each arrest represents roughly $1/.045 = 22$ different offenses.

The implicit assumption is that q_i is the same for all offenders, but this is probably not true. For example, given no other information we might reasonably suppose that q is lower for nonarrestees than for arrestees—they succeeded in avoiding arrest because their risks were somehow lower. Because q is the average for all offenders, arrested or not, this suggests that q for the arrestees should be higher and λ lower than estimated in Table 3.3. On the other hand, there is solid evidence that frequent offenders learn through experience to avoid capture, and that q is highest for novices (see Chapter 5). This suggests that q is probably higher for nonarrestees (who are never arrested because they commit few crimes), and that λ is higher than shown in Table 3.3. For this population, it is hard to tell which of these two stories is most credible.

A third problem is that we cannot be sure how long one-time arrestees should be considered criminals. Although there are clever ways to avoid this issue (Greenberg, 1975), most of these estimates require some estimate of the time at risk. The longer the average criminal career lasts, the lower λ must be during that career (and vice versa). Chapter 4 presents evidence that the average adult criminal career lasts 5 or 6 years, and that it is slightly longer for recidivist and incarcerated populations. The estimates of Table 3.3 are based on estimated career lengths of 5 years (for one-time arrestees) and the time between first and last recorded arrest (for recidivists), so this does not bias our answer if the estimates in Chapter 4 are correct. But the evidence is inconclusive, and the errors could run in either direction.

We may reasonably conclude that, for the roughly 16 percent of the adult population that is arrested for an index crime, the average offense rate is around 6 crimes per year during the period when the average offender is active. Although this figure is the right order of magnitude, it is probably low, and may easily be 50 percent or more off in either direction.

Recidivists

The problem of imputing a career length to once-arrested offenders may be avoided if the sample consists only of twice-arrested criminals. It is reasonable to presume that, unless the period is very long, offenders are active throughout the period between their first and last arrests. And arrest records suggest that this period averages between 5 and 10 years in length, which matches alternative estimates fairly well. But the problem of comprehensive arrest records becomes, if anything, more serious, because frequent and persistent offenders are the most likely to cross jurisdictional lines (Rhodes & Conly, 1981). Further, q for recidivist populations is fairly certain to be smaller than q for the entire criminal population. So, although there may be less random noise in our estimates of λ for recidivists, there is probably more bias. The true value of λ is probably higher than the measured value.

Estimates based on arrest records are shown in Table 3.4. They range from 12 to 14 index crimes per year; given the biases, 15 to 20 might be more realistic estimates. We may reasonably conclude that two-time losers commit three times as many crimes as one-time losers, perhaps more.

First offenders are very unlikely to be imprisoned in most jurisdictions, so the recidivist population is more useful for purposes of estimating incapacitation benefits than the arrestee population. Still, many arrests do not result in convic-

TABLE 3.4
Mean Offense Rates for Recidivists

	Violent	Property	Total
Philadelphia, 1963	—	—	12.6
Washington, DC, 1973	3.2	10.5	13.6
Washington, DC, 1977	—	—	12.2

Sources. Philadelphia: *Delinquency in a Birth Cohort,* by M. E. Wolfgang, R. M. Figlio, & T. Sellin, 1972, Chicago: University of Chicago Press. Washington: "Age, Crime and Punishment," by B. Boland & J. Q. Wilson, 1978, *The Public Interest, 51,* 22–34. Washington: "Estimation of Individual Crime Rates from Arrest Records," by A. Blumstein & J. Cohen, 1979, *Journal of Criminal Law and Criminology, 70,* 561–585.

tion, so some recidivists never receive punishment of any kind; and in many states jail and prison cells are sufficiently scarce that many two-time losers are unlikely to be incapacitated, anyway. Thus the population of incarcerated offenders (or else of offenders who stand a reasonable chance of incarceration) will probably commit crimes at higher rates than this. Although offense rates for these populations could be estimated from official records, available estimates are based on self-reports of imprisoned offenders.

Active Offenders

If we define the active offending population to be the offenders who stand a reasonable chance of going to jail or prison at any given time, we can weight an in-prison or incoming cohort sample to resemble this group. Although errors in the weights may introduce some biases, conceptually this group is identical to the offenders who are incarcerated for some period during their careers; the reciprocal of each individual's weight corresponds to the proportion of his or her career spent behind bars. Two sets of λ estimates are available for this group, shown in Table 3.5.

The highest estimate (California, 1978) is seven times higher than the largest official records estimate. Given low rates of conviction and incarceration given arrest, this is at least possible (although somewhat unreasonable). But the highest estimate is also six times higher than the lowest, which is reported for the same jurisdiction only 2 years previously. Clearly the disparity is driven by differences in the data collection methods used in the two studies. As described in Chapter 2, respondents to the 1976 California study were asked to estimate the number of crimes in which they had taken part in recent years; the offense rate was calculated by dividing this figure by the number of years during which the offender was free to commit them. The other estimates were derived from a modified questionnaire that asked offenders to specify the rate at which they

TABLE 3.5
Mean Offense Rates for Offenders

	Violent	Property	Total
California, 1976	2.1	16.2	18.3
California, 1978	14.7	113.9	128.6
Michigan, 1978	12.7	60.4	73.1
Texas, 1978	4.8	86.5	91.3

Sources. California, 1976, *Doing Crime: A Survey of California Prison Inmates,* by M. A. Peterson, H. B. Braiker, & S. M. Polich, 1980, Santa Monica: Rand. All others: author's calculations.

committed crimes. The first method probably stifled most impulses offenders may have had to make up crimes that never happened; on the other hand, offenders who committed many crimes may only have been able to recall the most interesting or profitable. So the 1976 California figure is almost certainly too low. As described in Chapter 2, the other figures, while closer to the truth, are probably too high. Frequent offenders overestimate their rates of offending, swamping the underestimates of infrequent offenders. So these two sets of estimates bracket the true values. Nevertheless, the figures based on rate-estimation methods can be adjusted to account for these and other biases, resulting in reasonably valid estimates.

One simple problem may be dispensed with immediately. The 1978 Rand estimates all include offense rates for forgery and fraud. These are important crimes that cause serious financial losses for victims and often result in incarceration. (In a survey of sentencing in 12 states, Perez, 1990, found that 12 percent of offenders sentenced to incarceration for violent and property crimes were convicted of fraud and "other property" crimes, mostly forgery.) But because citizens rarely report them, the FBI does not count forgery and fraud among the index offenses, so it is difficult to include them in official records estimates of λ. Given the frequency with which property offenders are imprisoned for these two crime types, it would be inappropriate to remove them from our estimates. But if we were to do so for comparative purposes, the estimates in Table 3.5 would decrease by between 20 and 30 percent, with an average of 24 percent.

The solution to the second problem was suggested in Chapter 2, above. For the rate-specification questionnaire, the top and bottom 10 to 20 percent of the offense rate distribution are the least accurately reported. On the other hand, those who report committing crimes at the highest and lowest rates are providing useful information—they really are higher and lower than the others, although it is impossible to know how much. A conservative means of correcting for these errors is to presume that all offense rates greater than the (say) 90th percentile are exactly equal to the 90th percentile; all those lower than the 10th percentile are equal to the 10th percentile. This process (sometimes called "Winsorizing," after biometrician Charles Winsor) can be applied to any percentage of estimates on both ends of the distribution; as the percent Winsorized increases, we obtain more and more conservative estimates of mean λ.

After Winsorizing 5, 10, 15, and 20 percent from each end of the offense rate distributions, the average λ obtained from each state in the 1978 Rand survey was as shown in Table 3.6. The resulting estimates are certainly much closer to those obtained in the 1976 survey and in the official records studies. In addition, differences among states diminish in size as more and more observations are Winsorized, suggesting that the differences among states are due primarily to a few offenders who report committing crimes very frequently. Still, even after trimming a radical 20 percent from either end, the 1978 Rand estimates are much

TABLE 3.6
Winsorized Means Are Lower, Closer Together,
and More Reasonable

Property crimes; percentage trimmed	California	Michigan	Texas
No trim	113.9	60.4	86.5
5 percent	85.9	49.6	57.6
10 percent	70.0	41.1	47.6
15 percent	55.4	31.8	43.3
20 percent	41.7	29.0	32.5

Personal crimes; percentage trimmed	California	Michigan	Texas
No trim	14.1	12.7	4.8
5 percent	9.9	10.4	4.1
10 percent	5.6	5.3	3.0
15 percent	4.9	3.2	2.6
20 percent	4.0	2.5	2.2

All index crimes; percentage trimmed	California	Michigan	Texas
No trim	128.6	73.1	91.3
5 percent	95.8	60.0	61.7
10 percent	75.6	46.4	50.6
15 percent	60.3	35.0	45.9
20 percent	45.7	31.5	34.7

larger than the 1976 estimates. Given the known biases of the 1976 survey, the most reasonable conclusion is that active offenders—those who spend some of their careers in jail and prison—commit between 30 and 50 violent and property crimes per year free.

Incoming Cohort

Although it may be less useful for estimating the benefits of incapacitation policies, it is much more convenient to survey an incoming cohort to incarceration. Several researchers (including the initial Rand researchers) have produced estimates of λ for this population. Their estimates are shown in Table 3.7.

These estimates span 10 years during which crime rates climbed and sentencing policies changed nationwide and cover five states with greatly varying sentencing policies. Still, the similarities are much greater than the differences.

TABLE 3.7
Mean Offense Rates for Incoming Cohorts

	Violent	Property	Total	Prison commitments per 1,000
California, 1976	4.5	30.0	34.4	
California, 1978	14.6	139.5	154.1	15
Michigan, 1978	10.6	59.3	69.9	20
Texas, 1978	4.2	77.0	81.1	38
Colorado, 1986	6.3	93.7	99.9	27
Colorado, 1988[a]	6.0	80.1	86.0	38
Nebraska, 1989	2.7	102.0	104.7	49
Nebraska, 1990	1.7	73.9	75.6	49

Sources. California, 1976: Peterson, Braiker, & Polich (1980). California, Michigan, and Texas, 1978: author's calculations. Colorado, 1986: Mande & English (1988). Colorado, 1988: English (1990). Nebraska, 1989: Horney & Marshall (1991b). Nebraska, 1990: Horney & Marshall (1991b).
[a]Preliminary estimates only.

In each state, the average incoming prisoner committed between 86 and 150 crimes per year. As described above, these figures are probably too high. If the data were available to Winsorize these distributions, one could expect that they would be both closer together and some 40 to 60 percent lower on average.

This leaves some substantial differences, but it is reasonable to believe that these are due mostly to differences in sentencing practices among the five jurisdictions. For example, the state with the highest average λ (California in 1978) was also the state that sent the fewest proportion of its offenders to prison. Even if the state were not consciously selective in its use of incarceration, frequent offenders would be more likely to end up in prison just because they run higher risks of rare punishments. And if California were saving its prison beds for the most frequent and serious offenders, this would exacerbate the natural filtering of the criminal justice system.

The number of prison commitments per 1,000 index crimes (a rough indicator of the probability of imprisonment given a crime) is shown on the far right column of Table 3.7. The correlation between imprisonment rate and total offense rate is $-.45$—in the expected direction, but insignificant ($p = .31$). But the correlation between imprisonment and λ for violent crimes is $-.95$, which is significant ($p = .001$), even given the absurdly small sample size. Given that incarceration is much more likely for those convicted of a violent crime than a property crime, this suggests that most of the differences in λ among these states are due to differences in incarceration policy, rather than to differences in the underlying offender population.

In Prison

Two surveys have been taken of offenders in prison, and estimates are shown in Table 3.8. The first estimate (California, 1974) was a preliminary survey conducted by Rand and suffers from the same recall biases of the 1975 survey. The second (Wisconsin, 1990) used the 1978 Rand survey and produced results very similar to found in the incoming cohort samples. Note that the mean λ of 141 is larger than most of the incoming cohort means. This is to be expected, because Wisconsin has implemented both sentencing and parole guidelines. Judges are especially likely to give long sentences to offenders with multiple prior convictions; parole boards grant early release in part on the basis of predictions of future offending (DiIulio, 1990; Shane-DuBow, Brown, & Olsen, 1985). If the Wisconsin estimates were Winsorized at 10 to 20 percent, λ for this in-prison sample would probably be between 55 and 85.

Conclusions

All this suggests that there are not one, but several consensus values for the average offense rate, depending upon the population in question. Which population we choose depends on what we wish to do with the results.

Because the estimates cover a wide range—from 5 to nearly 100—it is vitally important that some way be found of reconciling them. Given the low rates of arrest, conviction, and incarceration characteristic of even the most punitive criminal justice system, it is not unreasonable to suspect that offenders who make it to prison commit crimes almost 20 times more frequently than the general offending population. But it may be entirely wrong. Whether these differing values can be reconciled depends upon the distribution of λ among the population, the distribution of criminal careers and arrest probabilities among offenders, and characteristics of the criminal justice system itself—all of which are considered below. So it would be premature to attempt to reconcile them

TABLE 3.8
Mean Offense Rates for Prisoners

	Violent	Property	Total
California, 1975	1.8	10.1	11.9
California, 1976	4.8	24.8	29.6
Wisconsin, 1990	—	—	141

Sources. California, 1975: Petersilia, Greenwood, & Lavin (1978). California, 1976: Peterson, Braiker, & Polich (1980). Wisconsin, 1990: DiIulio (1990).

here. Nevertheless, the analysis in Chapter 6 shows that it can be done and that the differing estimates match one another rather nicely.

In the meantime, let us close the circle on the interpretation of λ as a benefit/cost ratio. Recall that the offense rate, although a reasonable measure of the risks of incarceration an offender faces in a given year, is systematically too high to be a valid measure of the benefit/cost ratio of incapacitating an offender. That is, because many crimes are committed by groups of offenders, we cannot be reasonably certain that incarcerating an individual will prevent all of the crimes in which he or she would have taken part. A better estimate of this figure can be obtained by dividing the offense rate by the number of offenders participating in a typical adult crime—1.73 offenders in the typical personal crime, 1.39 offenders in the typical property crime. Thus incarcerating an average member of the (say) active offending population prevents .58 λ_V for personal crimes, or between 2 and 3 crimes per year, and .72 λ_P for property crimes, or between 22 and 32 crimes per year. Estimates of the effects of selective incapacitation should use these adjusted figures when computing the crime control benefits.

Although currently available estimates of the offense rate vary widely, most of the variation can be attributed to real differences in the populations sampled. The average offender commits something like 8 crimes per year; offenders who are incarcerated sometime during their careers typically commit 30 to 50; the average member of an incoming cohort commits 60 to 100 crimes per year, depending upon the state.

The Distribution of λ

There is good reason to believe that a few offenders commit crimes much more frequently than the average—that is, that the distribution of λ is skewed to the right. This result has been obtained in every study of the subject since at least the 1960s. And for a much longer period, police officers, prosecutors, and judges have believed that some hardened and frequent offenders are much more dangerous than the vast majority of casual offenders. There is no evidence at all contradicting the skewness of λ, and we may as well regard it as a fact. The initial analysis of the Rand inmate survey only confirms this long-held view. Why continue to beat this thoroughly dead horse? There are several reasons.

First, it is important to know how skewed the distribution of λ is, and that is not clear from previous studies. The extent to which selective policies could cut the crime rate depends critically on the amount of skew in the distribution of λ. If the distribution is only moderately skewed—the dangerous few are only slightly worse than the average—then it may even be counterproductive to concentrate criminal justice resources on a small percentage of criminals. By focusing too much attention on "dangerous offenders" who are not all that dangerous, the justice system may neglect to deter and incapacitate the majority of offenders who account for most of the crime. Preliminary investigation suggests that this scenario is neither implausible nor inconsistent with available evidence as to the skewness of the λ distribution (Spelman, 1983). So a precise definition of the distribution of λ is necessary before we can even decide whether selective policies are a good idea at all.

Even if we found a great deal of skewness in the distribution of λ, this would only begin to answer the important policy questions. Can we be selective everywhere, or only in certain jurisdictions? Should we focus on personal offenses such as assault and robbery, or does the distribution of larceny and burglary offense rates suggest that property offenders would be more promising targets? By doing one are we also doing the other? To answer these questions, it is necessary to know how the distribution of offense rates differs among different crime types, or among different criminal populations. Previous studies have had little to say about these questions.

Once we answer them, we are still faced with the problem of assessing the effects of various selective policies on the crime rate. Although knowing the distribution of offense rates across jurisdictions and offenders makes such an assessment possible, it doesn't make it easy. Unless the distribution of λ is remarkably simple, there are two methods available to us to help make the assessment.

- We can employ a simple analytic model that leaves out a lot of information, such as the model employed by Shinnar and Shinnar (1975) or Greenwood (1982). Unfortunately, the information we leave out may turn out to be critical.
- We can attempt to include the complications of reality in our assessment, either through an embellished version of the familiar analytical models, or through a computer simulation. This choice is equally unfortunate: if the analytic solution is sufficiently Baroque to model reality well, it will probably be almost impossible to use; a computer simulation would be easy to use, but difficult to interpret and explain.

We can avoid this Hobson's choice, however, if λ may be characterized by some functional form with known properties, such as the Pareto, gamma, or logNormal distribution. This would allow the analytic solution to be dramatically simplified, while maintaining most of its precision. Again, prior research is of little assistance.

With these objectives in mind, then, let us examine the distribution of λ

among offenders in the Rand inmate survey. First things first: How skewed is the distribution?

The Distribution of Offense Rates Is Very Skewed

Analysis of the Rand survey confirms that a very small proportion of offenders commit a very large proportion of crimes. Before examining these results in detail, let us first consider the results of prior studies as to the distribution of offense rates.

Skewness of Arrest Frequencies

It has long been known that some criminals commit crimes more frequently and persistently than others. "Habitual offenders" were identified as the root of the crime problem at least as early as the nineteenth century (Binny, 1862/1967). The problem of frequent, persistent offenders influenced American and British judicial policy throughout the twentieth century (Bruce, 1928/1968). Throughout the 1950s, for example, parole boards used explicit guidelines to identify offenders who were particularly likely to commit crimes upon release. Good risks were released more quickly than poor risks: In effect, sentences were selectively passed on the basis of expected dangerousness (Lanne, 1935; Ohlin, 1951). Nevertheless, few efforts were made to explicitly estimate how much these habitual offenders contributed to the crime problem.

Perhaps the first scientific attempt to estimate the contribution of habitual offenders to the crime problem was made by Marvin Wolfgang and his associates at the University of Pennsylvania (Wolfgang, Figlio, & Sellin, 1972). While studying the delinquent activities of a cohort of boys born in Philadelphia in 1945, these researchers were struck by the fact that many of the boys were arrested only once or twice, but only a few were arrested many times. A substantial number of the boys—35 percent—were arrested sometime before age 18. A smaller number—19 percent—were recidivists, who were arrested two or more times. And a smaller number still—the 6 percent who were "chronic recidivists"—were arrested five times or more. It is of course inappropriate to equate the number of arrests with the number of offenses—the vast majority of offenses never result in arrest, and people are sometimes arrested for crimes they did not commit. Even if all offenders committed crimes at the same rate, some offenders will be arrested more often than others. Still, on their face, these data suggest that many of the youths committed a few crimes, but that a few did many crimes.

Other researchers undertook similar cohort studies and obtained similar results: The distribution of arrests among offenders was skewed; many offenders were arrested once or twice, but a few were arrested many times. Box plots showing the distribution of arrests among arrestees for four of these studies are shown in Figure 3.1. Note that the upper half of the boxes (representing the 50th through 75th percentiles) and the upper "whisker" (representing the 75th through 90th percentiles) are longer than the lower box and whisker. In fact, there are no lower whiskers on any of these box plots.

This skewness suggests that those offenders in the upper half of the distribution contribute more than their share of the total arrests. Let us assume for the sake of argument that arrests are perfectly correlated with crimes. Clearly, if incapacitation of an offender is successful in preventing the crimes that he would have committed, then we can prevent a great many crimes with a relatively small investment in prison resources. How many crimes, and how small an investment? Probably the first attempt to answer this question was based on one well-publicized finding of the Philadelphia cohort study: The 6 percent of the cohort who were chronic recidivists were responsible for 52 percent of the arrests (Wolfgang, Figlio, & Sellin, 1972). Thus, a hasty policymaker might reason, the crime rate could be cut in half by simply incarcerating that 6 percent of the sample who committed crimes most frequently. This may well be true, but it is highly unrealistic: Incarceration of six percent of the teenage and young adult population of Philadelphia would require an enormous increase in prison capacity. Still, the logic of the decision is quite reasonable, and it makes sense to extend it to the other studies. In doing so, let us rely on the use of Lorenz curves, as described in Chapter 1.

Lorenz curves for the four cohort studies are shown in Figure 3.2. Like the distributions in Figure 3.1, they are almost identical among the four sites. In

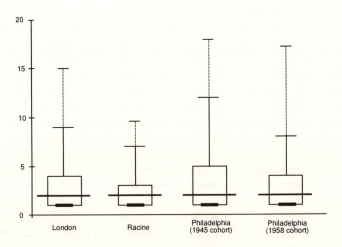

FIGURE 3.1. The distribution of arrests among arrestees is very skewed.

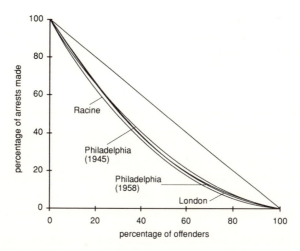

FIGURE 3.2. Ten percent of arrestees account for about 40 percent of all index arrests.

theory, incapacitation of the 10 percent of offenders with the most arrests could have prevented 38 to 41 percent of all crimes. Incapacitation of the worst 20 percent of offenders could have prevented 55 to 61 percent of crimes, depending on the jurisdiction.

This is a powerful result and suggests there is a lot to be gained by selectively focusing the resources of the criminal justice system on a few, frequent offenders. However, these studies are of limited usefulness, for several reasons. First, they count arrests, not crimes. These estimates require that we assume that all offenders face the same risk of arrest per crime they commit. As shown in Chapter 5, this is probably not true. Moreover, even if all offenders did face identical risks, the distribution of arrests would be less skewed than the distribution of offenses committed, just by chance (Moore et al., 1984).

Second, the total number of arrests an offender racks up, or the total number of offenses he or she commits, indicates a combination of frequency and persistence. But if the offenders with the most arrests or offenses have the most primarily because they are persistent, not frequent, then they may need to be jailed a long time before we can cut the crime rate by much.

Finally, the skew in the arrest distribution is not so dramatic that it may only be explained by large differences in the frequency or persistence of offending. In fact, it can be shown that all the skewed distributions shown in Figures 3.1 and 3.2 could have been produced, even if all offenders committed crimes at identical rates. The wide variations in arrests may be due solely to chance and minor differences in persistence (Blumstein, Farrington, & Moitra, 1984).

All this suggests that arrest data alone are unlikely to provide reliable estimates as to the usefulness of selective policies. Because our aim is to identify changes in crime rates, rather than arrest rates, we return to the self-report studies.

Skewness of Offense Rates

When researchers at Rand began to survey jail and prison inmates in the mid-1970s, they doubtless expected that the distribution of offense rates would be skewed. In their first survey of 49 armed robbers, the researchers distinguished between two groups: One-third of the sample were labeled *intensive* offenders; two-thirds were termed *intermittent*. The two groups differed primarily on the basis of offense rate and persistence:

> The adult offense rate exceeded one crime per month of street time for 94 percent of the intensive offenders but for only 21 percent of the intermittent offenders. Most striking, over his full career the average intensive offender committed about ten times as many crimes as the intermittent offender. (Petersilia, Greenwood, & Lavin, 1978, p. xi)

Less than one-third of the sample committed over 90 percent of the serious crimes.

Similar findings were obtained in the larger-scale survey administered in 1976. If anything, the results of that survey were even more striking: The most active 8 percent of offenders sampled committed over three times as many crimes as the least active 50 percent of the sample (Peterson, Braiker, & Polich, 1980). If these figures can be relied on, the distribution is even more skewed than the arrest studies would indicate.

To make the self-report and arrest studies easier to compare, consider Lorenz curves for the 1975 and 1976 Rand surveys, shown in Figure 3.3. The two curves are not strictly comparable because limited data were available as to the distribution of offense rates estimated from these surveys. (The 1975 survey curve includes nondrug crimes committed at the peak of the careers of imprisoned armed robbers; the 1976 survey curve includes only armed robberies for a sample weighted to replicate a sample of active offenders.) Still, the curves provide a general indication of the degree of skewness in the offense rate distributions. Moreover, they are almost identical: In each survey, the most active 10 percent of offenders committed between 50 and 60 percent of serious crimes; the most active 20 percent accounted for 75 percent of serious crimes. Leaving aside complications such as multiple offending and limited career length, it would appear that most crime could be prevented by incarcerating only 10 percent of active criminals.

The distribution of offense rates for active offenders in the 1978 Rand survey are even more dramatically skewed. Figure 3.4 uses a box-and-whisker plot to portray the distribution of λ for nondrug offenses (that is, personal and

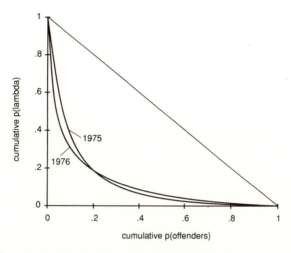

FIGURE 3.3. Ten percent of armed robbers report committing 50 to 60 percent of armed robberies.

property offenses added together). The graphs have the same distinctive shape of those in Figure 3.1: the upper portion of the "box" is much longer than the lower portion, and the upper "whisker" extends much farther than the lower. Although there are some real differences among the states (for example, high-rate Michigan and Texas offenders seem to commit crimes less frequently than their counterparts in California), all states and crime types are characterized by a very similar skewed shape.

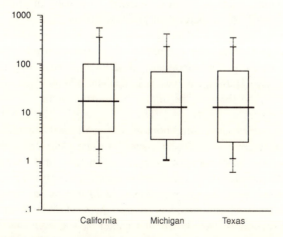

FIGURE 3.4. The distribution of nondrug offense rates is very skewed.

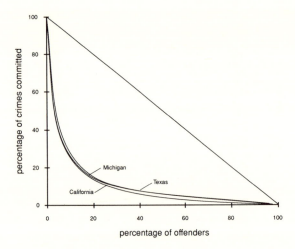

FIGURE 3.5. Ten percent of offenders report committing 70 percent of nondrug crimes.

Lorenz curves for nondrug crimes are shown in Figure 3.5. The figure shows not only the skew in the distributions of λ but also the limit on the usefulness of selective crime-control policies. As shown, at least in the limit, these policies may be very useful, indeed. Imprisonment of the most frequent 10 percent of offenders may cut the crime rate by about 70 percent. Because some offenders commit only property crimes and others commit only personal crimes, the results are even more dramatic if each crime type is considered separately: The most frequent 10 percent of personal offenders account for 75 to 80 percent of personal crimes, whereas the most frequent 10 percent of property offenders account for about 73 to 78 percent of property crimes.

These percentages are extraordinarily high, much higher than those obtained in any prior study. The magnitude of the potential gains from selective incapacitation confirms the importance of seriously considering such a policy. What is even more startling, however, is that the potential gain from selective policies—that is, the shape of the offense-rate distributions—is virtually identical in all of the three states sampled. This provides at least preliminary evidence that selective policies may work about equally well in all jurisdictions.

Of course, these results depend greatly on the estimates available for the offense rates of the most and least dangerous offenders. In the limiting case, for example, if 90 percent of the offenders committed no crimes, and 10 percent committed 100 per year, then 10 percent would do 100 percent of all crimes. But the highest- and lowest-rate offenders are also the least likely to report their rates of offending accurately. As shown in Chapter 2, the high-rate offenders are probably not so frequent as they claim, and the low-rate offenders are probably somewhat more frequent. The result is that the distribution of offense rates is probably not so skewed as it appears.

To test the sensitivity of our results to the veracity of these particularly low-rate and high-rate offenders, let us consider how the Lorenz curves change when the least reliable responses are trimmed as described above. The larger the proportion of offenders trimmed, the smaller the contribution of the high-rate offenders will be, and the less beneficial selective policies will appear to be. As before, we trim from zero to 20 percent from the top and bottom of the distribution and pay particular attention to trim rates of 5 to 15 percent.

Results for personal offense rates, aggregated over all states, are shown in Figure 3.6. (Again, the results are virtually identical for all states and crime types.) Although the exact number of offenses that may be allocated to the (say) worst 10 percent of offenders changes a great deal, in all reasonable cases it remains a large number. Even in the very unlikely event that the top and bottom 20 percent of offenders are each homogeneous, the worst 10 percent commit about one-fourth of the crimes. Clearly there is great room for selection, even if the self-reports of frequent offenders are unreliable.

Why Is the Distribution Skewed?

It is obvious enough that there must be differences among offenders as to their rates of offending. People differ: Some are highly motivated to commit crimes, others less so; some see many opportunities to commit crime (or have

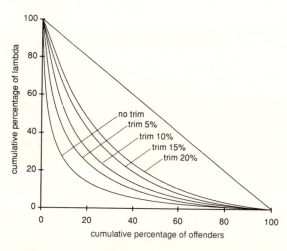

FIGURE 3.6. Measurements of skewness are sensitive to outliers.

many opportunities thrust upon them), others do not. And people change over time, as well: Some undoubtedly commit crimes more frequently as they get older, as they become more used to their criminal identity and overcome their inhibitions about breaking the law; others slow down with age, perhaps settling into a "straight" job and falling in with less antisocial companions. Because there are bound to be differences, there are bound to be some particularly dangerous offenders. But we have grown to expect that the distribution of most things is roughly Normal-distributed, or at least relatively symmetric (Yule & Kendall, 1950, p. 187). The distributions shown above are not at all symmetric. Why are they upwardly skewed? There are two classes of explanations: those that consider the λ distribution for one time period only, and those that consider changes in λ over time.

Cross-sectional Explanations

The simplest explanation may be that the distribution of motivations to commit crime really is Normal-distributed, but that we only measure this motivation among the top 1 or 2 percent of the population who actually commit crimes. That is, all of us have varying motivations to steal, threaten, and injure others, but 98 to 99 percent of us are sufficiently inhibited that we only do so in ways that are not serious enough to be criminal (see, for example, Allport, 1934; Schur, 1969). Thus the distribution of motivations among offenders is (roughly) the top 1 or 2 percent of a Normal distribution. Although the tail of a Normal distribution is very skewed, close examination reveals that it is not nearly as skewed as the distribution of offense rates. Additional explanations are necessary.

A closely related argument is that many offenders do not rely solely on illegal activities for their income. Of the 2,000-odd offenders sampled in the Rand survey, for example, only 26 percent of them were never employed in the 2 years prior to their most recent incarceration. Most were employed some of that time, and fully 20 percent were employed throughout the 2-year period. There is also evidence that many spent long periods in which they committed no crimes (Chaiken & Rolph, 1987). So it may be that the distribution of offense rates, given that an offender was committing crimes, is much closer to Normal-distributed. The long right-hand tail would consist of those offenders who both committed crimes at high rates when they were active and were active throughout much of that portion of the 2-year window they spent on the street.

There is a clear-cut parallel here to the distribution of income. Income is conceptually similar to offense rate: Income represents money received per unit time; λ represents crimes committed per unit time. And, like the offense rate, a lot of people make a little money, and a few people make a lot of it. But some of the skewness in the distribution of income is due to the fact that some workers only work part-time. In fact, the distribution of hourly and daily wages is much less skewed than the entire individual income distribution (Lebergott, 1959). Further, well-paid workers have an incentive to work more hours, contributing to the skewness of the total income distribution (Mayer, 1960; Staehle, 1943). Thus we might expect a positive correlation between the number of hours worked (proportion of street time active) and wage rate (offense rate while active).

The analogy works, at least to some extent. When offense rates are averaged over the entire 2-year period ("net" λ), the worst 10 percent of offenders commit 75 to 80 percent of the personal crimes, and 73 to 78 percent of the property crimes. But if only the active periods of each offender are considered ("active" λ), the worst 10 percent account for only 50 to 53 percent of personal crimes, and 65 to 70 percent of property crimes. So active λ is less skewed than net λ. And, as might be expected, offenders who were sufficiently motivated to commit crimes at high rates during their periods of activity were active more frequently than other offenders: The correlation between the proportion of months in which an offender was active and his level of activity in those months is .42 for personal crimes, and .39 for property crimes. So it is clear that at least some of the skewness in the distribution of (net) λ is due to the part-time nature of much criminal activity.

Even when part-time offending is accounted for, however, active offense rates remain substantially skewed. But the part-time argument exemplifies another principle that economists have found helps to explain skewness in the wage rate distribution—the Law of Proportionate Effect (Aitchison & Brown, 1954). This describes situations in which the measure of interest—wages, or momentary dangerousness—is the product of two or more elements. For example, income is the product of wages (dollars earned per unit of time worked) and the amount of time worked. If the amount of time an individual works increases by (say) 10 percent, then that person's total income will likewise increase by 10 percent. What makes this principle interesting is that economists have found it useful to consider wages to be a product of several other elements: Schooling, personality factors, intelligence, manual dexterity, and other elements all combine in a multiplicative way to predict an individual's wage rates (Boissevain, 1939; Burt, 1943). It is not difficult to show that, even if these elements are each Normal-distributed, the distribution of the resulting values will be very highly skewed to the right (Roy, 1950).

What evidence is available to help explain the production of offense rates suggests that a similar process is at work. For example, people will only commit a crime when all of three conceptually separate elements are present (Cohen & Felson, 1979):

- They must be motivated to commit the crime.
- They must have an opportunity to commit the crime.
- They must have the capacity to take advantage of the opportunity.

If any of these elements are absent, the crime will not be committed.

Clearly, this is a highly simplified model. For instance, there may be motivations of many different kinds, which may all be present in varying degrees in the same offender. Offenders may be motivated to obtain drugs to support habits; they may want money in order to feed, clothe, and house themselves; they may wish to demonstrate that they are not people who can be pushed around. Similarly, there are various kinds of capacities (an ability to crack safes, to plan escapes so that more difficult targets are less forbidding, or to work with others in order to do more complex jobs) and various kinds of opportunities (corresponding to different crime types, such as armed robbery of pedestrians, or suburban residential burglaries, for example). And the three are probably both empirically and conceptually related. People who want to commit a crime are more likely to learn how and also more likely to look for opportunities. Conversely, if one has the capacity and if the opportunity is good enough, many people with relatively ordinary motivations will take a chance and commit a crime (minor tax evasion, insurance fraud, and even embezzlement may fall into this category). Nevertheless, the point is clear enough: λ depends upon several different things, and not just on one thing.

Now suppose that these elements are (more or less) Normal-distributed. (The real distribution doesn't matter so much as the fact that the distribution need not be skewed. In fact, it would not be difficult to break down the elements so that they are Normal-distributed.) Call these "enabling factors" E, and reference each with the subscript i. Then we know that

$$\lambda_j = f(E_{1j}, E_2j, \ldots E_{ij}). \qquad (3.2)$$

In fact, it is probably most reasonable to suppose that this relationship is a multiplicative one. That is,

$$\lambda_j = \Pi_i E_{ij}. \qquad (3.3)$$

If one of the elements changes, the effect the change will have on the offense rate will be proportional to the offense rate before the change occurs. So the same change would have greatly differing effects on each individual, depending upon his or her prior level of activity. As it happens, the distribution of the product of a series of random Normal deviates will be upwardly skewed, like the distribution of offense rates. In fact, under the (admittedly ridiculous) assumption that the enabling factors are all identically distributed, the logarithm of the offense rate distribution will be exactly Normal-distributed (Haldane, 1942).

Although it seems pretty foolish to suppose that offense rates are really the product of a group of unmeasured and quasi-mythical "enabling factors," a good many things turn out to be at least roughly logNormal-distributed (Aitchison & Brown, 1962). And offense rates are roughly logNormal, as well. In fact, as will be shown later in this chapter, none of the deviations from logNormality are significant for either of the crime types or any of the states.

Time-Series Explanations

Differences in motivations, opportunities, and capacities are unlikely to remain stable. If the changes over time are (more or less) random, this provides a complementary explanation for the skewness in the offense rate distribution: Random changes in enabling factors affect individual offense rates in such a way that the highest-rate offenders are likely to become even higher-rate offenders, whereas the lowest-rate offenders are likely to maintain low rates of activity. After several years of changing conditions, the result will be the familiar, highly skewed distribution—even if all offenders began with identical motivations, opportunities, and capacities. In more precise terms, the argument goes like this.

Suppose that, for each offender, the relationship between this year's offense rate and next year's may be expressed as

$$\lambda_{t+1} = A\,\lambda_t, \tag{3.4}$$

where A is a random variable with an average value of 1.0. Suppose further that there is no "memory" in the random draws of A; last year's change is independent of this year's change. (Similar results are obtained unless the correlation of successive As is both large and negative.) Then by chance a few offenders will become increasingly dangerous over several consecutive years; because all changes are proportionate to the previous rate of offending, these offenders may eventually commit crimes at rates many times higher than they began. On the other hand, the median offense rate will not change at all. Thus as t approaches infinity, the distribution of offense rates will become more and more skewed; this will be true, even if all offenders began with identical λs at time zero.

This is a very simplistic model, but it is not difficult to extend it slightly and obtain results that fit the empirical data quite closely. Let us imagine that the population of active offenders consists of members of successive cohorts. Because offenders eventually die off or go straight, there will be more active offenders in the recent cohorts than in the earlier ones; for simplicity, let us assume that criminal careers are roughly exponentially distributed, so the number of offenders in each succeeding cohort will be smaller by some known proportion. (As shown in Chapter 4, this is not quite true; but Rutherford, 1955, shows that the basic results are not sensitive to moderate deviations from the exponential.) Also, suppose that the cross-sectional hypotheses cited above are all correct; due to differences in motivation, opportunity, and capacity, offense rates are very skewed, even at the beginning of a criminal career. Under these assumptions, it can be shown that the following statements are true.

- If the system is in steady-state, offense rates at any given point in time will strongly resemble a logNormal in the lower and middle ranges. However the tail—the top 10 to 20 percent of observations—will be too long (Rutherford, 1955).
- On average, there will be no relationship between age and criminal activity. Some offender careers will heat up, others will cool down, but the two effects will balance one another out.
- There will be a relationship between age and the variance of offense rates. For older offenders, the distribution of λ should be both more skewed and have a higher variance than for younger offenders (Kapteyn, 1903).

Figure 3.7 shows how the distribution of λ changes as offenders age. Note first that prediction (1) is borne out: The boxes for each group are nearly symmetrical about the median (as is true for the logNormal distribution), but the upper tail of each distribution is slightly longer than the lower. The second and third predictions seem to be correct, as well. After a "break-in" period of 2 to 3 years, the median offense rates hardly change at all. However, the 25th and 75th percentiles are further apart for older offenders than for younger ones. Thus there are both more low-rate and more high-rate of-

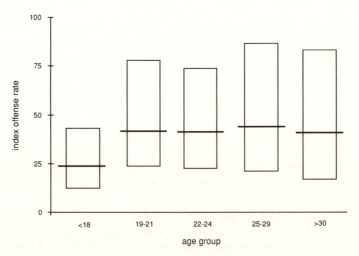

FIGURE 3.7. Offense rates are stable on average but increase in variance over time.

fenders in the older age brackets, just as we would expect if this "random proportionate change" hypothesis were correct.

These results suggest that it would not be unreasonable to suppose that λs change proportionately and randomly over time. But other hypotheses could account for these results, as well. For example, a frequently made assumption, that individual λs change hardly at all over time, is not necessarily ruled out. It may be that offenders who begin committing crimes at higher-than-average rates increase slowly in frequency, whereas criminals who begin at lower-than-average rates decrease. A third hypothesis—that medium-rate offenders drop out more quickly than low- and high-rate offenders—is explored in Chapter 4.

Even if equation (3.4) were undeniably true, it would be impossible to model changes in offense rates over an offender's career with any precision, because the variance and distribution of the A terms is unknown. These parameters may have important effects on the final result, too: If most of the random changes are small, then an offender's λ will change little over time, and predictions of his or her future dangerousness are likely to be valid for several years. On the other hand, if many of the random shocks are large, individual λs will fluctuate wildly, and predictions of future dangerousness will only be valid for short periods. If this were true, it is conceivable that it would be futile to give long sentences to predicted high-rate offenders: Even if they were dangerous at the time of sentencing, many would be no more dangerous than anyone else long before their prison term was over.

A conclusive test of this hypothesis would require reliable information on offense rates for two or more consecutive periods. Then it would be simple to identify the appropriate parameters through regression. We would estimate the equation,

$$\log \lambda_{t+1} = A' + B \log \lambda_t + u, \tag{3.5}$$

expecting the following of each parameter:

- A' would be zero, or nearly so (thus $A = \exp(A')$ would be close to the expected value of 1).
- B would be 1, or nearly so.
- The standard deviation of the distribution of random A's would be $\exp(u)$, and the value of this term would be most uncertain.

Rand collected reliable information on offense rates for only one period, covering the 2-year window prior to the most recent incarceration. Nevertheless, some information on two earlier 2-year windows was collected, including each individual's employment and marital status, drug history, prison record, and (most important) the types of crimes committed during the 2 to 6 years prior to the most recent incarceration. It is very likely that these characteristics have an important effect on an individual's rate of offending: As will be shown below, offenders who commit crimes of many different types probably commit more of each type than others; criminals probably commit fewer crimes when they have jobs, and more when they are addicted to hard drugs, than otherwise. So it may be possible to use information on these known characteristics to help make rough estimates of individual offense rates for the earlier periods. These estimates, called *instruments* (Kmenta, 1972), may then be regressed against the (known) λs for later periods; the final result will be a consistent and probably efficient estimate of equation (3.5).

First, let us use the available information to create the instruments. The first step is to identify the relationships between the variables which were measured in all periods and the offense rate, which was only measured in window 3. The results, shown in Table 3.9, are encouraging. Most of the variance in offense rates for Window 3 may be accounted for by knowing the type of crimes the offender committed during that period, characteristics of his living situation during that period, and some information on his juvenile and prior adult record. Note that the differences among states are very small and do not approach statistical significance.

This equation will probably not predict offense rates in Windows 1 and 2 with the same precision. For one thing, it may be that the relationship among the variables changes in a systematic way as an offender ages. For example, older offenders who live with women may commit crimes less frequently than other older offenders because they are more likely to have settled into a legitimate lifestyle that includes marriage and a straight job. In contrast, many younger offenders who live with women have not yet aged into legitimacy; the primary effect of their living situation may be a need for more money to support their spouse or girlfriend, with the result of higher rates of offending. If the effects of these variables really did change over time in ways like this, then we would expect the offender's age or career length-to-date to be important predictors of offense rates. However, as Table 3.9 shows, career length is only a statistically significant predictor of personal offense rates, not of property offense rates; and it is not a particularly important predictor for personal offenses. So it is probably safe to conclude that the instruments will work about as well at all stages of an offender's career.

A more important problem may stem from the fact that the parameters shown in Table 3.9 were obtained from a relatively small sample, reflected in the substantial standard errors for the regression coefficients. Through random variation, the same parameters will not predict quite so well on a second sample. So the correlation between the instrument and the real offense rate will probably be somewhat lower than indicated by the R^2 shown. This means that the results of the regression using the instrument will be falsely precise—the standard error of

TABLE 3.9
The Offense Rate Is Fairly Predictable

	Property	Personal
Criminal activity		
Log (*N* property types)	2.455	
	(.117)	
Business robbery		1.098
		(.074)
Personal robbery		1.088
		(.077)
Assault		.754
		(.061)
		.317
Hurt victim of burglary or robbery		(.103)
Drug dealer		.099
		(.064)
Used hard drugs	.502	
	(.114)	
Held job for more than 1 month	−.634	−.148
	(.126)	(.066)
Was locked up for more than one month	.497	
	(.111)	
Lived with a girl for more than one	.247	
month	(.119)	
Frequency of juvenile property crimes	.134	
	(.027)	
Frequency of juvenile personal crimes		.156
		(.024)
Juvenile drug-use index		.022
		(.011)
Log (career length to date)		.011
		(.004)
Years of schooling	.179	
	(.044)	
California	−.003	−.009
	(.027)	(.022)
Michigan	.007	.003
	(.028)	(.022)
Intercept	−.743	−.062
	(.226)	(.082)
Standard error of estimate	1.397	.728
R^2	.539	.687

the estimate (the u term) and the standard errors of the coefficients will both be slightly too low.

The final results—the relationship between λ_{t-1} and λ_t—are shown in Table 3.10. All expectations are met. Although some of the intercept terms are substantial, in no case can we be sure that they are not the expected value of zero. Each of the slope terms is insignificantly different from 1. And the standard error of each of the estimates appears well behaved as well: For property crimes, the standard deviation of the A distribution seems likely to lie somewhere between 1.1 and 1.2; for personal crimes, the standard deviation probably lies around 1.0. (The λ_3 equations are probably more reliable for this purpose.) Thus the hypothesis that offense rates change randomly over time, but neither systematically increase nor decrease as offenders get older, is confirmed.

These random changes in λ may have important implications for selective policies. Implicit in most previous work is the assumption that criminals commit offenses at constant rates throughout their criminal career (Greenwood, 1982; Shinnar & Shinnar, 1975; Zedlewski, 1987); this assumption is backed up by the finding that for all offenders, no matter what their offense rate, the most likely value for next year's offense rate will be the same as at present. However, the variation from year to year may well be substantial. Consider Figure 3.8. Our best guess as to an individual's personal offense rate 2 years from now, given his or her present offense rate, lies on the regression line in the middle of the graph. It is about the same as the offender's present personal offense rate. For example, offenders who commit 10 robberies and assaults this year are most likely to commit 9.3 such crimes 2 years from now, if they continue to commit crimes.

TABLE 3.10
Relationship between λ_t and λ_{t+1}: Best Guess Is No Change, but Standard Error Is Large

	Personal		Property	
	λ_3	λ_2	λ_3	λ_2
λ_t	.875	1.067	1.127	.944
	(.139)	(.077)	(.089)	(.068)
California	−.050	−.133	−.033	−.084
	(.065)	(.135)	(.216)	(.166)
Texas	−.008	−.321	.082	−.099
	(.065)	(.172)	(.231)	(.180)
Intercept	.218	−.068	−.367	.141
	(.224)	(.106)	(.269)	(.195)
Standard error of estimate	0.999	0.438	1.170	0.843
R^2	.187	.524	.584	.344

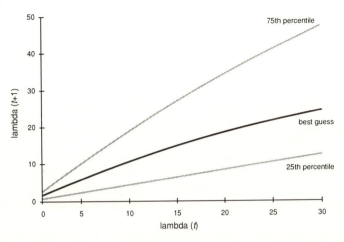

FIGURE 3.8. Offense rates vary substantially over time, but on average they remain constant.

But the future offense rates for only half of these offenders will lie between the shaded lines. Some will commit considerably more than 10 crimes per year—1 in 4 will commit more than 18 personal crimes, and 1 in 10 will commit 33 or more personal crimes per year. Similarly, one-fourth of these offenders will commit fewer than 5 personal crimes 2 years from now.

This variability does not affect the crime-control effectiveness of selective policies. True, our predictive measures will sometimes be very wrong—but on average, they will be right. If the predictive scale indicates that an individual has participated in 10 crimes per year in the past, we can count on the likelihood that he or she will participate in a similar number of crimes in the future (so long as that offender remains active).

Nevertheless, this variability may well affect our assessment of the justice of these policies. One of the claims often made by critics of selective sentencing is that the predictive scales make many "Type-2 errors." That is, they identify some individuals as high-rate offenders who in fact commit crimes at low or moderate rates. Variability over time obviously exacerbates the problem of Type-2 errors: Even in those cases where the present identification is correct, it may not stay correct. This is particularly worrisome if apparently high-rate offenders receive very long prison sentences, because the extent of inaccuracy— and injustice—will be higher for long-range than for short-range forecasts.

Policy Implications

Theory and the available data are consistent: The distribution of offense rates is highly skewed. And because a few offenders commit crimes at much higher-than-average rates, the potential gains of selective criminal justice action—in particular, selective sentencing—are great. Due to the natural filtering of the criminal justice system, we can also expect that the effectiveness of collective incapacitation policies will be greater than previously measured (Cohen, 1978, 1986). But the maximum potential gains can only be achieved if the criminal justice system has perfect information as to the true offense rates of individuals. Perfect information is, of course, never available. Thus it is important to ask how well judges and other decision makers can do, given what information is typically available.

Methods for estimating and predicting criminal activity date back over sixty years (Bruce, 1928/1968). And recidivism prediction and similar scales are still in use in most jurisdictions. The well-known 7-point scale developed by Greenwood (1982) was in fact based on one of these recidivism scales (Hoffman & Stone-Meierhoefer, 1979). Although the relationship between recidivism and offense rate is complicated, the two are closely related; a scale that predicts recidivism will also predict offense rates with about the same level of accuracy (Maltz, 1984). So the results of 60 years of recidivism research are directly relevant to the policy implications of a highly skewed distribution of offense rates.

The problem is, despite 60 years of research, the criminal justice system still cannot do a very good job of predicting future criminal activity. Greenwood's scale, for example, only explains about 20 percent of the variance in offense rate. To put it another way, when the scale was used to assign offenders to one of three groups (corresponding to low- , medium- , and high-rate offenders), only 45 percent of the offenders were correctly assigned. And many of the errors were large: 15 percent of true low-rate offenders were incorrectly assigned to the high-rate group, whereas 9 percent of true high-rate offenders were incorrectly assigned to the low-rate group (Greenwood, 1982, p. 53).

Such results raise a number of questions as to the ethics of assigning prison sentences (or police and prosecutorial resources, for that matter) to offenders on the basis of scales that are certain to be wrong some of the time (von Hirsch & Gottfredson, 1983). More important for our purposes, the inaccuracy of these scales cuts deeply into the crime-control gains that can conceivably be achieved through selective activity. In the limiting case, where the prediction is no better than flipping a coin, the fact that the distribution of offense rates is dramatically skewed would do us no good whatever. No information would be available as to which offenders were in fact dangerous, so we would be unable to take advantage of the differences among offenders. Of course, present methods are considerably better than chance, so we can expect some crime-control gains. How large can we reasonably expect them to be?

For the sake of illustration, let us use Greenwood's 7-point scale. (Although it is no better than most prediction methods now in use, it is probably no worse;

Gottfredson & Gottfredson, 1986.) This scale uses past criminal activity, drug abuse, and employment information to assign each convicted offender to one of three groups:

- Those in the lowest group are predicted to commit crimes at rates lower than the median for all offenders.
- Those in the middle group are predicted to commit crimes at between (roughly) the 50th and 75th percentile of the offense rate distribution.
- Those in the highest group are predicted to commit crimes at rates greater than (about) 75 percent of all offenders.

Let us assume, rather conservatively, that all offenders in a predicted group commit crimes at exactly the same rate.

Because the method is not always accurate, some offenders will be incorrectly assigned to the wrong group. Because there will be mixing across categories, each of the predicted groups will be more like the average over all offenders than the "true" groups to which they correspond. This means that the distribution of predicted offense rates will have less variance and less skew than the distribution of true offense rates. One might think of the inaccuracy of prediction as "shrinking" the whole distribution toward the middle.

As a result, the maximum potential gains of selective incapacitation are considerably less than they would be, were perfect information available. Figure 3.9 compares the potential tradeoffs between crime rate and prison population for perfect information to the tradeoffs when the only data available are the imperfect

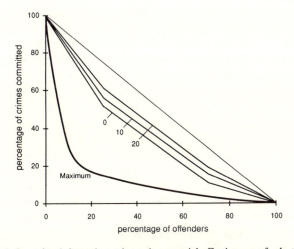

FIGURE 3.9. Imperfect information reduces the potential effectiveness of selective policies.

predictions of the Greenwood scale. For each proportion of offenders in jail and prison, the maximum potential decrease in the crime rate is considerably lessened due to the inaccuracy of the prediction scheme.

As shown earlier in this chapter, our best guess as to the potential tradeoffs given perfect information is very sensitive to small deviations in the skewness of the offense rate distribution. Because the distribution of offense rates reported by participants of the Rand survey was probably too skewed, a more accurate distribution could only be achieved by trimming the top and bottom 5 to 20 percent of the offense rates from the distribution. One might expect that the potential tradeoffs given imperfect information would also be sensitive to the amount trimmed from the distribution. But, as Figure 3.9 indicates, the value of imperfect information is considerably less sensitive to the amount trimmed (compare Figure 3.6, above). So, although there is still considerable uncertainty as to the true distribution of offense rates, this uncertainty may not be particularly important for policymaking.

The distribution of offense rates is highly skewed—a few offenders commit crimes at much higher-than-average rates. Thus incarcerating the most frequent 10 percent of offenders could prevent the commission of between 40 and 80 percent of personal crimes, and between 35 and 65 percent of property crimes.

These differences may stem from the part-time nature of criminal offending, differences among individuals in motivations, capacities, or opportunities, or random, proportionate changes in offense rates over time. Most likely, all of these explanations are correct.

Although large changes in individual offense rates from year to year indicate that predictions of future dangerousness based on past conduct must often be wrong, frequent offenders on average remain frequent as time goes on. So predictions will still be right, on average.

Although the potential for crime control through selective incapacitation is enormous, much of this potential cannot be achieved because information about individual offense rates is so inaccurate.

Offender Specialization

So far we have only considered the offense rates of offenders who commit offenses of two kinds—personal and property. That is, we have characterized the robbery and assault rates among personal offenders, and the burglary, theft, forgery, and fraud rates among property offenders. But we have said nothing about the relationship among these offense rates. And it is possible that this relationship has important policy implications, both for the structure of selective policies, and for the very desirability of these policies.

For example, it may be that most offenders specialize in either personal or property offenses. So if our aim is to prevent the crimes the public sees as particularly threatening—say, personal and business robberies—then we must concentrate our efforts primarily on offenders with a history of personal crimes. Incapacitation of repeat burglars or auto thieves would be unlikely to affect the robbery rate much. On the other hand, more flexibility is called for if many offenders are "generalists" who commit both personal and property crimes. When faced with a repeat burglar, for instance, it would be reasonable to suspect that he or she is also a frequent robber or con artist. So selective programs should be structured differently under specialization than under generalization.

Perhaps more important, if specialization is nearly complete, then even the most selective policies may not be cost-effective. Suppose that property offenders commit only property crimes. Then the most frequent property offenders—those whose offense rate puts them in the top 25 percent of the λ distribution—commit about 80 crimes per year. Most of these crimes will be small-time thefts and cons, at a few dollars a job; let us assume the average victim loses $500, including direct monetary losses, inconvenience, pain and suffering, and a slight risk of serious injury or even death (Cohen, 1988; Shenk & Klaus, 1984). Then the costs to society of letting such offenders stay free are about $40,000 per criminal. But the social costs of jailing them, if we include the marginal costs of prison construction and operation, pretrial detention, lost employment, and increases in welfare payments to the offenders' dependents, may be well in excess of $40,000 apiece (Cavanagh, 1990). This does not mean we should not imprison these offenders, of course—other costs and benefits must be considered, and deterrence and retribution count for something, even if they are difficult to measure. But we should certainly think twice before investing in a crime policy that (nominally, at least) costs more than it benefits.

Such objections as these largely disappear if most offenders are generalists. Under this scenario, the high-rate burglar/thief/con artists also commit fear-inspiring, emotionally traumatizing, and physically dangerous crimes such as robbery and assault—so the gains to society of incarcerating these offenders are demonstrably greater than the monetary costs of imprisonment. And, because the benefits are demonstrable, we have fewer qualms about selecting them out for special punishment. The point is, although it makes sense to describe λs in a disaggregated fashion (because different motivations, opportunities, and capacities are associated with each crime type), it only makes sense to base policy on the combination of them that best describes the dangerousness of each individual to society.

Until recently, the prevailing view of criminal offenders was that they were fairly sophisticated specialists. Criminologists such as Edwin Sutherland (1937) examined the careers of "professional thieves" and found high degrees of specialization in skills, attitudes, and experiences. More systematic studies found stable patterns in the criminal activities of juveniles (Frum, 1958) and adults (Peterson, Pittman, & O'Neal, 1962). Some idealized crime to be a kind of medieval trade: Juvenile delinquents served apprenticeships to experienced, skillful master-fiends; everyone respected the guild rules ("Thou shalt not rat on thy brother" is perhaps the most celebrated), lest they be rebuked by their fellows (Irwin, 1970). And this view was shared by the police, who relied on such factors as the offender's presumably stable "M.O.," or method of operations, to identify and arrest him. As an influential study prepared for the International Association of Chiefs of Police put it:

> Human behavior being as it is, provides us with the knowledge that a great number of human beings in this world perform certain things in their daily lives almost out of instinct, especially if they are successful in their endeavors. . . . Criminals are no different. They employ methods they know to be tried and true, and as a result, these methods are as significant as a signature. (Chang et al., 1979, p. 67)

This consensus broke down in the mid-1960s. Rapid rises in crime rates could not be explained in terms of increased activity among a few, romanticized criminals; with the riots of Watts and Detroit, the attention of (white, middle-class) America was drawn to the "conventional" criminal activities of the poor and the blacks. And, for the first time, researchers began a systematic investigation of empirical evidence. After examining what empirical evidence was available, most researchers concluded that the typical criminal was an unsophisticated, opportunistic generalist. Little "apprenticeship" was required to gain the skills needed to commit most crimes; little planning was needed to escape capture (Einstadter, 1969; Shover, 1973).

The most persuasive evidence of the generalist hypothesis came from "arrest-switch matrixes." These indicate the probability that an offender whose last arrest was for a crime of one type will next be arrested for a crime of another type. Consider this simple switch matrix:

	Next crime	
Last crime	Personal	Property
Personal	.90	.10
Property	.10	.90

If this is the matrix that best describes the offender population, it is easy to see that offenders tend to specialize, at least for a short period of time. People who commit a personal crime are likely to continue to commit personal crimes, property criminals will continue to commit property crimes, and only rarely shall the twain meet. If the twain never met (if the row elements were 1.0 and 0.0, rather than .9 and .1), specialization would be complete.

Although the criminologists of 20 years ago probably expected a specialized matrix like this one, what they found in arrest records suggested much greater movement between crime types. This matrix is taken from data provided by Blumstein and Cohen (1979, p. 582):

Last crime	Next crime	
	Personal	Property
Personal	.44	.56
Property	.13	.87

Two things are evident from this matrix. First, offenders commit property offenses more often than they commit personal crimes (which is only reasonable, because people are victimized by property crimes more often than personal crimes). Second, offenders do not seem to restrict themselves to crimes of only one type. If the arrest-switch probabilities were the same for all offenders, then few criminals would specialize in crimes of one type only. Criminologists congratulated themselves on their perspicacity, and roundly shot down the long-standing specialization hypothesis as unrealistic (Hood & Sparks, 1970; Wolfgang, Figlio, & Sellin, 1972).

No one seemed to notice the (usually implicit) assumption—that the probabilities applied equally to all offenders. There was no evidence whatever that it did; in fact, the matrices were also consistent with the hypothesis that most offenders were personal or property specialists. For example, the second matrix shown above can also be obtained if 5 percent of offenders are personal specialists and 65 percent are property specialists, but the remaining 30 percent of criminals commit crimes of both types, according to a Markov process defined by the following crime-switch matrix:

Last crime	Next crime	
	Personal	Property
Personal	.24	.76
Property	.65	.35

An infinite number of alternative solutions are available, subject only to very broad restrictions on the number of personal and property specialists. Such a result is even easier to devise if one drops the (again, implicit) assumptions that all offenders commit crimes at identical rates and stand identical chances of arrest. In this case, it is theoretically possible that all offenders but one are specialists; however, the sole generalist commits crimes so much more frequently or is so likely to be captured that he or she accounts for all the arrest switches in the matrix.

The underlying problem, of course, is a chestnut among social scientists termed the *ecological fallacy*: Data on aggregates cannot be applied directly to individuals without some information as to the distribution of individuals within the aggregate (Robinson, 1950). Because the question to be answered centers on the distribution of individuals, the only way to use (aggregate) arrest-switch matrices to identify the degree of (individual) criminal specialization is to assume some degree of criminal specialization. When the problem is phrased in this way, it is clear that few criminologists (or even economists) would be willing to go that far.

So, although the arrest-switch matrices helped to solidify a consensus around the position that criminals were opportunistic generalists, they are not much help in answering the question of specialization. Fortunately, the individual-level data collected in the Rand survey can help to answer this question.

How many offenders are found to specialize depends on how specialization is defined, of course. A few criminals probably specialize in pursesnatches from old women on city streets; a larger number probably confine their efforts to robbery of all sorts from pedestrians; a still larger number commits various kinds of robberies; and so on. The larger the categories that comprise "specialties," the more specialists there will be. Here, as elsewhere, all kinds of property crimes are considered to be identical, as well as all kinds of personal crimes. Although these categories are broader than those usually associated with criminal specialization, the reasons for making only this broad distinction are the same as before: This is probably the most important distinction to be made, and it keeps the analysis simple.

Table 3.11 shows the proportion of offenders in each state who were generalists and specialists of each of two types. Of every 100 offenders,

- 43 committed only property crimes during the 2 years before their current incarceration.
- 20 committed only personal crimes.
- 37 committed both personal and property crimes.

Most of the offenders specialized. The exact proportions differed among the three states. The Texas sample included more property specialists, and fewer personal

TABLE 3.11
*Most Offenders Commit Either Property or Violent
Crimes but Not Both*

	Property only	Violent only	Both property and violent
California	40.6%	19.6%	39.7%
Michigan	42.2	25.7	32.1
Texas	52.2	14.4	33.3
Total	44.7	20.0	35.4

specialists than the other two states. But in all three states, only between 34 and 40 percent of criminals chose to commit crimes of both types.

This result answers only part of the question, however. The policy implications of criminal specialization depend not only on the proportion of offenders who specialize and of those who do not but on the proportion of offenses committed by specialists and generalists. As suggested above, the greater the relative frequency of offending among generalists, the better selective policies will work; if generalists commit crimes relatively infrequently, selection may not be cost-effective at all. So now we must ask whether generalists are more or less dangerous than criminal specialists.

Generalists Are More Dangerous

For a long time, research on career criminals has emphasized their versatility. In the typology of Clinard and Quinney (1973), for example, the career criminals are clearly differentiated from noncareer offenders. "Occasional" offenders commit either "violent and personal" acts motivated by momentary anger or a culture of violence, or they commit property offenses largely for recreational purposes. "Conventional" (career) criminals, in contrast, "are likely to have a diversified criminal record. These offenders commit a series of offenses which may include theft, larceny, robbery, and burglary" (p. 134). So high-rate offenders commit several kinds of crime, whereas low-rate offenders are specialists. Similar findings have been presented by numerous other observers (e.g., Gibbons, 1968; Normandeau, 1972).

Although such typologies as these made sense on their face, they were based on anecdotal evidence. The hypothesis that versatile offenders were more dangerous was confirmed with the more systematic evidence provided by the Rand inmate surveys, and particularly by the analysis conducted by Chaiken and Chaiken (1982). The Chaikens found that some 10 percent of the offenders surveyed—the "violent predators"—were particularly versatile criminals. These offenders all committed robbery, assault, and drug deals; most of them also did burglaries, thefts, and auto thefts; many did forgeries and frauds. But what best characterized the violent predators was not their versatility, but their activity: The median violent predator committed robberies more than twice as frequently as the average robber who was not a violent predator and dealt twice as many drugs as the typical nonpredator drug dealer. The combination of versatility and activity made the violent predators considerably more dangerous than other offenders: The average violent predator committed more than six times as many crimes as the average nonpredator.

There are good reasons why generalists such as the violent predators should be more dangerous than more specialized offenders. Most researchers agree that the typical offender starts out committing relatively minor property offenses, such as petty theft. The most highly motivated thieves then progress to crimes requiring more skill and guts, such as burglary. And the most highly motivated burglars eventually progress to personal crimes, which require the presence of mind and skill to confront the victim. In this way, offenders' motivations to commit crimes lead them to develop a variety of criminal abilities. Once their careers have fully developed, these offenders will have both the motivation and the capacity to take advantage of most of the criminal opportunities available to them—they will be both versatile and dangerous. Criminal specialists, on the other hand, are either those who have not yet developed fully, or have gone the full cycle but are no longer so motivated as they once were. This progression was confirmed by the initial analysts of the 1978 Rand survey: Over a 2-year period, offenders were about three times as likely to progress to a more serious offending group than to regress to a less serious group (Chaiken & Chaiken, 1982).

Reanalysis of the Rand survey confirms the Chaikens's basic result: Generalists are much more active offenders than specialists. As shown in Figure 3.10, offenders who committed both personal and property crimes commit each at rates about twice as high as criminals who specialize in one or the other. Seriousness indexes indicate that the average personal crime is three times as serious as the average property crime (Sellin & Wolfgang, 1964), whereas jury awards and direct victim losses suggest that personal crimes may be as much as 27 times as serious as property crimes on average (Cohen, 1988). This means that the typical generalist is much more dangerous than the average specialist offender. In fact, even if we rely on the relatively moderate weights of the seriousness index, generalists are more than twice as dangerous as property specialists, and over 10 times as dangerous as criminals who only do robberies and assaults. If jury awards can be taken seriously, property specialists are less dangerous than robbers and assaulters; but generalists are still over three times as dangerous as personal specialists.

The increased activity of versatile criminals is a weighty argument in favor of selection, but there is a better one. Offense rates for personal and property

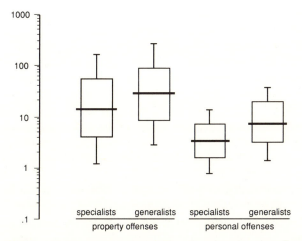

FIGURE 3.10. Criminal specialists are less dangerous than generalists.

offenses, among offenders who commit both offense types, are strongly positively correlated. That is, if we find that a particularly active property offender
also has a history of robbery or assault, chances are good that he or she does
these crimes at much higher-than-average rates, even for a generalist. More
precisely,

$$\log \lambda_V = 1.076 + .231 \lambda_P \pm 2.132 \qquad (3.6)$$
$$(.102) \quad (.034)$$

This equation explains 9.5 percent of the variation in the logarithm of personal
offense rates; the relationship does not differ significantly or substantially among
the three states in the Rand sample.

We may safely conclude that, if incapacitation and punishment should be
concentrated on a relatively elite group of versatile offenders, there is an elite of
even this group who commit crimes of all types at much higher-than-typical
rates.

Conclusions

If all offenders were specialists, it would easy to estimate the effects of
incapacitation. For example, we could assume that robbers and assailants commit only robberies and assaults, and can only be arrested, convicted, and incarcerated for the robberies they commit. Incapacitation of convicted burglars, auto
thieves, or flashers would have no effect on the robbery rate, because all of these

offenders specialize in only one kind of offense. Such an assumption was (implicitly) made by Greenwood (1982) in his estimate of the effects of selective policies, and this assumption dramatically simplified his analysis.

Of course, the assumption is not even wrong. As shown above, most personal criminals are also property criminals. Many commit property crimes more frequently than personal crimes; some are undoubtedly more likely to be jailed for burglary than for robbery. In any case, generalists are certain to be in jail a greater proportion of time than we would expect from their personal offense rates, simply because they run some risk of incarceration due to the other offenses they commit. We could be sure that the criminal justice system is preventing more crimes through incarceration than a one-crime model would estimate. We could also be sure that a greater proportion of offenders are in jail or prison. All else equal, then, the crime-control effectiveness of the present system would be greater than that estimated through use of a one-crime incapacitation model.

One solution is to create a model that specifically accounts for multiple crime types. Offenders would commit personal and property crimes at varying rates, get arrested, convicted, and incarcerated for each, and serve sentences based on the crime type for which they were convicted and on (perhaps erroneous) predictions of their offense rates for each type. Such a model would be considerably more accurate, and it would not be difficult to make such assumptions in a computer simulation (Spelman, 1983). Unfortunately, accounting for multiple crime types would complicate an analytical model considerably. In addition, the capacity of existing selection methods to predict offense rates of multiple types is rarely specified in the research literature. Given the difficulties associated with simultaneously predicting multiple events (e.g., Rossi, Berk, & Lenihan, 1980), this is understandable. But the overwhelming importance of generalist offenders suggests that this issue needs more attention.

Simulation results suggest a workable alternative. Within the current range of uncertainty, the effectiveness of collective and selective policies does not appear to be sensitive to differences in the degree of specialization among the offending population. That is, whether the proportion of specialists is as large or as small as is consistent with available data does not seem to matter much. Thus an analytic model that assumes offenders commit crimes of only one, homogeneous type will predict changes in aggregate crime rates reasonably well, so long as obvious corrections are made for arrest, conviction, and incarceration probabilities and expected sentence lengths (Spelman, 1983).

Such a homogeneous crime model obviously leaves out some important parts. In particular, it will not be possible to estimate the relative effectiveness of selective methods that are particularly accurate at identifying generalists; neither will it be possible to estimate the benefits of increases in jail and prison beds if these beds are earmarked for certain types of offenders. If current policies are already especially likely (unlikely) to imprison generalist offenders, the homogeneous crime model may overestimate (underestimate) the effectiveness of both selective and collective incapacitation. This is a significant price to pay for simplicity.

On the other hand, we may be able to predict the significant biases in the model in advance. For a variety of reasons, selective sentencing will probably be more effective at reducing personal crimes than property crimes. Personal offenders are more likely to get caught per crime committed than property offenders; as shown in Chapter 5, personal offenders appear to learn less from experience than frequent property offenders. Thus a history of repeat personal offending is likely to be easier to substantiate than a history of repeat property crime. And it appears to be easier to differentiate between frequent and casual personal offenders on the basis of other offender characteristics than is true for property offenders (Chaiken & Chaiken, 1982).

If high-rate robbers and assaulters are disproportionately singled out by the predictive scale, selective sentencing may reduce the crime rate by less than the homogeneous-crime model will estimate. Conceivably, it could increase the crime rate, by giving systematically lenient sentences to frequent burglars and auto thieves. On the other hand, an increase in the aggregate crime rate may be a substantial benefit to the public if accompanied by a reduction in robberies and assaults. Thus, though the homogeneous crime model may overestimate the size of reductions in the aggregate crime rate, this would be compensated by underestimates of the importance of these reductions. The benefits of collective incapacitation would be biased in similar ways.

This is admittedly a second-best solution, but the alternative would be complex, and would require additional assumptions as to the ability of selective scales to differentiate among offenders of different types. Until further data are available, a one-crime model should do tolerably well.

About two-thirds of active offenders are specialists, committing only property crimes or only personal crimes. But the typical generalist—an offender who commits crimes of both types—is 3 to 5 times as dangerous as the typical specialist. The most frequent offenders are also most likely to be versatile. As a result, selective methods that predict high-rate generalists are likely to be especially effective at reducing crime.

Mathematical Models of Offense Rates

Up to this point, the analysis results have been complicated. The offense rate distributions differ slightly and unpredictably from state to state; the Lorenz curves are full of funny kinks and bends. This makes it hard to use all of the results. For example, it would be difficult to design an analytic model that relied on the entire idiosyncratic distribution of Michigan property offense rates. The approach taken by previous analysts—simplifying the data so that they fit easily into an uncomplicated policy model—certainly makes the results easier to use and may be practically necessary to obtain any usable results at all.

There is another reason for simplifying the data analysis results—some of them are wrong. Some of the kinks, bends, and inconsistencies in the observed offense rates are due to chance variations; some are due to biases in individual estimates. So it would be wrong to pay too much attention to all the idiosyncracies, even if they could be included in a model of the offending population. A simpler form that smooths out the inconsistencies and compensates for the biases may well be more accurate.

Of course, any simplification leaves out some information. This poses two problems: First, the results of policy analysis may be less precise than they need be; second and more important, it is impossible to be sure whether leaving out some of the data affects the policy implications. All this suggests that any simplification of the offense rate distribution—or any other characteristic of the offending population—must balance ease-of-use against accuracy. There are no hard and fast rules here. But the fact that these objectives may conflict should be kept in mind throughout the discussion.

There are many ways of simplifying complex distributions like those identified above. The method likely to prove most useful is to fit the empirical distributions to known functional forms. Once it is known that the data (approximately) follow some known formula, it is possible to substitute the formula for the data in further analysis. Few attempts have been made to do this in the past; most analysts have made "not-unreasonable" assumptions and trusted to providence that they were (about) right. The Rand survey data provide the information needed to test whether such assumptions are really reasonable or not.

Another way to simplify the analysis is to combine the data from two or more states if the distribution of offense rates seems to be very similar in each. Although there is no particular reason for thinking that the distributions are really the same in all states, the differences may be so small that they are overwhelmed by random fluctuations in the survey data. So combining states where the results are similar not only simplifies later analysis; it decreases the contribution of random error by increasing the sample size. Although combining data from similar states is likely to be a good idea, it is only strictly appropriate (and, if the policy model is less blunt an instrument than the Avi-Itzhak and Shinnar model, it is only safe) when the data are similar in three ways:

- The distributions of personal offense rates are similar.
- The distributions of property offense rates are similar.
- The relationship between personal and property offense rates is similar.

In the remainder of this chapter, an attempt will be made to lay the foundation for better models of the effectiveness of selective criminal justice policies. Attempts will be made to fit the univariate and bivariate distributions of offense rates to various functional forms; and comparisons will be made between states to identify whether important information would be lost, should the distributions from each state be combined.

Functional Forms for Modeling Offense Rates

Three distributional forms have been suggested for the purpose of classifying these results. The gamma distribution has been found to fit a variety of data conceptually similar to offense rates. In particular, service times in queueing systems and individual accident-proneness seem to be close to gamma-distributed. The logNormal distribution has proven particularly useful in economics work. Income and wealth seem to be about logNormal-distributed throughout the population in most countries. Another form often used in mapping the distribution of income and wealth is the Pareto distribution. First proposed as an "iron law" of income at the turn of the century, the Pareto is still used to fit the distribution of incomes in the highest ranges—those over the 80th percentile or so.

The only prior attempt to fit distributional forms such as these to empirical data was made by researchers at the Rand Corporation in their first analysis of the 1978 inmate survey. They found that offense rates for some crime types were roughly gamma-distributed, and that others were about Pareto-distributed (Rolph, Chaiken, & Houchens, 1981). Although their results suggest that these forms will probably work here as well, they may not. There are several reasons for this.

First, the previous Rand results were obtained by fitting distributional forms to each of the 10 crime types covered in the survey. Thus a different form was obtained for the distribution of offense rates for each of the five property crimes included—frauds, forgeries, burglaries, larcenies, and auto thefts. For simplicity, however, our interest here is in fitting a distributional form to the distribution of offense rates for all property crimes. If the shape of the offense rate distribution for each property crime were about the same, and all property offenders committed each of these crime types, then we should expect that the same functional form would fit the aggregate distribution. But some offenders do not commit all of these crime types, and the shapes of the distributions are very different (although many of them may be described by the same form). So it is entirely possible that the aggregate distribution will look very different from the component distributions.

The second reason is that cases were not weighted in the previous Rand work. Some of the effects of weighting have already been noted: High-rate offenders are systematically more likely to be in prison; thus the upper tails of the (unweighted) offense rate distribution are too long; and thus a distributional form with long tails is less likely to fit the weighted offense rate distribution. In addition, it may be that offenders with high rates of arrest and conviction, or offenders who commit crimes that tend to draw long sentences commit crimes at systematically different rates than others. And it has already been shown that the variance of offense rates is higher among older offenders than among youthful offenders, and the unweighted incoming cohort sample will include too many younger criminals. So the effects of weighting the sample are unpredictable.

Enough caveats. Let us now consider how the distribution of offense rates among younger offenders may be fitted to these three distributional forms.

The gamma distribution is a flexible form with a great variety of uses. One special case of the gamma is the χ^2 distribution—the distribution of the sum of squared, Normal deviates. Another special case is the Erlang distribution, which is often used in queueing models and other operations research work. If one adds α random variates, each of which are exponentially distributed with a mean of β, the result will be Erlang-distributed with parameters of α and β. And the gamma has been found to describe many social and physical phenomena. Examples include the distribution of rainfall (Kotz & Neumann, 1963), the lifetime of building materials (Birnbaum & Saunders, 1958), and accident proneness (Beard, 1948).

The analogy to accident proneness is particularly apt. For years, actuaries have relied on the convenience of the gamma when describing the frequency of accidents in analytic models. Suppose that Z_i is an underlying proneness to auto accidents. It may represent a combination of carelessness, slow reactions, a tendency to speed, and so on; assume this combination is gamma-distributed. Suppose further that accidents occur according to a Poisson process. Then it can be shown that the distribution of the number of accidents in which each member of the population is involved during some time period will be negative binomial-distributed. (In fact, Irwin, 1968, shows that the empirical distribution is nearly negative binomial.) The practical implication of this result is that, if accident proneness changes only slowly over time, actuaries can predict from past accidents the likelihood that an individual will become involved in another, and charge appropriate insurance premiums. Although such a prediction could be made, no matter what the distribution of underlying accident proneness, the gamma-Poisson-negative binomial regularity makes the mathematics of modeling and prediction much simpler.

A similar process may be used to describe the relationship between λ—an underlying propensity to commit crimes—and the number of offenses actually committed during some period of time. Applications and some extensions of the gamma-Poisson model were considered at length by the initial analysts of the Rand 1978 survey (Rolph, Chaiken, & Houchens, 1981). Although the most realistic of these models are elegant and seem to be reasonable, they are too complicated to be tested here. Let us be content with examining the likely fit of the (none too simple) univariate gamma distribution.

The density function of the (two-parameter) gamma distribution is

$$p(\lambda_i) = \beta^{\alpha} \lambda_i{}^{\alpha-1}\, e^{-\beta\lambda i}/\Gamma(\alpha), \qquad (3.7)$$

where α determines the shape of the distribution, β the scale (roughly, the variability) of the distribution, and Γ denotes the gamma function. α and β are restricted to be greater than zero; the Erlang variant of the gamma has an identical density, except that α is restricted to be a positive integer. The distribution function of the gamma is complex; one of the advantages of the Erlang is that restricting α to a positive integer makes the density function integrable.

Although there are many ways of fitting a gamma to an empirical distribution, most of them are very sensitive to small deviations in the tails. That is, even if the empirical data are exactly gamma-distributed, the fitted parameters can be very wrong, simply because a few very high or very low observations are in error. Because the discussion in Chapter 2 suggested that the tails of the offense rate distribution are the least reliable sections anyway, it is necessary to find a more robust method of fitting. If possible, the method should rely mostly on observations in the middle of the distribution.

One such method was proposed and used by the initial Rand researchers. They relied on the fact that, for all gamma distributions with the same shape parameter, α, the ratio of sample quantiles is identical. For example, for all gammas with $\alpha = .30$, the 75th percentile divided by the median is 4.80. Moreover, the ratio of the 75th percentile to the median will not be 4.80 for any gamma with $\alpha \neq .30$. So the shape parameter may be (roughly) estimated from order statistics (Rolph, Chaiken, & Houchens, 1981). Once α has been estimated, β may be computed through a rather complicated equation that uses three quantiles of the empirical distribution (Saerndal, 1964). So, in order to estimate gamma parameters, it is sufficient to know (for example) the 25th, 50th, and 75th percentiles.

These quantiles were used to estimate gamma parameters for the distributions of personal and property offense rates, for each of the three states. Before examining the results, let us first consider more closely the other two candidates for describing these distributions—the logNormal and the Pareto.

The logNormal distribution is, not surprisingly, the most frequently used distribution for describing skewed phenomena. This is due in part to the familiarity of its parent, the Normal distribution. Another reason is that the Normal may result from applications of the law of proportionate effect. This regularity forms the basis of the cross-sectional and time-series explanations for skewness in λ explained above. Finally, many phenomena seem to be roughly logNormal-distributed, even when the law of proportionate effect cannot be expected to hold. The number of syllables in words used in spoken English (Herdan, 1958) and the abundance of species in a biosystem (Gundy, 1951) are both close to logNormal. And the fact that the critical dose of a drug is often logNormal-distributed among different individuals in a species led to the development of probit analysis for qualitative dependent variables (Bliss, 1934).

The density function of the logNormal is a slight variation of the familiar Normal density.

$$p(\lambda_i) = (\sigma\lambda_i)^{-1} (2\pi)^{.5} \exp (-(2\sigma^2)^{-1} (\log(\lambda_i) - \lambda_.)^2), \qquad (3.8)$$

where $\lambda_.$ is the mean, and σ the variance, of the distribution of logarithms of offense rates. Although the distribution function is not generally integrable, tables are available in any statistics book.

The most obvious method of estimating the parameters of the logNormal relies on the fact that it is almost identical to the Normal: $\lambda_.$ and σ may be estimated by the first and second moments (that is, the sample mean and variance) of the empirical distribution of logarithms of offense rates. Such estimates are consistent, and in fact are the maximum likelihood estimates. Unfortunately, they are very likely to be far from precise for small samples, especially when offense rates in the tails are imprecisely measured. As with the gamma distribution, a more robust method would be more appropriate.

Again, a more accurate method for estimating the parameters, for all but the largest samples, relies on sample quantiles (Aitchison & Brown, 1962). Any quantiles will do, but the power of the resulting estimates depends upon the quantiles chosen. The further apart the chosen quantiles are, the more powerful will be the estimate of the variance; the closer together they are, the more powerful will be the estimate of the mean. Given the relative imprecision of estimates in the top and bottom 20 percent of the offense rate distribution, the 25th and 75th percentiles seem to be a good compromise choice; experimentation showed that they usually resulted in the best-fitting parameters, as well.

The Pareto distribution is the brainchild of Swiss economist Vilfredo Pareto. Working at the turn of the century, Pareto used this form to describe the distribution of income for a variety of populations. Amazingly (and purely by coincidence), Pareto found that the shape of the income distribution was virtually identical for populations ranging from 1471 Augsburg burghers to 1890s Central European countries (Pareto, 1897/1972). Although his initial hypothesis—that the shape of the distribution was independent of technology, culture, and government policy—has been thoroughly disproven (Cowell, 1977; Pigou, 1932), the Pareto form is still useful for describing the distribution of individual incomes. It is particularly useful for describing the upper tail of the income distribution—the top 20 percent of earners. In addition, researchers have shown that a variety of other social phenomena are approximately Pareto-distributed: Examples include the population of cities (Cowell, 1977), the assets of firms in an industry (Simon & Bonini, 1958), the frequency of word usage in American Indian languages, and even the billiards scores racked up by faculty members of Indiana University (Johnson & Kotz, 1967).

One reason the Pareto has been used so frequently is that it may result from a variety of processes. For example, the Pareto has proven useful in operations research because it can be the result of a mixture of exponential distributions (Harris, 1968). In the long run, any distribution will tend to Pareto if the variates change over time according to certain random processes (Champernowne, 1953; Pen, 1974). And reasonable hypotheses about corporate policies of compensating executives suggest a Pareto distribution for incomes within a corporate hierarchy (Simon, 1957). Unfortunately, close examination of these processes reveals that none of them could very well be working in the production of offense rates.

The density function of the (two-parameter) Pareto distribution is

$$p(\lambda_i) = [\gamma \, \kappa^\gamma \, \lambda_i]/(\kappa + \lambda_i)^{\gamma+1}, \tag{3.9}$$

where γ provides the shape of the distribution, and κ provides the scale. For all γ and κ greater than zero, this form ensures that all offense rates will be greater than zero. The distribution function of the Pareto is

$$F(\lambda_i) = 1 - (1 + \lambda_i/\kappa)^{-\gamma}. \tag{3.10}$$

Like the gamma and logNormal, there are several ways of fitting the parameters γ and κ to empirical data. Once again, at least for small samples, the most reliable results are obtained by using sample quantiles (Quandt, 1966). Using quantiles has the usual advantage: γ and κ are unlikely to be much affected by unreliable estimates or chance deviations in the tails. For sample quantiles λ_1 and λ_2 at the P_1 and P_2 percentiles of the distribution, respectively, an estimate for γ may be obtained by finding the roots of the equation,

$$\lambda_1 \{(1 - P_1)^{1/\gamma} - [(1 - P_1)(1 - P_2)]^{1/\gamma}\} - \\ \lambda_2 \{(1 - P_2)^{1/\gamma} - [(1 - P_1)(1 - P_2)]^{1/\gamma}\} = 0. \tag{3.11}$$

This equation may be easily solved through use of the Newton-Raphson method. Once γ is obtained, simple arithmetic yields the other parameter:

$$\kappa = \lambda_i \, (1 - P_i)^{1/\gamma}/[1 - (1 - P_i)^{1/\gamma}], \tag{3.12}$$

where P_i and λ_i may be either P_1 and λ_1 or P_2 and λ_2. Estimates obtained in this way are consistent; Monte Carlo experiments show that the most efficient estimates are produced when P_1 and P_2 are the 25th and 75th percentiles (Quandt, 1966).

Fitting the Univariate Distributions

One last problem must be considered before fitting parameters to our empirical offense rate data. The problem may be summarized as follows. Some active property offenders may have committed no property crimes during the (up to) 2-year sampling window, just because they never got around to it. Some active personal offenders may never have gotten around to committing personal crimes. So some of the "zeroes" in each empirical distribution may not really be zeroes at all—they may be small but positive offense rates. It may even be that all offenders who committed any index crimes should really be considered to be active personal offenders. So the proportion of apparent zeroes that are really nonzero could possibly be anywhere between 0 and 1. It could even conceivably be greater than 1.0, if some offenders who committed only drug crimes or only nonindex crimes ran a reasonable risk of committing an index crime within the sampling window.

One is tempted to call this a question for philosophers rather than for data analysts. But recall that the only reason for fitting these parametric distributions in the first place is to make the empirical results easier to use. The usefulness of selective policies—and the usefulness of any incapacitation strategy—is driven by the number and offending frequency of the medium- and high-rate offenders, not by the proportion of offenders who commit crimes at low rates. So if including a few too many or too few low-rate offenders in the characterization ensures a better fit in the middle and high end of the distribution, the implications for policy will be about right.

As a result, it seems prudent to try several different values for the proportion of empirical zeroes that are really nonzero. For simplicity, let us estimate parameters when all zeroes are excluded, when all zeroes are included, and when 25, 50, and 75 percent of the zeroes are included in the empirical distribution. Then we may choose that combination of parametric form and included zeroes that best fits the empirical data. If some form appears to fit the empirical distribution progressively better as more zeroes are added, we might even consider adding some nonindex offenders to the sample, thus increasing the included "proportion" to some figure greater than one.

Estimated parameters are shown in Tables 3.12 (for the distribution of personal offense rates) and 3.13 (for property offense rates). Goodness of fit statistics—χ^2 and the associated significance level—are shown in Tables 3.14 and 3.15. In addition, a significance value that summarizes the goodness of fit for each distribution among the three states is shown in Tables 3.14 and 3.15. This summary value is the cumulative probability that the results in each of the

TABLE 3.12
Fitted Parameters for Personal Offense Rate Distribution

	Proportion of zeroes included				
	0	25	50	75	100
Gamma parameters					
California	.623	.548	.474	.467	.443
	.0727	.0878	.0724	.0958	.1152
Michigan	.651	.595	.552	.536	.558
	.1080	.1099	.1238	.1575	.2446
Texas	.627	.619	.535	.532	.544
	.1136	.1376	.1332	.2034	.2937
LogNormal parameters					
California	1.273	1.121	.821	.494	.266
	1.464	1.779	2.028	2.056	2.144
Michigan	1.133	.959	.642	.336	.002
	1.550	1.639	1.768	1.815	1.748
Texas	.784	.777	.498	.099	−.214
	1.493	1.571	1.822	2.176	1.792
Pareto parameters					
California	1.159	.778	.580	.564	.521
	5.114	2.062	.899	.615	.416
Michigan	1.397	.978	.791	.740	.814
	5.082	2.522	1.312	.865	.727
Texas	1.818	1.124	.733	.726	.764
	3.406	2.580	1.001	.660	.527

Note. For gamma and Pareto distributions, first figure given is shape parameter, second figure is scale parameter; for logNormal-distribution, first figure is mean, second figure is standard deviation.

three states could have been achieved, if the empirical data were in fact distributed according to the parametric distribution in question (Edgington, 1972). This is the most powerful method available when the number of significance levels to be combined is small (Rosenthal, 1978).

Rather than examine these (rather dense) tables in gruesome detail, let us summarize the important results.

First, note that the gamma form does not fit the empirical offense rate distributions very well at all. Of the 30 cases tested in Tables 3.14 and 3.15 (five proportions of included zeroes, multiplied by three states, multiplied by two crime types), we can reject the hypothesis that the data were really gamma-distributed in 29 cases at the 5-percent significance level. In half the cases, we may reject the hypothesis at even the .001 level of significance. In some ways the gamma is the most convenient of the distributional forms in question, but it gives unquestionably the worst fit to these data. Although this appears to conflict with

TABLE 3.13

Fitted Parameters for Property Offense Rate Distribution

	Proportion of zeroes included				
	0	25	50	75	100
Gamma parameters					
California	.374	.361	.369	.337	.270
	.00468	.00496	.00669	.00638	.00580
Michigan	.336	.296	.264	.262	.244
	.00523	.00509	.00496	.00619	.00744
Texas	.344	.327	.297	.262	.241
	.00585	.00555	.00501	.00443	.00456
LogNormal parameters					
California	3.159	2.900	2.671	2.435	1.929
	2.413	2.499	2.460	2.616	2.994
Michigan	2.705	2.312	2.035	1.759	1.415
	2.498	2.839	3.0343	3.044	3.170
Texas	2.519	2.509	2.352	2.144	1.886
	2.661	2.665	2.833	3.049	3.193
Pareto parameters					
California	.418	.402	.412	.375	.309
	4.109	3.215	2.717	1.689	.594
Michigan	.374	.333	.304	.303	.287
	2.090	1.082	.626	.469	.280
Texas	.383	.364	.334	.302	.284
	2.058	1.693	1.141	.684	.436

Note. For gamma and Pareto distributions, first figure given is shape parameter, second figure is scale parameter; for logNormal-distribution, first figure is mean, second figure is standard deviation.

results reported by Rolph, Chaiken, and Houchens (1981), they did not weight their cases, but only analyzed a small subset of the data, and relied on less-robust methods of fitting the Pareto and logNormal parameters.

The Pareto and logNormal fits are much better. Probability values combined across states (denoted as p in Tables 3.14 and 3.15) show that the logNormal provides an excellent fit for the distribution of personal λs with 0, 25, and 50 percent of zeroes included; the Pareto works quite well for the distribution of property offense rates with 50 and 75 percent of zeroes included, and tolerably well for the distribution of personal λs with 0, 25, and 50 percent of zeroes included. On the basis of fit alone, a case could be made for either form.

Unfortunately, the mean of a Pareto distribution is infinite when the shape parameter is less than 1. The shape parameters of the fitted Paretos are consistently less than 1 for all property λ combinations, and for most personal λ

TABLE 3.14
Goodness of Fit of Parametric Distributions: Personal Crimes

	Proportion of zeroes included				
	0	25	50	75	100
Gamma parameters					
California	9.634	4.855	6.177	6.131	23.639
	.008	.088	.046	.047	≪.001
Michigan	13.136	17.493	13.665	9.205	13.305
	.001	<.001	.001	.010	.001
Texas	10.256	7.233	6.615	15.047	26.567
	.006	.027	.037	<.001	≪.001
Combined probability	≪.001	<.001	≪.001	≪.001	≪.001
LogNormal parameters					
California	.381	1.743	2.004	4.674	13.897
	.826	.418	.367	.097	.001
Michigan	1.780	3.058	2.118	3.689	10.119
	.411	.217	.347	.158	.006
Texas	6.113	1.790	3.718	9.140	17.558
	.047	.409	.156	.010	<.001
Combined probability	.353	.190	.110	.003	≪.001
Pareto parameters					
California	.669	2.166	4.278	4.686	10.428
	.716	.339	.118	.096	.005
Michigan	6.777	4.775	1.276	2.213	10.791
	.034	.092	.528	.331	.004
Texas	7.820	2.550	4.663	3.611	17.057
	.020	.279	.097	.164	<.001
Combined probability	.076	.060	.068	.034	≪.001

Note. First number provided is χ^2 with 2 degrees of freedom; second number is significance level associated with that χ^2.

combinations. So, although the Pareto form fits the empirical data well, it would be very awkward to use.

This leaves (more or less by default) the logNormal distribution. The best logNormal fit for personal λs includes no zeroes; the least-worst fits for property λs include none and 75 percent of the empirical zeroes. Neither of the property fits are particularly satisfying, but they are at least defensible. Moreover, the logNormal distribution fits these empirical distributions relatively well in the critical upper tails but fails in the bottom 40 percent of the distribution. If we have to use a distributional form that is in error, this is where we would like the errors to be. Because the logNormal form fits the 0 and 75 percent inclusion levels about equally well, let us (a bit grudgingly) choose the fits that include no zeroes since this will simplify the bivariate analysis.

TABLE 3.15
Goodness of Fit of Parametric Distributions: Property Crimes

	Proportion of zeroes included				
	0	25	50	75	100
Gamma parameters					
California	20.362	15.009	14.919	21.521	46.120
	<.001	<.001	<.001	<.001	<.001
Michigan	7.568	15.778	12.856	17.605	12.972
	.023	<.001	.002	<.001	.002
Texas	12.186	12.000	9.367	13.080	26.497
	.002	.002	.009	.001	≪.001
Combined probability	≪.001	≪.001	≪.001	≪.001	≪.001
LogNormal parameters					
California	8.120	11.344	13.736	6.977	2.976
	.018	.003	.001	.030	.226
Michigan	1.924	3.501	4.762	2.400	9.697
	.382	.174	.092	.300	.008
Texas	7.456	7.188	4.628	4.095	14.029
	.024	.028	.099	.129	.001
Combined probability	.013	.001	.001	.016	.002
Pareto parameters					
California	19.236	3.917	2.619	2.627	12.966
	≪.001	.141	.270	.269	.002
Michigan	5.702	9.166	4.698	1.708	5.855
	.058	.010	.096	.426	.054
Texas	1.789	1.403	.906	3.472	4.925
	.409	.496	.636	.176	.085
Combined probability	.017	.045	.167	.110	<.001

Note. First number provided is χ^2 with 2 degrees of freedom; second number is significance level associated with that χ^2.

Modeling the Bivariate Distribution

To characterize the bivariate distribution we must answer two kinds of questions. First, we must identify the univariate distributions of personal and property offense rates among members of three groups: personal crime specialists, property specialists, and generalists. Second, we need to know the relationship between (that is, the bivariate distribution for) personal and property offense rates among offenders who commit crimes of both types. As shown above, the average generalist commits crimes more frequently than the average specialist, and the relationship between personal and property offense rates for generalists is positive. In this section, these relationships are described in somewhat more detail. Let us consider these two questions in turn.

Offense Rates among Generalists and Specialists

Because the distribution of offense rates for both crime types is best characterized by the logNormal form, it is easy to define the distributions for each of
the three groups of interest. We need only estimate the mean and the variance of
each distribution and measure the differences in each parameter among the three
groups. The need for measuring differences in means is obvious—results presented in Chapter 1 showed that small changes in the mean value of the offense
rate can have important effects on the effectiveness of selective criminal justice
action. But differences in variances may also be important, because the variance
is a measure of the concentration of offense rates among offenders. The higher
the variance, the more concentrated the motivations for crime commission
among a small number of offenders. In fact, all logNormal distributions with the
same variance have identical Lorenz curves, even if the means are very different
(Aitchison & Brown, 1954).

Consider first differences among means. Table 3.16 shows the results of an
analysis of the variance in the logarithm of personal and property offense rates,
respectively. This analysis tests the assumption that average offense rates for
each crime type differ between generalists and specialists, and among states. As

TABLE 3.16
Generalists and Specialists Behave Differently in Each State

Personal crimes

Explanatory variable	df	Sum of squares	F	p(F)	Percentage variance explained
States and λ_P	5	137.091	11.230	.000	11.25%
Specialist	1	99.724	70.014	.000	8.19
States	2	15.761	5.533	.004	1.29
Interaction	2	21.606	7.585	.000	1.77
Residual	759	1081.072			88.75
Total	764	1218.163			100.0%

Property crimes

Explanatory variable	df	Sum of squares	F	p(F)	Percentage variance explained
States and λ_V	5	191.173	11.230	.000	5.00%
Specialist	1	126.848	37.527	.000	3.31
States	2	53.740	7.892	.000	1.40
Interaction	2	11.142	1.636	.195	0.29
Residual	1069	3639.631			95.00
Total	1074	3830.804			100.00%

shown, we can clearly reject the hypothesis that the average value of each offense rate is the same for generalists as for specialists. Although it appears to be more reasonable, we can also reject the hypothesis that the average value does not differ from one state to the next. But interactions between these factors do not seem to be very important. That is, generalists and specialists behave differently in each state, but the amount by which they differ is about the same in all states.

The mean and standard deviations of these distributions are shown in Table 3.17. The differences in average value between generalists and specialists are clear and consistent in each state: The typical generalist commits crimes of each type considerably more frequently than the typical specialist. Table 3.17 also shows results of tests of the homogeneity (that is, the similarity) of the variances of the offense rate distributions between generalists and specialists. Here, the results are more ambiguous, but the most reasonable conclusion is that the concentration of property offense rates is higher among generalists than among

TABLE 3.17

Pattern of Differences between Generalists and Specialists Is Similar among States

1. Distribution of personal offense rates given different values of property offense rates

	$\lambda_V \vert \lambda_P = 0$ $s(\lambda_V)$	$\lambda_V \vert \lambda_P > 0$ $s(\lambda_V)$	eta(λ_V) p(eta)	Bartlett–Fox F $p(F)$
California	1.098 (0.882)	2.210 (1.331)	4.10 ($p < .001$)	10.926 ($p = .001$)
Michigan	1.433 (1.363)	1.955 (1.298)	.192 ($p = .029$)	.327 ($p = .567$)
Texas	1.024 (0.693)	1.615 (1.083)	.258 ($p = .014$)	5.741 ($p = .017$)
All states	1.218 (1.082)	1.972 (1.277)	.286 ($p < .001$)	4.642 ($p = .031$)

2. Distribution of property offense rates given different values of personal offense rates

	$\lambda_V \vert \lambda_P = 0$ $s(\lambda_V)$	$\lambda_V \vert \lambda_P > 0$ $s(\lambda_V)$	eta(λ_V) p(eta)	Bartlett–Fox F $p(F)$
California	2.901 (2.018)	3.559 (1.737)	.173 ($p = .013$)	2.309 ($p = .129$)
Michigan	2.605 (1.842)	3.169 (1.717)	.156 ($p = .043$)	0.425 ($p = .515$)
Texas	2.413 (1.896)	3.164 (1.888)	.193 ($p = .014$)	0.000 ($p = 1.000$)
All states	2.644 (1.927)	3.333 (1.777)	.182 ($p < .001$)	1.805 ($p = .179$)

property specialists and that the concentrations of personal offense rates are about the same for generalists as for personal specialists.

The fact that the pattern of these results is very similar in each state suggests that it may be possible to construct an algorithm that converts information about univariate offense rate distributions into bivariate distributions. After a little trial and error, it turns out that the following algorithm works quite well in all three states. Let λ_V and λ_P reference the average offense rate for personal and property crimes among all offenders; denote the standard deviations of the distributions personal and property offense rate distributions by σ_V and σ_P. Then

- $\lambda_P(\text{specialists}) = .88\ \lambda_P;\ \lambda_P(\text{generalists}) = 1.1\ \lambda_P$
- $\sigma_P(\text{specialists}) = \sigma_P(\text{generalists}) = \sigma_P$
- $\lambda_V(\text{specialists}) = .72\ \lambda_V;\ \lambda_V(\text{generalists}) = 1.16\ \lambda_V$
- $\sigma_V(\text{specialists}) = .80\ \sigma_V;\ \sigma_V(\text{generalists}) = 1.1\ \sigma_V$

These results, combined with the finding that the proportion of street offenders who are specialists and generalists is about the same in each state, makes it easy to describe the univariate distributions for each group in each state. They also make it easy to assign random offense rates to simulated offenders. This algorithm is neither elegant nor particularly likely to be exactly confirmed by future work, but it is a convenient summary of the relationships described here.

The Bivariate Distribution among Generalists

The obvious parametric approximation for the bivariate distribution is the bivariate logNormal. Although two logNormal-distributed variables are only bivariate logNormal-distributed if the relationship between them is linear (Derman, Glaser & Olkin, 1973), the scatterplot between log λ_V and log λ_P for each of the three states showed no substantial deviations from linearity. The formula for the bivariate Normal (and, by obvious extension, the bivariate logNormal) is complex:

$$f(\lambda_{Vi},\lambda_{Pi}) = [(2\Pi\ \sigma_V\ \sigma_P)^2\ (1\ -\ R^2)]^{-.5}\ \exp\ [-Q(\lambda_{Vi},\lambda_{Pi})/2], \quad (3.13)$$

where

$$Q(\lambda_{Vi},\lambda_{Pi}) = (1\ -\ R^2)^{-1}\ \{(\lambda_{Vi}\ -\ \lambda_{V.})^2/\sigma_V^2\ +\ (\lambda_{Pi}\ -\ \lambda_{P.})^2/\sigma_P^2\ -$$
$$2R[(\lambda_{Vi}\ -\ \lambda_{V.})(\lambda_{Pi}\ -\ \lambda_{P.})/(\sigma_V\sigma_P)]\} \quad\quad (3.14)$$

(R refers to the correlation of λ_{Vi} and λ_{Pi}.) Needless to say, this makes the bivariate logNormal difficult to use in an analytic model. What is worse, the distribution of Poisson samples from a univariate logNormal a priori distribution is itself quite complicated; one can only imagine what the a posteriori distribution for the bivariate case would look like.

All this suggests that it may be simpler (if less elegant) to use a computer simulation, rather than an analytic model, in future work. As it happens, it is easy to generate random draws from the bivariate Normal distribution:

- First, generate a random logNormal λ from the marginal distribution of one of the two crime types (say, λ_V); then
- Use the conditional probability function (that is, the distribution of λ_P given the just-generated value of λ_V) to calculate the expected mean and standard deviation of λ_P; finally
- Generate a random logNormal λ_P with the proper mean and standard deviation.

What makes this easy is that the conditional probability function is very nicely behaved. The distribution of λ_P, given λ_V, is exactly logNormal, with the mean

$$E(\lambda_P|\lambda_V=V) = \lambda_{P.} + R \, \sigma_P \, (V - \lambda_{V.})/\sigma_V, \tag{3.15}$$

and the variance

$$\sigma^2(\lambda_P|\lambda_V=V) = \sigma_P{}^2 \, (1 - R^2). \tag{3.16}$$

As noted earlier in this chapter, $R = .308$; it does not differ substantially or significantly from one state to the next. So computer generation of a bivariate logNormal distribution would be quite simple.

There are, of course, advantages to use of an analytic model. The benefits and costs of analytic and simulation models will be discussed in some detail in Chapter 6. For now, suffice it to say that fairly realistic models of the multivariate distribution of offense rates among offenders would be easy to simulate, but difficult to include in an analytic model.

The distributions of personal and property offense rates for all states are roughly logNormal-distributed. Although offense rates are close to Pareto-distributed, use of that functional form would be awkward. Offense rates are too skewed for the gamma form to provide a good fit. It is reasonable to assume that offenders who reported committing no crimes of a given type during the 2-year window were not active offenders of that type.

Although the univariate distribution of offense rates differs from one state to the next, the differences are not very large. Also, the pattern of differences among generalists and specialists is quite similar in all states. This makes it easy to simulate patterns of criminal offending with a computer, but difficult to construct analytic models that use these results.

4

The Criminal Career

The effectiveness of selective strategies depends to large extent on the length of time the average criminal remains active. It is easy to see why: If the average "career" were long—say, 20 years or so—then a judge could pass sentences of 5 or 7 years with relative impunity, confident that most offenders would very likely have committed crimes throughout their incarceration period had they been free. On the other hand, if most adult offenders went straight 5 years after they began to commit crimes, much of a 5-year sentence would very likely be wasted unless the offenders were convicted immediately after they started. So the average length of a criminal career might matter a great deal.

Of course, the average length of a career is only a place to start. Not all offenders are average, and the exceptions may prove as important for public policy as the rule. For example, if a few offenders commit crimes for very long periods, the arithmetic average may be high, even though the vast majority of careers are short. Unless long sentences are disproportionately meted out to those offenders with the longest careers, most long incarcerations would still be wasted on offenders who were no longer dangerous. So the entire distribution of career lengths must be taken into account.

It may be possible to avoid much of the waste if the probable length of an individual career can be predicted. Although parole boards have been attempting to do this for years, recent proposals for selective incapacitation have chosen instead to focus on λ, the rate of offending. This emphasis is at least potentially misplaced, because the parole board's emphasis on "rehabilitation" and the end of an offender's career is in many ways more relevant to selective incapacitation than is the offense rate. Frequent and dangerous offenders, those with high values of λ, are the ones we want to make most certain we incarcerate for the length of their career. But it is the most persistent offenders, those with the longest careers, that we want to incarcerate for the longest periods. If λ and career length (often called T for short) are closely and positively related, there is little to be lost by focusing directly on λ. But if there is little relationship between the two parameters, or if the relationship is negative, then a selective focus only on the most frequent offenders is certainly inefficient, and possibly entirely ineffective. So it is important to consider the relationship between λ and T, and possibly the potential accuracy of means of predicting the end of a career.

Before considering the results of prior research on these questions, it makes sense to define terms. What exactly is meant by a *criminal career*? The notion of a career has a certain commonsense value, but a close examination shows that it is difficult to operationalize. Moreover, *career* is a loaded word that is in many ways inappropriate.

Defining the Criminal Career

A potential offender's criminal career is perhaps best defined as the length of time he or she runs a substantial risk of committing a serious crime. As noted previously, everyone runs some risk at virtually all times; only an extraordinary set of circumstances will induce the average person to commit a serious crime, however. Rather than define something so amorphous as *substantial risk*, previous researchers have adopted a working definition of career length that begins with the offender's first offense and ends with the last. This operational definition is certainly precise, but it differs from the best definition in at least a few cases. Consider the following criminal careers.

- Kevin commits a series of burglaries and thefts in the company of bad companions before he is 18. Once he becomes an adult, however, he gets a job, marries, and commits no crimes for some time. When he is laid off and unable to find a job at age 25, however, he returns to theft—in the form of writing bad checks—to support his family and his growing drug habit (Lemert, 1958).
- Alan, a retired police officer, commits no crimes until age 23, when he marries. Shortly afterward, he begins to beat his wife, takes out insurance on her life, and eventually attempts to kill her. She escapes and divorces him, but presses no charges because she is unsure he is responsible for the attempts on her life, and is afraid of him. Seven years later, Alan marries again, takes out insurance on the life of his second wife, and murders her for the insurance money. In the interim, he is a successful businessman and commits no crimes (Bugliosi, 1978).
- Eugene, a corporate vice president and electrical engineer with an honorary doctorate, conspires over a period of twenty years to fix prices of heavy electrical equipment. Much of his work day is taken up in furthering the conspiracy, but he is only arrested once, and commits no crimes other than at work (Geis, 1967).

These three case histories may not be typical of criminal careers as we usually consider them. Nevertheless, they do represent clear types of offenders who are seen more or less regularly in the populations of prisoners and arrested offenders.

Kevin is a "square John," a sometime criminal with essentially noncriminal values, who commits his offenses when the conventional alternatives he would prefer are blocked. Should a job become available, Kevin will probably stop committing crimes and take it; but this may be followed by another spurt of criminality if he loses his next job or finds his habit too expensive (Irwin, 1970).

Alan typifies Norval Morris's one-liner about the most difficult case for sentencing policymakers to agree on—the "wife murderer with no plans to remarry" (Morris, 1982). Most people who commit assault or murder have never been arrested before. Those who are arrested more than once usually confine their attacks to close friends or family members (Peterson, Pittman, & O'Neal, 1962; Pittman & Handy, 1964; Wolfgang, 1958). For Kevin and Alan, the arrest record may bear a strong relationship to the offending history, but the history does not constitute a "criminal career" in the usual sense.

Eugene, on the other hand, exemplifies a different set of problems. He is a typical corporate offender: His criminal career may be well defined, but it bears no relationship whatever to his arrest record. For Eugene, the concept of a criminal career is perfectly reasonable, but it makes little sense to use arrest data to define it.

Because criminal behavior encompasses such a wide range of activities, criminologists have made many attempts to categorize it (e.g., Roebuck, 1967; Gibbons, 1968). Most of their typologies emphasize the varied nature of criminal careers and show that many offenders are not at substantial risk of committing crimes except for a few periods in their lives. The categorization of Clinard and Quinney (1973, pp. 16–21) is representative:

> *Violent personal criminals*, like Alan, commit crimes sporadically, but neither consider themselves "real" criminals nor actively seek criminal opportunities. Their acts are typically motivated by sudden anger resulting from disputes or arguments.
> *Occasional property offenders*, like Kevin, commit crimes for profit rather than emotional reasons; but they, too, neither consider themselves criminal nor seek opportunities for criminal activity.
> *Occupational and corporate offenders*, like Eugene, also commit crimes for profit, and may commit them over long periods of time; but they are able to rationalize their actions to themselves so that they need never consider themselves criminals, despite their long periods of criminal behavior. Because they are rarely caught (and their criminal career often ends with their first arrest), arrest records are of little help in identifying the seriousness of their offending careers over time.
> *Conventional and professional criminals* are those that most of us think of as "real" criminals. These offenders actively seek criminal opportunities, and largely define their identities on the basis of their criminal activity. Only for this group are arrest records useful indicators of the length and seriousness of their criminal career, for they alone have well-defined criminal careers and a substantial chance of being caught for each crime they commit.

In short, many offenders commit crimes so sporadically over the course of their lifetimes that the concept of criminal career has little meaning. Although this is most likely to be true for offenders whose motivations to commit crimes change dramatically over time, the same sporadic pattern of criminality may be found among offenders whose motivations remain at the same low level for a long period (Moore et al., 1984, pp. 33–34). And even when it makes sense to consider an offender's criminal activities as part of a career in crime, it may be very difficult to measure the career's length.

To the degree that use of the word *career* conjures up images of purposive behavior, with well-defined onset and desistance, areas of specialization, and levels of effort and accomplishment, the word is clearly inappropriate. If our concern were with the causes of individual criminality and the reasons for its changing over an individual's lifetime, the career metaphor may be of dubious value (Gottfredson & Hirschi, 1990).

And even if we define career in its narrowest sense—as, for example, the time between first offense and last—we find that the concept does not provide a realistic map of offender behavior. For example, the incapacitation model presumes that each offender commits crimes at a constant rate so long as he or she remains active. Thus when the career begins, the offense rate jumps from zero to λ_i; when the career ends, the rate drops immediately to zero. It is clearly more reasonable to suspect that offenders work their way into and out of crime, committing offenses more and more often as their careers progress, and less and less often as they abandon crime (Cornish & Clarke, 1986).

On the other hand, the concept of a criminal career can be helpful even if it is not an accurate metaphor. It may be true that an offender begins a slowdown at age 30 that does not result in total desistance until age 40, and that we are incorrect when we simplify this as offending at a constant rate until she quits at (say) age 35. But the policy implication is the same in either case: We get far fewer benefits from incapacitating this person in her 30s than we did from incapacitating her in her 20s, and we risk wasting scarce resources if we assign her a long sentence. (In fact, our estimates of the number of crimes committed will be nearly identical to the true number over a wide variety of scenarios.) Thus we can consider the criminal career to be simply a theoretical construction that simplifies our calculations. If it is unbiased and reasonably accurate, we have little to lose by using it. And, as the analysis of the Greenwood model described in Chapter 1 indicates, we have much to lose by failing to use it.

In taking desistance into account in this analysis, three kinds of information are important.

- The average length of a criminal career, $\overline{T}$.
- The distribution of T about the average value.
- The relationship between T and the offense rate, λ.

For simplicity, let us examine the simplest and most basic of these questions first—the average criminal's career length.

The Length of the Average Criminal Career

As shown in the previous chapter, arrest data provide a woefully incomplete picture of the nature of criminal offending.

- Offenders are only arrested for a fraction of the crimes they commit.
- Some offenders are more prone to arrest than others.
- Many arrests may never even be recorded.

So creating a picture of criminal offending from arrest data is a lot like piecing together a jigsaw puzzle with some of the most interesting pieces systematically removed from the box. Still, most of the information available to us about T is derived from arrest data. In addition, the best methods available for estimating the length of criminal careers from the Rand survey were first applied to arrest records. So it makes sense to turn first to the early arrest-based studies, paying particular attention to the validity of the assumptions required. Next, a method of analyzing arrest data is presented that does not require many of these assumptions and requires even fewer when applied to the Rand survey data set. Finally, the method is applied, and the reanalysis results compared to previous applications to arrest records in Washington, D.C.

A First Cut at $\overline{T}$

The simplest approach to using arrest records is simply to count the time between the first and most recent arrests and call this the length of the criminal's career to date. This is easy to do if the records are available, and the Federal Bureau of Investigation did it for years. Three estimates of the partial career lengths for personal and property offenders are shown in Table 4.1. Judging from these data, the average criminal career appears to last between 5 and 10 years; the average criminal who commits property crimes appears to be active for a shorter period than the typical personal offender. Although these estimates obviously only reflect a partial criminal career, they are unbiased estimates of the full career length if careers are exponentially distributed. That is, if the likelihood that an offender will retire from the criminal population in the next year is unrelated to the number of years he or she has been committing crimes, then 5 to 10 years is a good estimate of the entire career length, not just a piece of it (Shinnar & Shinnar, 1975, p. 597).

TABLE 4.1

FBI Records Show Average Criminal Career
Lasts 5 to 10 Years

Period	Personal	Property
1966–67	9.5	8.8
1968–69	8.9	8.4
1970–72	5.5	4.7

Source. 1966–1967: Federal Bureau of Investigation, 1968, p. 33. 1968–1969: Federal Bureau of Investigation, 1970, p. 37. 1970–1972: Federal Bureau of Investigation, 1973, p. 37.

These estimates must be taken with a grain of salt, however, for a number of reasons. First, consider that virtually all offenders commit some crimes without getting caught, even offenders whose criminal career is well defined, and for whom the arrest record represents their offense history rather well. If they commit crimes at rates that are low enough, they may commit many crimes before their first arrest, and many more after their most recent arrest. So the partial career lengths of Table 4.1 (that is, the time from first arrest to last) will always be smaller than the total career length (the time from first crime to last). In addition, the Bureau only collected information on adult arrests. Because many (and probably the great majority) of active adult offenders were also active as juveniles, these figures will not even include information on the first arrest, only on the first adult arrest. For these reasons, the numbers in Table 4.1 underestimate the total career length; the error will be greatest for sporadic and low-rate offenders, and for offenders who were active as young people. The errors will of course be smaller if we respecify the estimates as "adult career lengths."

Although the figures in Table 4.1 are underestimates for the applicable population, they may still be too large for the population of active offenders. Although there are several reasons for this (Ward, 1970), the primary problem is that all of the offenders included in the Bureau's sample had been arrested at least twice: once to mark the beginning and once to mark the end of their adult career. But some offenders are not arrested twice: Those who commit crimes at very low rates and those who commit crimes for only a very short time are likely to be arrested only once. If there are enough of these sporadic or short-term offenders, the figures in Table 4.1 may be right on target, or even *overestimates* of the typical career length. So the average criminal career may conceivably be less than 5 years in length.

Another objection to use of these estimates is somewhat more subtle. Note that between 1966, when the Bureau began to compile these estimates, and 1972, when it completed its "Careers in Crime" program, estimated career lengths dropped steadily. Although this may in fact indicate a trend toward shorter careers, it seems more likely that the decrease reflects the influx of "baby-boom" offenders who came of age in the mid-1960s. Many of them had not completed their careers by 1972, but the baby-boom cohorts were so much larger than previous cohorts that the estimates for their partial careers overwhelmed the estimates for the more advanced careers of the older offenders. This steady decrease reveals a hidden assumption behind use of aggregated career lengths to estimate the length of the typical criminal career—the group of offenders must be in steady-state. That is, the number of offenders who retire from the offending population each year must equal the number who enter the population. If more offenders are leaving the population than are entering (as may well have been the case through most of the 1980s), then most of the criminals in the population will be older offenders, and the aggregate partial career length will overstate the average for offenders active at that time. On the other hand, if more offenders are entering the population than are leaving (as was almost certainly the case in the late 1960s and early 1970s), then most of the criminals in the population will be young, and the aggregate length will underestimate the average for active criminals.

Finally, there is no empirical justification for the assumption that criminal careers are exponentially distributed. It is true that many time intervals can be modeled as though they were exponential: Operations researchers have used the exponential to model the length of telephone conversations, the life of electronic components, the time between arrivals for service in banks, grocery stores, and hospital emergency rooms, and a variety of other situations (Moder & Elmaghraby, 1978). Nevertheless, there is good reason to suspect that the premier feature of the exponential—its memoryless property—does not apply to criminal careers. One might suspect, for example, that offenders who have committed crimes for many years may "burn out': They may become tired of the uncertainties of a life of crime and seek a more certain (if prosaic) existence as a cab driver or caterer. Opportunities for employment in the straight world will probably increase as offenders get older, as will the need for a steady income if they take on family responsibilities. On the other hand, offenders who are successful enough at crime to avoid burnout, or are unable to obtain employment due to long prison or arrest records, may for a time become less likely to cease committing crimes: They have chosen crime as their profession and are likely to stick with their choice for a few more years, at least. So the assumption of a constant "dropout rate" at each stage in an offender's career may systematically either understate or overstate the likelihood of retirement for each individual offender. If the systematic biases are related to the individual's rate of offending, then estimates of the crime-control effects of selective policies may be very wrong, in either direction. And plausible stories can be made up to explain both under- and overestimates of the dropout rate.

So, although a first-cut estimate of the length of the typical offending career remains 5 to 10 years, these estimates are very uncertain. It is worthwhile to revise the analysis techniques if it will help to reduce the uncertainty as to this important parameter.

A Second Cut at $\overline{T}$

The problems inherent in the simple estimates described above have been evident from the beginning. Several researchers have attempted to revise the estimates, primarily by adjusting the basic results to account for different assumptions. For example, Shlomo and Reuel Shinnar (1975) adjusted these estimates to include offenders arrested only once and also adjusted the data to account for crimes committed before the first recorded arrest and after the latest recorded arrest. David Greenberg (1975) devised an entirely different method to obtain estimates of $\overline{T}$ including both once- and multiple-arrested offenders. And a number of cohort samples have been drawn that could be used to eliminate the problem of differences among cohorts (e.g., Van Dine, Conrad, & Dinitz, 1979; Wolfgang, Figlio, & Sellin, 1972; Wolfgang & Tracy, 1983).

But by far the most comprehensive solution has been offered by Alfred Blumstein and his associates (Blumstein, Cohen, & Hsieh, 1982). Their approach builds on the Shinnars' work but requires fewer assumptions about the distribution of career lengths and the underlying system producing this distribution. This method may be used to estimate the shape of the entire T distribution, and it will be used for that purpose in the next section. For now, let us concentrate on how the method may be used to estimate $\overline{T}$ only.

Suppose, first, that the number of active criminal offenders is in steady-state. That is, the active criminal population is about the same size, year after year. Because new offenders are constantly entering the system, and old ones are constantly leaving, the steady-state assumption implies that the number of new offenders who enter the population each period is the same as the number of old offenders who quit offending each period. If we can measure one, we will also be measuring the other.

If this basic assumption is approximately true, then our estimates of $\overline{T}$ and the distribution of T among offenders will be quite robust. If the assumption is wrong, then our results will be biased in the same way as were the FBI estimates of the mid-1960s and the early 1970s, and for exactly the same reasons. Fortunately, Blumstein and associates used a data set that applied to the late 1970s, and the Rand survey data were collected in 1978. Although the number of 18- to 21-year-olds and the crime rate both increased slowly between 1975 and 1981, the annual rate of increase was less than 1 percent (Brown, Flanagan, & McLeod, 1984, p. 307; U.S. Bureau of the Census, 1982, p. 25). Thus the relative stability of nationwide crime rates and demographics during this period suggest that steady-state assumptions are not unreasonable for this period.

Now, suppose that we can use official records, or offender interviews, or some other means to identify p, the yearly proportion of new entrants and recent quitters. So long as everyone who commits crimes eventually quits (in the long run, we're all dead), it can be shown that the average criminal career length is $\overline{T}$ = $1/p$ (Cox, 1962, pp. 45–60).

A formal proof is beyond the scope of this work, but a couple of examples may demonstrate why this should be true. Suppose first that criminal careers are exponentially distributed; that is, there is a constant probability that an active offender will cease his criminal activity at any given time. For simplicity, let us express this constant probability, p, in terms of yearly intervals. So there is a p probability that each active offender will quit this year, and a $1 - p$ probability that he will continue into the next year. If there are N active offenders, then it is obvious that pN will quit this year; if our steady-state assumption holds, then pN will enter the offending population, as well. Given this information, it is easy to see that

$$\overline{T} = 1 + (1-p) + (1-p)^2 + \ldots + (1-p)^i + \ldots = \Sigma_i\,(1-p)^i, \quad (4.1)$$

which reduces to

$$\overline{T} = 1/p. \quad (4.2)$$

If the proportion of new offenders entering the population each year were (say) 20 percent, then 80 percent of offenders active in one year would still be active in the next, and $\overline{T}$ would be $1/.20 = 5$ years.

Another special case is easier to visualize. Suppose all offenders commit crimes for exactly the same length of time; there is no variance about $\overline{T}$. Then we might consider offender careers to be analogous to the steadily moving lines in an exceptionally well-run grocery store. If the system is in steady-state, the lines are the same length at all times; as soon as someone joins a line at the back, another shopper is checked out at the front. A shopper's position in line (second, first, checked out) corresponds to the number of years left in an offender's career (2, 1, no longer active). And the proportion of shoppers in line who have entered the line within some duration of time is equal to the proportion who have checked out in that duration and is analogous to p, the proportion of offenders who enter and leave the offending population each period.

$\overline{T}$ is easy to calculate for this system. Say that the line is five shoppers long and that one person joins, and one person is checked out, each minute. For this example, $p = .20$, and all shoppers advance in their waiting "career" by exactly

20 percent each minute. After $1/.20 = 5$ minutes, all will have advanced to the front of the line and be out the door. Again, $\overline{T} = 1/p$.

The application of this principle to criminal careers is obvious: If we can identify the proportion of offenders who are new entrants to the offending population—first-time offenders—then we can determine the average career length for all offenders, provided the system is in steady-state. Although this is very easy to do when offender self-reports are available, Blumstein, Cohen, and Hsieh (1982) show that it can be done, using only official records.

Estimating $\overline{T}$ from Arrest Records

Any attempt to estimate p (and thus $\overline{T}$) from official records requires that two tasks be undertaken. Since p is a ratio, one task is to find the denominator— a random sample must be drawn from the offending population. The second task, logically enough, is to define and identify the numerator—those members of the sample who have recently entered the population. Because criminals go to some pains to avoid identification, it is difficult to do either of these with much precision, or even to know how well one is doing. As usual, the best tack to take is to make assumptions that seem reasonable and do the best one can with what is available.

Consider first the denominator. The population of arrestees is probably the best available sample of active offenders. And if all offenders commit crimes at identical rates, are all equally likely to be arrested for each crime they commit, and are all equally likely to be on the street, free to commit crimes—then the sample is certainly random. Of course, the results of Chapter 2 show that some offenders are much more likely to be on the street than others; in Chapter 3 it was shown that offenders commit crimes at greatly differing rates; as will be shown in Chapter 5, they are arrested at greatly differing rates, as well. So the population of arrestees will be a biased sample of the entire offending population. However, it would surely be complicated to adjust for all of these potential sources of bias. If we are willing to assume that offender career lengths are unrelated to the likelihood of incarceration or the product of offense rate and arrest probability, then the sample is unbiased for our purposes. The credibility of these assumptions will be discussed and empirically tested on the Rand survey data below.

Now consider the numerator. Suppose we know that all offenders begin their careers at age 18; if we can estimate the proportion of 18-year-olds in the (adult) offending population, this proportion will be (by definition) the proportion who enter the population each year; as the steady-state assumption implies, it will also be the proportion who leave. Most index offenders commit their first crimes when they are minors, so the 18-year-old starting age for adult offending is correct most of the time. Nevertheless, some criminals begin their careers in their 20s, or even their 30s. It is relatively easy to adjust for the effects of this assumption, and Blumstein, Cohen, and Hsieh (1982, pp. 24–28) make the necessary adjustments before presenting their estimates.

Despite this nitpicking, it is probably reasonable to expect that useful indicators of the proportion of offenders entering and exiting the population each year can be obtained from official records. When Blumstein and associates applied their method to Washington, DC arrest data, they obtained the results shown in Table 4.2.

As noted above, previous estimates of the length of the average criminal career ran from a low of 4 years to a high of 15 years; a consensus value, based on findings published before 1982, would be about 7 years (Spelman, 1983). Blumstein, Cohen, and Hsieh's findings fit nicely into this consensus: The mean property offender commits crimes for a shade over 4 years, whereas the mean personal offender commits crimes for about 7 years. The average criminal commits crimes over about a 5-year career.

Although these estimates are clearly more reasonable than any estimates previously published, they would be more convincing if fewer assumptions were required. Although reliance on a sample survey of incarcerated offenders probably requires that more assumptions be made, if anything, at least the assumptions are different ones.

Application to the Rand Data

The Rand survey data hold two major advantages over estimates based on arrest records. First, the sampling bias problem is specifically addressed through use of the weighting scheme detailed in Chapter 2. Although imperfect, the

TABLE 4.2

Average Criminal Career of Washington, DC Arrestees Lasts 4 to 7 Years

Crime type	T in years
Personal crimes	7.0 years
Homicide	7.8
Rape	5.5
Robbery	4.6
Aggravated assault	8.6
Property crimes	4.2 years
Burglary	4.3
Auto theft	3.8
All crimes	5.2 years

Source. Blumstein, Cohen, & Hsieh, 1982, pp. 60, 62.

weights at least represent an explicit attempt to control the problems of differences in street time, offense rate, and arrest probability among offenders. In addition, because offenders indicated the age at which they committed their first crime, fewer assumptions about the beginning of active criminal careers were required. Because we are only concerned with adult criminal activity, the following assumptions were made:

- Offenders who indicated that they first committed crimes as a minor, but were included in the Rand sample due to an incarceration received when an adult, were assumed to have committed their first adult crime at age 18.
- Offenders who claimed to have committed no crimes until after the age of 18 were assumed to have committed their first crime at the age they said they did.
- Offenders who entered their present period of incarceration as juveniles were ignored for purposes of identifying career length.

All careers were assumed to end at the time the offenders entered prison, since this is the last time at which we can be reasonably certain they were still active offenders.

Blumstein, Cohen, and Hsieh's arrest data hold one major advantage over the Rand data. Their sample sizes are considerably larger, including over 20,000 cases in their Washington, DC, data set, and over 60,000 cases in their Michigan data set. Thus their estimates will be extremely precise. The Rand sample, by contrast, included only a shade over 2,000 cases, and many of these offenders claimed never to have committed an index crime. This has three practical effects on the reanalysis.

First, confidence intervals are extremely important, because they provide a lower bound on the accuracy of the estimates. The figures obtained may of course be less precise if any of the assumptions required by the method differ significantly from reality.

Second, it is probably not realistic to base estimates of such an important figure as $\bar{T}$ on only the 10 to 15 percent of offenders who are still in the first year of their careers. Instead, let us combine the proportion of first-year offenders with the proportion of second-year offenders, and use this as a basis for estimating $\bar{T}$. If r_1 represents the dropout rate for year 1, and r_2 represents the dropout rate for year 2, then

$$r_{12} = r_1 + (1 - r_1) r_2. \tag{4.3}$$

That is, r_{12} (the total dropout rate for the first two years) includes all those who did not survive the first year, plus those remaining who did not make it through the second year. If we assume that the dropout rates for the first two years are equal ($r_1 = r_2$), we may simplify (4.3) so that

$$r_{12} = r_1 + (1 - r_1) r_1$$
$$= 2 r_1 - r_1^2. \tag{4.4}$$

This is a simple quadratic equation. It is easy to show that

$$r_1 = r_2 = 1 - (4 - 4 r_{12})^{.5}/2. \tag{4.5}$$

So, for 2-year intervals,

$$\overline{T} = 2/[2 - (4 - 4 r_{12})^{.5}]. \tag{4.6}$$

Blumstein, Cohen, and Hsieh (1982, pp. 35–37) compared career lengths for seven years of data—1970 to 1976—and found $\overline{T}$ to be stable throughout the period studied. In addition, the arrest data and demographic information both suggest that the population of active offenders was approximately in steady-state during the mid-1970s. So, though the Rand sample is not large enough to control for differences among cohorts, this is probably not too serious a problem.

Estimates of $\overline{T}$ for the Rand data set are shown in Table 4.3. Average total career length ranges from 7 to 10 years for property offenders, and from 7 to 9 years for personal offenders. Although Michigan careers appear to be shorter than California and Texas careers for both crime types, the differences are not statistically significant.

Contrary to Blumstein and Cohen's findings, the average career for personal offenders is consistently shorter than the property offender careers. However, the difference is not large. Judging from the Rand survey data alone, it would be

TABLE 4.3
Average Criminal Career of Active Offenders Lasts 7 to 10 Years

	State			
	California	Michigan	Texas	Total
Property offenders	9.6	7.1	10.1	8.8 7.6 to 10.2
Personal offenders	9.3	6.6	8.2	8.0 6.8 to 9.5
All offenders	9.4	6.9	9.3	8.4 7.6 to 9.3

reasonable to conclude that the average career runs for between 7 and 10 years; our best guess should be about 8.5 years.

Both the Rand reanalysis results and the Washington, DC, arrest data results are well within the range of prior estimates; both sets of findings are reasonable. But they are not identical—the difference between 5 and 8 years may even have important effects on the policy implications of the Greenwood model. So it pays to ask why the two sets of findings may be different. Although there are any number of possible explanations, the simplest of these focus on the most obvious differences between the two studies—the samples from which the results are drawn.

Certainly neither sample is an exact mirror of the active criminal population. Both samples are likely to systematically exclude infrequent offenders, becuase they are unlikely to be arrested in a given year and are very unlikely to accumulate a record long enough to justify a jail or prison sentence. In this respect, the biases of the two samples are likely to be similar; as will be shown later in this chapter, these biases are probably not too serious.

In addition, however, the arrest sample includes greater numbers of young offenders who have not yet accumulated a record long enough to incapacitate them, and (as will be shown in the next chapter) inexperienced offenders who have not yet learned to avoid capture. The Rand sample is biased in exactly the opposite way: Even if the sampling weights were assigned perfectly, the Rand sample (or any inmate sample) would include too few young and inexperienced offenders, since these criminals are very unlikely to be sent to jail or prison. This is probably particularly true for offenders who only commit property crimes: Even property convicts with several offenses are typically sentenced to probation in many jurisdictions. This effect is exacerbated by errors in the weights. As the analysis detailed in the next section indicates, young, inexperienced criminals are much more likely to drop out of the offending population; on average, their careers will be shorter. The arrest sample should include more of these offenders with short careers than the active criminal population, and the Rand sample should include fewer of them than the active population. So it makes sense that the average career length is shorter for the arrest sample than for the inmate sample; the most appropriate estimate will lie somewhere between the two.

Implications

It makes sense to mete out long sentences to high-rate offenders if we can be fairly certain that they would have been active throughout the period of incarceration. And if the typical criminal career were very long—say, 20 years—then this would seem to be a reasonable assumption. The chances that an offender would drop out in any given year would be a scant 5 percent; so we would intuitively guess there to be a very good chance he or she would have been active throughout the period of a 5- or 6-year prison term. This would have prevented that offender's crimes for the whole period; if we could give 5- or 6-year prison terms to enough frequent offenders, we could reduce crime considerably.

As shown above, however, the typical offender does not commit crimes over a career nearly as long as 20 years. The most liberal estimate is half that long; depending upon the population of interest, more reasonable estimates run from 5 to 8 years. Suddenly long sentences do not look so good: If most offenders run a 15 to 20 percent risk of dropping out in any given year, it is very likely that they would have dropped out sometime during their 5- or 6-year prison sentence. If so, then we would have wasted some of our scarce prison resources on offenders who would have been entirely harmless, had they been on the street.

How much will we waste, on average? To get a precise answer, it is necessary to know whether all offenders' careers are about the same length, or whether some careers are much longer than others. It is also necessary to know whether judges and parole boards will give all high-rate offenders the same sentence, or whether some will get stiffer sentences than others. The distribution of career lengths among offenders will be considered in greater detail in the next section; for purposes of illustration, let us assume for the moment that all offenders run a constant risk of dropout throughout their careers—that criminal careers will be exponentially distributed. Similarly, let us assume that the sentences passed on each class of offenders are exponentially distributed, as well. That is, judges and parole boards will be very selective in their incarceration policies, on average; but they will maintain a great deal of discretion in matching sentences to offenders. This is more realistic than it sounds; Chaiken (1981, pp. 245–252) has shown that sentences served in California during the 1970s were approximately exponentially distributed.

Under these assumptions, it is easy to show that the proportion of a sentence of length S that will be wasted if the typical offender commits crimes over a career $\overline{T}$ years in length is

$$\theta = S/(S + \overline{T}). \tag{4.7}$$

So the longer the sentence, S, the more of it will be wasted; the longer the average career, $\overline{T}$, the less will be wasted. Values of θ for reasonable values of S and $\overline{T}$ are shown in Figure 4.1.

In most states, the typical personal offender who is sentenced to jail or prison receives a sentence of about 2.5 years; the typical property offender receives a sentence of between 6 and 12 months (Langan & Dawson, 1990). Figure 4.1 suggests that present sentencing policies waste little: Between 80 and 90 percent of jail and prison cells are filled by offenders who would be actively committing crimes were they to return to the street. Now consider the wastage of a 5-year prison term for predicted, frequent offenders: At any given time, be-

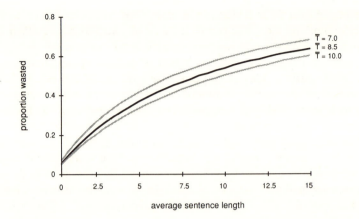

FIGURE 4.1. Long sentences waste prison time on no-longer dangerous offenders.

tween 35 and 50 percent of the apparently frequent offenders in prison would be (more or less) harmless has-beens. And the most radical selective incapacitation schemes—those that would imprison predicted frequent offenders for 15 years or more—would waste 60 to 70 percent of these long prison terms.

These findings do not, by themselves, indicate that selective sentencing schemes are a bad idea. It may be that frequent offenders commit crimes over longer careers than their less dangerous comrades; it may be that dropout from a criminal career can be predicted with sufficient accuracy to reduce the waste. Perhaps more important, it may be that the benefits of even the most radical selective sentencing schemes outweigh the costs. These questions are considered later in this chapter and in Chapter 7.

Still, the relative shortness of the average criminal career does suggest that there are limits to the utility of selective sentencing. Further, these results make clear that the proportion of jail and prison terms wasted on no-longer active offenders must be specifically included in any model of the benefits of incapacitation.

Between 10 and 20 percent of active, adult offenders drop out of the offending population each year. Estimates from arrest data, that the average adult criminal career is about 5 years in length, are probably slightly too low; estimates from inmate data, that the average career is about 8.5 years in length, are probably too high. Thus the most likely value is probably 6 or 7 years. In any case, the typical criminal career is relatively short, so it is likely that long prison terms would be wasted on offenders who would no longer be active, were they to be released.

The Distribution of T among Offenders

Until recently, virtually nothing was known about the distribution of T among offenders. Shinnar and Shinnar (1975, p. 597) provided (not very persuasive) evidence that T was roughly exponentially distributed. But there were no good theoretical reasons why this should be true; any number of alternative distributions would have worked as well, and the exponential was chosen simply because it was convenient.

Of course, if one must assume any distribution, it is hard to find one more convenient than the exponential. If all offenders are equally likely to quit offending at all times, then an offender's age need not be considered when we decide what sanctions to apply. Neither need we introduce such complications as correlations among career length and offense rate, arrest and prison record, or other factors that bear on decisions to incapacitate. Finally, any analytical incapacitation model requires an estimate of the likelihood that offenders will "survive" their sentence, that they will still be active when they are released. It is very easy to estimate this likelihood if careers are random and exponential.

No matter how convenient an assumption, there is little justification for making it if more realistic assumptions provide different policy implications. And alternative assumptions about the distribution of T do influence the effectiveness of selective incapacitation policies. For example, suppose that all offenders commit crimes for the same length of time and then quit. If the system is in steady state, then τ, the time remaining in each offender's career, will be uniformly distributed among active offenders; for each offender i, $p(\tau_i) = 1/\overline{T}$. If sentences are exponential-distributed with mean S, the probability that any offender i will still be active once his or her sentence has run out is

$$1 - \theta = p(S < \tau_i) = 1 - \exp[-(\overline{T} - \tau_i)/S]. \qquad (4.8)$$

The average probability is

$$1 - \theta = \int_\tau \{1 - \exp[-(\overline{T} - \tau_i)/S]/\overline{T}\}\, d\tau, \qquad (4.9)$$

and the proportion of the sentence that is wasted reduces to

$$\theta = S\,[1 + \exp(-\overline{T}/S)]/\overline{T}. \qquad (4.10)$$

Because $\exp(-\overline{T}/S)$ is positive for all positive $\overline{T}$ and S, it is obvious that this probability is always greater than the probability for exponential S and T given in equation (4.7). If sentences are short relative to careers, the difference is unimportant. But for sentences of 5 or 10 years, the proportion of the average sentence wasted is much higher for uniform T.

Alternatively, suppose that frequent offenders commit crimes over a longer career than less-frequent criminals. If this were true, a model that assumed all offenders faced identical risks of career dropout at all times would underestimate the benefits of selective criminal justice actions; a smaller proportion of the long sentences doled out to these high-rate offenders would be wasted than the model would predict. If these differences among offenders are large, they can have an important effect on estimates of the crime-control benefits of selective policies.

Of course, it is difficult to estimate the entire distribution of career lengths from cross-sectional arrest data. (Recall the difficulties inherent in estimating just the average value of T.) Nevertheless, by extending the method used above to obtain $\overline{T}$, it is possible to obtain a reasonable guess as to dropout rates over time and among offenders. Applying this method to Washington, DC, arrest data, and to the Rand survey data shows that offender careers are clearly not exponential and suggests that there may be a consistent relationship between dropout rates and offense rates.

Criminal Dropout and Age

The Simple Mechanics of Changing Arrest Rates

The approach used here makes direct use of renewal theory. Although this branch of stochastic process analysis is complex, the basic ideas are easily explained. Let us begin with a very simple question, indeed: How many arrests are made at time t?

Note that t may reference an offender's career-to-date (that is, it may be the time since an individual's first arrest, or first crime), or the age of the offender, or the year on the Mayan calendar. The theory is perfectly general for all changes over time. For our purposes, it makes most sense to use t to reference an offender's career-to-date. Thus "how many arrests at time t?" may be translated to mean "how many arrests are made now of offenders who were first arrested exactly t years ago?"

Suppose λ_t is the average offense rate for offenders whose careers have run t years, q_t is the probability that these offenders will be arrested per crime committed, η_t is the likelihood that each of these offenders will be on the street, free to commit crimes at any given time, and N_t is the number of active offenders with career lengths-to-date of t years. Then the expected number of arrests in time t is

$$E(A_t) = \lambda_t \, q_t \, \eta_t \, N_t. \tag{4.11}$$

That is, crimes per offender in year t, times arrests per crime, times street offenders, yields arrests in year t. So this is perfectly general.

Because the point is to explain changes in the number of arrests from one t

to the next, it makes sense to consider changes in these components over time. It is reasonable to suppose that all four of them will change, at least somewhat.

- λ_{t+1} may be different from λ_t—the average offender may commit crimes more or less frequently as his or her career progresses.
- q_{t+1} may be different from q_t—as offenders age, they may learn to evade arrest, or the police may learn to catch them.
- η_{t+1} may be different from η_t—older offenders may be systematically more or less likely to be in jail or prison at any given time than younger offenders.
- Finally, N_{t+1} may be less than N_t—some offenders may drop out of the population. Note that N_{t+1} can never be greater than N_t, due to the way we have defined t.

We can express each of the $t+1$ terms as the sum of the t term and the change from t to $t+1$. That is,

$$\lambda_{t+1} = \lambda_t + \delta\lambda_t/\delta t,$$
$$q_{t+1} = q_t + \delta q_t/\delta t,$$
$$\eta_{t+1} = \eta_t + \delta\eta_t/\delta t, \text{ and}$$
$$N_{t+1} = N_t + \delta N_t/\delta t.$$

All this means that we can express $E(A_{t+1})$, the expected number of arrests for offenders whose careers have lasted $t+1$ years since their first arrest, as

$$E(A_{t+1}) = (\lambda_t + \delta\lambda_t/\delta t)(q_t + \delta q_t/\delta t)(\eta_t + \delta\eta_t/\delta t)(N_t + \delta N_t/\delta t). \quad (4.12)$$

The change in arrests from t to $t+1$ is simply

$$E(A_{t+1} - A_t) = E(A_{t+1}) - \lambda_t\, q_t\, \eta_t\, N_t. \quad (4.13)$$

This is rather messy, but it is easy to see that, in order to solve the system entirely (that is, to find the expected number of arrests in each period), it is necessary and sufficient to know the starting point and the changes over time of each of the four components of the arrest production function. Alternatively, given empirical time-series data on arrests and the starting point and changes over time for three of the components, it is possible to solve for the fourth component.

Of course, it is difficult to collect data on all of these changes over time, particularly because such things as the frequency of offending (and thus the number of offenses and the likelihood of arrest, given an offense) are really known only to the offenders themselves. But some of these things are more likely to change than others. In particular, the number of active offenders, N_t, is certain to decrease as offenders drop out of the offending population or "go straight." That is, $\delta N_t / \delta t < 0$ for all t. If we are willing to make the (rather cavalier) assumption that each offender commits crimes at a constant rate throughout his career, given that he is active, and also assume that the average q_t does not systematically change as an offender gets older, either, then we have defined two of the "change" terms:

$$\delta q_t / \delta t = 0, \text{ and}$$
$$\delta \lambda_t / \delta t = 0,$$

for all t. Further, if λ_t and q_t really do not change, then it would not seem unreasonable to suppose that the proportion of time an active offender spends on the street, η_t, is relatively constant, as well.

Because our aim is to estimate $\delta N_t / \delta t$, we still need data on arrests over time. As it happens, time-series data are available from the Federal Bureau of Investigation on the number of offenders arrested in the District of Columbia, broken down by age. If we know each offender's present age (call it a) and the age at which their career began (call it a_0), then their career length at age a is simply

$$t = a - a_0.$$

That is, we may convert data on offender ages to data on offender careers-to-date. If these assumptions are reasonable, then, it is possible to estimate $\delta N_t / \delta t$.

A more directly applicable restatement of $\delta N_t / \delta t$ is the dropout rate, r_t. The dropout rate represents the proportion of offenders active in time t who become permanently inactive over the course of the next year. Stated mathematically,

$$r_t = (N_t - N_{t+1})/N_t$$
$$= 1 - N_{t+1}/N_t. \tag{4.14}$$

Solving equations (4.11) and (4.12) for N_t and N_{t+1}, respectively, and substituting into (4.14), we find that

$$r_t = 1 - A_{t+1}/A_t,$$
$$= -(\delta A_t / \delta t)/A_t. \tag{4.15}$$

All this is pretty simple algebra, but a graph may explain the concepts even more directly. Consider Figure 4.2, which shows the number of offenders who have been active for between 1 and 10 years. Twenty offenders have been committing crimes for 5 years, but there are only eighteen 6-year offenders. Now suppose we are interested in identifying how many of the 5-year actives will drop

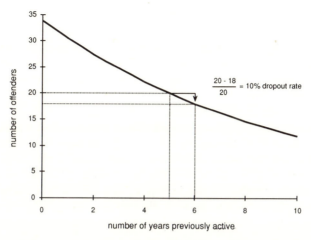

FIGURE 4.2. The dropout rate is the proportion of last year's offenders who are now missing.

out in the next year. If this system is in steady-state—that is, if this distribution does not change from year to year—then only eighteen of the twenty 5-year actives will be around next year, and two will have dropped out. So the dropout rate will be $2/20 = 10$ percent. In general, if N_t is the number of offenders active for t years, and N_{t+1} the number active for $t+1$ years, the dropout rate, r_t, may be expressed as

$$r_t = 1 - N_{t+1}/N_t. \qquad (4.16)$$

If the number of arrests made each year is equal to the number of offenders multiplied by a constant (the constant is equal to $\lambda q \eta$), then we may substitute A_{t+1} for N_{t+1} and A_t for N_t, and measure the dropout rate from official records.

There are three kinds of problems associated with using equation (4.16) to measure dropout rates.

- The system may not be in steady-state. Next year's distribution may look different than this year's.
- The data used to measure the distribution may be inaccurate.
- The basic assumptions of the model may be wrong. For example, the average values of λ, q, and η may not be the same for offenders of different ages.

The first assumption probably poses no serious problems. It is true that demographic or economic changes in society will radically affect entry to and exit from criminal offending. But demographic changes are slow, and crime rates seem independent of short-term changes in economic conditions, although they are probably greatly affected by such long-run changes as the movement from the Frost Belt to the Sun Belt, or from a manufacturing to a services economy (Wilson & Herrnstein, 1985, pp. 312–336). Moreover, what empirical evidence there is indicates that one year's distribution is about like the next year's (Blumstein, Cohen, & Hsieh, 1982, pp. 35–37).

Similarly, the second assumption is probably reasonable. It is true that records of individual arrests are very unreliable; that is, different police agencies define "arrest" in very different ways, and sometimes individual officers produce arrest reports in situations that would not be sanctioned by official agency policy (Sherman & Glick, 1984). On the other hand, these individual errors will not affect the career length estimates so long as they are made in a consistent way over time. In the absence of dramatic changes in arrest policies, or in enforcement of unchanging policies, it is most reasonable to assume that the errors will wash out.

Although aggregate arrest data for offenders of different ages may be sufficiently reliable, they will be of little help if they cannot be converted to arrest data for offenders with different career lengths-to-date. Luckily, this information is available for each of the arrests included in the F.B.I. data set. In fact, it is possible to compare dropout rates and career lengths for offenders who started their careers at different ages.

The big problem, of course, is the third assumption. λ_t, q_t, and η_t may change over the course of an offender's career. For a variety of reasons provided in Chapter 2, very young adult offenders are unlikely to be in jail or prison at the start of their careers; the likelihood that they will be incarcerated at any given time increases quickly at first, then levels off. Even if there were no dropout among young adults, we would expect fewer arrests among 23-year-olds than among 18-year-olds: Some proportion of them will have gone to prison, and thus won't be liable to arrest.

Expected changes in q_t are likely to produce the same apparent results. As will be shown in Chapter 5, criminals who have committed more crimes are less likely to be arrested for each crime they commit, because they are more experienced at evading the police. Again, this suggests that analysis of arrest data would lead to fewer arrests among 23-year-olds than among 18-year-olds: At least some of these youthful offenders are staying in the offending population, but learning to avoid capture.

It is less clear how (or even whether) λ_t will change over time. There is little evidence to suggest that young offenders commit crimes at increasing or decreasing rates as get older, and our best guess (as shown in Chapter 3) is that λ_t is roughly constant for offenders who choose to continue offending. On the other hand, it may be that frequent offenders tend to drop out in higher numbers, so that the average offense rate among active offenders decreases. A case can be made for the opposite effect, as well.

In any case, it is certain that the number of arrests is a "noisy" measure of the number of offenders. And there are good reasons to suspect that the apparent dropout rates resulting from this analysis will be biased high for the youngest offenders. So it is good to take results of the arrest analysis with a grain of salt and to look for ways of overcoming the problems of bias and noise.

Arrest Analysis

Blumstein and Cohen used (4.16) to estimate dropout rates over the careers of offenders who commit different kinds of crimes. A representative sample of these results is shown in Figure 4.3. If the distribution of career lengths were really exponential, then the true likelihood of dropout would be constant over an offender's career. As Figure 4.3 shows, however, the dropout rate appears to differ greatly over the course of a career. Young offenders (and, to a lesser degree, very old offenders) are very likely to drop out: Fully 40 percent of the 20-year-old offenders no longer commit crimes by the time they are 21. In contrast, crooks who are between (roughly) 30 and 45 are much less likely to retire in the next year or so: Only about 10 percent of offenders who are over 30 drop out each year. The rate of dropout continues to drop throughout the 20s and 30s, only beginning to increase somewhat for offenders in their 40s.

If one is to take these results at face value, the obvious conclusion is that the few criminal offenders still active at age 30 are more or less committed to making crime their profession. So one of the most frequently heard objections to selective policies—that they focus on older offenders who are just about to stop committing crimes—would be dead wrong. The 30- to 45-year-old offenders who are the principal target of selective policies would be the least likely of all offenders to stop committing crimes in the near future.

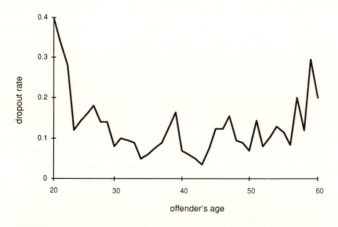

FIGURE 4.3. Dropout rates fall, then rise, for Washington, DC arrestees.

These results are striking, if they are reliable. But they are in large part the results we would expect to see, even if true dropout rates were constant over the course of an offender's career. As expected, young offenders are those who appear to drop out at the highest rates. To some degree, at least, we can be sure that the high dropout rates among the youngest offenders are due to their going to jail and prison for the first time, and to their learning to avoid arrest. On the other hand, the effect appears to be much larger than would be expected from examination of the relatively moderate effects of aging on q_t and η_t. Moreover, there is no obvious reason why dropout rates should increase for offenders over 45. It would be prudent to suspect that something is going on here, even if it is not quite so dramatic as Figure 4.3 would lead us to believe.

Application to the Rand Survey

The Rand self-report data provide (in some ways) better information for estimating the distribution of dropout rates over an offender's career. The career length itself may be measured directly from information supplied by the offenders; arrests need not be used as an indicator of the number of active offenders, since it is possible to count them directly. So the biases that are more or less guaranteed to produce high dropout rates among the youngest offenders are not a problem.

In other ways, however, the data are worse. Though the sample has been weighted to reflect the distribution of all active offenders, only those who stand a reasonable chance of going to jail are included in the sample; thus the "faint of heart," young offenders who commit crimes for a short time and quickly stop, are not likely to be included. Thus analysis of the Rand data set may well underestimate the relative dropout rate among the youngest offenders. Offenders may lie about their age, introducing a new source of uncertainty, if not obvious bias. And—most important—there may be too few data points to identify differences in dropout rates with any reliability.

Despite the problems, replicating the dropout rate analysis on the Rand data set may help us decide how much salt to sprinkle on the results produced by official records; differences between the two may suggest that the chances of arrest, or the average offense rate, or the chances of being free to commit crimes are systematically different for different offender age groups. Moreover, it may be useful to compare career lengths among different definitions of active offenders. The set of active criminals defined by official records is identical to the group of "once-arrested" offenders considered in Chapter 3; the active offenders included in the Rand data set are similar to the "twice-arrested" offenders. Because the point to examining career lengths is to provide parameters for analysis of incapacitation policy and because the once-arrested group includes many offenders judges would be very reluctant to incapacitate, the twice-arrested group is more appropriate for our purposes.

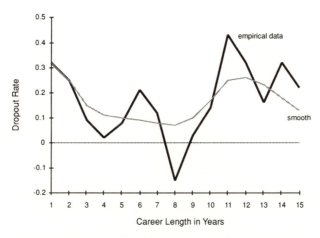

FIGURE 4.4. Dropout rates fall, rise, level off for prison inmates.

Figure 4.4 shows dropout rates over the course of a criminal career, as estimated from the Rand data set. The similarity between Figures 4.3 and 4.4 is striking. In both the official records and the Rand survey results, the dropout rate decreases after roughly the first 5 years of activity, then levels off. At some point—for the arrest data it is after some 20 years of activity, for the Rand data it is after about 10 years—the dropout rate begins to rise again. Neither the arrest analysis nor the self-report analysis is without problems, but the fact that they both result in functions with the the same shape suggests that this shape is roughly correct.

The two functions are not identical. As expected, the reduction in dropout rate for the youngest offenders is most dramatic for the (biased) analysis of arrest records. The true function probably lies somewhere somewhere between the two estimates. In addition, the increase in dropout rate for older offenders seems to be somewhat more stable for the arrest analysis than for the self-report analysis. Here, the self-report analysis is liable to be in error: An offender who had been active for 10 years at the time the Rand survey was conducted would very likely have been born in about 1949, at the beginning of the post-World War II baby boom. Because relatively few children were born during the Depression and war years, we would expect there to be relatively few offenders with careers more than 10 years in length. The self-report results have not been corrected for demographics, so they are probably less reliable on this score than the official records results, which have. For the most part, however, the similarities between these two figures are more marked than the differences.

At first blush, these results appear counterintuitive in the extreme. It is not difficult to imagine how the risks of dropout could decrease over the course of an offender's career; neither is it difficult to imagine how they could increase. But these results—showing that dropout rates first decrease, then increase—are less easy to explain away. And the fact that these results are found in both arrest and self-report data make it unlikely that they are a statistical aberration. Nevertheless, dropout functions such as these are encountered frequently in biological and engineering systems. A mathematical model may be constructed that both explains these counterintuitive results and makes them easier to use in analytical incapacitation models.

A Mathematical Model of Dropout Rates

Dropout functions like those of Figures 4.3 and 4.4 are sometimes called "bathtub-shaped," for obvious reasons. The bathtub shape is characteristic of a great variety of electronic, mechanical, and biological systems. For example, age-specific mortality rates are bathtub-shaped: Newborns and the very young run high risks of death; the risks flatten out quickly, so that individuals between 2 and 35 are about equally likely to die at any given time; the risks increase steadily and at an increasing rate for persons older than 35, as the various body systems begin to wear out (U.S. Bureau of the Census, 1982, p. 72). For mechanical and electronic systems, these three periods of decreasing, steady, and increasing likelihood of failure are called the "break-in," "useful life," and "fatigue" stages (Billington & Allan, 1983, pp. 134–135).

Following Blumstein, Cohen, and Hsieh (1982), let us try and interpret the meaning of these three stages in the context of criminal offending. The first stage, characterized by decreasing risks of dropout, may correspond to a weeding-out period. People who commit a few crimes may decide that they are not really cut out for a life of crime. Many of these would drop out quickly: The proportion of individuals dropping out due to such a "faintness of heart" can be expected to decrease steadily as individual careers increase in length. After the first few years, these risks would probably have diminished to minimal levels. One such "weed-out" function is shown as the downward sloping line in Figure 4.5.

The third stage, characterized by increasing risks of dropout, has sometimes been called "burnout." Older offenders experience a number of stresses that make it increasingly difficult to continue their criminal behavior. Some get married and accept family responsibilities; some become tired of the erratic and low income they eke out of their criminal activities; some slow down, become careless, and begin to run higher risks of arrest; as old associates begin to drop out, it becomes more difficult to find partners, fences, and drug connections (Clinard & Quinney, 1973; Shover, 1985). Although offenders may burn out at any time, it is likely that the risks of burnout are very low for the first few years of a criminal career, but increase steadily as one's career progresses. One example of a burnout function is shown as the upwardly sloping line in Figure 4.5.

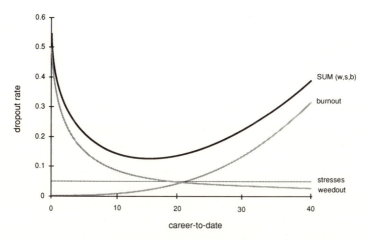

FIGURE 4.5. If offenders quit for a variety of reasons, bathtub dropout functions may result.

Finally, offenders run a more or less steady risk of dropout due to reasons unassociated with the length of their career. Sudden stresses or unusually severe conditions such as the death of a friend or relative, rehabilitation due to incarceration in jail or prison, religious conversion, or similar circumstances are about equally likely to come up at any time. If these risks are really constant throughout an offender's career, they may be modeled by the straight line in Figure 4.5.

If weeding out, burnout, and sudden stresses are (more or less) independent, then the total dropout from all causes is equal to the sum of the three lines in Figure 4.5.

This logic may be operationalized as follows. Suppose that the relationship between career length and dropout rate due to each of these three classes of causes is a power function. That is, the dropout rate at time t due to cause i is

$$r_{it} = \alpha_i \, t^{\beta i}, \tag{4.17}$$

where t represents career length-to-date, and α_i and β_i are parameters. For r_{it} to be positive, α_i must be greater than zero. However, β_i may be either less than or greater than zero. If β_i is greater than zero, the line will be upwardly sloping (like the burnout function); if β_i is less than zero, the hazard function will slope downwards (like the weedout function). If β_i is exactly zero, r_{it} will be a straight line (like the stresses function). Then $r_{.t}$, the dropout rate at time t from all of these three causes, will be

$$r_{.t} = \alpha_0 + \alpha_1 \, t^{\beta 1} + \alpha_2 \, t^{\beta 2}. \tag{4.18}$$

α_O represents the dropout rate due to factors that do not change over the course of an offender's career. α_1 and β_1 represent weed-out, and α_2 and β_2 represent fatigue and burnout. Further,

$$\alpha_O,\ \alpha_1,\ \alpha_2,\ \beta_2 > 0,\ \text{and}$$
$$\beta_1 < 0.$$

The internal structure of this model may be clearer if the coefficients are reexpressed. Let $a_O = 1/\alpha_O$; $b_1 = \beta_1 - 1$; $b_2 = \beta_2 - 1$;

$$a_1 = (\beta_1/\alpha_1)/(1 - \beta_1),\ \text{and}$$
$$a_2 = (\beta_1/\alpha_2)/(1 - \beta_2).$$

Thus r_t may be reexpressed in terms of these new coefficients as

$$r_t = 1/a_O + b_1\ t^{\ b1-1}/a_1{}^{b1} + b_2\ t^{b2-1}/a_2{}^{b2}. \tag{4.19}$$

The general formula for the hazard rate of a distribution that is frequently used for reliability and mortality problems, the Weibull, is

$$r_t = b\ t^{b-1}/a^b.$$

So the dropout model expressed by (4.18) assumes that aggregate dropout rates are the sum of three, independent Weibull variables, where $b = 1$ for the first of these three distributions. Given the parameters of (4.18), it is possible to solve for the parameters of the underlying system.

Of course, this is by no means the only mathematical description of the bathtub-shaped dropout function. Many others are possible, and probably provide equally good fits to the empirical data. For example, Blumstein, Cohen, and Hsieh (1982, pp. 41–46) obtained good results with a piecewise linear function. Nevertheless, the mixed-Weibull formula provides a reasonable description of the processes underlying the dropout function. Moreover, it has the advantage of (relative) objectivity: The parameters are determined entirely by the data, and not through a (potentially arbitrary) combination of expert guesswork and data analysis.

Because the dropout rate can be estimated for all values of t within the relevant range, parameters of equation (4.18) may be estimated through regression. Although the model could be applied to the Rand survey data, too few cases were available to allow reliable estimates to be made. So we consider only the official records data further.

Empirical dropout rates are most reliable for the youngest offenders—there are more cases available from which to estimate the rate. This does not affect

TABLE 4.4
*Parameters for a Mixed Weibull
Dropout Function*

Component	Coefficient (standard error)
Sudden stresses	
A_0	0.000
	(0.000)
Weedout component	
A_1	1.261
	(0.180)
B_1	−1.013
	(0.201)
Burnout component	
A_2	4.42×10^{-6}
	(4.70×10^{-5})
B_2	2.819
	(2.781)
Standard error of estimate	.109
R^2	.900

regression estimates of the parameters, but it will bias the standard errors of these estimates. To control this bias, each observation was given a weight proportionate to the reciprocal of its variance.

Regression results for the Washington, DC arrest data are shown in FIGU-Table 4.4 and Figure 4.6. Note that the regression converged on a solution for

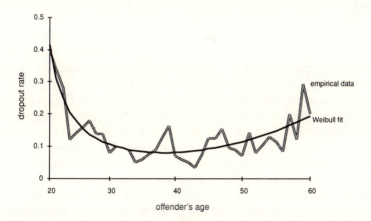

FIGURE 4.6. The "weedout/burnout" model fits the Washington, DC data well.

which the stress function is zero. Thus only four parameters were needed to fit the empirical data. Although the two coefficients representing the burnout function are not significantly different from zero, this is because they were negatively correlated; the fit is significantly better with the burnout function included than without it. As the figure shows, the mixed-Weibull model appears to fit the data quite well; fully 90 percent of the variance in dropout rates over time can be accounted for by this model. We may conclude that the dropout function is described reasonably well by a mixture of two Weibull distributions, at least for a sample of arrestees in Washington, DC.

Implications

Age matters, and selective policies will be most effective if age is somehow accounted for in the selection process. This is because typical young-adult offenders are particularly unsuitable for a long prison sentence: Left to their own devices, they will very likely quit offending soon, anyway. But the yearly dropout rates are considerably lower for offenders aged 25 to 40 or so. Thus a randomly selected 30-year-old who is given a 5-year prison sentence is more likely to have been active for the entire duration of the sentence than a randomly selected 20-year-old. All else equal, then, it is more efficient to concentrate scarce prison resources on "confirmed" offenders, 25 years and over, who have survived the shakedown period of their early 20s.

The most obvious way to use these results is to include age as one of the variables in the predictive equation or scale. And some jurisdictions have included age as an explicit criterion (Hoffman & Beck, 1984). However, offenders have no control over their age; there is considerable debate as to whether such variables are a proper and just basis for determining the amount of punishment (Moore, 1986). An alternative scheme that may do almost as well is to include age implicitly, by focusing on offenders who have accumulated longer prior criminal records. Such criteria are considered proper and just by virtually everyone and are widely used already. It may even be that present "career criminal programs" that use prior record to indicate future criminality are close to optimal solutions to the problem of accounting for age differences.

The Greenwood predictive scale (and, by inference, other scales that use the same characteristics) is biased neither in favor of nor against young offenders. That is, the predicted high-rate, medium-rate, and low-rate categories all include about the same number of young and old offenders. Nevertheless, age must still be considered when assessing the benefits and costs of this scale. The reason is that a thorough analysis requires a reliable estimate of the amount of wastage, and this in turn requires some knowledge of the shape of the career-length distribution. In the analysis at the end of the last section, it was assumed that career lengths are exponentially distributed; this is not generally true, and the resulting estimates are biased. But the size and direction of the bias depends upon the age of the offenders in question.

Figure 4.7 makes this clear. The figure shows the proportion of 24-, 30-, and 36-year-old offenders who are still active after committing crimes for 1 more year, for 2 more years, and so on up to 30 more years. For 24-year-old criminals, this "survival function" is extremely skewed: Few survive the weeding-out period, but those who do are likely to commit crimes for many years. If there is no way to predict which young offenders would have dropped out and which would have remained active, a very large proportion of any long sentences meted out to those offenders would be wasted.

On the other hand, criminals in their late 30s are more likely to go on their merry way for several years, until they run into the wall of burnout. At this point, the remaining older offenders drop out in large numbers; thus the survival function is much less skewed for old criminals than for young criminals. (For offenders aged 40 or so, the burnout function is so strong that the distribution is skewed to the left. Because few of these offenders will drop out right away, waste is considerably less of a problem.)

Finally, offenders around 30 years of age face approximately constant risks of dropout for the foreseeable future. This is indicated by the fact that the survival function for 30-year-olds is closer to a straight line. For these offenders, remaining career lengths will be about exponentially distributed—about midway between the extremely skewed distribution of remaining career lengths for younger offenders, and the much less skewed distribution for older offenders.

All this means that the exponential assumption will be about right for 30-year-old criminals; estimates of waste will be unbiased. But the exponential

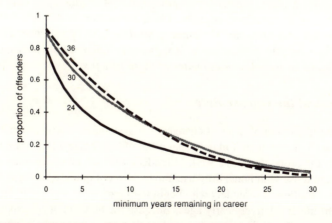

FIGURE 4.7. Expected remaining career length is probably longest for older offenders.

assumption will systematically underestimate the waste in sentences for offenders younger than 30, and systematically overestimate the waste in sentences for offenders older than 30. The error can be considerable, especially for long sentences. For example, the exponential assumption underestimates wastage in 6-year sentences by 20 percent for 24-year-old criminals, but overestimates it by 10 percent for 36-year-old offenders; the error is less than 1 percent for 30-year-olds.

The obvious solution is to derive a formula for sentencing waste, assuming the weedout/burnout dropout function and resulting distribution of remaining career lengths. Although this is difficult to do, an alternative works almost as well: simulate the careers of a large number of offenders of various ages who are sentenced to jail and prison terms of varying lengths. This provides a direct estimate of the wastage for each combination of age and sentence length. Then, since the age distribution of active offenders is known (it is, after all, the sand upon which this house was built), results for each age may be aggregated, weighting by the appropriate proportion of offenders. The final result may be described by a simple equation that maps the relationship between sentence length and waste, for the population of active offenders:

$$\theta = 1/(1 + 4.903 \ S^{-0.927}).$$

Computational details are available upon request. This equation may be used in place of the at-risk equation employed in the last section, and will in fact be used in the analysis shown in Chapters 6 and 7.

Young and inexperienced offenders—those in the first 5 years of a criminal career—are much more likely to drop out of crime each year than older offenders. After 5 years, the rate of dropout levels off, rising again only after the twentieth year as an active offender. These variations in dropout rate over a career do not obviously bias the crime-control benefits of selective sentencing; still, the age-varying dropout model is sufficiently different from the usual model that it should be included in estimates of these benefits.

Dropout and the Offense Rate

If the likelihood of dropout changes in a systematic way over the course of an offender's career, then it may be that other offender characteristics are associated with the dropout rate, as well. Offenders with job prospects may drop out sooner than those with none; drug users may burn out quickly, whereas nonusers have more resilience; offenders who begin their careers at early ages may return to straight life at relatively early ages. Because the benefits of selective policies depend on an offender's persistence no less than his offense rate, it would seem wise to combine predictions of future offense rates with predictions of an offender's persistence in pursuing criminal behavior.

This idea is by no means new. Parole boards have been explicitly predicting dropout, in the form of "recidivism," for years. And recent efforts to predict future offense rates owe much to the example provided by "salient factor scores" and similar recivism-prediction schemes. In fact, scales used for the two purposes bear a striking resemblance to one another. Both recidivism and offense rate prediction scales use the same characteristics, and weight these characteristics in much the same way (Gottfredson & Gottfredson, 1986). It is almost as though "recidivism" and "offense rate" were different names for the same beast.

A close look at how recidivism scales are formed suggests why this may be true. Most often, offenders are found to have "recidivated" if they are arrested for a serious crime within some arbitrarily chosen time limit after their release from prison. U.S. Parole Board guidelines are based on studies using follow-up intervals ranging from 2 to 6 years. An offender who commits a felony or whose parole is revoked within the follow-up period is considered a recidivist; an offender who commits no felony is not, and is presumed to have dropped out of the criminal population (Hoffman & Beck, 1984; Hoffman & Stone-Meierhoefer, 1979). Such a definition of dropout has some face validity—offenders who really do drop out of the criminal population will probably never be arrested again. Unfortunately, the reverse is not true. An offender may continue to commit crimes for years and not be caught—and not be considered a recidivist—so long as he or she does not commit very many crimes. Because so few crimes result in arrest, parole boards may confuse low offense rates with career dropout when creating their guidelines. And, as shown in Chapter 5, frequent offenders are systematically less likely to be arrested than others—further confounding the issue.

This is not necessarily a weakness of the prediction method. It would not be difficult to argue that the recidivism approach better predicts the usefulness of long-term confinement than the more recent approaches that focus only on the current offense rate. Nevertheless, the point is the same, whether we construct a scale that predicts recidivism or offense rates: High-rate offenders may drop out at higher rates or lower rates than low-rate offenders; if the difference is large, it will diminish substantially the effectiveness of selective incapacitation policies. So it is important to measure the relationship between λ and dropout.

Although it is clear that the relationship between offense rate and dropout rate is important, it is by no means clear what the relationship should look like. A number of conflicting theories of the end of a criminal career have been posited. For example, theories emphasizing burnout (Inciardi, 1975; Shover, 1985) suggest that high-rate offenders stand a greater risk of dropping out of crime than low- and medium-rate offenders. Because they run greater risks and undergo more severe physical and mental distress, one might argue, frequent offenders are unlikely to keep up the pace for very long. Other theories (Krohm, 1973; Meisenhelder, 1977) suggest that offenders zig-zag in and out of criminal behavior before they quit crime entirely. Because low-rate offenders have more attachments to conventional lifestyles, they are more likely to enter this "cool-down" period. It is even reasonable to suggest that offenders who commit crimes at moderate rates drop out at the highest rates: They commit too many crimes to allow them to hold down a straight job, but commit too few to make much money from them. Because all of these theories are based on anecdotal evidence, there is little to recommend one over another. In short, our uncertainty as to the nature of this relationship is near total. Even the flimsiest of evidence can only help.

A Model of Dropout Rates and Offense Rates

Suppose we have obtained a fabulous crystal ball from a friendly genie. With it, we can positively identify whether an offender who is active today will still be active next year. Given these miraculous powers, we would quite naturally divide the criminal population into two groups—*quitters* and *persisters*. Quitters are all those we are certain will quit offending entirely within the next 12 months. Everyone else is a persister. Although omniscient, our genie is a tad pedantic; she insists on referencing the persisters with P and the quitters with Q. If N is the total number in the criminal population, it is obvious that

$$N = P + Q. \tag{4.20}$$

Now suppose that we break down these aggregate figures by the offense rate, λ. $N(\lambda)$ is the number of active offenders with offense rates of λ, $P(\lambda)$ is the number of λ-rate persisters, and $Q(\lambda)$ is the number of λ-rate quitters. Then, for all λ,

$$N(\lambda) = P(\lambda) + Q(\lambda). \tag{4.21}$$

So the probability that an offender with offense rate λ will quit in the next year is just

$$\begin{aligned} r(\lambda) &= Q(\lambda)/N(\lambda) \\ &= 1 - P(\lambda)/N(\lambda). \end{aligned} \tag{4.22}$$

Figure 4.8 shows this graphically: Of 20 offenders who commit 10 crimes per year, 5 are quitters. So the probability of dropout in the next year, given an offense rate of 10, is 5/20 or .25. If we can identify the distribution of lambda among all offenders who are certain to be active one year from now, we may obtain the dropout rate by simple arithmetic.

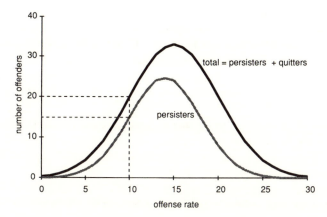

FIGURE 4.8. Dropout rate is the proportion of last year's λ-rate offenders who are now missing.

Of course, all this arithmetic is liable to be rather tedious in practice. It is particularly inconvenient to have to rely on the frequency of persisters and quitters at each offense rate. It would be much easier to estimate $r(\lambda)$ if the probability density function of lambda for persisters and quitters could be used, instead. If P_λ is the density function of offense rates for persisters, and Q_λ is the density function for quitters, then it is not difficult to show that

$$P(\lambda) = P_\lambda \, (1 - r) \, n, \qquad (4.23)$$

and that

$$Q(\lambda) = Q_\lambda \, r \, n, \qquad (4.24)$$

where r is the dropout rate averaged over all offenders, and n is the total number of offenders in the sample. Thus

$$
\begin{aligned}
r(\lambda) &= 1 - [P_\lambda \, (1 - r) \, n]/N_\lambda \, n, \\
&= 1 - (1 - r) \, P_\lambda/N_\lambda.
\end{aligned}
\qquad (4.25)
$$

Although this equation is correct for all density functions, let us examine more closely the special case where both N_λ and P_λ are logNormal. That is, suppose that

$$
\begin{aligned}
P_\lambda &\sim \text{logN} \, (\lambda_P{}', \sigma_P), \text{ and} \\
N_\lambda &\sim \text{logN} \, (\lambda_N{}', \sigma_N),
\end{aligned}
$$

where λ' is the natural logarithm of λ. (As shown in the previous chapter, the logNormal is a reasonably good approximation of the distribution for all offenders. As shown below, it is a good guess for the distributions of persisters and quitters, as well.) Then $r(\lambda)$ can be rewritten as

$$r(\lambda) = 1 - \{[(1-r)\sigma_N/\sigma_P \exp [(\lambda'-\lambda_N')^2/\sigma_N^2 - (\lambda'-\lambda_P')^2/\sigma P^2]/2\}. \quad (4.26)$$

Given r and the parameters of P_λ' and N_λ', we can solve for all $r(\lambda)$. How can we identify these parameters?

Estimation of Parameters

The best way would require two independent measurements. First, we would round up a random sample of active offenders, ask them about their offense rates, and estimate the distribution of lambda for this year. Then, we would follow up their careers for several years and pick out those offenders who committed crimes more than 12 months after the sample was drawn. Finally, we would estimate the distribution of offense rates for the persisting offenders and compare it to the distribution for all offenders. If both distributions are about logNormal, then we may use equation (4.26); in any case, we may readily alter the equation to fit the appropriate functional form.

Although a large cohort sample is as yet unavailable, an alternative method will do almost as well provided we are willing to make a few (not too unreasonable) assumptions about changes in the distribution of offense rates over time. The purpose, of course, is to obtain a reasonable estimate of $r(\lambda)$ from the Rand survey data.

First, assume that the distribution of lambda among all offenders is relatively constant from year to year. Over a long period (say, 5 years or more), there is reason to believe that the distribution may change due to changes in criminal justice or economic policies, or in demographics. But, barring very dramatic events such as wars or major depressions, these changes should happen gradually. To phrase this steady-state assumption in the notation used above,

$$N(\lambda_t) = N(\lambda_{t+1}).$$

If we are willing to stretch the assumption to a 2-year period, we may use the distribution of λ among all offenders active in Window 3 as an approximation for the λ distribution among all Window 2 offenders. So λ_N' and σ_N may be considered known.

Although the Rand researchers did not ask their inmate sample to estimate their rates of offending for Windows 1 and 2, they did ask a variety of questions about the offending activities and living circumstances of these offenders in each of the two windows. So it is possible to identify those inmates who were active in Windows 1 and 2—that is, we can identify the persisters.

If offenders commit crimes at a constant rate over their career, this solves the problem. Each offender committed crimes at the same rate in Window 2 as in Window 3. Offenders active in both windows represent a random sampling of all offenders active in Window 2 who persisted into Window 3. So the distribution of lambda for Window 2 persisters is the same as the Window 3 distribution for these offenders, and λ_P' and σ_P may be readily estimated, too.

This is very neat, but there are good reasons to believe that it won't work. As shown in the previous chapter, older offenders do commit crimes at about the same rates as younger offenders, on average. But the variation among older offenders is greater, suggesting that some offenders become more dangerous, while others becomes less dangerous as they age. It may be that variation increases because offenders with moderate rates of offending are more likely to drop out, leaving disproportionate numbers of high- and low-rate crooks. But we cannot discount the hypothesis that λ changes over an offender's career.

As always, there is another way to solve this problem. Recall that, in the last chapter, it was necessary to estimate the offense rates of individuals active in Windows 1 and 2. It turned out that the offender's demographic characteristics, living circumstances, and number of different crime types committed were together excellent predictors of offense rates in Window 3. By applying the regression parameters to data available for these offenders in Windows 1 and 2, it was possible to estimate their offense rates for these windows with fair precision. If this method can be used to predict individual offense rates, it is a simple matter to aggregate the predictions for all active individuals and estimate parameters of the offense rate distribution. So the two independent measurements required are available; in fact, three independent measurements are available.

So long as each prediction is unbiased, the errors will balance out. So the estimate of λ_P'—the initial offense rate of the eventual persisters—will be on target (Chaiken, 1984). Unfortunately, the other parameter of interest, σ_p, will be biased low. This, because the predicted value of λ for each offender will lie right on the regression line; each offender's true λ will be some distance away from the regression line. So the predicted distribution will have only 54 or 69 percent the variance of the real offense rate distribution for these periods, the percentage of the real variance that could be accounted for by the characteristics included in the regression. Of course, the R^2 for each regression provides an estimate of the proportion of variance due to unincluded factors, or "errors." That is, if s^2 is the variance of the distribution of predicted values, and σ^2 is the true variance, then

$$s^2 = R^2 \sigma^2,$$

where R^2 is .539 for property crimes, and .687 for personal crimes. Because s^2 may be measured directly from the distribution of predicted values and R^2 is known, a reasonable estimate of the true variance is

$$\sigma^2 = s^2/R^2.$$

We will want to break down the distribution for each state separately. Thus we must assume that the R^2 for each regression is about the same for California, Michigan, and Texas.

Through this (rather Rube Goldbergesque) method, all the parameters of interest may be estimated. Let us now apply the method to the Rand survey data.

Application to the Rand Data

The equations shown in Table 4.4 were applied to the Window 1 and 2 characteristics of all offenders who were actively committing index crimes in Window 3. This resulted in 12 distributions: A distribution of the logarithm of personal and of property offense rates, for each of the three states included in the Rand sample, for Window 1 and for Window 2. None of the distributions were significantly different from logNormal.

Moments of each distribution were calculated in the usual way and compared to a mean and standard deviation calculated using the method of quantiles explained in the last chapter. The values were very similar; for consistency, the quantile calculations were used and are shown in Table 4.5. Because the variance of the distribution of predicted values was smaller than the true variances, each predicted variance was divided by the appropriate value of R^2. This resulted in an unbiased estimate of the variance of the distribution of true values. The third figure shown for each cell—the standard deviation of the variance in λ— demonstrates that the variance is also relatively robust. Sensitivity analyses (not detailed here) revealed that the results described below were insensitive to random sampling errors.

As Table 4.5 shows, the means and standard deviations do not change consistently over time. Moreover, the differences between windows are relatively small. So the effect of lambda on the dropout rate cannot be identified through simple inspection.

Although (4.26) could have been used to calculate dropout rates for the entire distribution of offense rates, it was simpler to restrict the calculations to a few, selected percentiles of offense rates. Percentiles selected were the 10th, 30th, 50th, 70th, and 90th percentiles of the distribution for each window. Thus the calculated rates represent the likelihood that an offender active in a particular window, who committed crimes at a rate equal to the 10th (or whatever) percentile of the offense rates for all offenders active in that window, would stop

TABLE 4.5
Mean and Standard Deviation of Logarithm of Offense Rates for Active Offenders, Windows 1, 2, and 3

State	Personal crimes		
	Window 1	Window 2	Window 3
California	1.251	1.573	1.273
	(1.554)	(1.666)	(1.464)
Michigan	1.272	1.545	1.133
	(1.815)	(1.867)	(1.550)
Texas	0.737	0.990	0.784
	(1.531)	(1.314)	(1.493)

State	Property crimes		
	Window 1	Window 2	Window 3
California	2.858	3.067	3.159
	(2.725)	(2.716)	(2.413)
Michigan	2.637	2.798	2.705
	(2.970)	(2.761)	(2.498)
Texas	2.580	2.647	2.519
	(2.820)	(2.637)	(2.661)

Note. First figure listed is mean; figure in parentheses is standard deviation.

committing crimes over the next 2 years. Two-year dropout rates were then converted to 1-year rates, using formula (4.3). Finally, the pattern of dropout rates for Windows 1 and 2 was similar in all states; the average of the two, for each state and crime type, is shown in Table 4.6.

The rates form a clear pattern: They are highest for moderate-rate offenders and are considerably lower for the most-frequent and least-frequent criminals. This characteristic pattern holds for both crime types in all three states. Average career lengths, also shown on the table, suggest that the relationship between dropout and offense rate may be large enough to be policy-relevant. High-rate and low-rate property offenders commit crimes over a career that averages 3 years longer than middle-rate offenders; for personal offenders, the difference is about 2 years.

This provides a very neat explanation for changes in the distribution of offense rates between older and younger offenders. In the previous chapter, it was shown that the average older offender commits crimes at about the same frequency as the typical younger offender, but that there are relatively more high-rate and low-rate older offenders. Although differences between cohorts or polar-

TABLE 4.6
*Dropout Rates Lowest, Criminal Careers Highest
for Low-, High-Rate Offenders*

	Percentile of personal offense rate				
State	.10	.30	.50	.70	.90
California	.090	.115	.119	.137	.115
Michigan	.145	.179	.191	.179	.122
Texas	.124	.133	.123	.134	.119
Average r	.116	.140	.143	.150	.118
Average T	8.63	7.15	6.99	6.68	8.46

	Percentile of property offense rate				
State	.10	.30	.50	.70	.90
California	.076	.103	.127	.133	.111
Michigan	.115	.167	.180	.172	.126
Texas	.095	.116	.118	.110	.083
Average r	.094	.116	.118	.110	.083
Average T	10.67	7.90	7.12	7.25	9.35

ization among offenders as their careers progress may still be partial explanations for this phenomenon, the dropout rate analysis suggests that one reason for the change is that the offenders in the middle drop out at higher rates.

Two Reasons Why

As previously noted, it is not difficult to make up a plausible explanation for virtually any consistent pattern of dropout and offense rates. So the fact that these results make some sense is hardly proof of their validity. Still, there are two complementary reasons why dropout rates may be highest for moderate-rate offenders.

First, note that offenders who commit economic crimes (that is, property crimes plus robbery) may or may not hold down a job in the straight economy. Those who work commit crimes at lower rates than those who do not work— there is less time in which to plan and carry out their offenses, and (probably) they have less need for money. This suggests that criminal offending may be looked upon as either a full-time job in itself or as a spare-time avocation. Because the average "take" for a burglary or a robbery is very low, a criminal must commit many offenses in order to make enough money to live on. Further, it suggests that it may be difficult to maintain a moderate level of offending: An offense rate of (say) one burglary or robbery per week may take too much time or emotional energy for the typical criminal hobbyist. So the low-rate, spare-time offenders and the high-rate professionals continue, whereas moderate-rate offenders are more likely to quit.

A second explanation relies on the unproven but theoretically reasonable principle of special deterrence. Special deterrence theory states that offenders are most likely to quit committing crimes just after they are caught. The threat of punishment drives home to offenders their vulnerability; they weigh the risks of continuing, perhaps overestimating the chances that they will be caught again; they may decide that continued criminal activity is not worth the trouble. If special deterrence is an important reason why crooks go straight, it could well result in the dropout/offense rate pattern shown here. Low-rate offenders can go for years without an arrest, because they put themselves at risk so infrequently. As a result, they are unlikely to be specially deterred over any given period of time. High-rate offenders, on the other hand, are very likely to be arrested over a given period; but precisely because they commit crimes at high rates, some (Claster, 1967; Schmideberg, 1960) have maintained that they are less likely to be deterred by an arrest. Criminals who commit crimes at middling rates may be arrested rather often but do not have the immunity to arrest of the high-rate professionals. So special deterrence acts most heavily on them.

High-rate and low-rate offenders are less likely to drop out of criminal offending at any given time than offenders with moderate offense rates. Consequently, they commit crimes over careers that are 2 to 3 years longer. This relationship may result from the inconvenience to offenders of maintaining moderate offense rates, or from differences in the way offenders are specially deterred.

Production of Arrests

Perhaps the most stringent restrictions on the potential for selective incapacitation are caused by the inability of the police to solve crimes and arrest the perpetrators. Low rates of arrest cause a variety of problems for the rest of the criminal justice system. Only partial information is available as to the criminal activities of most offenders, because they can only be tied to a fraction of the crimes they commit. Even if a group of offenders can definitely be labeled as habitual, criminal justice agencies will be unable to incapacitate them if they cannot find them. And, at least partly because arrest rates are so low, police have been unable to determine whether their activities are more or less likely to lead to arrest of habitual offenders: If the most experienced criminals are consistently able to evade the authorities, even the most selective prosecution policies, bail-setting and sentencing guidelines, and parole regulations are unlikely to reduce crime by much.

All this suggests that there are two questions of interest. First, exactly how low are arrest rates? Current estimates range from a low of 3 percent to a high of 20 percent; clearly, the likely effectiveness of predictive restraints will be different at the low end than at the high end of this range. Second, how do arrest rates differ among offenders? In particular, are habitual or frequent offenders able to evade arrest, or do the police succeed in catching them with greater facility? Let us consider each of these questions in turn.

Average Probability of Arrest

Conceptual Problems

Up until this point, the most serious problem encountered in measuring the values of the parameters at issue have been conceptual. In the case of λ, the offense rate, the biggest problem was defining the population of active offenders. In the case of T, the career length, the major problem was identifying the beginning and end of a criminal career that may include long periods of inactivity. It was necessary to consider these relatively sticky conceptual questions before turning to empirical measurements.

This is not the case with the probability of arrest. Here, the population is relatively well defined: It includes all crimes that have been committed in a particular jurisdiction (whether city, state, or nation) over a particular period of time. Some crimes may be more likely to result in arrest than others; but there are no conceptual reasons for excluding any crimes from our sample. Similarly, there are few conceptual problems in defining an arrest. It may be difficult to define an arrest operationally (Sherman & Glick, 1984), but any clear operational definition will serve our purposes nicely, so long as it is used consistently. Finally, once these basic elements have been identified, there is no dispute over how they combine to form arrest rates: The average probability that an offender will be arrested, given that he or she has committed a crime, is simply the number of arrests divided by the number of crimes. Had λ and T been this simple, this book would have been over pages ago.

Data Problems

At first glance, the data required seem to be readily available, as well. Virtually all local police departments report the number of crimes committed and arrests made in their jurisdictions each year to the Federal Bureau of Investigation. So it is a simple matter to find the number of arrests for a given crime type, divide by the number of crimes, and estimate the probability. Police typically use this "clearance rate" as a measure of investigative productivity, and researchers have used it many times as an estimate of arrest productivity. For example, James Q. Wilson and Barbara Boland (1976) used Washington, DC, crime and arrest statistics for this purpose. Their result: About 20 percent of serious felonies resulted in an arrest. Probabilities estimated in this way differ greatly from one jurisdiction to the next. However, the commonsense nature of the procedure suggests that these represent real differences among police departments.

Unfortunately, the clearance rate may not really measure the chances that an offender will be arrested. One obvious problem concerns timing: Offenders may only be arrested for a crime after they have committed one, and sometimes the delay between crime commission and capture is considerable. This means that many of the people arrested in (say) 1981 did not commit all of their crimes in 1981. Some doubtless committed the crimes for which they were arrested in 1980, 1979, or even earlier. Although this is disconcerting, it is a trivial problem unless the probability of arrest fluctuates greatly from year to year, or unless the number of crimes committed each year changes greatly. FBI-reported clearance rates have been stable for the past 15 years, and annual changes in crime rates are generally small for large jurisdictions; so this is probably not a major problem.

A more serious problem concerns errors in the data. It has long been known that crime statistics are relatively sensitive to (apparently) minor changes in reporting and recording procedures. Police departments can encourage crime reporting or discourage it by making reporting procedures easy or difficult; they may alter internal procedures on "unfounding" and case classification; if the political stakes are particularly high, they can simply lie outright, and no one will be the wiser (Black, 1970; Cook, 1971; Seidman & Couzens, 1974). Although one might reasonably assume that arrest records are more consistent and reliable, careful research shows that internal reporting procedures can have an enormous impact on the number of arrests for each type of crime that a police department records (Conklin, 1972; Sherman & Glick, 1984). So differences between departments or over time in arrests, crimes, or the ratio of the two may be due more to police procedures than to police arrest productivity. Offenders may run about the same risks in all jurisdictions.

Although these problems suggest that one should cast a cold eye on measurements of arrest probability, they do not demonstrably bias the results. However, two, more subtle problems strongly influence this measure of the arrest probability to be too high. First, most crimes are never reported to the police; second, many crimes are committed by groups rather than by individuals.

Victimization surveys show consistently (if not quite convincingly) that 60 percent of property crimes and over 50 percent of personal crimes go unreported to the police. The biggest reasons are that citizens believe that reporting the crime will be inconvenient or unlikely to yield results, and that the issue is a personal matter and not the business of the police (see, e.g., Bureau of Justice Statistics, 1986, pp. 85–103). Whether victimization surveys should be taken at face value is an open question; but there is no doubt but that officially reported crime statistics greatly understate the amount of crime in a jurisdiction. Thus C, the denominator of the arrest probability, will be too low if estimated from official records; the probability itself will be too high.

The second biasing problem is a bit more subtle. We are used to equating "victimizations" with "crimes committed"—looking at crime from the victim's point of view. But if we are interested in measuring the risks run by each offender, we must examine crime from the criminal's point of view. Many serious crimes are committed, not by individual offenders, but by offending groups. For example, two or more offenders are involved in 54 percent of reported robberies, 60 percent of reported burglaries, and 24 percent of reported assaults (Reiss, 1980; Spelman, Oshima, & Kelling, 1986). Each member of the group may be held liable for his or her participation in the incident, and each runs a risk of arrest. Thus, from the viewpoint of the offenders involved, each robbery victimization really represents 2.0 robberies committed, each break-in represents 1.6 burglaries committed, and so on. Use of victimization data to estimate the number of offenses committed will systematically understate the number of offenses, and systematically overstate the probability of arrest.

Empirical Estimates

Because of these problems, it is fairly certain that the true probability that a randomly selected offender will be arrested for his or her deed is considerably less than 20 percent. Two methods are available that may lead to unbiased estimates:

- Official records may still be used, if adjustments are made to control the problems of citizen nonreporting and multiple offending.
- Offender self-reports may be used, so long as the offenders represent a random sample of all criminal offenders.

The first method was employed by Alfred Blumstein and Jacqueline Cohen, using Washington, DC, arrest, crime, and victimization statistics; it was also employed by Peter Greenwood, using official records from the State of California. The second method is employed here on the Rand survey data. Although both data sources are likely to be in error in different ways, virtually identical results are obtained from each. This suggests that each of these studies may have converged on the correct value.

Let us consider the official records estimates first. Blumstein and Cohen (1979) broke down clearance rates by crime type, while correcting for the fact that many crimes are not reported to the police and that several offenders are responsible for many crimes. They conclude that the average chances of arrest for personal crimes are 8.3 percent, and that average arrest probabilities for property crimes are 3.4 percent. Of course, these figures are, strictly speaking, only applicable to the District of Columbia; nevertheless, there is no particular reason to suspect that arrest probabilities are particularly high or low in Washington.

Greenwood replicated the Blumstein and Cohen analysis, using official records from California. He found that the average chances of arrest for robbery were 6.4 percent, and that the average arrest probabilities for burglary were 5.5 percent (Greenwood, 1982). (Because Greenwood was concerned only with the crimes of burglary and robbery, he did not identify the arrest probabilities for any other serious crimes.) The estimated arrest risks for California are very similar to the risks of arrest faced by burglars and robbers in Washington, DC.

Both of these results are confirmed by reanalysis of the Rand data set. The average probability of arrest, given that a crime was committed, is shown in Table 5.1 for eight different crime types for each of the three states included in the data set. For comparison, Blumstein and Cohen's results for the District of Columbia and Greenwood's results for California are also shown. Although there are a few obvious differences, the probabilities are remarkably similar. Note particularly that arrests are made in one of every six to nine assault cases, but in only one of every 50 thefts and frauds. This reflects the fact that both the identity of the suspect and the very fact that a crime is being committed are often known to a victim or witness while an assault or robbery is happening, especially because the offender is often a family member or friend. In contrast, thieves

TABLE 5.1
Offender Self-Reported Estimates of the Probability of Arrest Are Consistent with Official Records

	Self-reports				Official records	
	California	Michigan	Texas	All Rand	DC	California
Personal crimes	.088	.054	.114	.077	.083	na[a]
Robbery	.073	.042	.099	.062	.069	.064
Assault	.180	.161	.190	.175	.111	na
Property crimes	.019	.023	.019	.020	.034	na
Burglary	.033	.032	.021	.028	.049	.055
Larceny	.014	.019	.012	.015	.026	na
Auto theft	.031	.024	.095	.032	.047	na
Forgery	.016	.031	.025	.019	na	na
Fraud	.007	.013	.021	.010	na	na

[a]na = not available.
Sources. Self-reports: author's calculations. Washington, DC official records: Blumstein & Cohen, 1979. California official records: Greenwood & Abrahamse, 1982, p. 109.

and burglars try to avoid detection, whereas forgers and con artists try to prevent recognition on the part of the victim that a crime is being committed in the first place.

Note also that the probabilities are lower for the Rand sample than for the others. This is probably due to differences in the population included in each sample: Even after weighting, the Rand sample includes more frequent and serious offenders than the Washington and California samples, which include (by definition) all arrestees. As shown below, frequent and serious offenders probably run lower risks than infrequent amateurs.

Although the probabilities are similar in each of these cases, it may be that they differ greatly from one locality to the next. The Rand and Greenwood estimates are averaged over all jurisdictions within each state, so local deviations may be masked. Washington, DC, may be a peculiarly typical city. Still, the similarities suggest that these probabilities represent something like a nationwide average. In the absence of information to the contrary, the average of these estimates may be considered to be the most likely value for any given jurisdiction.

It is reasonable to expect that estimates of the effectiveness of incapacitation strategies will be fairly sensitive to small variations in arrest probability. The higher the probability, the more effective the present, relatively unselective criminal justice system ought to be, because a greater proportion of offenders would be in jails and prisons at any given time.

Moreover, the better the system is doing already, the better it can do by increasing its reliance on general incapacitation. Suppose the chances of arrest were sufficiently high that 40 percent of active offenders were in jail or prison at a given time. Then a 10 percent increase in prison space would bring another 4 percent of all active, adult offenders behind bars, and reduce the number of active, adult offenders on the street by

$$.04/(1.0 - .40) = 6.7 \text{ percent.}$$

If the chances of arrest were half that, then only 20 percent of active, adult offenders would be incarcerated. A 10-percent increase in prison space would reduce the number of street offenders by

$$.10(.20)/(1.0 - .20) = 2.5 \text{ percent.}$$

So a 50-percent reduction in arrest rate implies a reduction in the effectiveness of incapacitation of more than 50 percent. Perhaps more important, this also suggests that incapacitation strategies may be more effective when applied to crimes that the police are particularly likely to solve (such as robbery and assault), rather than those that are rarely solved (forgery or fraud).

The average probability that an offender will be arrested, given that he or she commits a property crime, is between .02 and .03; the probability of arrest, given a personal crime, is about .08. However, these probabilities may differ from one jurisdiction to the next. The higher the arrest rate, the more effective incapacitation strategies are liable to be.

Differences among Offenders

Although average arrest probabilities are clearly a good place to start, the analysis in Chapters 2 through 4 has emphasized the enormous variation about the average values. Relatively few criminals commit crimes at an average rate, or over a career of average length; it seems likely that few should risk arrest at an average rate. The Rand survey data bear this out. Box plots of the arrest probabilities reported by offenders in the Rand survey, shown in Figure 5.1, show a wide variation among offenders. Some of this variability is no doubt due to random error; even if all offenders ran identical risks with every crime they committed, a few would be arrested much more often than others, purely by chance. However, random errors become relatively unimportant as the number of crimes committed increases; it would not be difficult to show that the enormous variability shown in Figure 5.1 cannot be the result of random chance alone. Moreover, as shown below, individual arrest probabilities are correlated with

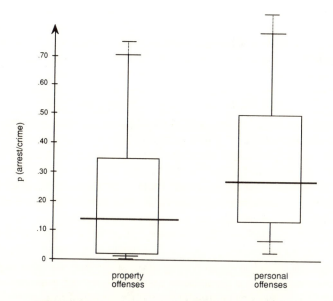

FIGURE 5.1. Arrest rates vary dramatically among offenders.

other offender characteristics. For one reason or another, some offenders are particularly likely to be caught, whereas others are particularly likely to get away with their crimes.

Before attempting to use the data available to find out why this is so, let us first consider how police tactics could lead to results like these. Police use their resources to arrest criminals in two, fundamentally different ways. Random and directed patrol tactics include stakeouts, surveillance, decoys, interception patrol, and rapid response; they are used to increase the chances of arresting the offenders at the scene of the crime. Follow-up investigations rely on physical evidence and witness accounts to identify and apprehend the criminals after they have made good their escape.

How Arrests Are Made

Patrol

Through random preventive patrol, police seek (among other things) to intercept crimes while they are in progress and apprehend the offenders in the act. Though there is persuasive evidence that preventive patrol is a very inefficient use of police resources (Kelling et al., 1974; Schnelle et al., 1977), some offenders are caught in the act by patrol officers. Even if the offenders are not caught in the act, the police may still make a quick arrest if a victim or witness reports the crime while it is being committed or shortly afterward, and the police respond quickly to the scene. Alternatively, a victim or witness may be able to catch the perpetrator, or tell the police where they can find him immediately (Kansas City Police Department, 1977; Spelman & Brown, 1984).

Although random patrol is the mainstay of most police patrol activity, many departments have experimented with directed-patrol activities in recent years. Like random patrol, the aim of directed patrol is to increase the likelihood that police will be on the scene when an offender commits a crime. However, directed-patrol tactics differ from random tactics in that police use information available before the crime is committed to help direct their actions. For example, patrol officers may use crime analysis data or informants to help them predict in advance when and where a crime is going to be committed and stake out the location. Police may follow offenders suspected of being particularly active, in hopes that they will attempt to commit a crime while under surveillance. And the police may bait offenders by providing decoys—targets that look especially promising. Although most departments make some use of stakeouts, surveillance, and decoy tactics, they usually view directed patrol as a supplement to, rather than as a replacement for, random preventive patrol (Gay, Schell, & Schack, 1977; Schack, Schell, & Gay, 1977).

Investigation

It would be pleasant if the police could manage to appear on the scene of many crimes while they were being committed, but this will never be possible. Crime analysis specialists and informants are notoriously vague (Gay, Schell, & Schack, 1977); there are far too few police officers to protect more than a tiny fraction of the promising targets (Riccio, 1974); many crime victims are understandably slow to call the police (Spelman & Brown, 1984). But the police may still identify and arrest the perpetrators if the offenders leave behind sufficient traces at the crime scene—fingerprints, tool marks, and so on. More important, a victim or witness may be able to describe the criminals, identify them in police lineups or mug books, or (occasionally) give the police their name and address. Again, there is evidence that much follow-up investigative work is wasteful and inefficient; but many offenders are caught as a result of successful detective work (Eck, 1983).

About half of all crimes that are solved and result in arrest are "cleared" as the result of an on-scene arrest; arrests are made in the other half of cases as a result of a follow-up investigation (Greenwood et al., 1975). And the productivity of patrol and investigative activities seems to be roughly the same for all police departments (see, e.g., Eck, 1979). Yet police departments that rely to a greater degree on one set of tactics than on another are likely to arrest systematically more or fewer high-rate, dangerous offenders; two departments with identical arrest rates may be vastly different in the selectivity of their arrests. This is because experienced and inexperienced offenders have different weaknesses, which these police strategies exploit in different ways.

Police Learning and Offender Learning

As already noted, high-rate offenders are neither specialists nor particularly "professional." Nevertheless, there is evidence that more experienced criminals plan their escapes more carefully, "case" their jobs more thoroughly, and more reliably avoid identification by a victim or witness. For example, the habitual armed robbers interviewed in the 1975 Rand survey became less likely to be caught soon after the crime as they became more experienced. And they were more likely to credit their ability to avoid arrest to their skill, mobility, or imagination as their careers progressed. Results of the 1976 survey reinforced the view that experienced, high-rate offenders believe skillful planning cut their risk of arrest (Petersilia, Greenwood, & Lavin, 1978; Peterson, Braiker, & Polich, 1980).

One might suspect, then, that the offenders apprehended at or near the scene of the crime as the result of random patrol or rapid response will be largely those who did not plan their escape very well or were identified by others while committing the crime. To the degree that these "unprofessional" errors are the hallmarks of inexperienced offenders, the police will apprehend mostly low-rate or young criminals through on-scene arrest. In short, as criminals develop in their careers and begin to commit crimes at high rates, they learn to commit crimes that are harder to solve through random-patrol methods.

Many directed-patrol activities, on the other hand, probably focus police resources on the higher-rate offenders. This is because they make use of information that is typically only available about more active criminals. For example, before a location may be staked out, police must have a reasonable suspicion that a crime will be committed there within a limited time. They may glean this information through analysis of recent crime patterns, or through informants. Though it is conceivable that low-rate offenders or groups may be active enough to establish recognizable patterns, crime analysis is most obviously useful when an offender is committing crimes frequently within a limited area (Chang et al., 1979). Similarly, police informants are most likely to monitor the activities of known, full-time criminals rather than small-time, sporadic offenders (Spelman, 1986, pp. 333–334). Thus one would expect that an offender arrested as the result of a typical stakeout will probably commit crimes at a higher-than-average rate. The same logic applies to surveillance tactics: Because police typically only follow offenders they are reasonably sure commit crimes frequently (otherwise, the returns are too low), the typical surveillance arrestee should also be a relatively frequent offender (Pate, Bowers, & Parks, 1976, pp. 6–8).

Evidence is scanty, but what there is suggests that offenders apprehended through stakeouts and surveillance do, in fact, commit crimes at higher rates than offenders caught through interception and rapid response (Boydstun et al., 1981, p. V-63; Pate, Bowers, & Parks, 1976, pp. 81–91). Police appear to learn who the dangerous offenders are and arrest them with greater frequency through directed tactics.

If the offender succeeds in committing the crime and fleeing the scene, detectives take up the case. When follow-up investigations are successful, it is usually because someone tells the police who committed the crime: A victim or witness knows the culprit's name or address in over half of the felony cases that are eventually solved (Eck, 1983; Greenwood, et al., 1975). For the remaining half, investigators develop suspect information from a variety of sources, including physical evidence, informants, and departmental records. The key to use of these alternative information sources is that they are aimed primarily at offenders who have previously been identified by the police. Fingerprints or toolmarks are of no help in identifying criminals who have never been booked and whose methods of operation have never been filed; a physical description of the suspect by a victim or witness rarely leads to an arrest unless the citizen can identify the suspect in a book of mug shots or can otherwise match the description of a known offender (Gay, Beall, & Bowers, 1984). So one would suspect that follow-up investigations lead mostly to capture of relatively experienced, high-rate offenders who have already been identified by the police as habitual criminals. Again, police learn who the dangerous offenders are and catch them with greater facility.

Thus two trends are evident in this analysis of police arrest practices. First, experienced offenders learn to evade capture, by picking targets that are less risky and by planning their crimes more thoroughly. Second, police learn to identify and arrest offenders they have arrested before, by using the information they have gathered to plan their actions either before or after a crime has been committed. To the degree that frequent offenders garner lots of experience, one would expect that they evade capture; thus they should be less likely to be arrested for each crime they commit. Because they place themselves at risk much more often than the typical offender, however, one would expect that they will be arrested more often as well. So the police will assemble more and more information about them, and ultimately they may become more likely to be arrested for each offense they commit (Willmer, 1970).

Prior Research on the Learning Hypotheses

How strong are these two effects? Is one substantially stronger than the other, or do they balance each other out? Because the best available estimate of a criminal's rate of offending is usually his or her arrest record, the evidence is scanty and inconclusive. However, two results suggest that the offender learning effect is relatively strong and dominates the police learning effect. The first relies on the aggregate distribution of motivations, crimes, and arrests among offenders, whereas the second links individual crime histories with arrest histories.

Filtering Estimates of Arrest Selectivity

As shown in Chapter 2, frequent offenders are more likely to be arrested, convicted, and incarcerated at any given time than others, even if police, prosecutors, and judges are not at all selective in their actions. In effect, the various stages of the criminal justice system act as a filter, leaving behind the infrequent offenders, but passing through the worst criminals (Moore et al., 1984).

It is comforting to find that a completely nonselective system can still be selective in its results, but what makes this result useful is that the degree of filtering in the system is predictable. Suppose we know that the most frequent 10 percent of robbers commit 40 percent of the robberies; further, offenders are arrested for 10 percent of the robberies they commit, and half of these arrests result in conviction and incarceration. Then it is not difficult to show that the 10 percent of offenders who rack up the most arrests will account for about 46 percent of the arrests, and the 10 percent of offenders who are most often convicted account for some 54 percent of all convictions.

Once benchmarks like these are established, the selectivity of any part of the system can be estimated by comparing the concentration of sanctions among offenders. For example, if the police are focusing their resources on the most frequent offenders, then the distribution of arrests will become concentrated in a smaller proportion of offenders; the 10 percent of arrestees with the most arrests will acount for more than 46 percent of all arrests. If, on the other hand, the most frequent offenders are more successful than others in evading identification and capture, then the arrests will be spread over a larger number of offenders— the worst 10 percent of arrestees will rack up fewer than 46 percent of the arrests.

The relative concentration of offenses and arrests among offenders is shown in Figure 5.2. (Although the offense- and arrest-rate distributions are not identical among California, Michigan, and Texas, they are very similar; the states have been aggregated for simplicity.) As shown in Chapter 3, the worst 10 percent of offenders accounted for roughly 70 percent of all crimes committed by respondents to the Rand survey. So if the police are neither selective nor counterselective, filtering indicates that more than 70 percent of the arrests should be concentrated in the 10 percent of arrestees with the most arrests. Instead, the most frequently arrested 10 percent account for only about 40 percent of all arrests. Thus the police do not seem to be filtering the low-rate offenders out of the criminal justice system—on the contrary, they seem to be filtering them in. This

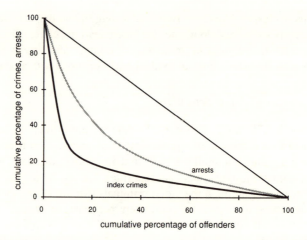

FIGURE 5.2. The distribution of arrest rates is less skewed than the offense rate distribution.

apparent counterselectivity suggests that frequent offenders are learning to commit crimes more efficiently than police are learning to catch them.

Individual Estimates

The second piece of evidence is more direct, but biased. Because our interest lies in estimating the relationship between the chances of arrest and the offense rate, the most obvious method of estimation would seem to be simple regression. If data were available on the number of offenses an individual had committed and the number of times he had been arrested, then we could estimate

$$q = a + b \lambda, \tag{5.1}$$

or perhaps more reasonably,

$$p(A|C) = \alpha \lambda^\beta, \tag{5.2}$$

where $q = p(A|C)$ is the number of arrests divided by the number of crimes. When equation (5.2) is applied to juvenile self-report data (Cohen, 1986; Dunford & Elliott, 1984), the results shown in Figure 5.3 are obtained. (Midpoints of each range have been interpolated under the assumption that the λ distribution is logNormal; $\chi^2 = 5.894$ with 7 degrees of freedom, showing no significant difference from the logNormal.) The data themselves are a bit suspect; the arrest probabilities are an order of magnitude lower than those presented in the previous section, suggesting that these juvenile offenders exaggerated their criminal activ-

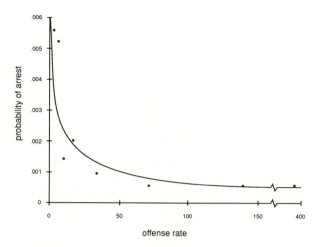

FIGURE 5.3. Arrest rates appear to be lower for frequent offenders.

ities considerably. Whether the average is biased or not, frequent offenders appear to run lower risks than the others. This finding backs up more general results from the first Rand inmate survey (Peterson, Braiker, & Polich, 1980) and from more recent surveys of arrestees (Chaiken & Chaiken, 1987; Greenwood & Turner, 1987).

This looks straightforward, but it may be misleading. Note that equation (5.1) may be rephrased as

$$A/C = a + b \ (C/T), \tag{5.3}$$

where A is arrests, C crimes, and T the time the offender spends out on the street, free to commit crimes. The coefficients measure what they are supposed to measure, so long as A, C, and T are measured without random error. However, if our meaure of C is imperfect, the errors in measurement of the independent variable, C/T, will be negatively associated with errors in measurement of the dependent variable, A/C. Suppose, for example, the true C is 20 for all cases, but due to measurement errors some offenders reported committing 25 crimes and others reported only 15. Then, even if all offenders were arrested exactly once and ran identical risks, there would appear to be a strong negative correlation between crimes committed and the likelihood of arrest. The size of the bias depends on the amount of error in measurements of C; given that the measurements were obtained from a survey of convicted criminals, the errors are likely to be large, even if the cons are doing their best to tell the truth. As a result, it is best not to take these results too seriously.

In summary, available evidence suggests that offenders learn to evade arrest, that the effect is moderately strong, and that it is somewhat greater than any police learning effect. But the evidence is by no means conclusive. A full test of the two hypotheses would require (yet another) survey of criminal offenders that tracked both the number of crimes and the number of arrests throughout an offender's career. Such a survey would be difficult to administer at best; considering the length of the typical criminal career and the number of offenses and arrests included within it, much of the data would be of dubious validity, anyway. Luckily, an unbiased (and relatively robust) test of the two hypotheses can be developed, using the Rand inmate surveys. Although the individual strength of the police and offender learning effects cannot be determined, the net effect can be estimated precisely enough to allow unbiased modeling of the arrest process.

A Test of the Learning Hypotheses

Mathematical Background

Suppose that q_i, the probability that our old friend, Ishmael, will be arrested given that he has just committed a crime, consists of four parts. Let P_i be a "police multiplier," an indicator of how well the police have learned his identity, and how much more likely they are to catch him than the average offender. P_i may be any number greater than zero; if it is 1, Ishmael is an average offender from the police point of view; if greater than 1, they are more likely to catch him than average; if less than 1, they are less likely. Likewise, let O_i be the "offender multiplier," a measure of how much more or less likely Ishmael is to be arrested, given his motivations to avoid arrest, his avoidance activities, and his experience. Then

$$q_i = q\, P_i\, O_i\, e_i, \tag{5.4}$$

where q is the average probability of arrest given a crime, and e_i is a random error term.

P_i and O_i both depend on a variety of characteristics. For example, P_i may increase with the number of prior arrests, convictions, and jail terms, whereas O_i may decrease with the number of prior crimes committed, or with the amount of preparation per crime. One reasonable form for these relationships between the multipliers and their determinants is

$$P = X_1^{B1}\, X_2^{B2}\, X_3^{B3} \ldots X_n^{Bn}. \tag{5.5}$$

where each X refers to a determinant of the multiplier (in this case, P) and each B refers to a predictive coefficient. Although other forms may fit the data, they are inconsistent with learning theory (Eysenck, 1960; Hill, 1963). Due to the skewed distribution of arrest rates, they are also less convenient. In practice, the actual functional form probably doesn't matter very much.

Because two of these variables are of particular importance—the number of prior arrests, and the number of prior crimes—let us rephrase P and O to make these components explicit. Thus

$$P_i = A^{Ba} X_1^{B1} X_2^{B2} \ldots = A_i^{Ba} \Pi_j X_{ij}^{Bj}, \tag{5.6a}$$

and

$$O_i = C_i^{Bc} X_1^{B1} X_2^{B2} \ldots = C_i^{Bc} \Pi_j X_{ij}^{Bj}, \tag{5.6b}$$

where A is the number of prior arrests and C the number of prior crimes.

Then equation (5.4) can be rephrased as

$$A_i/C_i = q A_i^{Ba} C_i^{Bc} \Pi_j X_{ij}^{Bj} e_i. \tag{5.7}$$

Solving for A, we obtain

$$A_i^{1-Ba} = P_i C_i^{Bc+1} e_i, \tag{5.8}$$

where $P = q \Pi_j X_{ij}^{Bj}$. Taking logs, again solving for A, and omitting subscripts for simplicity,

$$\begin{aligned} \log A = \log P/(1 - B_A) + [(B_C + 1)/(1 - B_A)] \log C \\ + \log e/(1 - B_A). \end{aligned} \tag{5.9}$$

The most interesting part of this result is the coefficient on $\log C$. Let us simplify by setting the first set of terms in equation (5.9) to B_O and rephrasing the error term such that $e^* = \log e/(1 - B_A)$. Then

$$\log A = B_O + (B_C + 1)/(1 - B_A) \log C + e^*. \tag{5.10}$$

This equation is linear in the parameters; moreover, because C and A are both roughly logNormal-distributed (that is, the logarithms of the values are roughly Normal-distributed), the usual difficulties of regressing on highly skewed variables are lessened (Mosteller & Tukey, 1977).

Note that the coefficient on $\log C$ consists of two parameters—B_A, corresponding to the amount of police learning from prior arrests, and B_C, a measure of the amount of offender learning from prior crimes. By estimating the single coefficient $(B_C + 1)/(1 - B_A)$, we can determine which of these two effects is stronger. Because the chances of arrest are expected to increase with prior arrests, B_A is greater than zero and (probably) less than 1; because the chances of arrest are expected to decrease with prior crimes, B_C is less than zero and (probably) greater than -1. Now suppose that police learning is more important than offender learning in determining the likelihood of arrest given a crime. Then

$$|B_A| > |B_C|,$$

and

$$(B_C + 1)/(1 - B_A) > 1.$$

The opposite result obtains for $|B_C| > |B_A|$, whereas if the absolute values of the two coefficients are equal,

$$(B_C + 1)/(1 - B_A) = 1.$$

Not only is this derivation satisfyingly easy, it is intuitively reasonable as well. Consider Figure 5.4, which plots three possible relationships between A and C. If the police and offender learning effects just canceled one another out (or were both insignificant), then the chances of arrest per crime—and the average ratio of arrests to crimes committed—should be a constant over all crimes and offenders. In this case, the relationship between A and C should be exactly linear, and the coefficient on C should be exactly 1 (Curve 1). If the offender learning effect dominates, then the ratio of arrests to crimes should decrease with the number of crimes committed—offenders who rack up lots of crimes should rack

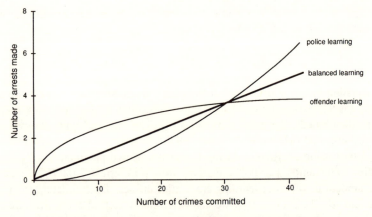

FIGURE 5.4. Three possible relationships between arrests and crimes.

up proportionately fewer arrests (Curve 2). And if police learning is dominant, then the ratio of arrests to crimes should increase with the number of crimes—the typical experienced offender has been caught several times before, and so is more likely to be caught again than the others (Curve 3).

Estimation of the Parameters

Of course, there is no information in the Rand data set (or any other data set) as to the chances of arrest for any particular crime, or the number of prior offenses and arrests at any particular time. If one is willing to make the simplifying assumption that the chances of arrest are relatively constant over a 2-year period, however, some reasonable estimates of each of the critical parameters may be made.

- q_i is just the number of arrests recorded over the latest two-year window, divided by the number of crimes in which the offender participated during that period.
- A_i, the number of prior arrests, is the number of arrests recorded over the latest 2-year window. This is a reasonable estimate of the number of prior arrests during the previous 2 years at any point in the 2-year window, if the chances of arrest and the rate of offending do not change greatly from period to period. The analysis detailed in Chapter 3 suggested that offending rates are sufficiently stable that this is not unreasonable.
- C_i, the number of crimes committed in the preceding 2 years, may be reasonably estimated by the number of crimes committed over the entire 2-year period. The logic is the same as for setting A equal to the number of arrests in that period.

Although there is no reason to suspect that either A_i or C_i is a biased estimate of the real value, it is quite likely that each has been measured with considerable error. More specifically, let $\hat{A}_i$ be our best guess as to the true number of arrests garnered over the 2-year period, and let $\hat{C}_i$ be our best guess as to the true number of crimes committed. Then, if A_i and C_i are the true figures,

$$\log \hat{A}_i = \log A_i + \log a_i, \text{ and}$$
$$\log \hat{C}_i = \log C_i + \log c_i,$$

where a_i and c_i are random errors that are independent of A_i and C_i, and are also independent of one another. (Although they are probably not independent of one another, as shown below, this probably does not affect empirical parameter estimates much.) So the model we really want to estimate is

$$\log A_i = B_O + (B_C + 1)/(1 - B_A) \log C_i + u_i, \quad (5.11)$$

but we may only estimate it through use of $\hat{A}$ and $\hat{C}$. Thus the estimating equation is

$$\log \hat{A}_i = b_O + (b_C + 1)/(1 - b_A) \log \hat{C}_i + e_i, \tag{5.12}$$

where

$$e_i = \log a_i - (B_C + 1)/(1 - B_A) \log c_i + u_i. \tag{5.13}$$

Unfortunately, all this means that the slope term, corresponding to the balance of police and offender learning effects, is biased toward zero. In fact, if c_i is roughly logNormal distributed, then

$$E[(b_C + 1)/(1 - b_A)] = [(B_C + 1)/(1 - B_A)] R^2, \tag{5.14}$$

where

$$R^2 = \sigma^2(\log C)/\sigma^2(\log \hat{C}). \tag{5.15}$$

That is, R^2 is simply the proportion of the variance in the log of $\hat{C}$, our measurement of the number of crimes committed that is due to variation in the true number of crimes. Because we have assumed that there may be errors of measurement in C (that is, c has a nonzero variance), then R^2 must be less than or equal to 1. When R^2 is close to 1, the errors are small, our measure of C is an excellent approximation, and the bias toward zero is small. When R^2 is close to zero, $\hat{C}$ is not a very good approximation of C, and the bias is substantial. So the size of the bias is directly proportional to the size of the errors of measurement in $\hat{C}$—the reliability of $\hat{C}$ (Guttman, 1945).

Does this cause any difficulty in interpreting the slope coefficient? Most certainly. The closer the true slope is to zero, the stronger the offender learning effect. If the apparent slope is biased toward zero, then the offender learning effect will be systematically overstated. In general, the greater the errors in measurement of $\hat{C}$, the greater will be the tendency to falsely accept offender learning rather than police learning as dominant.

However, if we can estimate R^2—if we can determine the reliability of $\hat{C}$—then we can use the apparent slope to solve for the true slope (Theil, 1971). Specifically, if R^2 is known, then

$$(B_C + 1)/(1 - B_A) = [(b_C + 1)/(1 - b_A)]/R^2. \tag{5.16}$$

How may the reliability of $\hat{C}$ be estimated?

One fairly straightforward way is to compute the reliability of some quantity that has been measured in about the same way as $\hat{C}$. The obvious example is $\hat{A}$, which was measured by both surveying prison inmates and by examining official records. The apparent reliability of survey arrests is between .13 (for property crimes) and .27 (for robberies and assaults). However, the usefulness of this straightforward approach is tempered by two facts. First, this represents a lower bound on the reliability of $\hat{A}$, because official records are themselves likely to be in error: They will systematically exclude many out-of-state arrests, for example. In this case, the R^2 between official records (R^2_O) and offender self-reports (R^2_S) will not be the reliability of the self-report estimate alone, but will equal instead

$$R^2_{OS} = R^2_O \cdot R^2_S.$$

If the ratio of the two reliabilities—roughly corresponding to the relative "correctness" of each estimate—may be estimated, then the reliability of $\hat{A}$ may be obtained from the reliability of the two together. Suppose, for example, that we know official records to be often wrong, but we find it inconceivable that they could be worse on average than offender self-reports. Then the ratio

$$R^2_S/R^2_O < 1,$$

and

$$R^2_S < (R^2_{OS})^{.5}.$$

This suggests that, if R^2_{OS} is a reasonable lower bound for the reliability of the number of crimes committed, the square root of this lower bound might be a reasonable upper bound on the reliability.

Although clever, this adjustment relies heavily on the assumption that the reliability of arrest estimates is similar to the reliability of offense estimates. This may not be so. At first glance one is tempted to suggest that the crime measurements are probably less reliable because so many more crimes are committed than arrests made, and there is more room for error. On the other hand, the Rand researchers chose to estimate the number of crimes committed in a rather circuitous way that proved to be more reliable on a control group than the method used to estimate the number of arrests (Peterson et al., 1981). The two measurement methods are not necessarily comparable, and the reliability estimates provided above are of uncertain quality.

But there is another way to skin this cat. If our measure of C really consists of two elements—C plus random error—then it is possible to estimate the proportion of the variance in $\hat{C}$ that may be attributable to C by regressing $\hat{C}$ on variables likely to be correlated with C. In Chapter 3, for example, it was shown that the rate of property crimes committed over a 2-year period was associated with the number of different kinds of property crimes committed, with employment status, living situation, drug use, and other factors that change from period to period, and with stable characteristics such as certain psychological and demographic attributes. There is every reason to believe that these attributes are associated with the number of crimes committed, as well. Because these variables will not be correlated with random measurement errors, the R^2 of the result will be a reasonable estimate of the reliability of C. If only a few independent variables are available, then they may not be sufficient to account for all of the variance in $\hat{C}$ due to C, and the estimate of the reliability of $\hat{C}$ will be too low. On the other hand, if many independent variables are available, the reliability of $\hat{C}$ may be overstated due to spurious correlations between $\hat{C}$ and variables that are randomly associated with the error term, not with C. On balance, these two types of errors seem about equally likely and will probably about cancel one another out.

Of course, this method will give incorrect results if $\hat{C}$ also includes a third element—nonrandom response error that pervades all measurements in the survey. For example, suppose that some of the offenders are macho guys who systematically overstate how bad they are; we are unsure (and don't much care) whether these errors are due to distorted self-perceptions, deliberate lying, or both. Then these offenders are likely to systematically overstate the number of property crimes they committed, as well as the number of different property crime types they committed, their use of drugs, their tendency to be unemployed, and so on. As a result, these variables may be more highly associated than their true values, and the assessed reliability of $\hat{C}$ may be biased high.

These arguments provide three estimates of the reliability of $\hat{C}$. One is too low, the others probably too high. The three groups of estimates are shown in Table 5.2. We may conclude that the reliability of $\hat{C}$ for personal crimes is between .3 and .5; reliability for property crimes is lower, between .15 and .35. These figures may be used to adjust the parameters of any regression between arrests and the number of crimes committed.

Taken literally, use of this specification requires the assumption that experience gathered more than 2 years ago is useless. Because this assumption is almost certainly wrong, let us include two additional terms: C_{t-1} specifies crimes committed between 2 and 4 years previously (in Window 2), whereas C_{t-2}

TABLE 5.2
Three Estimates of the Reliability of $\hat{C}$

Estimation method	Personal crimes	Property crimes
Lower bound (arrests)	.269	.133
Upper bound (arrests)	.519	.365
Upper bound (crimes)	.524	.365
Approximate range	.30 to .50	.15 to .35

specifies crimes committed between 4 and 6 years previously (in Window 1). Information on the actual number of crimes committed in these two periods is not available in the Rand data set; nevertheless, reasonably precise and unbiased estimates may be made similarly to the method outlined in Chapter 3. (Note that these coefficients have no particular bearing on the relative strength of the police and offender learning hypotheses; they are included only to avoid biasing the coefficient on $\hat{C}_t$.)

This would be enough if we were certain that the only way offenders learned was through experience, and that the only way police learned was by making arrests. Although these are probably the most important elements of the learning process, there are others. Both offenders and police must be motivated to learn; they must have the capacity to learn; and they must take actions that make use of their knowledge if learning is to have any effect. Indicators for each of these additional elements were available in the Rand data and added to the specification whenever they proved useful.

Indicators of the Probability of Arrest

In order to identify indicators of high and low probabilities of arrest, two multiple regressions were run. In the first regression, the logarithm of A_V, the number of arrests for personal crimes in Window 3, was regressed against the logarithm of C_V, the number of personal crimes committed during that period. The residual of this result was then regressed against a number of other potential indicators in steps; only those indicators that were significant at a .05 probability or better entered the equation. The second regression was similar, except that the logarithm of A_P, the number of arrests for property crimes, was regressed against the logarithm of C_P, the number of property crimes, and then against the stack of potential indicators. Potential indicators included a variety of variables describing each inmate's offending history, criminal record, and demographic characteristics. Dummy variables representing each of the states were also included in the stack.

Results are shown in Table 5.3. Let us consider these findings in two parts. First, the impact of the number of crimes committed on arrest probabilities will be considered. It will be shown that, on balance, frequent offenders learn to evade capture more effectively than police learn to arrest them. Second, the effects of all other indicators are considered. A portrait is drawn of those personal and property offenders who are best able to avoid the clutch of the authorities.

Learning and Arrest Probabilities

As demonstrated above, the coefficient on C is a biased estimate of the true impact of learning on the likelihood of arrest. However, the bias may be corrected by dividing by the reliability of the empirical estimate of $\hat{C}$. Thus,

TABLE 5.3
Indicators of Arrest Probability

	Personal	Property
Offense history		
Personal crimes, Window 3	.202	.137
	(.029)	(.029)
Personal crimes, Window 2	.073	
	(.031)	
Property crimes, Window 3		.105
		(.015)
Property crimes, Window 2		.026
		(.016)
Total homicides committed	.170	
	(.070)	
Use of weapon in crimes		−.053
		(.019)
Percentage of income from crime	−.064	.038
	(.022)	(.019)
Total career length-to-date	.106	−.148
	(.032)	(.037)
Criminal record		
N of adult jail/prison terms		.066
		(.023)
N juvenile incarcerations		.061
		(.027)
Committed to drug treatment	−.128	.144
	(.067)	(.059)
Individual characteristics		
Anxiety about arrest	−.110	−.053
	(.034)	(.028)
Percentage of time employed	−.076	
	(.021)	
Salary at legitimate job		.092
		(.032)
In military, Window 3		−.201
		(.103)
Hispanic		−.165
		(.077)
Years of schooling	−.102	
	(.020)	
Intercept	.386	
	(.089)	
R^2	.268	.335
Standard error of estimate	.589	.549

$$B_{AC} = b_{AC}/R^2. \qquad (5.17)$$

(Note that, for convenience, B_A and B_C have been combined.) Then, since B_{AC} represents the proportionate marginal increase in A associated with an increase in C, an equation predicting the probability of arrest may be obtained by dividing both sides by C. So

$$A = B_O \, C^{Bac},$$

and

$$q = A/C = B_O \, C^{Bac-1}. \qquad (5.18)$$

Estimates of B_{AC} are liable to be very sensitive to the value of R^2. So let us estimate the relationship between the probability of arrest and the number of crimes committed for three values of R^2—a lower bound, an upper bound, and a value about halfway between the two. Following Table 5.2, reasonable values of R^2 for property crimes are .15, .25, and .35; for personal crimes, reasonable values are .30, .40, and .50. A case can be made that the true value of R^2 is closer to the upper bound than to the lower, since it seems more reasonable that there are errors or gaps in official records than that certain classes of offenders report consistently biased estimates. Nevertheless, the expected final results of these calculations are that $B_{AC} < 0$, that the offender learning effect will predominate over the police learning effect. Since this is more likely to be true for higher values of R^2, we may think of the lower bound estimates as conservative; they are biased in favor of the null hypothesis that $B_{AC} = 0$.

The resulting equations are shown in Table 5.4; these relationships are shown in graphical form in Figure 5.5. Even assuming the (very conservative) lower bound for the reliability of $\hat{C}$, frequent, experienced offenders run a lower risk of arrest than do infrequent, novice offenders. The decrease is steepest for the first few crimes committed: The risks of arrest decrease swiftly after each of

TABLE 5.4
Estimates of Police and Offender Learning Effects,
Holding All Other Factors Constant

Reliability of C	Personal crimes	Property crimes
Low	$.134 \, C^{-.325}$	$.033 \, C^{-.303}$
Moderate	$.180 \, C^{-.494}$	$.077 \, C^{-.582}$
High	$.215 \, C^{-.595}$	$.111 \, C^{-.701}$

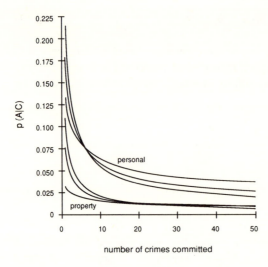

FIGURE 5.5. Offender learning dominates: arrest rates lower for frequent offenders.

the first 10 to 15 personal crimes, and after the first 5 to 10 property crimes; additional crimes committed beyond this number do not seem to contribute substantially to offender learning.

The strength of the relationship is very similar for each crime type—the curves in Figure 5.5 are nearly parallel. Moreover, there is no evidence that the relationships differ among states: Dummy variables representing California and Texas were insignificant predictors of the log of arrests at even a 25-percent significance level.

Throughout this chapter, it has been assumed implicitly that the probability of arrest is influenced by the number of crimes committed. Whether police or offender learning predominates, the learning hypothesis assumes that the chances of arrest change with each additional crime an offender commits. Although this explanation is certain to be at least partially true, it may be that the causal links work in the other direction, as well: An offender's probability of arrest may influence the number of crimes he commits. Two such explanations are particularly important—special deterrence and incapacitation.

Special deterrence is certainly consistent with the findings shown in Table 5.4 and Figure 5.5. Offenders who run into a streak of particularly bad luck or who are arrested for their first few crimes may decide that they are not cut out to be criminals and drop out of the offending population. Or their apparent incompetence may prevent other offenders from wanting to work with them, limiting their opportunities for further activity (Irwin, 1970). Such explanations square nicely with conclusions reached in the last chapter: Young and inexperienced offenders are particularly likely to drop out; offenders who survive the early shakedown period become more experienced and more committed to a life of crime.

The special deterrence interpretation implies a somewhat different set of policies for police action than the learning interpretation. However, the implications for the crime-control effectiveness of selective prosecution and sentencing are the same: Frequent, dangerous offenders are less likely to be linked to each crime they commit; thus an offender's prior arrest record is unlikely to indicate the true extent of his prior criminal activity with much reliability. In addition, present prosecution and sentencing policies are less selective than they appear because they are largely applied to a sample of fairly infrequent offenders.

Incapacitation provides another alternative explanation for these findings but implies a different conclusion for public policy. Offenders who are arrested are sometimes convicted of their crimes and sent to jail or prison. They are physically constrained from both committing more crimes and racking up more arrests, at least for some portion of the remainder of the 2-year window. Thus offenders who are arrested are likely to commit fewer crimes, simply because they average less time on the street. It is easy to see that this could produce a relationship between arrests and crimes that resembles offender learning, even if all offenders ran identical risks.

This would be a serious objection to the estimates obtained here if punishment were more or less swift and certain following an arrest. If that were the case, the relationship between arrest and street time would be strong. But, of course, one of the reasons selective incapacitation is an attractive policy is because the criminal justice system cannot guarantee swift and sure punishment, given present resources. Most arrests do not lead to conviction; many convictions do not lead to imprisonment; many terms of imprisonment are very short; even if the offender is imprisoned, it is often not until 6 months or a year have elapsed since his arrest. All these factors tend to weaken the empirical relationship between arrest and street time, and thus the effects of previous arrests on the number of crimes committed.

A complete description of the arrest/crime relationship would require a separate, simultaneously determined equation; crimes committed would be a function of street time, which would in turn be determined by previous arrests. As it happens, this is a needless complication because the empirical relationship between arrest and street time is too small to measure with the available data. This hardly proves that arrests never lead to incarceration, nor does it show that none of the relationship between arrests made and crimes committed can be attributed to incapacitation. But it does indicate that the size of the incapacitation effect is very small, relative to the net offender learning effect.

A related objection appears at first glance to be more serious. The results of Table 5.4 apply only to offenders in this data set, all of whom were eventually arrested and incarcerated for their crimes. One may argue that all high-rate offenders eventually do some time, as do low-rate "losers" who are repeatedly arrested. But there may be a population of low-rate "winners" who get away with crime repeatedly (if infrequently). We obtain a negative relationship between q and λ because these low-rate winners are missing.

This problem is at least somewhat ameliorated by the sample weights developed in Chapter 2. If a group of offenders stands any reasonable chance of imprisonment, some members of the group will be in the data set, and the weights will account for their underrepresentation. On the other hand, the weights are imperfect. Due to errors in measurement and truncation, they probably do not adjust fully for the lack of infrequent but clever offenders.

Still, this does not matter a bit so long as we (1) can account for the crimes committed by low-rate winners (and anyone else who is not incarcerated), and (2) consider only policies that will not affect the number of low-rate winners who go to jail and prison. As shown in the next chapter, a substantial but predictable number of crimes are committed by people now unlikely to go to prison; these crimes are accounted for in the estimates produced in Chapters 6 and 7. Small increases in prison capacity will not widen the net sufficiently to increase the number of imprisoned winners by much, even if they exist. And, because the selective policies considered in Chapter 7 deal only with offenders already likely to be imprisoned, they will not affect the low-rate winners, either. No doubt the possible existence of this group limits the contribution of these findings to criminological theory, but it does not limit their applicability here.

These findings are admittedly exploratory. When combined with previous results suggesting that frequent offenders are more facile at avoiding arrest, however, there is good reason to believe that they are correct. At least for the population relevant to our purposes, offenders probably do learn more effectively through experience than do the police.

Other Indicators of the Probability of Arrest

The coefficient on $\hat{C}$ and the resulting equations shown in Table 5.4 are useful for identifying the net result of police and offender learning. As shown, offender learning appears to be predominant for both crime types. But these equations do not say much about the size of each of these effects. For example, it may be that police do not learn at all, but that offenders learn at the rates suggested by the equations. On the other hand, it may be that both police and offenders learn a considerable amount about one another's actions, but offenders learn faster or better. To estimate the degree to which each of these two hypotheses is true, let us consider other indicators of learning. These include the offender's criminal history, prior record, and demographic characteristics.

Consider personal offenses first. On the whole, prior record, offense history, and demographics suggest that police are successful in identifying at least certain classes of dangerous offenders. Note, for example, that criminals who commit homicide run higher risks of arrest. Police typically expend far more resources investigating each homicide than they expend investigating each robbery or aggravated assault. Clearance rates for murder are higher as a result. So this may be viewed as a result of police activity. Similarly, criminals who have committed crimes over long careers run higher risks. It may be that robbers and assailants get sloppier as they get older, committing crimes that are more likely to lead to their identification and arrest. But it seems more reasonable to suppose that long-term robbers are identified as career criminals by the police and are scrutinized more closely.

Employment characteristics reinforce the view that both police and offender learning are working in personal crimes. All else equal, the criminals who run the highest risks are those who are chronically unemployed but still derive much of their income from their legitimate job. Such criminals are likely to be conspicuous to police and residents of their neighborhoods as having no visible means of support. But, because they do not receive much money from crime, either, they are also likely to be low-λ, occasional crooks who do not commit crimes often enough to get very good at it. They may be opportunists who choose relatively unlucrative targets, for instance. Or they may support themselves largely by sponging off of friends or relatives. Although there is evidence that unemployed offenders are more dangerous than others (Gottfredson & Gottfredson, 1986), the fact that these characteristics show up even after controlling for the number of crimes committed suggests that police may be making too much of unemployment.

Probably the most intriguing characteristic that influences the frequency of arrest is what might be called "anxiety about arrest." The anxiety measure is a scale derived from factor analysis of offender's attitudes about the consequences of doing crimes. Offenders with high anxiety measures are likely to agree that events like the following are very likely to happen as a result of their doing crimes: going to prison for years; getting injured or killed; and getting arrested. As shown in Table 5.3, personal offenders who say they are very worried about the consequences of their criminal behavior are substantially less likely to be arrested per crime they commit. This suggests that those who work to make themselves hard to catch are successful in their efforts.

The picture is hardly cut-and-dried, but these characteristics do suggest that both offenders and police learn from their experience with personal crimes. The picture is similar with regard to property crimes.

All else equal, generalists (offenders who commit both personal and property crimes) are caught more frequently for their property crimes than are property specialists. It may be difficult to avoid risks efficiently for too many different kinds of crimes at once; or it may be that property offenders who develop special skills at breaking locks and safes or forging checks become comfortable with these crimes and stick with them.

The longer the property offender's career, the less likely he or she is to be caught for each property offense committed. This suggests that there are substantial cumulative effects of experience.

Property offenders who have been caught before are likely to be caught again. The more adult and juvenile jail and prison terms offenders have served, the higher the chances that they will be caught again. Similarly, offenders who have been committed to drug treatment programs are apprehended at high rates. It may be that police (formally or informally) identify property offenders who have already done jail or prison time for property crimes as active property offenders. Or else offenders clumsy enough to have been caught once stay clumsy.

Finally, a few demographic characteristics are associated with the likelihood of arrest as well. However, the indications seem inconsistent and hard to characterize. Offenders who have relatively many years of schooling are arrested at lower rates; perhaps offenders who are smart enough to stay in school are smart enough to outwit the police. Lower probabilities of arrest are also associated with relatively low salaries in legitimate jobs, but relatively small proportions of income from criminal activities. Hispanics are less likely to be caught than blacks or whites, and offenders who are in the military are much less likely to be caught than civilians. It may be that police are relatively indifferent to crimes committed in Hispanic or military communities; more likely, police find it more difficult to gather information about the activities of these offenders. In general, it is difficult to conceive how response biases could have caused such an inconsistent pattern, and each of these effects makes sense on its face. But it is even more difficult to create a consistent portrait of the infrequently caught property offender from this pattern. It is probably wise to take none of these indications too seriously.

With the exception of these demographic characteristics, these indicators all fit our stereotypes as to the offenders who are able to evade the police. They are experienced. They are specialists. They have consistently avoided the police throughout their career. And they are concerned about the consequences of arrest—they are motivated to use their experience to help them commit crimes that are more difficult to solve. These indications reinforce the view that offenders learn through experience, and that the criminal justice system consistently arrests and incapacitates the least dangerous of property offenders.

Implications

Differences among offenders in their risks of arrest would be important, even if these differences had no effect whatever on estimates of the effectiveness of selective incapacitation. Those concerned with the ethics of criminal justice actions will find it simply unfair that some offenders are consistently able to beat the system. For the strictest retributivists, in particular, it is important that all offenders run the same risks of punishment for each crime they commit. The evidence presented above suggests that, under the present system, some offenders are punished systematically more harshly than others who commit crimes of equal severity just as often.

The unfairness of differing arrest risks is exacerbated by the fact that those who run the smallest risks are those who have committed the most crimes. Perhaps one would not much mind a system of differing risks, so long as the risks were randomly distributed; but a system that puts the least frequent and dangerous offenders at the highest risk is unlikely to be preferred by anyone.

These results also suggest that selective action would be more appropriately taken by the police than by judges and parole boards. Better use of official police records, greater use of informants and community watch programs, and better coordination among police agencies may all help police identify who the most dangerous offenders are, and catch them with greater facility. Some specific proposals, and the potential crime reductions that may result from their adoption, are considered in Chapter 7.

As offenders gain experience committing serious crimes, they learn to avoid capture by the police. Police probably learn to identify experienced offenders, as well, but their efforts are overwhelmed by the effects of offender learning. In addition, certain classes of offenders are particularly likely to avoid arrest, no matter what their previous experience. This suggests that police and prosecutor efforts to focus on frequent offenders may be both more effective and more equitable than selective sentencing and parole schemes.

6

Collective Incapacitation

The discussion to this point has focused on characteristics of the criminal population. Questions about rates of offending, offense specialization, likelihood of arrest, and the like have been paramount. All this is intrinsically interesting, and these findings may by themselves suggest lines for further work. The point of learning about the world is to change it, however, and it is to questions of criminal justice effectiveness that we now turn.

The analysis of the effectiveness of incapacitation covers three chapters. In Chapter 6, the results of Chapters 2 through 5 are used to assess the likely crime-control effects of the present criminal justice system. The selectivity of current policies and the expected utility of changes in present levels of imprisonment are considered.

Chapter 7 deals with the nature and effectiveness of selective criminal justice programs. Two kinds of policies and programs are considered: those that aim to increase the likelihood of incarceration and those that aim to increase the length of incarceration for the most frequent and dangerous offenders. The goal is not to make a definitive estimate—the only way to be sure that selective policies work is to try them out. Nevertheless, a reasonable range of estimates may be obtained as to the crime-control effectiveness of various selective policies.

Finally, it is important to recognize that these estimates are incomplete. In Chapter 8, a short account of what has been left out—and an assessment of its importance—is developed. The requirements of a better model, and the probable findings of that model, are also discussed.

First, let us summarize the results of Chapters 2 through 5. Chapter 1 described the considerable uncertainty as to the critical parameters of the adult criminal population. As shown in Table 1.1, the range of previous estimates often spanned one and sometimes two orders of magnitude. Secondary analysis of the Rand 1978 inmate survey, combined with a critical look at other previous studies, has helped to narrow these ranges considerably. Table 6.1 shows a more reasonable range of possible values.

For each critical parameter, Table 6.1 provides three values: a lower bound, an upper bound, and a best guess. Although the range has narrowed considerably from Table 1.1, there is still substantial uncertainty about most of these parame-

TABLE 6.1

Most Reasonable Assumptions about the Adult Criminal Offending Population

Parameter	Range
Lambda (violent)	2.0 to 5.0 violent crimes per year. Best guess is 3.5.
Lambda (property)	9.0 to 15.0 property crimes per year. Best guess is 12.0.
Skew (λ)	Most frequent 10 percent of offenders would commit 50 to 70 percent of crimes if left free to do so. Best guess is 60 percent.
Corr (λ_V, λ_P)	Most offenders are occasional specialists; but most crimes are committed by frequent generalists.
Offending groups	Typical adult offender usually commits crimes alone; average group size 1.2 to 1.6, depending upon the crime type.
Career patterns	Frequent offenders start early, develop; infrequent offenders start late and drop out.
Average career length	6 to 9 years. Best guess is 7.5 years. Longest for property offenders.
Distribution of drop-out rates	Decreasing, then increasing dropout rates over time; careers slightly longer for low- and high-rate offenders.
Pr(arrest)	Experienced offenders learn to evade police; coefficient on crimes committed lies between $-.30$ and $-.70$, with a most reasonable value of $-.50$.

ters. It may be that the typical street offender commits as few as two rapes, robberies, or aggravated assaults per year; it may be he or she commits as many as five. Note that, although 3.5 has been called a "best guess," there is nothing particularly persuasive about this term; 3.5 is simply a reasonable compromise among the remaining values. The other "best guesses" should be viewed with similar caution.

Given this uncertainty, it would obviously be imprudent to claim that additional prison beds or particular selective policies could reduce the crime rate by any particular amount. Instead, it makes more sense to identify a range of possible effects, corresponding to the range of reasonable assumptions that could be made about the criminal population. The extent of this range, and the most likely results within it, are explained in the analysis that follows.

Modeling the Effectiveness of the Present System

As explained in Chapter 2, even a criminal justice system that has implemented no selective policies or programs will be selective in effect. That is, the most frequent and persistent offenders will bear the brunt of the punishment, simply because they put themselves at risk of punishment more often than others. Returning to the language of Chapter 1, the production possibilities frontier is convex, or bowed inward, with respect to the origin. Hypothetical examples of such production possibilities frontiers were provided in Figures 1.3 and 1.4.

There is another reason for expecting the production possibilities frontier to be bowed inward: Some parts of the criminal justice are already consciously selective. The most widely implemented examples are provided by sentencing and parole systems. In all states, individual characteristics of some offenders are taken into account when allocating jail and prison space; in most states, taking these characteristics into account is the norm (Shane-DuBow, Brown, & Olsen, 1985). Many of these procedures are explicitly predictive. Few of the procedures that have been implemented are as far-reaching and sophisticated as current selective sentencing proposals, but they are identical in form.

As shown above, however, the effects of filtering and selective decision making will be offset by other factors. Frequent offenders are less likely to be arrested, per crime committed; many offenders commit crimes in groups, reducing the crime-control benefits of incapacitating any of the group members. But it is not obvious whether these factors are substantial enough to overwhelm the effects of filtering and explicit selectivity.

A second problem does not affect the shape of the production frontier but does affect the current system's position on that frontier. Incapacitation policies only affect adult offenders, and many crimes are committed by juveniles. And, as noted in Chapter 3, some adult offenders commit crimes so infrequently or so intermittently that they run virtually no chance of imprisonment. Thus incapacitation policies—at least given current levels of imprisonment—cannot conceivably prevent all crimes. The effectiveness of any increase in the jail and prison population will thus be limited to a (probably large) fraction of crimes. The size of that fraction is not obvious, however.

The analytical model described in Chapter 1, combined with the results described in Chapters 2 through 5, will help to shed some light on these questions. By explicitly accounting for filtering and explicit selectivity on the one hand, and for such countervailing influences as offender learning and group offending on the other, it may be possible to identify which of these effects is most important. It may also be possible to estimate the proportion of crimes committed by offenders who stand some chance of imprisonment. At least we can expect to identify the range of possible results consistent with the available data.

For purposes of measuring the effectiveness of the present criminal justice system, the only particularly important assumption required is that the system is the same in all jurisdictions. This is clearly wrong: There are substantial differences among jurisdictions in arrest rates (Federal Bureau of Investigation, 1990), conviction rates (Boland, Brady, Tyson, & Bassler, 1983), and incarceration rates (Cohen, 1991). Nevertheless, the only alternative is to produce many different sets of estimates, corresponding to conditions in different local areas. Rather than complicate the analysis still further, a generic criminal justice system was modeled that represents something like a nationwide average.

Other assumptions will be required when the model is extended to measure the effectiveness of changing the criminal justice system. All are one variant or another of one principal assumption: Characteristics of the offending population are unaffected by changes in the justice system. In particular, it must be assumed that there are no special deterrence or rehabilitation, no general deterrence, and no effect of sanctions against adults on the behavior of juvenile offenders. Common sense suggests that deterrence and rehabilitation effects not only exist but are an important reason why the distributions of offense rates, career lengths, and arrest probabilities are as skewed as they appear to be. Unfortunately, researchers have found precise measurements of deterrent and rehabilitation effects to be elusive (Blumstein, Cohen, & Nagin, 1978; Sechrest, White, & Brown, 1979). Rehabilitation and deterrent effects could be accounted for in some version of this model if further information becomes available, however; some thoughts as to what data are needed and how they could be included are considered in the final chapter.

The mathematical model used to estimate the effectiveness of criminal justice policies was developed by Avi-Itzhak and Shinnar (1973). Several adjustments and improvements were made to account for the heterogeneity of offense rates among offenders and for dropout from criminal careers. The most important improvement elaborates on Peter Greenwood's (1982) basic insight that, if the model works for a homogeneous population of offenders, it can be made to work for a heterogeneous population by dividing the population into a number of homogeneous groups and separately estimating incapacitation effects for each group.

This description of the incapacitation model is in three parts. First, methods are developed for using the characteristics of a homogeneous offending population to estimate the incapacitation effects of any given criminal justice system response. Then two enhancements of this basic model are considered: methods of accounting for heterogeneity in the population, and methods of accounting for dropout from offending.

Basic Incapacitation Effects

Conceptually, the basic model is simple. If we know both an individual's offense rate and the average time served per crime committed, then it is possible to estimate the proportion of time that offender spends in jail and prison. If we also know the number of similar offenders currently incarcerated, then it is possible to estimate the number of these offenders who are on the street and the total number of crimes they commit. A variant of this model was used to estimate weights for each participant in the Rand survey, as shown in Chapter 2.

Because the number of crimes committed by these offenders depends entirely on their offense rate and the average sentence served, we can manipulate the total number of crimes committed by changing the average sentence. Although this may in turn affect the offense rate through deterrence or rehabilitation, for the time being let us assume that these effects are unimportant.

Now let us operationalize this logic. Let λ_i be the offense rate per year for offender i. The average sentence that offender i will serve per crime committed can be thought of as a combination of several elements:

- q_{Ai}, the probability that offender i will be arrested, given that he or she has committed a crime.
- q_{Ci}, the probability of conviction, given an arrest.
- q_{Ji}, the probability of incarceration, given a conviction.
- S_i, the average sentence received by offender i, given that he or she has been incarcerated.

If we assume that offenders are only incarcerated after conviction, convicted after arrest, and arrested after committing a crime, then the probability of incarceration given an offense is

$$p(\text{inc} \mid \text{crime}) = q_{Ai} \, q_{Ci} \, q_{Ji}, \tag{6.1}$$

and the expected number of years spent in jail or prison per crime is simply

$$E(S \mid \text{crime}) = S_i \, p(\text{inc} \mid \text{crime}). \tag{6.2}$$

Note that $E(S \mid \text{crime})$ is expressed in terms of years spent in jail or prison per crime. λ_i is expressed in terms of crimes per year spent outside of jail and prison. Thus $\lambda_i \, E(S \mid \text{crime})$ will be expressed in terms of years not free per years free. If we then add one and take the reciprocal, we find that the proportion of time an offender spends free is

$$p(\text{free}) = 1/(1 + \lambda \, q_A \, q_C \, q_J \, S). \tag{6.3}$$

(For convenience, the subscripts have been dropped.) Let us call the probability that an offender will be free at any given time η.

This is not a rigorous derivation. In fact, it hides an assumption basic to the model as it most often has been used: $\lambda \, E(S \mid \text{crime})$ only expresses time not free divided by time free if all the offenders in question would have been active throughout their jail or prison terms. Now suppose some of these offenders would have permanently dropped out of the offending population sometime during that sentence—that is, they would have committed no crimes, even if they had been free to do so. Then the denominator of λ E(S | crime) will remain unchanged, but the numerator (number of years not free) will be systematically overestimated. Thus η will be underestimated. Further, we will systematically overstate the effects of increased punishment. Some ways to adjust for dropout are considered below.

The rest of the basic model follows easily. Suppose N_i is the number of criminals of type i; R_i is the number of i-type offenders who are in jail or prison at any given time. Then

$$R_i = N_i (1 - \eta_i). \tag{6.4}$$

If none of these N_i offenders were ever incapacitated, they would commit

$$C_i' = N_i \lambda_i \tag{6.5}$$

crimes per year. Because they are incapacitated on average $(1 - \eta_i)$ of the time, they will actually commit

$$C_i = N_i (1 - \eta_i) \lambda_i \tag{6.6}$$

crimes per year, and C_i/C_i' will be the proportion of potential crimes that really were committed. The proportion of i-type offenders in jails and prisons will be $1 - \eta_i$.

All this means that we may more or less completely describe the incapacitative effects of the current system of punishment, if we know the components of η for each group of offenders and the proportion of all offenders who are members of the group. Summing over all groups i gives the total number of crimes committed and the total number of jail and prison inmates.

This also means that we can describe the incapacitative effects of any given change from the current system, so long as the change is specified in detail. We need only estimate the following for each group i:

1. The total number of offenders and the potential number of crimes committed, given no incapacitation.
2. The predicted number of jail and prison inmates and crimes committed given the current system.
3. The predicted number of jail and prison inmates and crimes committed under the proposed system.

The results of (1) can be used to calibrate the axes of the basic choice model; (2) will provide the coordinates of the current criminal justice system; and (3) will provide coordinates for the proposed system. If a social preference function were defined in sufficient detail, this would allow us to evaluate whether the proposed system is preferable to 2). Even if the preference function is not well defined, it may be that the proposed system would result in both fewer offenders in jail and prison and at the same time fewer crimes committed, and thus would be preferable no matter what the preference function. In economic terms, the proposed system would *dominate* the current system. (Of course, it is also possible that the proposed system could itself be dominated by current practice.)

There are three important problems with this basic model. One is that the heterogeneity among offenders—the definition of the groups—must be operationalized. Another problem is clear from the preceding paragraph. Unless one strategy dominates another, it will be very difficult to choose among competing proposals. A third was alluded to earlier: Criminals do eventually quit committing crimes, so the estimates of η will be systematically too low. As it happens, all of these problems can be solved with relative ease; the first two problems can even be solved with only one set of adjustments. Let us consider methods for accommodating heterogeneity first.

Adjusting for Heterogeneous Offense Rates

Heterogeneity among offenders is the reason selective programs are implemented in the first place. Because the most important of the variations among offenders is the variation in offense rates, offense rates will be used to define (more or less) homogeneous groups. Although such parameters as arrest probability and career length are related to offense rate, the relationship is not perfect. Thus the members of a group that is homogeneous with respect to offense rate will have a systematically different average arrest probability and career length from other groups, but all the members of the group will not have identical arrest probabilities and career lengths. This makes no practical difference, so long as the effectiveness of the current and proposed selective criminal justice systems depends mostly on the heterogeneity of offense rates. This is almost certainly true and is much less complex than the alternative—defining groups on the basis of two or more dimensions.

As shown in Chapter 3, the greater the variability in offense rates among offenders, the greater the opportunities for crime control through incapacitation. Because high-rate offenders risk jail more often, all else equal they are more likely to be in jail at any given time. The higher their λs relative to the average offender, the greater their relative risks, and the higher the proportion of jail and prison beds these high-rate crooks will fill. Offense rates are continuously distributed among offenders, so the most accurate results would be obtained by using an infinite number of groups. (A model that relies on only one group assumes all offenders are identical and eliminates all variability.) Thus the larger the number of groups used, the larger (and more accurate) estimates of inca-pacitation effects will be.

Although use of many groups may be more accurate, it will also make estimation more time-consuming. But the number can be held to a minimum if groups are defined efficiently. The solution adopted here was to define groups on the basis of their contribution to the total number of crimes committed. That is, i groups were formed by dividing the Lorenz curve for offense rates into i pieces, such that the members of each piece would commit exactly $1/i$ of the crimes if they were never incapacitated. Each group thus contained a different number of offenders, and the groups with the highest offense rates contained the fewest number of offenders. Then it was possible to experiment with the number of groups, to determine the best combination of accuracy and convenience.

This solution was much simplified by the fact that offense rates are (rough-ly) logNormal-distributed among offenders and that the Lorenz curve for a log-Normal distribution is particularly well behaved. The cumulative proportion of offenses that would be committed for any logNormal distribution of offense rates is equal to

$$C = N (N^{-1}(F) - \sigma), \tag{6.7}$$

where F is the cumulative proportion of offenders, N is the logNormal distribu-tion function, N^{-1} is the inverse logNormal distribution function, and σ is the standard deviation of the distribution. Although the logNormal (like the Normal) is completely defined by the mean and standard deviation, the Lorenz curves for all logNormals with the same standard deviation are identical (Aitchison & Brown, 1954).

As a result, given some number of groups, i, it was a simple matter to define the upper and lower limits for each group and the proportion of all adult offenders who are members of each group. Once the high and low bound for each group was established, Simpson's Rule was used to determine the average offense rate for members of each group. The means and skewness estimates shown in Table 6.1 are easily converted to logNormal distribution parameters. If λ_T is the aver-age "true" offense rate, and λ_L and σ_L are the mean and standard deviation of the accompanying logNormal distribution, then

$$\lambda_T = \exp(\lambda_L + .5 \, \sigma_L{}^2). \tag{6.8}$$

From equation (6.7) it is easy to show that

$$\sigma_L = N^{-1}(1 - C') - N^{-1}(F), \tag{6.9}$$

where C' is the number of crimes that would be committed by the worst F offenders, if no one were incapacitated. Consistent with Table 6.1, we set $F = .10$, and the second term of (6.9) reduces to 1.2816.

Experimentation with the number of groups indicated that the results were usually identical to three decimal places for numbers greater than 10 groups. Due to an excess of caution, all of the results described below rely on analysis of 20 groups.

Note that all of this discussion assumes only one, homogeneous crime type. This is patently wrong, but the error makes little practical difference so long as variations in the seriousness-weighted offense rates of different offenders are adequately captured by the standard deviation of the offense rate distribution, and so long as probabilities of incarceration and expected sentences are adjusted appropriately.

These adjustments were made to produce the findings shown below. Parameters for the current criminal justice system were set to a reasonable average of the personal and property values. But as shown in Chapter 3, the skewness of the seriousness-weighted distribution of offense rates for all offenses is somewhat less skewed than the distributions for property or personal crimes alone. (This is because most offenders only commit crimes of one type; the effects of specialization are somewhat offset by the fact that generalists commit all types of crimes at higher rates.) Thus the finding stated in Table 6.1, that no more than 60 percent of seriousness-weighted offenses would be committed by the top 10 percent of index offenders, may be somewhat conservative.

These adjustments will not bias the results, but they will limit the scope of the findings. For example, some have suggested that additional jail and prison beds should be reserved for offenders convicted of particular crime types (robbery and burglary are usually those singled out). This analysis will be unable to estimate the potential effectiveness of such policies. Because providing for more than one crime type would have added considerably to the complexity of the model, however, it seems more reasonable on balance to consider only one crime type.

Defining groups on the basis of offense rates not only solves the problem of heterogeneity, it also solves the problem of comparing among various policies. In Chapter 3 it was shown that the Lorenz curve for offense rates (appropriately adjusted for group offending) is a reasonable estimate of the production possibilities frontier given perfect information. Further, the (roughly) logNormal distribution of offense rates means that only one parameter (and thus only 1 point on the Lorenz curve) is needed to specify the entire frontier. If we are willing to make the (not too heroic) assumption that the production possibilities frontier for imperfect information is likewise a logNormal Lorenz curve, then we may specify the entire frontier given only one point on it. Such a frontier is shown in Figure 6.1.

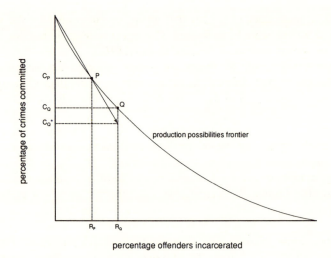

FIGURE 6.1. Resource levels change but selectivity is the same along entire production possibilities frontier.

Now suppose the current criminal justice system is operating at point P—imprisoning an R_P proportion of active offenders and thus preventing a C_P proportion of potential crimes. Unless there is a change in either the criminal population or the selectivity of the criminal justice system, an increase in the number of jail and prison cells to R_Q would move the system down the production frontier to point Q, preventing C_Q crimes. Thus we can estimate the effects of changing resource levels while holding selectivity constant.

Note that if we estimated the marginal effectiveness of changes in the system to be the same as the average effectiveness of the current system (Cavanagh, 1990; Zedlewski, 1987), we would predict that C_Q^* crimes would be prevented. That is, we would presume constant returns to scale as prison resources increased. Because the returns to scale probably decrease—in the limit, if there were only one prison cell it would hold Charles Manson or Sirhan Sirhan—this assumption systematically overstates the benefits of increasing prison resources.

This solves two of the problems inherent in the basic incapacitation model. Let us now consider the third—dropout from offending.

Adjusting for Finite Career Length

Every criminal career ends, sooner or later. Thus we cannot be sure that putting an offender in prison for (say) 2 years will prevent 2 years' worth of

crimes. Had the offender been out on the street, he or she may have quit sometime during that 2-year period, anyway. So a prison sentence will only prevent
crimes for that fraction of the sentence during which the offender would have
been active, had he or she been out on the street. To adjust the Avi-Itzhak and
Shinnar model to reflect finite career length, we must compute this proportion
and take it into account.

In Chapter 4, this proportion was termed θ. Clearly θ will depend upon the
time remaining in the criminal's career and the length of the sentence he or she
receives. θ will be largest for short sentences and long careers; it will be smallest
for long sentences and short careers. In addition, the exact formula for computing θ depends upon the distribution of sentence and career lengths. For example,
θ is calculated differently if all criminal careers are the same length than if some
are much longer than others.

For a group of similar individuals, θ represents the proportion of these
offenders that are expected to still be active upon release from prison. Thus if R_A
refers to the number of imprisoned offenders who will still be active, and R_T
represents the total number imprisoned, then

$$R_A = R_T \, \theta. \tag{6.10}$$

This means that we can adjust the number of crimes not committed due to
incarceration of members of this group, even though we do not know which
members we may safely let out and which we dare not.

Because some of the offenders in jails and prisons are no longer members of
the offending population, θ also influences our best estimates of the fraction of
active offenders who are on the street at any one time. Shinnar and Shinnar
(1975) showed that this fraction is

$$\eta = 1/(1 + \lambda \, q \, S \, \theta), \tag{6.11}$$

where q now refers to the probability of incarceration given a crime. Since η
represents the fraction of active offenders only, we must also change our calculation of N, the total number of offenders in this group, so that it reflects only those
offenders in jail and prison who are active. That is,

$$N = R_A/(1 - \eta). \tag{6.12}$$

Given these modifications to the formulas presented above, it is possible to
calculate the proportion of once-active and now-active group members who are
in jail and prison. If we also have some measure of the total number of offenders
in the group—R_T, R_A, or N—we can compute the other measures of group size,
the number of crimes committed by group members, and the number of crimes

they would have committed had all of them been free to do so. So this is all that is needed to estimate the incapacitative effects of punishment for offenders of this type.

Avi-Itzhak and Shinnar (1973) showed that, for exponential-distributed careers with mean $\overline{T}$ and exponential-distributed jail and prison sentences with mean S,

$$\theta = \overline{T}/(S + \overline{T}). \tag{6.13}$$

So only S and $\overline{T}$ are needed to calculate θ. The analysis of Chapter 4 suggests that T is roughly mixed-Weibull-distributed, rather than exponential-distributed, so equation (6.13) is not strictly correct. To examine the practical significance of these deviations from the exponential, a mathematical experiment was conducted.

Several thousand mixed-Weibull-distributed offender careers were simulated with varying S and $\overline{T}$, and θ was measured for each. Then regression was used to fit the function

$$\theta = \alpha_T S^{\beta_t} \, T/(S + T), \tag{6.14}$$

where $\alpha_T S^{\beta_t}$ represents a correction factor applied to equation (6.13). Note that, for $\alpha_T = 1$ and $\beta_T = 0$, equation (6.14) reduces to (6.13). Parameter estimates and standard errors for α_T and β_T were $\alpha_T = .93919 \pm .00576$ and $\beta_T = -.04201 \pm .00291$. Although the differences are small, α_T and β_T are significantly different from 1 and 0. The regression explained 97.2 percent of the variance in θ and was significant at $p \ll .001$. So it characterizes the simulation results quite well.

A second finding of Chapter 4 was that low- and high-rate offenders appear to commit crimes over careers that are significantly longer than moderate-rate offenders. A close examination of Table 4.6 suggests that the relationship between offense rate and career length might be quadratic—that is, it might increase as the square of the deviation from the middle value. One convenient way of characterizing this finding was to regress the logarithm of mean residual career length against the square of the (logarithm of) offense rate Z-score, using the data shown on Table 4.6. That is, coefficients were estimated for the equation,

$$\log T = \alpha_L + \beta_L \, Z^2. \tag{6.15}$$

The intercept term defines the expected value of T for the median offender; it will clearly depend upon the average value of T for all offenders, which is a separate variable. So the only parameter needed to define the size of this relationship is β_L; if there were no correlation between offense rate and career length, β_L would be zero.

Three regressions were run, resulting in the following values for β_L:

- Personal crimes: $\beta_L = .13924 \pm .02314$.
- Property crimes: $\beta_L = .20442 \pm .03986$.
- All index crimes: $\beta_L = .17183 \pm .03407$.

Despite the absurdly small sample sizes, all coefficients were significant at $p < .05$; the coefficient for all index crimes was significant at $p < .001$. R^2 was above .90 for both the personal and the property crimes samples. So these coefficients characterize the results of Table 4.6 rather well. Given the speculative nature of these findings, it seems reasonable to consider three potential values for β_L: an upper bound of 0.20, a best guess of 0.10, and a lower bound of zero. For each distribution of offense rates, α_L was determined through an iterative process that ensured the proper value of $\overline{T}$ averaged over all offenders. Because the adjustment for bathtub-shaped hazard functions requires that $\overline{T}$ be known for each group of offenders, the adjustment for offense-rate-dependence was made first.

Current Criminal Justice System

Parameters and estimation algorithms were necessary for two elements of the current criminal justice system: the risks of incarceration per crime committed, and the probable sentence, given incarceration.

As described above, the likelihood of incarceration can be thought of as the product of the probabilities of arrest given a crime, conviction given arrest, and incarceration given conviction. Average values of the q_A, the probability of arrest given a crime, were presented in Chapter 5. Recent data from 12 states on the risks of conviction and incarceration are shown in Table 6.2. Because the model developed here aggregates over all index crimes, a weighted average was used for each probability. Combining the results of Chapter 5 with those of Table 6.2 produces three reasonable values for the average risks of incarceration per crime: a lower bound of .010; an upper bound of .015; and a best guess of .0125. In all further analysis the best guess is weighted as twice as likely as either the upper or the lower bound.

As shown in Chapter 2, limited empirical evidence suggests that the probabilities of conviction and incarceration are unrelated to the offense rate in most jurisdictions. As shown in Chapter 5, however, there is good reason to believe that arrest probabilities vary systematically with offense rate: The average high-rate offender stands a lower risk of arrest, per crime committed, than the average low- and moderate-rate offender. This relationship may be described by the equation

$$q_A = \alpha_Q \, C^{\beta q}, \tag{6.16}$$

TABLE 6.2
Nationwide Estimates of Criminal Justice System Characteristics

	Arrests	Probability of convictions	Probability of incarceration	Expected time served
Personal crimes	138,011	.498	.680	2.478
Robbery	40,943	.540	.800	1.975
Assault	66,455	.462	.560	0.964
Other	30,613	.519	.744	5.431
Property crimes	190,133	.623	.660	.744
Burglary	66,379	.713	.780	.927
Larceny	47,911	.659	.590	.558
Auto theft	20,838	.466	.780	.489
Fraud	24,853	.611	.530	.624
Other	30,152	.534	.598	.504
All crimes	328,144	.570	.667	1.393

Sources. Columns 1–3: Perez (1990). Column 4: Langan & Dawson (1990).

where C represents the number of crimes committed within the last 2 years, and the coefficient β_Q lies between $-.30$ and $-.70$. Simplifying slightly, we may substitute λ, the current offense rate, for C in the same equation and achieve almost identical results. And, because the probability of incarceration is simply the probability of arrest multiplied by a constant, we may choose whatever value of α_Q we need to reconcile equation (6.16) with the appropriate value of β_Q and the average q_A. Again, given q_A and β_Q, α_Q was determined according to an iterative process that maintained the proper value of q_A when averaged over all crimes committed.

Estimates for the probability and expected length of jail and prison sentences served given incarceration are also provided in Table 6.2. The nationwide average is 1.4 years per index incarceration, identical to Greenwood's (1982) estimate from California records. This figure also squares reasonably well with the estimates presented in Chapter 2, suggesting that jail and prison sentences are about the same today as they were in the late 1970s (Langan & Dawson, 1990).

Sentencing practices in many states are now explicitly selective; Greenwood's California sentencing data suggested that convicted frequent offenders served longer terms than others, primarily because they were more likely to be sent to prison than to jail. This suggests that the relationship between sentence length and offense rate could be well characterized by an equation similar in form to (6.16); that is,

$$E(S|\lambda) = \alpha_S \, S^{\beta_S}, \tag{6.17}$$

where again α_S represents an intercept that may vary depending upon the distribution of offense rates among offenders. On the other hand, regression on the Rand data (described in Chapter 2) shows that β_S is insignificantly different from zero for most crime types, and selective practices in most states appear to focus on persistent offenders rather than frequent offenders (McDonald, 1985). In the analysis that follows, several values of β_S were tried, ranging from zero to .30. The principal results were unchanged throughout the range, so β_S was assumed to be zero to maintain consistency with the Rand data.

Limitations of the Effectiveness of Incapacitation

With this model and the available data, it is not difficult to estimate the probable effects of marginal increases in the number of jail and prison beds—the benefits of collective incapacitation. First, however, it is important to consider an important limitation on the usefulness of these strategies: Many crimes are committed by people we cannot reasonably expect to incapacitate.

The clearest example is juvenile crime. With very few exceptions, the juvenile and adult corrections systems are entirely separate. Although some juveniles are treated as adults by the courts and eligible for sentencing to (adult) jails and prisons, they amount to only 0.6 percent of all juvenile cases processed (Snyder, 1989). It may be that juvenile crime can be prevented through incapacitation strategies, but it will not be prevented by increasing the number of adult jail and prison beds, or reallocating the use of these beds.

This puts a serious limitation on the utility of adult incapacitation. About 27 percent of arrests for serious crimes are of juveniles (FBI, 1990). The number of crimes committed by these offenders is probably somewhat less: Juveniles tend to commit crimes in larger groups (more offenders to be caught per crime); and they are probably more likely to get caught (less experienced offenders run higher risks). Nevertheless, even supposing that juvenile groups are 50-percent larger than adult groups and that the average juvenile offender runs 50-percent higher risks than the average adult, 17.1 percent of crimes are committed by juvenile offenders.

Victimization records confirm these figures: 18.4 percent of violent victimizations reported in 1989 were committed by juveniles or predominantly juvenile groups (Bureau of Justice Statistics, 1991a). Because adults are somewhat more likely to commit violent crimes than juveniles, this probably understates the proportion of all crimes committed by juveniles. Given all the evidence, 20 percent would be a reasonably good guess as to the true proportion.

Of the remaining 80 percent of crimes, some are committed by adults who cannot be incapacitated. Before offenders can be incarcerated, they must be identified, arrested, and convicted. An offender may commit crimes for years, suffer several arrests, and—through cleverness or good luck—never be convicted. Infrequent and impersistent offenders may never even be arrested. Extrapolating from the results of Chapter 3, we would expect that there are many more low-rate offenders than moderate- and high-rate ones in the total population of adult offenders. If their number is large enough, it is conceivable that most crimes are committed by people who are never convicted.

Such objections have been made before (Gottfredson & Hirschi, 1990), but it is difficult to know how seriously to take them without additional data. Specifically, what proportion of adult criminals are arrested, convicted, and incarcerated? What proportion of crimes are committed by those who are never arrested, convicted, or (currently) incarcerated?

Estimating the Limits of Adult Incapacitation

Any answers are bound to be speculative, but the Avi-Itzhak and Shinnar model can be used to estimate the size of these limitations. Three principal assumptions are needed.

First, it is most convenient to assume that the criminal justice system in every state incarcerates the same proportion of arrestees for about the same length of time. (That is, q_{Ci} and q_{Ji} are everywhere the same.) This is clearly not true, but use of a nationwide average will at least show the magnitude of the problem.

Second, the model is much simpler if we are willing to assume that all crimes are alike, and that an individual's probability of arrest does not change from one crime to the next (although it may differ among individuals). These are probably reasonable simplifications. But if low-rate offenders are especially likely to commit serious crimes that are very likely to result in incarceration (homicide, for example), this may cause the model to overstate the proportion who never get caught, convicted, and jailed. If low-λ offenders tend to commit minor crimes (shoplifting, joyriding), we may understate the proportion.

Finally, we need to assume that the total adult offending population is like the "street-offender" population in many respects. The distribution of offense rates is very skewed; the average criminal "career" (such as it is) lasts several years; probabilities of arrest are related to offense rates in about the same way as they are for street offenders, and so on. Although none of these assumptions are likely to be quite correct, they seem reasonable enough. Note that the only assumption we need make about the distribution of offense rates—the most critical parameter of the offending population—is that it may be reasonably approximated by a logNormal distribution with unknown mean and standard deviation. Given the results of Chapter 3, this seems close enough for a rough cut.

If we are willing to make these assumptions, we can reconstruct what the total adult offending population must look like, if it is to be consistent with official records. Arrest distributions for juvenile offenders (that is, the number of juveniles with one arrest, two arrests, and so on) have been available since the cohort studies of the early 1970s, and some were provided in Figure 3.1 of Chapter 3. More recently, an arrest distribution for adults has been derived from California records (Tillman, 1987).

It is easy to show that adult arrest distributions are inconsistent with a homogeneous offending population. There are too many offenders with many arrests, and these offenders must commit crimes at higher rates than others. To account for this, we may specify plausible estimates of the mean and standard deviation of a logNormal distribution of offense rates for the entire offending population. Given the distribution of offense rates, the arrest probabilities for offenders with different rates (q_A), and the proportion of time that each offender spends in jail or prison (η), we may estimate the number of offenders with no arrests, one arrest, two, and so on, if the mean and standard deviation are correct. Some means and standard deviations will fit the arrest distribution better than others. The distribution that fits best is most likely to be correct. In practice, we may use mean absolute percent error (MAPE) as an indicator of fit (Blumstein & Graddy, 1982).

Given the distribution of offense rates for a population that includes all criminal offenders, we can then work our way forward to estimate the proportion of offenders that are arrested, convicted, and incarcerated; we can also estimate the proportion of crimes committed by each of these offenders. Finally, we can estimate the average offense rate for each group of offenders. This will help to reconcile the disparate estimates of λ found in Chapter 3.

There is no way to validate these calculations directly, but we can compare other model predictions to published figures derived from other sources. For example, parameters of the total offending population are manipulated to match published arrest records, so the model should track the prevalence of arrest among adults quite closely; if it also matches self-reports of the prevalence of offending and published records of the prevalence of incarceration, however, we may reasonably believe that the model is accurately predicting similar characteristics that cannot be independently validated.

Filtering Estimates

Experiments with a wide variety of criminal population characteristics showed that three factors are the primary predictors of the proportion of offenders and offenses that filter through to each stage of the system:

1. The length of the criminal career ($\overline{T}$, assumed to be between 6 and 9 years, with a best guess of 7.5 years).

2. The relationship between career length and offense rate ($0 < \beta_L < 0.2$, with a best guess of 0.1).
3. The distribution of career lengths among offenders with similar offense rates ($0 > \beta_T > -.04$).

The average probability of arrest and the relationship between arrest probabilities and offense rates were relatively unimportant predictors. In all cases, the model fit the arrest distribution data reasonably well; MAPE averaged 10.5 percent.

To get a better handle on the range of possible solutions, a more formal experiment was conducted. Three values each of $\overline{T}$ and β_L and two values of β_T were chosen; "best-guess" values were weighted twice as heavily as outside range values. (The mixed-Weibull and exponential assumptions were assumed to be equally likely for purposes of this analysis.) For maximum resolution, a full-factorial design ($3 \times 3 \times 2 = 18$ cases) was chosen.

The results, shown in Table 6.3, suggest that a relatively small proportion of offenders are filtered through to incarceration. Fewer than half of the offenders were ever arrested; only one-third are ever convicted, and one-fourth are ever incarcerated. On the other hand, those who do filter through are by and large the most frequent and persistent: Offenders who are incarcerated account for 58 to 68 percent of all crimes committed by adults; only 8 to 17 percent of crimes are committed by the majority of people who never get caught. If these results are correct, most criminals commit a few offenses and quit before they are found out.

Note that this does not mean the current system prevents 58 to 68 percent of adult crimes. Many of those incarcerated are only in jail or prison for a short

TABLE 6.3
Current System Filters Out Most Offenders, Especially Low-Rate Offenders

Offending group	Percentage of offenders	Percentage of crimes	Average λ	Expected λ
All offenders	100.000%	100.00%	9.712 (1.566)	na[a]
Ever arrested	47.193 (0.688)	87.226 (3.477)	18.739 (2.890)	4 to 11
Ever convicted	32.668 (0.432)	74.938 (3.718)	24.302 (3.603)	na
Ever incarcerated	24.027 (0.264)	62.851 (3.854)	28.581 (4.121)	33 to 59
Incoming cohort	5.509 (0.734)		53.615 (4.490)	32 to 68
In prison	9.494 (1.066)		65.360 (5.961)	60 to 70

[a]na = not available.

part of their careers, so the proportion of adult crimes prevented is bound to be lower.

Speculative as these results are, they square well with independent assessments of the degree of filtering obtained from different data sets. For example, in California, about 16 percent of all adult males are arrested for an index crime (Tillman, 1987). Similar estimates were obtained from samples in Philadelphia and Washington, DC (Blumstein & Graddy, 1982). Combined with the results of Table 6.3, this suggests that about 35 percent of adult men commit crimes at some point, and about 8 percent go to jail or prison. These coincide closely with published figures of the prevalence of crime among adults (Visher & Roth, 1986) and the prevalence of imprisonment (Langan, 1985). In addition, the model predicts that each year's incoming cohort should be about half the size of the current jail and prison population, which is approximately correct (Beck, 1991; Bureau of Justice Statistics, 1991b). Thus the proportion of offenders who graduate to each stage seems to be about right.

The experimental results are also consistent with the number of crimes reported each year. In 1989, 450,564 adults were sentenced to jail or prison (Beck, 1991; Bureau of Justice Statistics, 1991b); if this really represents 5.5 percent of active adult offenders, then 8.2 million adults were responsible for 80 percent of the index crimes reported to police that year. For the 7.7 million who were free to commit crimes, the average index offense rate must be about 5.8; assuming further a reporting rate of 36.8 percent (Bureau of Justice Statistics, 1991a) and an average adult criminal group size of 1.45, this represents 11.4 million reported index offenses. In fact, 14.2 million offenses were reported to the police (FBI, 1990), and 80 percent of this is 11.4 million. So the results are remarkably close.

There is less information about the proportion of offenses committed by each group of offenders, but what information is available fits the experimental findings rather well. Offense rate estimates from Chapter 3, shown in the right-hand column of Table 6.3, are close to the figures predicted by the model. Estimates of λ for arrestee, incoming cohort, and in-prison samples are very close; the only estimate available for the ever-incarcerated group is the weighted Rand survey, which is higher than the experimental figures. This suggests that "active street offenders" (the group the weights were designed to mimic) resemble the group of offenders who were incarcerated at some point in their careers, but that the weighted sample underrepresents minor offenders who were unlikely to be incarcerated. More direct evidence bears this out: The average (unadjusted) weight for the Rand survey was 3.272, suggesting that the average respondent represented about 2.3 street offenders who were not in jail or prison; if "active street offenders" were equivalent to "ever-incarcerated offenders," this experiment suggests that the average weight should be 24.027/5.509, or about 4.4. As suggested in Chapter 2, much of the difference may be due to errors and limits placed on the weights; on balance, the two groups are remarkably similar.

When juvenile crimes are accounted for, we find that the Rand survey (and other surveys of jail and prison inmates) excludes the 82 percent of offenders who are either juveniles or are never sentenced to imprisonment during their careers. Further, about 50 percent of all crimes are committed by people too young, infrequent, or impersistent to be incarcerated. So the bulk of the information presented in Chapters 3 through 5 applies only to a fraction of the criminal population.

On the other hand, this is by far the most important fraction, particularly for estimating incapacitation effects. Taken together, these results suggest that we may take the Rand figures more or less at face value when estimating incapacitation benefits, so long as we are careful to adjust for the offenders who are never incarcerated and the offenses they commit. This will produce reasonable estimates of the effectiveness of current system. Estimates of the effects of marginal increases in the number of jail and prison beds will also be reasonable, because a marginal change would not widen the net of imprisonment sufficiently to include many offenders who are not now incapacitated. Larger increases would widen the net, however, and the additional offenders will be for the most part less frequent and serious than those now jailed. Thus incapacitating them would provide lower benefits than expected, and we would systematically overestimate the effectiveness of large increases in jail and prison capacity.

With these adjustments and caveats, let us look more closely at the effectiveness of the current system.

Effectiveness of the Current System

To get accurate estimates of the effectiveness of collective incapacitation, the focus of the mathematical model was restricted to the ever-incarcerated population. Results from the previous section were then used to extend the analysis to all crimes and all criminals. Combining the two analyses produces more accurate results, for two reasons:

- By focusing on a smaller population, the incapacitation analysis more precisely models the effects of heterogeneity in the ever-incarcerated population.
- Since parameters of the offending population have been developed primarily from a survey of ever-incarcerated offenders, this avoids extending (most of) the results to a population for which they may not be appropriate.

Some of the parameters described in Table 6.1 were likely to have a large effect on the final results—the mean value of λ or the skewness of the λ distribution. The importance of the others was not so obvious. To get a feel for the importance of each parameter—and to see whether some parameters could be eliminated from further consideration—each was plugged into the model, one at a time. Deviations of T from the exponential had little impact on estimates of the effectiveness of the current system, but each of the seven remaining parameters were sufficiently important to merit further scrutiny.

To further test these seven parameters, a formal experimental design—the 7-factor Box-Behnken design—was chosen (Box & Behnken, 1960). This design is much more efficient than a full factorial design and has the advantage of being equally precise at all points surrounding the most likely estimate (Mason et al., 1989). Sixty-two separate experiments were conducted at various levels of the seven parameters. As is usual in such designs, the central point (the case representing the "best-guess" value of each parameter) was given a weight of 6.0 to represent its greater likelihood of fitting reality.

Results are shown in Figure 6.2. To make the results easier to read, curves have been drawn to show the envelope of possible locations of the current system. If the model's assumptions are met, the present criminal justice system is about 50 percent likely to be acting within the innermost (dark gray) ellipse; it is about 90 percent likely to be acting within the outer (light gray) ellipse. As shown, the present system is preventing about 21 percent of potential crimes by incarcerating about 8 percent of the active offenders. There is considerable uncertainty as to the exact point, but it is very unlikely that the present system is preventing fewer than 15 percent or more than 28 percent of potential crimes; it is

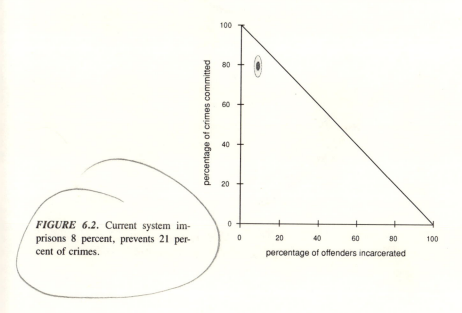

FIGURE 6.2. Current system imprisons 8 percent, prevents 21 percent of crimes.

equally unlikely that fewer than 6 or more than 12 percent of offenders are in adult jails or prisons at any given time.

Selectivity of the Current System

These results are consistent with the notion that the current system is selective in its effects; that is, they all lie on an inward-sloping, rather than an outward-sloping production frontier. This is illustrated by the production frontiers of Figure 6.3. The model suggests that the production possibilities frontier available to the typical state or local criminal justice system is about 50 percent likely to be in the dark, shaded area; it is about 90 percent likely to be in the light, shaded area. So it is almost certain that filtering and explicitly selective procedures bow the production frontier slightly inwards.

Statistical analysis of these results confirms that the selectivity of the current system depends crucially on parameters of the offending population. Selectivity is measured by the standard deviation of the logNormal Lorenz curve that describes the production possibilities frontier; positive values mean positive selectivity, or an inward-sloping frontier (Aitchison & Brown, 1954). As shown in the left-hand column of Table 6.4, three factors in particular influence selectivity: the skewness of the offense rate distribution, the size of the average adult offending group, and the relationship between offender experience and ability to evade arrest (β_Q). (For convenience, all independent variables were coded in the same way: the most likely value was coded as a "0"; low values were coded as "-1" and high values as "$+1$." So the regression coefficients for each parameter are directly comparable with one another.) The more skewed the distribution of λ,

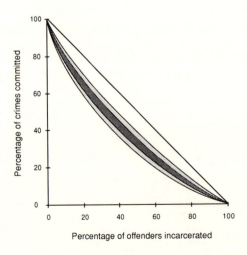

FIGURE 6.3. Worst offenders most likely to filter through the current system.

TABLE 6.4
Indicators of Selectivity and Elasticity
for the Current System

Descriptive statistics	Selectivity	Elasticity
Mean	0.6803	0.1557
Standard deviation	0.1062	0.0229
Kolmogorov–Smirnov Z	0.506	0.781

Regression coefficients		
Mean λ	−.00078	.02138
Standard deviation λ	.10985	.00829
Group size	−.07578	−.01418
Mean T	.02786	.01086
$r(\lambda, T) = \beta_L$	.04448	.00634
Mean q	−.00075	.01968
$r(\lambda, q) = \beta_Q$	−.08802	−.00680
Standard error (coefficients)	.00249	.00050
Standard error (estimate)	.01218	.00245
R^2	.98834	.98987

Note. Regression coefficients are shown for each independent variable. Due to the experimental design selected, all coefficients in each regression have the same standard error. Kolmogorov–Smirnov Z tests hypothesis that dependent variables are Normal-distributed.

the fewer offenders who participate in the typical crime, and the smaller the offender learning effects, the more selective the current system is likely to be.

One consequence of the selectivity of current criminal justice system practices is that collective incapacitation policies begin to look a bit better. Most past estimates of the effectiveness of collective incapacitation (e.g., Cohen, 1978) have assumed that the current system is neither positively nor negatively selective—that the production frontier is bowed neither in nor out. If the frontier is in fact bowed in, then the current system has already reduced crime by a larger amount than an unselective system would have by (wittingly or not) putting the most frequent and dangerous offenders behind bars. Unless a very large proportion of criminals are in jail or prison at any given time, marginal increases in capacity will continue to focus on worse-than-average offenders. In general, the more selective the current system, the fewer additional jail and prison cells will be needed to reduce crime.

Although small changes are more likely to be very effective, for a selective system the marginal returns will diminish as the changes grow larger. That is, increases in jail and prison space will move us further down the production frontier (see Figure 6.1, above); the further down the frontier we move, the flatter the curve becomes, and the smaller will be the resulting change in crime rates. Additional jail and prison cells may, of course, be used more selectively than they are now. For example, we may increase the average sentence served but hold steady the probability of incarceration given a crime (Cavanagh, 1990). But this represents a marked change from current practice. The prospects for crime reduction through increases in selectivity are considered in the next chapter.

Elasticity of Crime

Given a selective production frontier and a current state, it is easy to determine the effect of a marginal increase in jail and prison beds on the crime rate. The percentage reduction in crime that would result from a 1-percent increase in jail and prison space may be defined as the *elasticity* of crime with respect to incapacitative effort (Cohen, 1978). The higher the elasticity, the more effective additional jails and prisons will be in cutting crime.

As shown in the right-hand column of Table 6.4, the information available is sufficient to bound elasticity estimates within a fairly narrow range. We can be 90 percent confident that the true value is between 0.12 and 0.20, with a best, single guess of 0.16. As expected, these figures are much higher than previous estimates that do not account for heterogeneity of offending. For example, Blumstein et al. (1986, pp. 148–149) assumed a uniform offense rate of 10.0 and estimated a nationwide median elasticity of .053. These figures are also much lower than estimates that take the Rand survey data at essentially face value; Zedlewski (1987) implicitly assumes an elasticity of about 3.34.

Selectivity is only one factor influencing the elasticity of crime with respect to imprisonment. The other is scale: If the present system is incarcerating a large proportion of active offenders, then a 1-percent increase in imprisonment will clearly have a larger impact on the number of crimes committed. As described above, estimates of the proportion of offenders incarcerated cover a wide range; estimates depend upon average offense rate, skewness, and other parameters of the criminal population.

Indicators of elasticity are shown in the right-hand column of Table 6.4. The most important indicators are average λ, the size of the average offending group, the length of the average criminal career, and the average probability of arrest. Collective incapacitation policies are particularly effective when the average offense rate and arrest probability are high; these are the conditions under which many offenders will be in jail and prison. Little jail and prison space is wasted on no-longer dangerous offenders when the average criminal career is long. And incapacitation is least effective when many offenders work in groups, because all members must be incapacitated before we can be sure to stop the group's activities.

If additional information became available as to the size of these parameters, it would be possible to reduce our uncertainty as to the true effectiveness of collective incapacitation policies. These results suggest that further research focusing on the λ distribution, the average probability of arrest, and the frequency of multiple offending by different kinds of offenders, would be most helpful.

Costs and Benefits of Prison Expansion

Whether we should increase the number of jails and prisons by 1 percent, or by any amount, depends vitally on the costs of prison expansion and the benefits of crime reduction. The direct costs and benefits are reasonably objective and easily measureable, but a reduction in the crime rate would bring with it uncertain indirect benefits. One way to account for our uncertainty is to measure the direct costs and benefits and then determine the sensitivity of the final result to reasonable values of the indirect benefits.

Costs of Crime Reduction

The costs of building and operating these cells are straightforward enough. Cavanagh (1990) estimates the annualized cost of building a prison cell to be about $4,500, and the annual operating costs to be about $20,000. The costs differ greatly from state to state. For example, daily operating costs per cell range from $22 in Arkansas to $69 in Alaska. Although some of the disparity is due to differences in accounting for administrative costs (Cory & Gettinger, 1984), it is nearly certain that the costs of jail and prison expansion are much higher in some states than in others. To avoid needless complexity, let us continue to consider the nationwide average.

The newly incarcerated inmates and their dependents will also incur costs. According to a 1989 survey of prison inmates, most inmates worked full time at low-paying jobs before they were incarcerated (Bureau of Justice Statistics, 1991b). Cavanagh (1990) estimates the cost of lost employment to be about $9,000 per inmate per year, which fits the prison survey data fairly well. Welfare payments to dependents of inmates amount to about $8,400 (Cavanagh, 1990), but because welfare payments may be largely a result of lost employment, some of this double-counts the true economic costs. In addition, dependents incur costs of visiting and telephoning their relatives in prison and pain and suffering associated with temporary loss of their loved ones (offset in some cases by the family's share in the culpability for the inmate's crimes, or their own victimization at the inmate's hands). Inmates doubtless consider their own pain and suffering to be important factors, and they probably run higher risks of victimization themselves while in prison than when they are free. Any criminogenic effects of crime— either on the inmates themselves or on their families and friends—will also increase the costs of imprisonment. On the other hand, one may reasonably argue that inmates' costs are offset by their guilt and by the potential benefits of rehabilitation while in prison. Many of these costs to inmates and their families are difficult to quantify, but we can be fairly certain that they are at least $9,000 per year and may be several times higher.

These costs total to a minimum of $33,500 per inmate per year. A more realistic estimate is $40,000 (Cavanagh, 1990). Higher values are not unreasonable, but they are without a firm research basis.

Benefits of Crime Reduction

The costs of crime—and thus the benefits of crime reduction—are of two kinds (Conklin, 1975):

- Direct costs to potential victims, in terms of monetary expenses, pain and suffering, and risks of death foregone by preventing these crimes.
- Indirect costs, such as increased insurance and prevention expenses, increased avoidance and anxiety, and (more generally) reduced quality of life.

If a given crime is somehow prevented, the direct costs to the victims of that crime will clearly be saved. It is less certain that any indirect costs will be saved, but if so they are probably larger than the direct cost savings.

The measurement of direct costs is fairly straightforward. Property damages and losses, medical expenses, time lost from work, and so on can be obtained from victimization surveys. Juries award damages to persons suffering psychic and physical injuries in civil cases, and those awards can be extended to crime victims when the injuries are similar. And the risks of death from crimes of each type are known from official homicide records. Cohen (1988) estimated these costs for a variety of crime types. His results (for consistency, expressed in 1989 dollars) are shown in Table 6.5. Note that the average crime costs the victim (or the survivors) about $1,275.

The indirect costs of crime are larger than the direct costs to victims. The amount of money spent on crime prevention devices and insurance, and the economic and social value lost due to avoidance and anxiety, dramatically outweigh the direct costs of crime (Conklin, 1975). Nevertheless, it is not at all clear whether the indirect benefits of a reduction in crime would be greater than or less than the direct benefits, because so many factors affect indirect costs. For example, recent victims believe there is more crime in their neighborhood and that they are more vulnerable than nonvictims; they are also less likely to go out at night, more likely to buy burglar alarms, dogs, and guns, and more likely to ask their neighbor to watch their house when they leave town (Spelman, 1983). And

TABLE 6.5
The Average Crime Costs the Victim over $1,000[a]

Crime	Number of offenses	Monetary losses	Pain and suffering	Risk of death	Total
Robbery	1,012,830	$1,270	$8,503	$4,584	$14,357
Assault	1,752,683	481	5,610	7,621	13,712
Burglary	6,248,856	1,070	361	132	1,564
Larceny	29,157,193	201	0	2	203
Auto theft	2,137,705	3,499	0	66	3,565
Forgery/fraud	11,898,769	201	0	0	201
Total	50,418,513	$ 487	$ 411	$ 377	$ 1,275

Source. Column 1: Bureau of Justice Statistics, 1990. Columns 2–4: Cohen, 1988, p. 546.
[a]All costs expressed in 1989 dollars.

vicarious victimization—from crime descriptions provided by friends and relatives—can create indirect costs, as well (Skogan & Maxfield, 1981). So preventing crimes will help to prevent these second-order costs to victims and the people around them.

But people are not victimized often enough to judge their risks accurately on the basis of personal or even vicarious experiences. Instead, they must rely on highly visible (but possibly erroneous) indicators, or "incivilities." Trash on the streets, abandoned buildings and uncaring landlords, and noisy neighbors are reliable predictors of avoidance, prevention, insurance, and anxiety (DuBow, McCabe, & Kaplan, 1979; Taub, Taylor, & Dunham, 1984). Although some studies have found relationships between neighborhood crime rates and indirect costs as measured by housing prices (Hellman & Naroff, 1979; Thaler, 1978), none of them controlled for incivilities. When incivilities are controlled for, the relationship between crime rates and indirect costs disappears (e.g., Spelman, 1983). On the other hand, activities that reduce incivilities directly, such as some problem-oriented and community policing projects (Goldstein, 1990; Greene & Mastrofski, 1988), appear to reduce indirect costs even when they do not affect the crime rate at all.

This is not to say that there would be no indirect benefits to a reduction in crime, or even that they are not two, three, or more times larger than the direct benefits. In addition, there are numerous collateral costs of crime avoidance and prevention unlikely to show up in housing prices and burglar alarm sales figures: reduced social interaction and solidarity, reduced interpersonal trust, and ultimately the distintegration of any sense of community (Conklin, 1975; Wilson & Kelling, 1982). These costs are speculative and difficult to quantify, but they may be very real if perceptions of crime increase. But increases in interaction and trust—like reductions in avoidance and prevention—will only materialize if perceptions of crime drop, and this is by no means a certain result of a reduction in the crime rate.

Relying primarily on economic analyses of housing prices (and without controlling for incivilities), Greer (1984) estimated that the indirect costs of a recent increase in New York City crime were 2.5 to 3.5 times greater than the direct costs. As suggested above, if these figures are correct it is only coincidental. They seem reasonable, however, and may in fact be underestimates. Rather than arbitrarily pick one value, or even a range of values, it makes more sense at this point to work backwards. How large must the indirect benefits of a crime reduction be, before it makes sense to put more people in jail?

Breakeven Analysis of Indirect Benefits

We may rely on the results described above to help answer this question. First, we identify real end points for the axes of our production possibilities frontier. The end point on the Y axis—the number of crimes that would be committed if no one were incapacitated—is the number of crimes now committed (about 50 million per year) divided by the percentage of potential crimes committed. Similarly, the end point on the X axis is the number of offenders in jail and prison (about 900,000) divided by the percentage of all active offenders who are in jail and prison. For the most likely case, we find that 70.4 million crimes would be committed nationwide if all offenders were freed, and that 9.1 million offenders are responsible for committing them.

Now it is possible to take the derivative of the production possibilities frontier at the current level of incarceration, expressed in terms of crimes prevented per offender incarcerated. This is the number of crimes prevented by incarcerating the marginal offender for 1 year. For the most likely scenario, this figure is 8.8 crimes. Although this may appear to be low, keep in mind that it accounts for extended jail and prison sentences (some of which will be wasted on no-longer dangerous offenders) and for group offending. If we could be certain that this marginal offender would be active throughout the next year, he or she would participate in about 20 crimes—only slightly below the average for ever-incarcerated criminals.

Given the marginal benefits of incapacitating an additional offender in terms of crimes, it is easy to convert to dollar terms. If the direct benefits of preventing the average crime are $1,275, and the direct costs of incarcerating the average offender are $40,000, then benefit/cost ratio will just break even in the most likely case when

$$B/C = 8.8 \ (1275) \ (IBM) \ / \ 40000 = 1,$$

where IBM is the indirect benefit multiplier. A little arithmetic shows that the indirect benefit multiplier in this case must be at least 3.6, or that the indirect benefits must be 2.6 times greater than the direct benefits. In general, if we think the indirect benefits are greater than the breakeven level, then we need to build more prisons. If we think the indirect benefits are less, we should consider converting some portion of our current capacity to a higher-valued use and set some prisoners free.

Figure 6.4 shows the distribution of these breakeven levels for the 62 experiments described above. If the indirect benefits of preventing an average crime are 2.6 times the direct benefits, then there is a 50-percent chance that it makes economic sense to build more jails and prisons. (That is, 50 percent of the experiments conducted produced breakeven values less than 2.6, and 50 percent produced values greater than 2.6). If the indirect benefits are 3.5 times the direct benefits, there is a 90-percent chance that additional capacity would produce net benefits. On the other hand, if the indirect benefits are only 2.0 times the direct benefits we can be 90-percent certain that additional prisons will not be cost-effective.

Assuming for the sake of argument that the indirect benefits are 3.0 times greater than the direct benefits (the midpoint between Greer's lower and higher estimates), it is possible to estimate the benefits associated with a small change in prison capacity. A 1-percent increase in current capacity amounts to about 9,000 beds. At $40,000 per year, this will cost us $360 million. This will reduce crime by between 0.12 percent and 0.20 percent—between 60,000 and 100,000 crimes

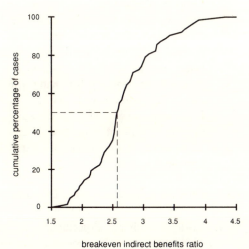

FIGURE 6.4. Breakeven indirect benefits ratios vary over a wide range.

breakeven indirect benefits ratio

per year. The social benefits will be between $306 million and $512 million per year. So the effect of this increase—the equivalent of one large prison—will be somewhere between a $54 million loss and a $152 million gain. Our best single guess is that it will produce net benefits of $41 million per year.

The benefits will be larger for states that imprison a relative small proportion of offenders but do so at a lower-than-average cost. For these states, the benefits of additional incarceration may be substantial (there are many frequent offenders on the street), but the costs will be fairly low. Similarly, cities and counties that jail a small proportion of offenders at low cost may benefit either from additional jail construction or from use of a greater proportion of their state's prison capacity.

Nevertheless, for most states and for the nation as a whole, the benefits of additional jail and prison construction are modest, at best. If Greer's figures are overestimates or if the indirect benefits will not be incurred without a substantial time lag, the benefits are probably less than the costs. And we can be virtually certain that the direct costs of prison construction and operations exceed the direct benefits to victims. If there were no other way of reducing crime, the returns may be worth the investment. Because they may well produce substantial losses, however, the investment is risky.

We can reduce our risks if we can learn more about the principal uncertainties: the size of the indirect benefits of a crime reduction and the elasticity of crime with respect to incarceration. Given the difficulties involved in reducing the proper elasticity value to even a factor of two, it will probably be easiest to resolve uncertainties about indirect benefits. Further study may shed additional light.

- Simplest would be a study of changes in avoidance, insurance, and prevention activities in communities that have undergone both steady increases and decreases in crime rates.
- A more ambitious effort would involve time-series analysis of housing prices and personal and business reactions to crime-rate increases and decreases, controlling for changes in neighborhood social composition, incivilities, and other factors.
- If these studies provide counterintuitive results, further investigation may be needed into the formation of and change in people's perceptions of crime rates, and the effect of these perceptions in forming opinions and provoking action.

Basic macroeconomics suggests that expectations of future crime may play a major role in motivating insurance, protection, and avoidance activities. If it proves difficult to change expectations, we may find that large increases in the prison population would be needed before we could obtain significant indirect benefits. If these increases are coupled with an increase in criminality among the population—as appears to have occurred in the last decade—crime rates may fail to drop, expectations may not change, and the indirect benefits may never materialize at all.

Further study will help, but it will always be difficult to be sure about the indirect costs of crime. We may be stuck with sizable uncertainty. Some will resolve this uncertainty in favor of more prisons; others will not. Even if a state decides against building more jails and prisons, it may still be able to reduce the crime rate simply by becoming more selective. The next chapter examines the potential effectiveness of some proposals to do that.

The present adult criminal justice system incarcerates between 6 and 12 percent of active offenders at any given time; the most reasonable single figure is 8.5 percent. This practice reduces the aggregate crime rate by anywhere from 16 to 28 percent, with a most reasonable value of 21 percent. As a result, a 1-percent increase in adult jail and prison populations would probably produce a 0.12- to 0.20-percent reduction in crime. Benefit/cost analysis suggests that, for most states and the nation as a whole, constructing additional jails and prisons is a risky investment with a very uncertain payoff.

7

Selective Incapacitation

All proposals for increasing the selectivity of the criminal justice system have two elements in common. First, some offenders—presumably the most frequent, serious, or persistent—are selected for special attention. Second, the resources of criminal justice agencies are reallocated so that these offenders in fact receive special attention; the presumably less dangerous offenders who are not selected receive correspondingly less attention. If the selection method is accurate and if resources are reallocated in a reasonable way, then the result should be a more efficient use of limited resources.

More important, successful selective policies and programs will change the entire structure of opportunities available to criminal justice practitioners. The production possibilities frontier will be shifted inward, toward the "bliss point" of no crimes and no criminal justice expenditures. It would be possible to capture the results of such a complex change by describing the difference between this frontier before and after the selective program; as shown above, a single statistic will do the job. But, owing to the importance of resource constraints on the current criminal justice system, there is a more straightforward way: We may simply estimate the reduction in crime rate that would take place, were the system to adopt these policies without committing any additional resources. Due to the nature of the distribution of offense rates, this "no-cost crime reduction" will completely describe the new production possibilities frontier (Aitchison & Brown, 1954). It is also easy to explain.

It is likely that the public, faced with a different set of opportunities than before, will want to change its allocation of resources to the criminal justice system. Because crime control will be cheaper, the public may be willing to pay for more crime control. In particular, the benefit-cost ratio associated with building additional prison cells will be more favorable. On the other hand, an increase in crime prevention efficiency also means that the public can cut taxes or spend more on other goods and services, while preventing the same number of crimes as it did before the increase. Although such shifts in resource allocation may be important, they are beyond the scope of this work. Let us concentrate instead on the potential of selective policies for reducing the crime rate and increasing the utility of prison construction, keeping in mind that the eventual outcome will probably be a more complex combination of crime and cost reductions.

Defining Selective Policies

The discussion will proceed in two parts. First, let us consider the selection methods available. A variety of methods have been proposed, and they appear to differ greatly as to their goals (that is, whether they aim to identify offenders who are frequent, serious, or persistent) and their effectiveness at achieving these goals (that is, the accuracy of selection). Second, consider two forms of resource allocation: reallocation of police and prosecutorial resources (changing the likelihood of arrest, conviction, and incarceration per crime committed), and reallocation of jail and prison space (changing the probable sentence that an offender will serve, given that he is to be incarcerated). Special attention will be given to the proper scale of selective efforts and to the effects of more- and less-accurate selective methods on the crime-control effectiveness of these efforts.

Selection Methods

The present criminal justice system is already selective. Police select some calls for service for fast response, and some crimes for extended investigation. Prosecutors pursue some cases but not others, and devote considerable resources to a few. Judges and parole boards mete out different sentences to different convicted offenders. Such discriminations are necessary to keep the system from being bogged down in unproductive activities.

The problem is that most of these discriminations are made on the basis of characteristics of the case, rather than on characteristics of the offender. Police devote more resources to a case when there are many leads, and they perceive the probability of arrest to be high; prosecutors devote resources to cases they think are likely to lead to convictions; when the offense is very serious, all stages of the system are willing to devote more resources to a case. Characteristics of the offender do enter into resource-allocation decisions, but they are usually unimportant relative to other factors. So making the criminal justice system more "selective" with respect to offender characteristics does not mean that anything qualitatively new need take place; it only requires that the weight given to offender characteristics be increased when making standard choices.

Many selective rules have been developed to help criminal justice agencies choose the most dangerous offenders. Descriptive, or backward-looking, rules have been adopted with just deserts in mind. They are particularly simple and amount to an accounting of past arrests or convictions. Offenders with a longer criminal record have presumably failed to learn the lesson provided by formal criminal conviction and thus are deserving of greater punishment. More complex rules, often taking the form of weighted scales, have been developed with crime control in mind; these are overtly predictive, or forward-looking. Predictive rules are distinguished by a variable to be predicted (usually either future offense rate or the persistence of criminal activity) and a procedure for identifying and weighting predictor variables. As it happens, many of these predictor variables are identical to those used in the just-deserts/descriptive scales—past arrest and conviction data. And the offenders selected by just-deserts rules are, by and large, the same as those selected by predictive scales. What distingushes the two types is the objective—crime control or just deserts. Because predictive scales have been developed with crime control in mind, let us consider only these in what follows.

Accuracy statistics for four representative scales are shown in Table 7.1. The statistic shown—the tetrachoric r^2—is like many such accuracy measures in that it varies from zero (for a scale that is no better than random chance) to 1 (a scale that discriminates perfectly between the worst and the least-bad offenders). However, it is more convenient to use than other, more familiar measures, for two reasons: First, unlike the "mean cost rating" (von Hirsch & Gottfredson, 1984), tetrachoric r^2 may be reasonably interpreted as the proportion of variance in the dependent variable (offense rate or persistence) that is explained by the scale; second, unlike the "relative-improvement-over-chance" statistic (Loeber & Dishion, 1983), the tetrachoric r^2 is relatively insensitive to changes in the proportion of offenders selected by the scale. The average correlations and their standard errors (shown in Table 7.1) assume that all deviations among construction and validation samples are the result of random sampling errors (Hunter, Schmidt, & Jackson, 1982).

As shown, the accuracy of the scales varies from .15 (that is, 15 percent of the variance in true "dangerousness" can be explained by the scale) to a shade above .5 (over 50 percent can be explained). The accuracy varies from one scale to the next for a number of reasons. For one, the scales measure somewhat

TABLE 7.1
Accuracy of Four Representative Selective Scales Varies Widely

	Accuracy	90% confidence interval
Salient factor score	.155	.136 to .170
Construction	.141	.111 to .173
Validation—1	.152	.110 to .198
Validation—2	.170	.130 to .223
Rand inmate scale	.226	.175 to .279
INSLAW prosecution scale	.397	.316 to .475
Iowa assessment scale	.524	.493 to .554
Construction	.506	.390 to .609
Validation	.610	.369 to .780

Source: Gottfredson & Gottfredson, 1986; author's calculations.

different things: Some scales predict recidivism, or arrest within some (essentially arbitrary) length of time; others predict the time before the next arrest; the Rand scale predicts self-reported offense rate. Another reason for the variation is the method used to develop the predictive scale: The methods used to develop the Iowa Assessment Scale and the INSLAW Prosecutor's Scale use information about the individual offender considerably more efficiently than the Rand and Parole Commission scales.

One problem with a statistic like the tetrachoric r^2 (or any similar statistic) is that it is almost mystically arcane. A scale with r^2 of zero is obviously useless, and higher r^2s are preferred to lower ones; but beyond this, there is little concrete one can say about individual values. So these results may make more sense if they are portrayed differently.

Suppose we were interested in dividing the offending population into two groups—more-dangerous and less-dangerous offenders. We might consider the offense rate, weighted for the seriousness of each crime committed, as an indicator of "dangerousness." An accurate scale would put most of the most dangerous offenders in one group, and we would expect that the average dangerousness of offenders in that group would be much higher than the average for the other. Then the accuracy of the test could be measured by the ratio of weighted offense rates of the "bad" group to the offense rates of the "good" group. As it happens, this ratio is the same, no matter what the relative size of the groups; so the translation of r^2 to dangerousness ratio is simple. Note, however, that the ratio does depend upon the skewness of the distribution of offense rates in the population: If the distribution is very skewed, the worst offenders commit crimes at much higher rates than the average; all else equal, the ratio of predicted high-rate to low-rate offenders will be much higher.

Results of this translation are shown in Figure 7.1. The three lines correspond to the dangerousness ratio for the cases of low, medium, and high skewness in the distribution of offense rates. For an r^2 of zero, the ratio is 1.0: There is no difference between the two predicted groups. The ratio increases steadily with r^2; in the most relevant range of r^2s from .20 to .40, the ratio is between 2.0 and 3.5. So if we relied on, say, the INSLAW Prosecution Scale, we could be nearly certain that the predicted high-rate offenders would be between two and four times as dangerous as the low-rate offenders; we could be fairly sure that this group was 2.5 to 3.5 times as dangerous. To be more certain than that, we would need to obtain more precise estimates of the accuracy of the scale and the true distribution of offense rates among offenders.

We will return to the subject of selective scales in the third section of this chapter. For now, let us take these accuracy ratings at more or less face value, and turn our attention to the uses to which the criminal justice system may put them.

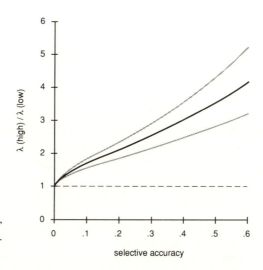

FIGURE 7.1. Even "inaccurate" scales can distinguish among offenders effectively.

Resource Allocation Policies

By allocating the resources of criminal justice agencies differently, we may inflict stiffer sanctions on selected offenders. The reason for developing predictive scales, of course, is to guide our resource-allocation decisions, to help ensure that the extra resources will be devoted to the worst offenders. Such policies may be adopted by any of several criminal justice agencies, and they may be quite complicated (see, for example, U.S. Sentencing Commission, 1987). Still, the questions we wish to answer are fairly simple. So let us consider a simple set of resource-allocation policies.

Changes in Risks and Sentences

The first step in the simplifying process is to reduce to a manageable level the number of potentially selective criminal justice decisions to be examined. Were the aim of this study to prescribe immediately useful policy implications to criminal justice practitioners, it would be appropriate to consider separately policies for (at least) police, prosecutors, judges, and parole boards. Any such practical implications would include consideration of program benefits (potential crime reductions), program costs (both tangible and intangible), management issues (organizational structure, staffing, supervision, performance evaluation, and the like), and program implementation (getting from here to there). All this is further complicated by the fact that the current structure and legal authority of each criminal justice agency differ from one jurisdiction to the next, and by the constraint that linkages between operational processes and program outputs are often mysterious.

Never fear—all this is well beyond the scope of this study. Instead, our present concern is with broader and more basic questions: a rough estimate of the potential benefits of these programs, and some indications as to the proper direction for policymakers interested in pursuing these benefits. Thus we shall start at the end of the line, considering the linkages between program outputs (such as arrests and convictions) and outcomes (such as crime rates)—and stay there. And, rather than consider many specific outputs, we consider only two: the risks of incarceration faced by each offender, given that he or she has committed a crime, and the probable jail or prison sentence each offender must serve, given that he or she has been incarcerated.

We are used to considering the functions of the police and the prosecutor separately; centuries of separate bureaucracies have persuaded us that catching crooks and bringing them to justice are different tasks. It may be true that these functions may be best administered if they are undertaken by separate agencies, but for our purposes it makes more sense to consider them together.

The reason is that, over many cases, each agency may compensate for the failings and errors of the other. Suppose our goal is to incarcerate frequent offenders at higher rates than at present. This may be done either of three ways. The police may identify and arrest frequent offenders at higher rates, who will then be convicted at higher rates than before even if the prosecutor does nothing special. Or the prosecutor may devote special attention to cases involving frequent and serious offenders when she sees them; even though she sees them no more often than before, the risks of conviction and incarceration will increase from the offenders' point of view. Or, of course, both the police and the prosecutor may focus their efforts on dangerous offenders. All else equal, focused programs and policies will be more effective if they are undertaken by both agencies working together (Spelman, 1990), but the brunt of the selective burden can be split among them in whatever way is most convenient.

The proper measure of the results of police and prosecutor dangerous offender efforts, then, should be the degree to which they increase the likelihood of incarceration, given that a crime is committed. In jurisdictions where judges have more or less free rein to sentence as they please, it may be fairer to both agencies to measure results on the basis of the likelihood of conviction, instead. For our purposes, though, it is simpler to estimate the crime-control benefits of a set of unified programs that alter the incarceration probabilities in various ways.

Similarly, it makes sense to combine the effects of judicial sentencing and parole-release decisions. In some jurisdictions, the parole board is relatively constrained to follow the decisions of the judges; in other jurisdictions, parole boards regularly release prisoners early despite a long judicial sentence. Clearly, the identity of the present sentencing decision maker is an important consideration for those attempting to design practical selective sentencing strategies. From our point of view, however, it is immaterial whether the decision is made before offenders begin their terms or as they end them. The output of interest is the time served, and it is on that variable that we should focus our attention.

Having slashed the scope of the analysis so that it includes only two, easily defined outputs, let us now take a meat cleaver to the wide variety of effects criminal justice policies and programs may have on these outputs. As it happens, these effects may be described simply, but in such a way that the analysis is still flexible enough to be of use.

Dichotomous Outputs

Our generic selective program entails only two levels of sanctions—low and high. Predicted high-rate offenders receive the high sanction; all others receive the low sanction.

As with more complex allocation schemes, this one allows us to control two important variables. The *selection rate* is simply the proportion of eligible offenders receiving the stiffer sanction; it may vary from zero to 1. The population of offenders eligible for selection depends upon the stage of the system in question. Police and prosecutors select from the pool of offenders frequent enough or serious enough to be arrested (the "ever-arrested" population of Chapter 6). Judges and parole boards select from among the offenders frequent or serious enough to merit incarceration (the "ever-incarcerated" population). Because only about one-half of arrestees are ever incarcerated, a sentencing selection rate of (say) 10 percent would focus on about the same number of offenders as a police/prosecution selection rate of 5 percent.

The second variable, the *disparity ratio*, measures the difference between the high and the low sanction. For sentencing, the disparity ratio is simply the average sentence given to predicted high-rate offenders, divided by the average sentence given to predicted low-rate offenders. That is,

$$dr = S_H/S_L. \tag{7.1}$$

For police and prosecutor programs, the disparity ratio is more complicated, because we do not generally have complete control over the likelihood of arrest and conviction. As a result, the likelihood for predicted high- and low-rate offenders are likely to be different before the selective program starts—not through a conscious decision of the criminal justice system, but because the crimes that high-rate offenders choose to commit may be more difficult to solve or prosecute. In this case, we may define the disparity ratio as the sanction ratio after the selective program takes effect, divided by the ratio before the program began. So if q_0 represents the average value of some police or prosecution sanction before the program begins, and q_1 represents the average value after the program is implemented, then

$$dr = (q_{H1}/q_{L1})/(q_{H0}/q_{L0}).$$

Alternatively,

$$dr = (q_{H1}\ q_{L0})/(q_{L1}\ q_{H0}). \tag{7.2}$$

Note that we can make any sanction as disparate as we want, at any level of the selection rate. We can even make the disparity ratio infinite, simply by dropping sanctions altogether for the predicted low-rate offenders. In practice, of course, it is doubtful whether very large disparity ratios would be considered ethical, even if they were more effective at controlling crime.

In summary, then, the selection-minded policymaker must make decisions on three factors: (1) the selection method to be used; (2) the scale of the program (that is, the proportion of offenders who receive the sanction); and (3) the level of disparity inflicted (the ratio of sanctions for the predicted dangerous divided by the sanctions for the predicted nondangerous). Such a program may be applied (in theory, at least) anywhere in the system—by police, prosecutors, judges, or parole boards. And, again in theory, it would be possible to use the model to define that combination of selection method, selection rate, and disparity ratio that provides the best results—maximizing the expected crime-control gains. Put mathematically, we could estimate or derive the function,

$$\Delta C = \mathrm{f}(r^2,\ sr,\ dr,\ \text{criminal population characteristics}),$$

where ΔC represents the change in crime rate. We may then set the derivative of this function with respect to the three control parameters equal to zero,

$$\delta(\Delta C)/\delta R^2 = 0$$
$$\delta(\Delta C)/\delta SR = 0$$
$$\delta(\Delta C)/\delta DR = 0,$$

and solve for the optimal selection method, selection rate, and disparity ratio, given different assumptions about the criminal population.

Although there is no reason why this couldn't be done, it is important to recognize that policymakers may find the optimal outputs impossible to achieve. The problem is that criminal justice agencies may be unable to use the optimal selection method, selection rate, and disparity ratio, because they are constrained by ethics, unavailability of resorces or information, and other factors. To obtain a more useful solution, let us consider how these constraints may be taken into account.

The Constraints on Selectivity

The criminal justice policymaker is faced with constraints at every turn. There are never enough staff, equipment, and time to do the job; the information needed to allocate resources properly is expensive to collect and analyze, or simply unavailable; some actions that are likely to be effective shift egregious burdens onto the public. These are all constraints on the optimum policy that may be adopted.

Another class of factors constrains the policy that is in fact implemented, regardless of the policy adopted. For example, subordinates may be unwilling to follow the new policy, or they may distort it for their own purposes; the policy-maker may find it impossible to monitor the subordinates' activities or to provide incentives for following the policies that are sufficient to motivate compliance. These constraints on implementation are important and may in fact be more important than those on policymaking itself. Nevertheless, they may only be realistically examined in the context of specific, selective policies; the scope of this work is more general. So implementation constraints will not be considered. Examination of the importance of these constraints and implications for handling them are, of course, worthy of further study (see, e.g., Spelman, 1990).

Constraints on the optimum policy to be adopted can be grouped into three categories: constraints on resources, constraints on knowledge, and constraints arising from ethical considerations.

Resources

One of the primary arguments favoring selective justice programs is that they are cheap: If we can achieve better crime control without spending more by simply revamping our procedures, we will have achieved a costless benefit. Given the present inability or unwillingness of the public to increase criminal justice spending, it seems most reasonable to test this argument by holding constant the resources of each criminal justice agency. If we like, we may later let this constraint slip, to estimate the resulting crime-control benefits if resources are added to the system—the elasticity described above.

Although this is conceptually simple enough, it is harder to measure and hold constant criminal justice resources than it may appear at first. One problem is that control of street crimes is not the only goal of the criminal justice system; thus it may be worthwhile to undertake some activities that are inefficient means of controlling street crime but help to achieve other goals instead. If we incorrectly assume that street-crime control is the only objective, we will systematically understate the utility of these apparently inefficient activities and thus systematically overstate the utility of selective policies.

Part of the problem is that street crimes are only a portion of all crimes committed. Domestic crimes such as wife-beating and child abuse, and "white-collar" crimes such as embezzlement and antitrust violations may pose serious costs for the public; they may sap a substantial proportion of the resources of the criminal justice system; they may even be committed primarily by a few frequent and persistent offenders. But they are not usually committed by the same individuals who commit burglaries and robberies. If resources remain constant, then a shift in focus to street crimes implies a shift away from domestic and white-collar offenses, with a concurrent loss in benefits that will probably not be reflected in reductions in the aggregate crime rate. These losses will certainly not be reflected in reductions in the rate of street crimes.

A more subtle problem comes from the fact that at least one of the agencies of the criminal justice system—the police—provides services that extend well beyond crime-fighting. In addition to identifying and catching criminals, police maintain order, enforce traffic ordinances, regulate businesses, and provide many other services. Again, if resources remain constant, then a shift in the focus of a police department to street crimes implies a shift away from these services. There is evidence that these services indirectly affect the crime rate in important ways (Wilson & Kelling, 1982, 1989); but even if they did, the costs of this shift would not be fully reflected in any reduction in the index crime rate.

For the police, at least, this "zero-sum" aspect of resource allocation is ameliorated by two factors. First, dangerous offenders commit many criminal acts that are never attributed to them. Even when police officers are not explicitly working repeat-offender cases, they will spend some of their time responding to these acts; if they succeed in incapacitating some of these offenders, this will free up some of this time. Second, the crimes of dangerous offenders are at least partly responsible for problems not explicitly criminal: Dangerous offenders are sometimes merely disorderly; their crimes inspire fear among citizens; they may be responsible for a large share of the drug dealing. Thus incapacitating these offenders may reduce the size of these noncriminal problems, reducing the officers' order maintenance and services workload. Unfortunately, the size of these ameliorating effects is anyone's guess.

These problems are readily overcome if we are willing to assume that the resources devoted to dangerous street offenders are obtained only by shifting those resources already devoted to control of street crimes. Thus adoption of selective policies and procedures implies no shift in emphasis for the agency and does not reduce the production of crime control for nonstreet offenses. If selective policies and programs succeed in making street-crime control more efficient, we may agree that more or fewer resources should be devoted to this objective; but that is a separate question.

A second problem is that the production function for most criminal justice agencies is complex, because most agencies produce crime control by undertaking a number of different activities, each with their own benefits and costs. Police catch criminals, but they do this by patrolling neighborhoods, responding to calls, investigating crimes after the fact, and (sometimes) investigating offenders before they commit crimes; prosecutors must allocate their time among preparation of briefs and motions, interviewing victims and witnesses, negotiating with defense attorneys and judges, and arguing their cases in court; judges may sentence convicted offenders to jail or prison, to probation of greater or lesser intensity, to restitution and community service programs, or to a panoply of presumably rehabilitative employment, education, and counseling efforts. The effectiveness of each of these classes of activities on crime control is (to say the least) poorly understood and probably differs greatly from one case or offender to the next.

Part of this problem may be solved by assuming (as we have, above) that there are no deterrent or rehabilitation benefits to any criminal justice activities. This simplifies the problem for the police, because several police activities (preventive patrol, in particular) are justified primarily on their deterrent value. And this assumption effectively solves the complexity problem for the corrections system, because the relationship between incapacitative effort and the crime-control result is particularly direct. Each day an active offender spends in jail or prison results in another day's crimes prevented; the number of crimes that an offender would probably commit, were he active, and the likelihood that a given offender will be active at a given time have already been accounted for in the incapacitation model. So it is easy to hold resources constant over the entire range of selection and disparity ratios, while comparing the benefits of incapacitating low-rate offenders with those of incapacitating high-rate offenders.

For the police and the prosecutor, however, the problem still remains: Selective agencies will forsake presumably inefficient present activities, the returns to which are poorly defined, in favor of presumably more efficient activities that are—if anything—more poorly defined because they are new.

Although little information is available about the police and prosecutor's production function, the basic form of the aggregate production function (like most production functions) probably will exhibit decreasing returns to scale. Each increment of resources devoted to a particular case increases the likelihood of arrest, conviction, or incarceration, but by a decreasing amount. The relationship between resources (R) and results (Q) for any given case i may be specified as $Q_i = R_i^{\beta_{pi}}$, where $0 < \beta_{P_i} < 1$ describes the slope of the production function for case i. Although this function clearly differs from one case to the next, it is reasonable to expect that all production functions will have this basic shape.

It now makes sense to ask how resources are allocated among cases. It is probably reasonable to assume that police allocate resources in order to maximize arrests and that prosecutors allocate resources in order to maximize convictions. True, some cases are more important than others—and serious and celebrated cases may absorb more resources as a result. But for classes of homogeneous cases at least, we can expect arrest and conviction maximization to be the rule. Within each of these homogeneous classes, the appropriate strategy is to pursue each case up to that point where the marginal value of adding more resources (the slope of the production function) is equal for all cases, and the resources available for handling all cases of this type have been used up. Such a strategy is illustrated in Figure 7.2.

Now consider resource allocation with the objective of maximizing crime control through incapacitation. Cases involving predicted frequent and dangerous offenders should receive more effort, since a successful result is more beneficial—the expected value of an arrest, conviction, or incarceration in terms of crimes prevented is greater. Due to marginally decreasing returns, however, these added resources will have smaller and smaller effects on the likelihood of arrest, conviction, and incarceration. The resources devoted to cases involving frequent offenders will be taken from cases involving less-dangerous offenders; due again to marginally decreasing returns, the reductions in the likelihood of arrest and conviction for these cases will be relatively large, more than offsetting the increases in cases involving frequent offenders. On aggregate, then, fewer arrests and convictions will be made, but because they will be made more often on cases involving the worst offenders, the police and the prosecutor may become more effective at controlling crime.

Perhaps it is needless to mention that little is known about the slope of the

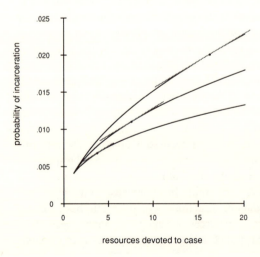

FIGURE *7.2.* Efficient police resource allocation equalizes marginal change in arrest rates.

production function. Economic studies of the work of police and prosecutors are rare. However, such a study has been conducted on the relationship between resources used and results achieved for one part of this question—police resources in response to burglaries and robberies. The data set, collected by John Eck (1983), includes information on the activities undertaken by patrol officers and detectives in response to all burglaries and robberies reported in DeKalb County, Georgia, St. Petersburg, Florida, and Wichita, Kansas, in 1980; the time required to undertake these activities, the information gained as a result, and the effect of this information on the likelihood of arrest were all considered in the primary analysis. Identification and analysis of homogeneous classes of cases would require another document of this size and hardly seems worth the trouble. But through secondary analysis it is possible to estimate an average value for β_P with little difficulty; so long as the relationship between β_{Pi} and the offense rate of the offender who commits case i is not too large, this simple average will be helpful. The data were used to estimate β_P in the following way.

First, the logistic transformation of the probability of arrest was regressed against information available about the crime and the suspect. This provided an estimate as to the relative importance of various pieces of information that could be obtained through police work. Next, the likelihood that any given activity would result in obtaining each piece of information was assessed; this was just straightforward arithmetic. Finally, the contribution of each activity to case solution was assessed by computing a weighted average of these probabilities, with the weights obtained from the logistic regression.

Some activities require more resources than others. In most big cities, it only takes a few moments to check departmental records through the computer; a stakeout may take hours. Thus the marginal effectiveness of each activity was divided by the average number of officer-minutes needed to undertake it. This resulted in a marginal efficiency rating for each activity. The most efficient activities were to interview potential informants, discuss the case with other patrol officers and detectives, and canvass the neighborhood of a crime in search of potential witnesses. The activity most often undertaken by detectives when assigned to a burglary or robbery—interview the victim to check the report taken by the patrol officer—was one of the least efficient, at least from the standpoint of crime solution.

If activities are undertaken in random order—time-efficient activities are no more likely to be undertaken first than last—then each increment of time available to spend on a case will be equally productive, and $\beta_P = 1$. On the other hand, if the most efficient activities are always undertaken first, each increment will produce less information and contribute less to case solution than the last, and $\beta_P < 1$. Eck's primary analysis suggested some tendency of officers to undertake efficient activities first, but the tendency was not pronounced. Thus we can think of the most efficient resource allocation as a limiting case that produces the lowest value of β_P. The true value will lie between this estimate and 1.0.

Results for patrol officer and detective activities for each crime type are shown in Table 7.2. The estimates are essentially identical: The relationship between resources used and the likelihood of arrest is about .77, for both crime types and bureaus.

These results are hardly definitive, of course. The size of the bias is difficult to estimate. Only three cities and two crime types are represented. The likelihood of conviction and the activities of the prosecutor are not considered. And proactive police activities such as preventive patrol, decoy operations, and surveillance are not included, even though they sometimes lead to arrests. Still, the figure seems reasonable. For the sake of argument, let us assume that β_P may be anywhere between 1.0 (nondecreasing returns) and .70, with a best-guess value of .85. Given the imprecision of these values, it would of course be prudent to examine closely the sensitivity of crime control estimates to changes in β_P.

Given the selection ratio, the disparity ratio, and β_P, it is easy to estimate the effects of the resource shift on arrest rates for different groups of offenders. Let R_0 represent the resources devoted to all cases before the focus on dangerous offenders begins. Then

$$Q_0 = (R_0)^{\beta_P} \tag{7.3}$$

is the likelihood of (let us say) incarceration given that an offender committed a crime. Some proportion of these offenders, sr, is predicted to be dangerous, and may be denoted by the subscript D; the rest are predicted nondangerous and may be denoted by the subscript N. If we increase resources devoted to cases in the predicted dangerous group by $R_D{}'$, the result is

$$Q_{D1} = (R_{D0}\, R_D{}')^{\beta_P} = Q_{D0}\, R_D{}'^{\beta_P}. \tag{7.4}$$

TABLE 7.2

Estimates of the Relationship between Police Resources and the Likelihood of Arrest

Crime type	Patrol officers	Detectives
Burglary	.774	.769
	(.040)	(.043)
Robbery	.784	.743
	(.042)	(.050)

Source. Eck & Spelman, 1983; author's calculations.

Resources devoted to cases involving nondangerous offenders are reduced to compensate. A little algebra shows that the total resources stay constant if those devoted to nondangerous cases change by the proportion

$$R_N' = (1 - sr\ R_D')/(1 - sr),$$

with the resulting incarceration probability of

$$Q_{NI} = Q_{NO}\ [(1 - sr\ R_D')/(1 - sr)]^{\beta_P}. \tag{7.5}$$

Because the disparity ratio for police and prosecution programs is defined as

$$dr = (Q_{DI}\ Q_{NO})/(Q_{DO}\ Q_{NI}),$$

we may plug in equations (7.4) and (7.5) to solve for R_D and R_N in terms of sr, dr, and β_P:

$$R_D = dr^{1/\beta_P}/(1 - sr + sr\ dr^{1/\beta_P}); \text{ and} \tag{7.6a}$$

$$R_N = (1 - sr + sr\ dr^{1/\beta_P}) - 1. \tag{7.6b}$$

R_D and R_N are the proportionate level of resources devoted to predicted dangerous and nondangerous cases, respectively. For any group of homogeneous offenders, i, suppose that sr_i are predicted to be dangerous and receive additional resources. Then the resources devoted to a case involving an average member of group i will be $R_i = sr_i\ R_D + (1 - sr_i)\ R_N$, or

$$R_i = (sr_i\ dr^{1/\beta_P} + 1 - sr_i/(1 - sr_i + sr_i\ dr^{1/\beta_P}). \tag{7.7}$$

From (7.3), we know that the probability of arrest after adoption of the selective police and prosecutor program for the typical member of group i will be

$$q_i^* = q_{0i}\ (R_i)^{\beta_P},$$

or the prior probability, multiplied by (7.7) taken to the β_Pth power. So if dr, β_P, and the selection rate for each group of homogeneous offenders i are all known, the effect of the program on arrest rates for members of each group can be identified.

To summarize, then:

- It makes sense to test selective strategies by holding constant the resources of each criminal justice agency.

- Prison resources may be held constant by keeping the number of economic offenders in jail the same, after adoption of selective allocation policies.
- Police and prosecutorial resources may be held constant by estimating the slope of the aggregate production function, and solving for changes in the probability of incarceration resulting from adoption of selective policies.

Although this both complicates the analysis somewhat and also requires that we make some rather cavalier assumptions, at least it takes into account the most important difficulties arising from scarce resources. Better assumptions about the production function for police and prosecutors may of course be obtained through further research.

Knowledge

As suggested by the preceding paragraphs, one reason we have found it difficult to reduce crime through incapacitation is that we are unsure how the activities of the criminal justice system work to achieve the arrest, conviction, and incarceration of offenders. For example, many observers believe that vertical prosecution, reduced plea negotiation, and increased willingness to go to trial are more effective means of ensuring the incarceration of arrested suspects; there is a consensus that surveillance, stakeouts, better use of informants, and similar schemes are effective ways of ensuring the arrest of selected offenders. But the details of these schemes are most often left up to tradition. A district attorney might ask, for example, how high the caseloads should be in her dangerous-offender unit, how tough a negotiating stance her assistants should take, what proportion of dangerous-offender cases should be taken to trial, and so on. Questions like these are addressed at best on the basis of standard practice, and no systematic research has been conducted as to how well different tactics will work.

Although it is tempting to state outright that incarceration is a known technology, even this isn't quite so. New schemes aimed at partial incapacitation in the community, such as community treatment centers, electronic monitoring, or intensive supervision probation show promise as less-expensive means of incapacitation. They are clearly not so complete in their incapacitative effects as imprisonment; still, they certainly incapacitate more than doing nothing, and they are cheaper. Whether they are cost-effective is a research question that has only recently begun to receive much attention (Byrne et al., 1989; Petersilia & Turner, 1990).

Another obvious case is the accuracy of selective scales. Until recently, the prevailing method for devising a selective scale was the Burgess method, essentially a crude way of combining the results of a series of contingency tables. In the past 20 years, criminologists have begun to apply more sophisticated techniques that use more and more of the information about offenders to form these scales. Multiple regression, partial likelihood, and pattern recognition methods are being used more and more frequently (Gottfredson & Gottfredson, 1986). At the same time, the criminal justice system is keeping more complete records of arrests, convictions, and incarcerations—providing more and more grist for the analytic mill. Thus it is reasonable to suspect that better scales will ultimately result. No matter how good the selection scales become, however, they will always be imperfect, and this will always constrain the effectiveness of selective activities.

Constraints as to knowledge are liable to become less binding in the long run. Up to a point, it is reasonable to expect that more accurate selection methods will be developed and that cost-effective tactics for police, prosecution, and corrections agencies will become better-defined. In terms of the model proposed here, this means that reasonable estimates of the r^2 term will increase and that β_P, the slope of the police and prosecutor production function, will increase. Should the accuracy of predictive scales grow high enough (or, what is the same thing, should the street information available to police agencies increase in quality and quantity), it is plausible that the slope may approach 1.0—that is, that additional resources would return additional results at almost a constant rate. This might happen if a police department were relatively certain who the most frequent offenders were, for example, and reoriented its activities from a case-oriented to an offender-oriented basis. On the other hand, such developments are a long way off. In the meantime, it is most reasonable to assume that the accuracy of selective methods is bounded by the figures shown in Table 7.1, and that the system will be constrained to producing arrests, convictions, and incarcerations according to a production function that exhibits strongly decreasing marginal returns.

Ethics

Ethics is the most-often-cited constraint on the effectiveness of selective criminal justice practice. Some feel that it is always inappropriate for the criminal justice system to be selective on the basis of individual characteristics; others feel that some degree of selectivity is appropriate, or that selection is more appropriate for certain parts of the system (arrest and prosecution) than at other parts (bail, sentencing, and parole-release decisions) (Moore, 1986).

For those who believe that some degree of individual selectivity is appropriate, the ethical concerns focus largely on the disparity of punishment resulting from application of selective policies. This is especially true for sentencing decisions, where selective decisions translate directly into unequal burdens among offenders. Such concerns are likely to be reflected in constraints on the disparity ratio. For example, it may be that the most-effective sentencing disparity ratio for some combination of criminal population characteristics, selection methods, and selection rate turns out to be 6.0. That is, predicted frequent offenders should get sentences six times as long as predicted infrequent offenders. But because we are concerned about the inaccuracy of the mathematical scale, or about the inherent unpredictability of human behavior, we may feel that the sentence disparity ratio should be constrained to a much lower level—perhaps 2.0 or 3.0.

Most of those who believe that selective criminal justice policies are ethical within constraints apply fewer constraints to the police and the prosecutor (Moore, 1986). Because no one is directly punished as the result of arrest or conviction, errors are less odious to the offender and thus to society as a whole. Higher disparity ratios are allowed. But ethics may still constrain the disparity ratio somewhat, so that we may come up with a suboptimal position from a purely crime-control standpoint.

Ethical concerns also constrain the accuracy of selection methods, in two ways. For one, they reduce the set of available predictors. For example, one might reasonably conclude that race is never an appropriate predictor, that unemployment is rarely appropriate, that arrests usually are, and that convictions always are. Methods that use all of these predictors are more accurate than those that use only the least objectionable (Chaiken & Chaiken, 1982). In addition, some feel that ethical constraints constrain the use of these variables. Few would quarrel with an apparently backward-looking scale, for example, whereas many will argue against a strict forward-looking scale. But forward-looking scales will clearly be more accurate at predicting future events. Because more accurate selection methods lead to more effective crime control, this reduces the effectiveness of selective strategies.

Accounting for Constraints

The impact of these constraining factors may be summarized as follows:

- The accuracy of selection methods is constrained by limitations of knowledge and (perhaps more important) by ethical concerns.
- The allowable disparity ratio may be constrained by ethical concerns, although these constraints will probably be tougher on selective sentencing schemes than on selective police and prosecution policies.
- The costs of selective activities may be summarized by a function of selection rate, disparity ratio, and (for the case of the police and prosecutor) an incarceration production function; these costs are offset by reductions in the costs of crime control for less-dangerous offenders. Total costs

are constrained to be the same under the selective system as they were under the unselective system.

All this suggests that the optimal program may be defined by the algorithm,

$$\min \Delta C = f(r^2, \; sr, \; dr, \; \text{criminal population characteristics}),$$

such that

[accuracy]	$r^2 \leq R^2$,
[disparity]	$dr \leq DR$, and
[resources]	$v = f(dr,sr) \leq V$,

where R^2, DR, and V are maximum levels of accuracy, disparity ratio, and cost consistent with the available resources and knowledge, and with ethical concerns.

As suggested by the discussion above, only the constraints imposed by resource availability are liable to be sufficiently well-defined to give reasonably precise results. Should additional resources become available, the resulting effects on crime rates may be measured by the elasticity statistic used above. On the other hand, various levels of accuracy and disparity are liable to be both practical and permissible, depending upon one's system of ethics and one's level of optimism with respect to prediction technology. As a result, it makes sense to consider the sensitivity of the crime-control benefits of selective policies with respect to changes in these levels.

So there are two important classes of uncertainty as to the benefits of selective criminal justice policies: uncertainties about the nature of the criminal offending population and uncertainties about the resource, knowledge, and ethical constraints on policymakers. And there are two important classes of selective policies: those aimed at increasing the likelihood of incarceration for dangerous offenders and those aimed at increasing the length of the sentences they serve. Let us now consider how these sources of uncertainty influence the effectiveness and optimal structure of these dangerous offender efforts.

Three dimensions characterize selective criminal justice policies: the accuracy of the selection method, the proportion of active offenders selected for special treatment (the selection rate), and the disparity between selected offenders and others as to the risks or sentences imposed (the disparity ratio). Selective actions are constrained by limited resources and knowledge, and by ethical concerns; the police and the prosecutor are also constrained by diminishing marginal returns. By examining the response of the aggregate crime rate to variations in these dimensions, we may identify optimal and constrained optimal selective policies.

The Effectiveness of Selective Policies

The adaptation of the Avi-Itzhak and Shinnar model described above allows for a variety of chracteristics of the offending population but cannot estimate the effects of changes in criminal justice policies and procedures. To make these estimates, the model was adapted further. Like the first version, the second version of the model assumes that the effects of special and general deterrence are small enough to be ignored, that all offenders commit crimes at constant rates throughout their careers, and that all states and localities are about the same.

Table 6.1 lists nine characteristics of the offending population; if selective programs and policies are characterized as described in the previous section, the number of parameters required is either three (for changes in sentencing) or four (for changes in the risk of incarceration). This is a lot of parameters to consider, and an experiment that included them all would be very complicated. So the crime-control estimation process was further simplified.

First, several selective programs and policies were posited, with widely differing selection and disparity ratios. Changes in risks and sentences were considered separately. The crime-control effects of implementing each of these selective programs were estimated for the most likely characteristics of the offending population—the "best guesses" of Table 6.1. Then the sensitivity of these effects to deviations from these best guesses was estimated, one characteristic at a time. The crime-control effects were very sensitive to changes in some offending characteristics and not very sensitive to changes in others. The most sensitive characteristics were singled out for further attention. A formal experimental design was developed and implemented that incorporated variations in both the structure of selective programs and in sensitive characteristics of the offending population. Finally, to simplify reporting and analysis of the experimental results, we use regression to fit a response surface among the experimental data points. The results of these experiments are presented below.

Because the mechanics of estimation are simpler for selective sentencing programs, let us consider these first.

Changing the Length of Jail and Prison Sentences

In preliminary analysis, the effectiveness of selective sentencing programs and policies proved particularly sensitive to reasonable changes in seven characteristics of the offending population:

- The average offense rate.
- The distribution of offense rates among offenders.
- The number of offenders participating in the average offending group.

- The average criminal career length.
- The relationship between career length and offense rate.
- The average probability of arrest, given a crime.
- The relationship between arrest probability and offense rate.

Changes in the distribution of career lengths had little effect on effectiveness. Sixty-two representative combinations of these seven characteristics were then assembled, according to a Box-Behnken design. This design ensures that the correlations among the seven characteristics at issue will be zero and that sufficient information is available to calculate quadratic effects and interaction terms. Some values of these characteristics are more likely to be true than others (for example, it is more likely that the average offense rate is about 40 per year than it is 30 or 50 per year); because the Box-Behnken design maintains the number of less-likely estimates to be the same for each experiment, the results need not be weighted. The central, "best-guess" point was replicated six times to represent its greater likelihood of representing reality, however. This inflated the sample size slightly, but had no practical effect on the results obtained.

For each of these 62 combinations, 15 selective policies were considered. These policies represented a combination of values for the accuracy of the selection method and selection ratio used, and the disparity ratio resulting from implementation of the program. As shown in Table 7.3, the values were chosen to represent a reasonable range of programs and policies. Combinations were chosen according to a 3-factor central composite design (eight "corner" points, six "star" points, and a central point). Like the Box-Behnken design, the central composite design has the advantage of being equally precise for all combinations of deviations from the central combination. It has the additional advantage of mapping five points for each program characteristic. This produces a somewhat better resolution of the effects of small changes in each characteristic on program outcomes (Box, Hunter, & Hunter, 1978).

A fair assessment of the crime-control benefits of selective sentencing requires that the resources available be kept constant; although added selectivity

TABLE 7.3
Range of Selective Sentencing Programs Considered

	Accuracy	Selection rate	Disparity ratio
Very high	.468	.301	9.364
High	.400	.250	8.000
Medium	.300	.175	6.000
Low	.200	.100	4.000
Very low	.132	.049	2.636

will change the elasticity of crime with respect to imprisonment resources, it is simpler to examine elasticity changes separately. Because the costs of imprisonment depend (almost) entirely upon the number of offenders in prison, costs can be kept (almost) constant by keeping the prison population constant. In theory, any reduction in crime rates should increase the effectiveness of the police and the prosecutor in handling those crimes that are still committed; nevertheless, the predicted reductions due to selective sentencing are sufficiently small, and the likely increases in police and prosecutorial efficiency sufficiently tenuous, that it seems reasonable to ignore this problem.

All told, then, estimates were obtained of the crime-control effectiveness of 930 combinations of offender and selective program characteristics. Regression was then used to map the response surface among the experimental data points. This provides a simple equation that captures the principal effects of each of these characteristics on program effectiveness. We may then use the equation to identify the best policies under given conditions. Although this is an unconventional means of simplifying the results of an analytic model, the model is too complex to obtain these results through direct derivation. Regression is frequently used for this purpose in simulation analysis (Larson & Odoni, 1981).

The functional form chosen was a translog specification—essentially a second-order polynomial on the logarithm of the dependent and independent variables (Christenson, Jorgenson, & Lau, 1971). The translog is the most flexible form for fitting a wide variety of response surfaces and is particularly appropriate for fitting a production function when the production process is complex or unknown (Guilkey, Lovell & Sickles, 1983; Heady, 1961). The complete specification includes 65 terms (9 program, 35 population, and 21 interaction terms). About one-third of these terms were insignificant at $p = .10$. When these terms were removed, the fit did not change significantly or substantially, and for simplicity results of the reduced model are considered below.

As shown in Table 7.4, the equation is quite precise; over 99.9 percent of the variance in the crime reduction resulting from adoption of these policies could be explained, and the average error in estimation was less than 1/10 of 1 percent. Although it would be more elegant to derive these results rather than to estimate them statistically, it is clear that there would be little practical difference between the derived results and these estimates. And, of course, statistical estimation is considerably simpler and more straightforward.

In broad outline, the results are fairly simple. Note first that 78 percent of the variance in the crime-reduction effects of selective sentencing schemes can be explained by knowing the selective policy used. That is, within the range of populations and policies considered here, effectiveness depends primarily on the accuracy of the selective scale, the selection rate, and the disparity ratio—and not on characteristics of the offending population or on interactions between population characteristics and program characteristics. Note also that population

TABLE 7.4

Indicators of Crime-Reduction Effectiveness of Selecting Sentencing Programs

	Coefficient	Standard error	Probability
Selective sentencing policy			
Explains 77.9% of variance			
Main effects			
Accuracy	.5618	.0325	
Selection	−.2711	.0233	
Disparity	1.0290	.0120	
Quadratic effects			
Accuracy	.0213	.0031	
Selection	−.2042	.0015	
Disparity	−.2565	.0031	
Interactions			
Accuracy/selection	−.0818	.0027	
Accuracy/disparity	−.0625	.0036	
Selection/disparity	−.2178	.0027	
Offending population			
Explains 21.8% of variance			
Main effects			
Mean offense rate	.4079	.0936	
Skew of offense rate	1.1538	.0948	
Mean group size	−1.2854	.1818	
Mean career length	.4178	.0051	
Corr (T,λ)	3.2865	.3027	
Mean arrest rate	.4650	.1034	
Corr (q,λ)	.2811	.0341	
Quadratic effects			
Mean offense rate	−.1565	.0105	
Skew of offense rate	−.4953	.0171	
Mean group size	.1959	.0626	.0018
Mean arrest rate	−.1573	.0124	
Corr (q,λ)	.0700	.0024	
Interactions			
Lambda/skew	−.2381	.0174	
Lambda/group	−.1398	.0334	
Lambda/arrest	−.3221	.0147	
Lambda/corr (q,λ)	.0666	.0062	
Skew/group	−.1448	.0429	.0008
Skew/arrest	−.2353	.0189	
Skew/corr (q,λ)	.4145	.0079	
Group/arrest	−.1354	.0364	.0002
Group/corr (q,λ)	.0427	.0153	.0053
Career/corr (T,λ)	−.4673	.1505	.0020
Arrest/corr (q,λ)	.0667	.0067	

(continued)

TABLE 7.4   (*Continued*)

	Coefficient	Standard error	Probability
Interaction of program and population characteristics			
Explains 0.2% of variance			
Accuracy/lambda	−.0447	.0058	
Accuracy/skew	.0244	.0074	.0011
Accuracy/arrest	−.0448	.0063	
Selection/lambda	.0678	.0041	
Selection/skew	−.1715	.0053	
Selection/arrest	.0678	.0045	
Selection/corr (q,λ)	.0166	.0019	
Disparity/skew	−.0881	.0074	
Disparity/corr (q,λ)	.0190	.0026	
Constant	−.1076	.3023	.7219

Note. Probabilities less than .00005 not shown. R^2 = .9992. F (41,888) = 27,673. Average crime reduction = 2.709 percent, with standard error of estimate = .026 percent.

characteristics explain nearly all of the rest of the variance. Taken together, these results suggest two conclusions:

- If we could reduce our uncertainty as to the nature of the offending population, it would help us to estimate the benefits of selective sentencing policies more precisely.
- Nevertheless, further research into the nature of the population will probably not help much in determining the optimal policy.

That is, we can expect one, close-to-optimal policy to work best, no matter what the offending population looks like.

This is a startling and powerful result, and will be examined more closely below. First, however, let us consider how we may determine the optimal sentencing policy for any particular combination of offending population characteristics.

Identifying the Optimal Policy

It is not difficult to imagine a sentencing policy that would reduce crime by the largest possible amount, were resource and knowledge constraints not binding. Such a policy was developed in Chapter 1, and we will return to it later. And, although crime control is not the only item on everyone's utility function, some would argue that perfect information as to which offenders are most dangerous, and sufficient jail and prison cells to give each offender his due, would reduce or even eliminate most of the ethical problems with which prison policy-makers must wrestle (e.g., Monahan, 1982; Moore, 1986; Morris, 1982).

In the real world of sentencing and corrections, of course, knowledge and resource constraints exacerbate ethical dilemmas; it is surely necessary to know something about all of these constraints if we are to develop appropriate policies. This poses a difficult problem for analysis, because some of these constraints are quite amorphous and difficult to make sense of except in light of a specific proposal.

For the moment, let us consider constraints on resources to be binding—that is, the number of jail and prison cells will remain constant. Because it takes several years to plan and construct a medium-security prison, these constraints are very likely to remain binding in the short run.

If we assume that resources remain constant, then we can use the results of Table 7.4 to determine the optimal sentencing policy. Note that we need not determine an optimal value of selective accuracy, because higher accuracy will always be preferred to lower accuracy. (Experiment confirms that optimal accuracy is always beyond the high end of the relevant range.) So we need only consider the selection rate and disparity ratio. Take the derivative of the logarithm of the crime reduction with respect to log sr and log dr, set the resulting equations to zero, and take the exponent of both sides. Since the interaction of sr and dr was a significant predictor, this produces equations of the form,

$$sr = A_1 \left(\Pi_i X_i^{Bi} \right) dr^{C1} \tag{7.8a}$$

$$dr = A_2 \left(\Pi_j X_j^{Bj} \right) sr^{C2}, \tag{7.8b}$$

where X_i and X_j are population characteristics with significant interaction terms with sr and dr, respectively, and B_i and B_j are proportionate to the coefficients on these terms. Substituting (7.8a) into (7.8b) and solving leaves equations of the form,

$$sr^* = \alpha_1 \, \Pi_i X_i^{\beta i} \tag{7.9a}$$

$$dr^* = \alpha_2 \, \Pi_j X_j^{\beta j}, \tag{7.9b}$$

where sr^* and dr^* are the optimal (highest crime reduction) values of sr and dr. Coefficients of these estimation equations are shown in Table 7.5.

Now that we have determined how the optimal selection rates and disparity ratios may be obtained, it is appropriate to ask two sets of questions. First, let us pretend that perfect information is available about parameters of the offending population. Note that we do not assume that perfect information is available about any individual, only that the true average offense rate, the true distribution

TABLE 7.5
Coefficients of Optimal Selection Evaluations (Sentencing)

	Selection rate	Disparity ratio
Constant	.1033	19.3190
Mean λ	.2109	−.0841
Standard deviation λ	−.5318	.2100
Group size	−.0001	.0002
Mean T	.0167	−.0034
β_T	−.1000	.0416
Mean q	.2110	−.0840
β_Q	.0270	.0256
r^2	−.1748	−.0476

of offense rates among offenders, and so on, are all available. If we are able to tailor our selective policy to these true values, how much could we reduce crime through selective sentencing? What would these "complete-information" policies look like, and how do they differ from one set of population characteristics to the next?

The limitations of our knowledge about characteristics of the offending population lead to the second set of questions. Given our ignorance, what policy should be adopted? What are the costs of our ignorance? Alternatively, what is the expected value of obtaining complete information about the characteristics of the offending population? Is the nature of the appropriate policy particularly sensitive to any of these characteristics? If so, it makes sense for us to devote more of our research resources to defining these characteristics more precisely.

Optimal Policies under Complete Information

For experimental purposes, let us assume that selective scales with r^2 between .20 and .40 are available, together with complete and accurate information as to the parameters of the criminal population. Then we may plug these parameters into equations (7.9a) and (7.9b) to identify the optimal selection rate and disparity ratio for each plausible population scenario and compare the results. Let us consider 186 representative combinations of population parameters and accuracy estimates (62 population combinations replicated for each of three accuracy estimates).

The first column of Table 7.6 shows the distribution of crime reductions that would result from implementation of the optimal policy in each of these 186 cases. Like everything else in this field, the distribution is upwardly skewed. It is very unlikely that selective policies would reduce crime by less than 2 percent, or

TABLE 7.6
The Optimal Selective Sentencing Program
Would Reduce Crime by 3 to 6 Percent

	Crime reduction	Selection rate	Disparity ratio
Maximum	7.488	0.151	22.232
90th percentile	5.735	0.135	21.447
75th	5.140	0.128	20.960
Median	4.359	0.119	20.511
25th	3.765	0.112	19.990
10th	3.287	0.106	19.573
Minimum	2.555	0.096	18.917
Mean	4.462	0.120	20.508
Standard deviation	0.942	0.012	0.737

by more than 7 percent, under these conditions; the median reduction would be 4.4 percent.

Of course, equations (7.9a) and (7.9b) will produce a different combination of selection rate and disparity ratio for each combination of criminal population parameters. The optimal values may cover a wide range, from 0 to 1.0 for selection rate, and from 1.0 upwards to nearly infinity for the disparity ratio. Nevertheless, as shown in the second and third columns of Table 7.6, the optimal values cover a relatively small range: Optimal selection rates range from .10 to .15, with a median value of around .12; optimal disparity ratios range from 19 to nearly 22, with a median of 20.5. Note that all of the optimal *dr*'s require extrapolation beyond the experimental range. Although the exact optima are thus unreliable, it is safe to say that the most effective program will be more disparate than any currently under consideration.

Sensitivity of the Optimal Policy

That the optimal selection rates and disparity ratios differ little from one scenario to the next suggests that there are few crime reduction benefits to be lost by relying on a compromise policy. Nevertheless, we can check this hypothesis explicitly, by comparing the benefits of the optimal policy under limited information to the crime reductions resulting from implementation of the compromise.

The box plots of Figure 7.3 show this comparison, again given 186 combinations of criminal population characteristics and accuracy rates, a selection rate of .12, and a disparity ratio of 20. The differences between the optimal and the compromise boxes are surprisingly small; in fact, the compromise policy retains 95 percent of the crime-reduction benefits of the optimal policy, on average. So

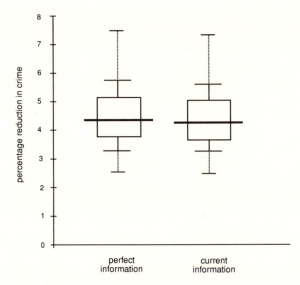

FIGURE 7.3. Perfect information about criminal population is of little value for selective sentencing.

the benefits of selective schemes are not very sensitive to small changes about these close-to-optimal values.

Simplifying slightly, we may conclude that the optimal scheme involves selecting the worst 10 percent of offenders for sentences 20 times longer than the remaining 90 percent. If jail and prison populations are kept constant, this is equivalent to giving 10-year sentences to the predicted high-rate offenders, and cutting the sentences of everyone else to 6 months. This would most likely reduce the aggregate, weighted crime rate by about 4.4 percent, and would very likely reduce it by between 3 and 6 percent.

Of course, it may well be that constraints on selective scales, selection rates, and disparity ratios prevent us from achieving these results. Let us next consider the effects of constraints in these parameters, to see whether the crime-control benefits of this and similar sentencing policies hold up.

Effect of Constraints on Selective Scales

As stated above, there are two primary constraints on the accuracy of selective scales. The first constraint is knowledge: It may be that the data needed are often unavailable, that the data are often unreliable or invalid, or that the statistical techniques for using the data are not sufficiently well developed to make accurate predictions. Even if the data may be found and analyzed to make (reasonably) accurate predictions, however, we may be constrained by ethics: We may decide that some of the variables needed are ethically inappropriate, perhaps because they discriminate explicitly or implicitly on the basis of suspect categories such as race or national origin or because they are not under the control of the offender and are thus unfair.

In the examples provided above, it was assumed that such scales as the INSLAW prosecution scale met the ethical requirements, and that the accuracy of such scales was likely to apply moderately well to other jurisdictions and over time. These conditions may not hold; alternatively, improvements to criminal justice records and statistical technqiues may improve the accuracy of scales available to us. So it is important to test the effects of both improvements and reductions in the accuracy of such scales.

All else equal, we would presume that the more accurate the scale, the less extreme the optimal policy need be: Fewer offenders would have to be selected for special treatment, and that treatment need not be so special. This is borne out by experiment. Figure 7.4 shows optimal values of the selection rate and disparity ratio for a variety of accuracy levels, for three sets of cases: those combinations that resulted in the median values of sr^* and dr^* for each accuracy level, and those combinations that provided 90-percent confidence limits. In fact, optimal selection rates and disparity ratios decline as the selection method becomes more accurate. But for the most relevant range—between accuracy levels of .20 and .40—the differences are small. Note also that the confidence intervals remain small throughout the range of plausible accuracy levels.

The crime reduction benefits from the model policy presented above are relatively insensitive to changes in accuracy. Figure 7.5 shows the crime-

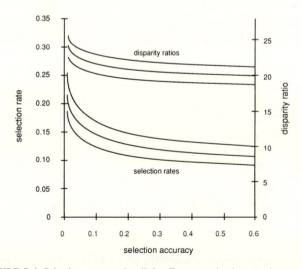

FIGURE 7.4. Selective accuracy has little effect on optimal sentencing program.

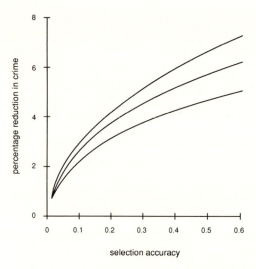

FIGURE 7.5. Effectiveness of compromise policy does not depend upon selective accuracy.

reduction benefits for the compromise policy for the median case and 90-percent confidence intervals, for the entire range of accuracy levels. The more accurate the scale, of course, the higher the crime reduction. But within the relevant range, marginal increases in accuracy have little impact on the benefits of selective sentencing. For example, the INSLAW scale is more than 100 percent more accurate than the Salient Factor Score, but using it instead of the Salient Factor Score would only increase the crime reduction benefits by 50 percent. Within the most relevant range of $.20 < r^2 < .40$, we can be fairly certain that the compromise policy will reduce crime by 3 to 6 percent, and very likely by 4 to 5 percent for a moderately accurate scale with $r^2 = .30$.

Because marginal increases in accuracy are of marginal importance, variables of uncertain ethical standing and marginal predictive utility—unemployment and age, for instance—can probably be removed from predictive scales without substantial costs. Similarly, the increased accuracy provided by powerful but complex statistical methods such as survival analysis (Witte & Schmidt, 1977) and pattern analysis (Fischer, 1984) may not be worth the increased complexity, especially if the complexity increases resistance to their use. A less-accurate scale that is simple enough to be readily accepted may be the better alternative, at least in the short run.

Effect of Constraints on Selection and Disparity Ratios

Disparity Ratio

Most who object to selective sentencing on ethical grounds argue that it is wrong to treat criminals who have committed similar crimes differently. In particular, it is unfair to sentence some offenders to long prison terms on the basis of often-inaccurate predictions as to their future conduct—in effect punishing them for who we think they may be, rather than what we are reasonably certain they have done. The essence of their argument, then, is that the disparity between offenders must be constrained.

Of course, different observers would constrain disparity levels by different amounts. For example, those who subscribe to Kantian ideals of strict retributivism, such as George Fletcher (1982) or Richard Singer (1979), would establish a strict punishment schedule corresponding to the amount of harm done to the victim (and, perhaps, to society). Fletcher and Singer would accept no deviations on the basis of offender characteristics whatever. Others would allow some disparity for ethical reasons; for example, Andrew von Hirsch (1985) would grant shorter sentences to first-time offenders, on the grounds that leniency is called for when an offender's previous conduct has been flawless. Still others, such as John Monahan (1982) or Norval Morris (1982), would balance the constraints of desert against the utilitarian goals of crime control. Observers in the Monahan/Morris "modified just-deserts" mold, in particular, could sanction or fail to sanction a wide variety of selective policies, depending upon such factors as the size of the crime reductions, the amount of disparity, and the accuracy of the selection technique. So it is necessary to consider the entire range of potential disparity levels, from the no-disparity case of 1.0 to the optimum levels of 10 or more.

Assume for simplicity that the selective scale is accurate with $r^2 = .30$; further, perfect information is available about the characteristics of the offender population, so it is possible to identify the optimal policy for that population. Suppose disparity ratios of 10 or more are considered too high: What effect will reductions in the disparity ratio have on the crime control potential of the selective policy?

As shown in Figure 7.6, constraining the disparity ratio has a big effect on the potential for crime reduction. The figure shows the percentage of possible crime reductions that can be obtained, for each value of disparity ratio between 1.0 and 10.0. Despite the high optimum values, 80 to 85 percent of the crime-reduction potential can be obtained if *dr* is as high as 10. Although the efficiency of selective sentencing strategies drops below this range, it drops less quickly than one might at first imagine. At a disparity level of 5.0, 60 to 65 percent of the potential crime reductions can be achieved; even at a level of 3.0, between 40 and 45 percent of the crime-reduction potential remains. This works out to a reduction of between 1.5 and 2.5 percent of all crimes. So a little disparity can go a long way.

If the disparity ratio is in fact constrained to single digits, the selection rate will have to change to compensate. As Table 7.5 shows, the less disparity there is between short and long sentences, the larger the proportion of offenders that should receive long sentences. The effect is not particularly large, however, and

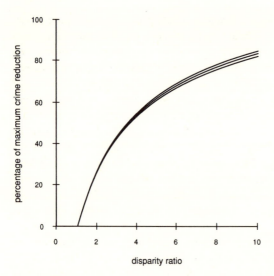

FIGURE 7.6. Disparity constraints reduce effectiveness of selective sentencing.

the optimal rate is close to .20 for most $dr < 10$. And, as shown in Table 7.6, the optimal selection rate is relatively insensitive to differences in criminal population characteristics. So even if the true values of the average offense rate, the likelihood of arrest, and so on can be obtained through further research, this information will be of little use in determining the best response to constraints on the level of disparity.

Selection Ratio

Other researchers, such as Don Gottfredson (1984) and Peter Schmidt and Ann Witte (1984), consider the problem of selection from a different angle. They advocate a policy of selective deinstitutionalization, arguing that the large number of predicted low-rate offenders should be given consistently lower sentences but that the predicted medium- and high-rate offenders should receive about the same sentences they do now. This policy clearly fits our definition of selective incarceration, because it would increase the selectivity of the criminal justice system; but it combines it with a policy of deincarceration, because it would reduce the number of incarcerated offenders by more than enough to compensate. Thus selective deinstitutionalization is certain to increase, rather than reduce the crime rate.

What makes the deinstitutionalization policies interesting for our purposes is that they would constrain the selection rate, rather than the disparity ratio. Specifically, they argue that it is wrong to single out a minority of offenders for consistently higher sentences; selection rates of less than .5 or so should not be allowed. Although a detailed analysis of their proposals would take up more space than is available here, their basic philosophical point—that the selection rate may be as important from an ethical viewpoint as the disparity ratio—is worthy of attention.

Figure 7.7 is the selection rate analogue to Figure 7.6: It shows the likely impact of constraining values of the selection rate on the potential for crime control. Small deviations about the optimal value of .10 have virtually no impact on the effectiveness of the policy, but large deviations of the sort advocated by Gottfredson, Schmidt, and Witte have sizable effects. If long sentences were provided to the 50 percent of offenders who were most likely to be frequent and dangerous—about four times the optimal value—the selective policy could only achieve 50 to 60 percent of the potential crime-reduction impact, for an expected reduction of around 2.5 percent in the crime rate. As with the disparity ratio, constraining the selection ratio reduces the size of the reductions considerably, but the reductions remain substantial.

Some Perspective

All this talk of constraints is intentionally fuzzy, for two reasons. For one, the parameters used to construct selective policies in this work—selection rate and disparity ratio—presuppose some manner of utilitarian selection. Desert purists, such as Andrew von Hirsch or Richard Singer, have typically adopted strong positions that argue against any predictive selection at all. In the few

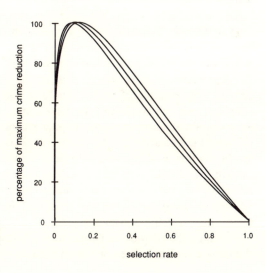

FIGURE 7.7. Best selective sentencing program selects only 10 percent of offenders.

instances when they have considered the objectives of crime control, it has been consciously

> a compromise of principles—a bone thrown to the political yahoos of the law and order right—and inferior on the merits to the more pristine pursuit of justice and justice alone. (Monahan, 1982, p. 35)

Because they seek a sentencing system where there is no place for utilitarian goals, the retributivists offer no guidance as to which utilitarian systems would be least odious.

The second reason is that, for those who would strike a balance between utility and desert, the nature of the balance has been difficult to define. As with pornography, it seems easiest to identify unbalanced policies after the fact. Still, at least some perspective can be added to this discussion by considering explicitly a proposal made by John Monahan (1982). He proposes that the range of reasonable punishments for a given crime be set on the basis of just deserts, but that within this range, the length of the sentence should be proportionate to the expected dangerousness of the offender. Thus the one-time offender who is very unlikely to commit another crime would receive the shortest sentence within the range; an offender who is extremely likely to commit serious crimes at high rates in the future would receive the longest.

Translated into the terms used here, the disparity ratio for a given crime should be no greater than either (1) the disparity between the expected dangerousness of an offender in the predicted high-rate group and the expected dangerousness of an offender in the predicted low-rate group, or (2) the ratio of the highest and lowest sentences that may be justified by desert, whichever is less. Although Monahan provides a procedure for determining the range of desert-based punishments, such a procedure has never been implemented. Given the limited statutory guidance given to judges in indeterminate sentencing states, however, it seems reasonable to presume that restriction (2) is not binding; so let us consider the constraints placed on selective sentencing by restriction (1) alone.

Restriction (1) is obviously most limiting when the selective scale is least accurate: For example, if we knew nothing about the relative dangerousness of offenders who had committed identical crimes, there would be no justification for giving them other than identical punishments; disparity ratios of greater than 1.0 would not be allowed. Restriction (1) also constrains policy more closely if the distribution of offense rates is relatively unskewed: Again to take the limiting case, if all offenders committed crimes at identical rates, there would be no difference in their dangerousness, and no justification for disparate sentencing. So both the accuracy of selective scales and the disparity of offense rates determine which selective sentencing schemes are ethical.

In fact, the allowable disparity ratio for each combination of accuracy and skewness has already been presented in Figure 7.1. If perfect information about accuracy and skewness were available, it would be possible to estimate the allowable disparity, and solve for the optimal selection rate and the resulting crime reduction.

The results of just such a calculation are shown on Figure 7.8. (Because accuracy and skewness are the primary issues here, these parameters are explicitly controlled for; but keep in mind that there would be a moderately large band about each of these lines corresponding to different possible values of the other population parameters.) For each case shown in the figure, the disparity ratio was set to the maximum allowable, and the selection rate was then set to the best value possible. The effects, although less impressive than before, are still substantial. Within the relevant range of selective accuracy and offense rate skewness, a modified just-deserts policy may reduce the crime rate by anywhere between 1 and 3 percent; a reasonable best guess might assume moderate skewness and an accuracy level of .30, for a crime reduction of 1.6 percent. In order to achieve such a reduction, it would be necessary to increase the sentences of the predicted worst 30 percent of offenders by 75 percent and to reduce the sentences of the rest by about 30 percent. For the average crime, then, the predicted low-rate offenders would get a 1-year jail term, whereas the predicted high-rate offenders would serve about 2.5 years.

The modified just-deserts policy would be roughly half as effective as the unconstrained optimal policy. Nevertheless, the constraints are much less limiting when the selective scale is accurate and the distribution of offense rates is quite skewed. This results from the fact that the disparity between predicted high- and low-rate offenders—and thus the allowable sentencing disparity ratio—is much greater under these conditions.

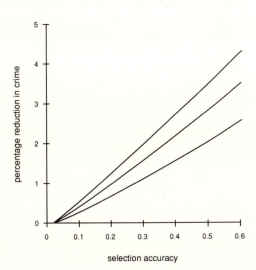

FIGURE 7.8. Modified just deserts sentencing about half as effective as optimal policy.

selection accuracy

Whether the added justice of restriction (1) is enough to justify an implicit 2-percent crime increase, or whether the injustice of any selective policy is worth a 1- to 3-percent crime reduction, are questions well beyond the scope of this study. And, as mentioned above, these figures are only very rough estimates, because they fail to account for deterrence, rehabilitation, and other factors that may influence crime rates. So a specific policy recommendation would be out of place. Still, the order of magnitude of the results is likely to remain about constant: The crime-control effectiveness of even the best sentencing policy is almost certainly less than 6 percent; a modified just-deserts policy would probably cut these reductions in half. If nothing else, even these rough estimates should help to provide a focus for discussing how the constraints of ethics, knowledge, and resources should be balanced against the probable crime control benefits.

Selectivity and Prison Construction

As described in the previous chapter, it is an open question whether it makes economic sense to build more jails and prisons. If the indirect benefits of some amount of crime reduction are 2.6 times greater than the direct benefits to would-be victims, prison construction is about 50 percent likely to pay off. If the indirect benefits are less than 2.6 times the direct benefits, the total benefits of reducing crime will probably not be sufficient to merit the construction and operating costs. If the indirect benefit ratio is greater than 2.6, prison construction is probably a good idea.

This changes if the criminal justice system becomes more selective. By using existing beds more wisely, judges and parole boards would increase the crime reduction effectiveness of each bed, and thus the benefits of building more. It is even possible that prison construction that is not cost-effective with current sentencing practices would become cost-effective if sentencing became more selective.

This is illustrated by Table 7.7, which shows the distribution of breakeven indirect benefits ratios associated with the current system, a modified just-deserts sentencing policy, and the optimum sentencing policy. The median breakeven value, currently 2.6, would drop to 2.4 with the modified just-deserts policy, and to 2.1 with the optimal policy. Alternatively, if we had persuasive evidence that indirect benefits really exceeded direct benefits by 2.5, there is only a 42-percent chance that additional prisons will be cost-effective now; but the probability increases to 56 percent under modified just deserts, and to 77 percent under the optimal policy.

Another way of portraying essential the same results is to use elasticities to calculate the return on investment associated with a 1-percent increase in prison space. If the indirect benefits ratio were 2.5, the benefits would be $351 million

TABLE 7.7
Distribution of Breakeven Indirect Benefits Ratios for Three Sentencing Policies

	Current policy	Modified just-desert policy	Optimum policy
Maximum	4.316	4.020	3.384
90th percentile	3.566	3.258	2.887
75th	3.028	2.781	2.442
Median	2.582	2.411	2.140
25th	2.320	2.139	1.910
10th	1.943	1.791	1.582
Minimum	1.762	1.545	1.354
Mean IBR	2.679	2.470	2.188
Standard deviation	(0.562)	(0.522)	(0.458)
Mean elasticity	0.156	0.164	0.179
Standard deviation	(0.023)	(0.024)	(0.025)

and the costs $360 million—a return on investment of -2.5 percent. Under the modified just-deserts policy, benefits climb to $363 million (a return of 0.9 percent), and under the optimum policy, benefits increase to $383 million (a return of 6.4 percent). Whether any of these returns are sufficient to merit the investment depends upon the alternatives available. And, of course, the correct indirect benefits ratio may be higher or lower than 2.5. But selective sentencing clearly increases the attractiveness of incapacitation, and this increase may well be policy relevant.

If judges and parole boards were unconstrained by ethical concerns, selective adult sentencing programs could reduce crime rates by 3 to 6 percent without increasing prison populations. Because predicted frequent offenders would receive sentences 20 times longer than predicted infrequent offenders, and many of the predictions would be wrong, most would consider such a scheme unfair. Proposals that balance desert against crime control would reduce crime by 1 to 3 percent without increasing prison populations, while reducing the potential for unfairness. Selective sentencing strengthens the argument for more prisons, but the cost-effectiveness of prison construction remains uncertain.

Changing the Risks of Incarceration

As with the sentencing analysis, the first step in assessing the effectiveness of selective police and prosecution programs was to identify the most influential population characteristics. In preliminary analysis, the same seven characteristics used in the sentencing analysis proved particularly important again. Although the eighth characteristic—the shape of the distribution of criminal career lengths—appeared to have an effect on police/prosecution effectiveness, it was less than any of the others and was dropped for simplicity.

Although sentencing programs can be described using only three parameters (disparity ratio, selection rate, and accuracy), police and prosecution programs require a fourth—the slope of the police and prosecutor's production function. As described above in the section on constraints, this parameter accounts for an expected reduction in overall incarceration rates should the police and the prosecutor choose to concentrate their resources on a few cases. Addition of this parameter made it possible to keep constant the amount of police and prosecutorial resources, while at the same time estimating the effects of dramatic shifts in the allocation of these resources. Reasonable low, medium, and high values for these parameters are shown in Table 7.8. Note that the maximum disparity ratio for police and prosecution programs is assumed to be about twice as high as the maximum ratio for sentencing programs; this reflects the findings of several program evaluations, as detailed below. Similarly, the accuracy estimates cover a broader range. This reflects the variety of information sources that may be legitimately used by police and prosecutors, but not by judges and parole boards: crime pattern and MO analysis, informant information, and the like.

In total, then, eleven parameters can be expected to affect the crime-reduction effectiveness of selective police and prosecution programs—seven population parameters and four program parameters. Again, a nested Box-Behnken/central composite design was used to identify representative and uncorrelated combinations of population and program characteristics; a total of 1,425 combinations were used in the analysis.

Regression was used to account for the effects of these parameters on crime-control effectiveness. Results are shown in Table 7.9. As with sentencing, a translog function described these results with excellent (99.9 percent) accuracy. Once again, program characteristics had by far the largest impact on effectiveness; interactions between program and population characteristics again had little impact, suggesting that the appropriate policy would be largely independent of

TABLE 7.8
Range of Selective Police and Prosecution Programs Considered

	Accuracy	Selection rate	Disparity ratio	Production function
Very high	.602	.301	14.89	1.00
High	.500	.250	12.50	0.94
Medium	.350	.175	9.00	0.85
Low	.200	.100	5.50	0.76
Very low	.098	.049	3.11	0.70

TABLE 7.9
Indicators of Crime-Reduction Effectiveness of Selective Sentencing Police and Prosecution Programs

	Coefficient	Standard error	Probability
Selective police/prosecution policy			
Explains 83.9 percent of variance			
Main effects			
Accuracy	.4647	.0267	
Selection	−.0854	.0234	
Disparity	.9077	.0117	
Production	.2727	.1242	.0283
Quadratic effects			
Accuracy	−.0872	.0019	
Selection	−.1633	.0010	
Disparity	−.2106	.0027	
Production	−.1381	.0549	.0121
Interactions			
Accuracy/selection	−.0582	.0018	
Accuracy/disparity	−.0515	.0024	
Accuracy/production	.0362	.0095	.0002
Selection/disparity	−.2175	.0020	
Selection/production	.4286	.0079	
Disparity/production	.2851	.0107	
Offending population			
Explains 15.8 percent of variance			
Main effects			
Mean lambda	.4858	.1081	
Skew of offense rate	1.1956	.1052	
Mean group size	−1.1429	.1953	
Corr (T,λ)	1.9602	.0196	
Mean arrest rate	.3263	.1195	.0064
Corr (q,λ)	.3219	.0380	
Quadratic effects			
Mean lambda	−.1700	.0124	
Skew of offense rate	−.5273	.0202	
Mean career length	.0667	.0026	
Mean arrest rate	−.1730	.0146	
Corr $(q,)$	.0805	.0029	
Interaction effects			
Lambda/skew	−.2281	.0193	
Lambda/group	−.1400	.0371	.0002
Lambda/arrest	−.3208	.0163	
Lambda/corr (q,λ)	.0574	.0069	
Skew/group	−.1444	.0476	.0025
Skew/arrest	−.2253	.0210	
Skew/corr (q,λ)	.4164	.0088	

(*continued*)

TABLE 7.9 (*Continued*)

	Coefficient	Standard error	Probability
Group/arrest	−.1357	.0404	.0008
Group/corr (q, λ)	.0425	.0170	.0124
Arrest/corr (q, λ)	.0575	.0075	
Interaction of program and population characteristics			
Explains 0.2 percent of variance			
Accuracy/lambda	−.0565	.0049	
Accuracy/skew	.0171	.0063	.0062
Accuracy/arrest	−.0565	.0053	
Accuracy/corr (q, λ)	.0109	.0022	
Selection/lambda	.0627	.0038	
Selection/skew	−.1440	.0049	
Selection/corr (T, λ)	.0101	.0048	.0360
Selection/arrest	.0627	.0042	
Selection/corr (q, λ)	.0156	.0018	
Disparity/skew	−.0880	.0071	
Disparity/corr (q, λ)	.0218	.0025	
Production/lambda	−.0572	.0227	.0117
Production/skew	.1112	.0291	.0001
Production/arrest	−.0572	.0246	.0204
Constant	.4965	.3520	.1586

Note. Probabilities less than .0005 not shown. R^2 = .9988. F $(49,1375)$ = 24,118. Average crime reduction = 3.706 percent, with standard error of estimate = .0519 percent.

the true characteristics of the population. As with the case of sentencing, then, we can anticipate that further research into the nature of the offending population will make estimates of the size of selective benefits more precise; but research will be much less helpful in determining the optimal policy.

Identifying the Optimal Policy

As before, we may consider constraints on resources to be binding for the moment, and use the results of Table 7.9 to determine optimal strategies for reallocating fixed police and prosecution resources. Because it is most reasonable to presume that the accuracy of the selection method and the slope of the production function are both beyond our control, at least in the short run, we may simplify matters by dividing our parameters into two groups: control parameters (the disparity ratio and the selection rate) and exogenous factors (including population characteristics, accuracy, and the production function slope). As before, we take the derivatives of the equation in Table 7.9 with respect to each of the control parameters, set them to zero, and solve simultaneously, producing equations of the form,

$$sr^* = \alpha_1 \, \Pi_i \, X_i^{\beta i} \qquad\qquad (7.10a)$$

$$dr^* = \alpha_2 \, \Pi j \, X_j^{\beta j}. \qquad\qquad (7.10b)$$

Coefficients are shown in Table 7.10.

As above, it makes sense to ask two sets of questions about the unconstrained optima. Suppose first that perfect information is available as to the characteristics of the offending population. How could we best tailor our selective policies to these characteristics, and how well would these policies work? Second, what is the best policy to adopt given that we are (largely) ignorant of these characteristics? How much does our ignorance cost us?

A related set of questions, concerning the optimal conditions when there are constraints upon the control parameters, will be considered later; for now, let us concentrate on the behavior of the optima under various combinations of population characteristics.

Unconstrained Optima under Limited Information

As Table 7.10 shows, the characteristics of the optimal selective police and prosecution program are bound to differ from one combination of population characteristics to the next. Relatively high selection rates are indicated when the average offense rate is high, the skewness of offense rates among offenders is low, the average probability of arrest is high, and when predictive accuracy is low and the production function is nearly linear. Similarly, high disparity ratios are indicated when the average offense rate and probability of arrest are both low.

Of course, the sentencing analysis developed above suggests that statistically significant differences may not be practically important. To find out,

TABLE 7.10
Coefficients of Optimal Selection Equations
(Police/Prosecution)

	Selection rate	Disparity ratio
Constant	.0753	32.8120
Accuracy	−.1476	−.0460
Production function	1.3131	−.0012
Mean λ	.2924	−.1510
Standard deviation λ	−.4598	.0284
Mean T	.0471	−.0243
Mean q	.2924	−.1510
Corr (q,λ)	−.0020	.0529

consider the results when equations (7.10a) and (7.10b) are applied to a sample of representative cases. The sample consists of the usual 62 combination of crime population characteristics replied by nine combinations of accuracy and production function values, for a total of 558 cases.

Results are shown in Table 7.11. As before, the optimal values of the control parameters all fall in a fairly narrow range: the optimal disparity ratio is probably between 30 and 32 and is almost certainly between 28 and 34; the optimal selection rate is probably between .03 and .05 and almost certainly between .025 and .06. And again, the predicted crime reductions fall in a much wider range, with 90-percent confidence limits of 3 and 8 percent. Our best guess as to the crime-control effectiveness of optimal selective police and prosecution policies—if we knew enough to identify what they were—would be about an 5.5-percent reduction in crimes committed.

It is revealing to compare these results to those obtained in the sentencing analysis, above. The most striking differences are in the control parameters. Recall that the optimal selective sentencing program would weed out the 10 to 14 percent of incarcerated offenders predicted to have the highest offense rates (equivalently, 5 to 7 percent of all offenders who are ever arrested and are thus known to the police), and give them sentences about 20 times longer than the other offenders. The optimal police and prosecution program, in contrast, would select 3 to 5 percent of the offenders known to the police and increase the disparity of incarceration risks to about 30 times their prior levels. Because the optimal disparity ratios for both programs require extrapolations beyond the ranges considered in this experiment, these estimates are not very precise. Nevertheless it is clear that, all else equal, the police and the prosecutor should focus more resources on fewer offenders than the judge.

The results of such selective activities, although comparable between the

TABLE 7.11

The Optimal Selective Police and Prosecution Program
Would Reduce Crime by 4 to 8 Percent

Percentile	Crime reduction	Selection rate	Disparity ratio
Maximum	10.624	.063	34.500
90th	7.848	.051	32.585
75th	6.921	.045	31.780
Median	5.799	.039	30.977
25th	4.799	.032	30.033
10th	4.125	.028	29.475
Minimum	3.039	.024	27.903
Mean	5.937	.039	30.956
Standard deviation	1.442	.017	1.127

two programs, appear to favor police and prosecution programs slightly. Specifically, the optimal "front-end" program will be about 25 percent more effective at reducing crime than the optimal "back-end" program. This is borne out in case-by-case comparisons: in about 90 percent of the population combinations, the police and prosecution program is more effective than the sentencing program. Particularly because most of the present debate concerns selective sentencing, this suggests that more attention should be given to targeted arrest and conviction activities.

Sensitivity of the Optimum

Rounding to even numbers, we may conclude that the most effective front-end programs would exhibit a selection rate of about 4 percent and a disparity ratio of about 30, on average. The narrowness of the range about the optimal figures suggests that little would be lost by applying these averages to all cases, but an explicit check would be more conclusive. Suppose a program with these characteristics were applied to each of the 588 combinations described above. How much would be lost through adoption of a suboptimal program?

The answer is, "So little it's not even worth a graph." As it happens, the compromise policy is 99.6 percent as effective as the optimum in the typical case; it is 98.7 percent as effective in 90 percent of the cases, and 98 percent as effective in all of them. As with sentencing, one size fits all remarkably well.

If we are not constrained by ethical considerations or knowledge, if police and prosecution selection schemes are about as accurate as those described above, if the slope of the production function is really between .70 and 1.0, and if the basic assumptions about deterrence, the course of criminal careers, and the criminal justice system itself are all (more or less) correct, then the optimal police and prosecution policy would be to target additional resources on 4 percent of the offenders, so that these offenders run a risk of arrest that is about 30 times what it is at present. This would reduce the aggregate, seriousness-weighted crime rate by 3 to 8 percent; the most likely crime reduction would be about 5.5 percent.

These are big "ifs." Selection rates, disparity ratios, and selective scales may all be constrained by knowledge and ethical considerations; the police and the prosecutor may already be more or less efficient than expected. Let us consider these assumptions next.

Effects of Constraints on Selective Scales

One would expect that the accuracy of the selective scheme used would affect the optimal selection rate and disparity ratio. The sentencing analysis confirmed the commonsense notion that accurate scales lead to more intensive programs: If our information is accurate, we can focus more attention on more people with greater confidence. Table 7.11 shows that the same holds true for police and prosecution programs.

Figure 7.9 shows the effects of changes in accuracy, for the median case and 90-percent confidence limits. As shown, the effectiveness of front-end selective programs is slightly more sensitive to small changes in accuracy than that of back-end programs. Suppose, for example, the compromise selective policy were applied to the most likely combination of population parameters (the middle line in the figure). If a scale as inaccurate as the Salient Factor Score were used, the program would reduce crime by a shade over 4 percent, but if a method as accurate as the INSLAW scale were used, the crime-reduction benefits would be 6.6 percent—65 percent higher. In sentencing, the crime reduction associated with the INSLAW scale is only 50 percent higher than that associated with the Salient Factor Score. This suggests that accurate target selection may be somewhat more critical to the success of front-end efforts than back-end efforts. Fortunately, more usable information is typically available to the police and prosecutor than to judges and parole boards, so it is probably easier for the front end of the system to make accurate judgments, or to find additional information when needed.

Effects of Changes in the Incarceration Production Function

At least in theory, the incarceration production function can have an enormous effect on the effectiveness of a selective program. The higher the slope of

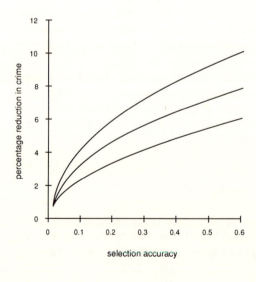

FIGURE 7.9. Accuracy is critical to effectiveness of selective police/prosecutor programs.

the production function—the closer it is to 1.0—the less is lost by shifting resources from cases involving predicted nondangerous to predicted dangerous offenders. When the slope is low and the production function exhibits strongly decreasing marginal returns, a shift in resources reduces the aggregate incarceration rate. Although more dangerous offenders will be incarcerated, fewer non-dangerous offenders will be. This will certainly offset and may even overwhelm the benefits of focusing on the worst criminals.

Marginal decreasing returns should affect the optimal values of the control parameters, as well. The lower the slope, the more is lost by shifting each incremental unit of resources from cases involving nondangerous (but easy-to-catch) offenders to dangerous (but more difficult-to-catch) criminals. Thus fewer resources should be shifted if the slope is low, and this will be reflected in lower optimal values of the disparity ratio. Judging from previous results, it is reasonable to expect that the optimal selection rate will increase to compensate. Simplifying our language slightly, we might expect the following:

> If the police and the prosecutor are very efficient at producing incarcerations, they should focus many resources on a few, especially dangerous offenders. The less efficient they are, the fewer resources they should focus on a larger number of dangerous offenders.

At very low levels of efficiency, it may be that the optimal selection rate is so high, and the optimal disparity ratio so low, that the optimal policy is indistinguishable from the current, unselective policy. If the slope of the production function is this influential within the relevant range of possibilities, it may be that we need to know much more about how police solve crimes and prosecutors obtain convictions before we can mount a selective campaign with confidence.

The back-of-the-envelope analysis described above suggested that the slope of the police production function was no less than .75 to .80. Hedging our bets slightly, we suppose that the slope could take on any value from .70 to 1.0. Applying these values to the standard set of 62 combinations, allowing r^2 to vary from .20 to .50, and solving for the optimal selection rate and disparity ratio, provides the crime reductions shown in Figure 7.10. The three lines correspond to the combinations that provided crime-reduction benefits at the 95th, 50th, and 5th percentiles.

As expected, the higher the slope, the greater the crime-reduction benefits. Selective policies are between 10 and 15 percent more effective at the high end of the range than at the low end; this works out to a difference in crime reduction of between 0.4 and 0.8 percent, depending upon the combination of population parameters. So the differences in result are small enough that they would probably not be noticed.

Perhaps more important, variations in β_P have little impact on the optimal values of sr and dr. The optimal value of the disparity ratio is almost identical at

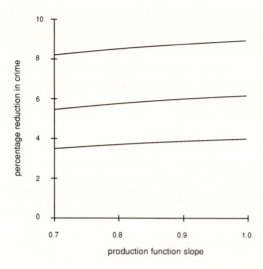

FIGURE 7.10. Within relevant range, police/prosecutor production function is unimportant.

the low end of the range of slopes as at the high end. The optimal selection rate is almost 40 percent lower when $\beta_P = .70$ as when $\beta_P = 1.0$, but this is a difference that makes no difference. Even in the worst case, the compromise policy ($sr = .08$, $dr = 30$) retains 97 percent of the crime-reduction benefits of the optimal policy. In most cases, it retains 99 percent or more of the benefits. Here, again, one size fits all remarkably well.

Of course, more research is needed into the incarceration production function, because it is bound to help police and prosecutors manage their workload more efficiently. But this analysis suggests that the findings of that research may not influence the shape of selective police and prosecution policies and programs by much.

Effects of Constraints on Control Parameters

In the case of selective sentencing policies, the primary constraints on the control parameters were ethical. Many feel it wrong to issue disparate sentences to some (presumably small) proportion of offenders on the basis of imprecise predictions. This led to calls for constraining the allowable disparity ratio and (sometimes) the allowable selection rate.

The constraints on selective police and prosecution programs are of an entirely different nature. For most observers, ethical concerns are not an issue: So long as the police and the prosecutor are careful not to adopt methods that infringe on the fundamental liberties of their suspects and so long as there is a rational basis for doing so, the courts (and most philosophers of law) have agreed that they may focus their attention as they will. The reasoning is that police and prosecutors do not themselves punish offenders; only when their actions begin to resemble punishment (e.g., when wire taps infringe on privacy, or when frequent street stops border on harrassment) should they be restricted. Presumably law enforcement officials would be just as thorough in investigating and prosecuting all offenders, if only they had the resources (Moore et al., 1984).

What constrains selective law enforcement programs is not ethics, but knowledge. It may be that the methods generally available to the police and the prosecutor to increase an individual's risks of punishment, given a crime, do not work so well as we would like them to. Clever offenders may recognize when they are being watched and wait until the watchers have gone home before committing their next crime. Vertical prosecution may help to ensure that the available evidence gets the best possible hearing in court, but sufficient evidence is not always available to convict an offender, no matter how well it is presented.

Such constraints may presumably be overcome if the police and the prosecutor devote enough resources to a case. This was one reason for including a description of the incarceration production function in the incapacitation model. But the range of values used in this analysis describe the activities typically adopted by law enforcement officials and not those that would be adopted if a new set of selective activities were adopted. Simply too little is known about the production function for selective actions. And the anecdotal evidence of especially difficult cases suggests that some cases are almost impossible to solve to everyone's satisfaction, no matter how many resources are put into a case. Many feel Bruno Hauptmann was framed, and that Lee Harvey Oswald worked with associates. D. B. Cooper is still at large.

These problems constrain the disparity ratio, but knowledge may also indirectly constrain the selection rate. Suppose a jurisdiction took the figures above more seriously than they deserve to be taken and decided to implement the compromise optimal policy, with disparity ratio of 30 and selection rate of .04. Suppose further that a slope of .85 reasonably fit the incarceration production function for adult offenders in this jurisdiction, not only for routine activities but for selective activities as well. Then from equation (7.6a), this jurisdiction would be devoting about 69.5 percent of its total street crime resources to dangerous offenders.

Of course, this means that only 30 percent of total resources are available for crimes involving other adult offenders. This may pose political problems for both the police and the prosecutor. For example, most agencies that have adopted a selective focus have done so by creating special units devoted to the purpose, but it is extremely unlikely that an agency would establish a special unit of this size. (If it did, it would clearly make more sense to call the rest of the agency "special.") A more promising alternative seems likely to be adopted in the long run: Special policies would be established to ensure that cases involving the most frequent and dangerous offenders receive the attention they deserve, drawing on the resources of the rank-and-file (Spelman, 1990). Still, given the need to satisfy victims, witnesses, and the general public that justice is being done, it seems unlikely that the police and prosecutors would be willing to devote so many resources to so few cases.

An even more important problem may not be solvable through simple changes in administrative practices: Focusing on certain offenders and their crimes requires that we know something about all offenders and all crimes, and it may prove impossible to obtain this information with the meager resources left available for this purpose. For example, much of the work in a criminal investigation is conducted by the patrol officers who take the crime report. The statements they take from victims and witnesses, and the physical evidence they collect, sometimes lead crime analysts and detectives to recognize that the crime was committed by a particular frequent offender. Sometimes they do not recognize who the offender is until after they have devoted substantial resources to following up the case. If the department were to restrict investigations in crimes not clearly committed by a target offender, it would reduce the depth of preliminary and follow-up investigations. This would reduce the number of arrests for target offenders resulting from routine investigation; it would also reduce the likelihood that the police could identify patterns that can help to identify and build strong cases against these offenders in the first place. To the degree that this information is needed to support the work of the other 70 percent of the department, the police may be unable to achieve the disparity ratios they seek.

Put in economic terms, we might say that fixed costs, some of them devoted to nontargets, must be paid before we can support a selective program of certain size. The larger the selective program, the larger these fixed costs would have to be. But the department simply may not have the resources needed to pay both the fixed costs and the variable costs associated with a given combination of selection rate and disparity ratio. Of course, if enough data were available, this fixed cost could have been taken into account in building the incapacitation model; unfortunately, selective police programs are a relatively new and untested technology, and no such information is available. The admittedly second-best response is to constrain the selection rate.

Yet another difficulty may result in larger-than-optimal selection rates. In the previous section, it was argued that the optimal selection rate for sentencing was about 12 percent of ever-incarcerated offenders. There are obvious administrative advantages to a program in which all criminal justice agencies focus on the same offenders. If a sentencing program were constrained to focusing on only 8 percent of the ever-incarcerated offenders (about 4 percent of all those known to police), Figure 7.7 shows that it would obtain only some 60 to 70 percent of the potential benefits. So it may be more reasonable to widen the net for police and prosecution programs than to narrow it for sentencing. This may be particularly attractive if the knowledge is not available to obtain disparity ratios of 20 to 30, but if disparity ratios of 8 or 10 can be achieved. In this case, a broadly cast net may actually be the most effective feasible strategy.

A close examination of evaluations of police and prosecution programs can help to identify the current constraints on these control parameters. But first, consider how constraints on these parameters affect the potential benefits of selective programs and policies.

Disparity Ratio

Figure 7.11 shows the relationship between disparity ratio and crime-control effectiveness, expressed as a percentage of the maximum possible crime reduction. The three lines shown correspond to those cases which are at the 5th, 50th, and 95th percentiles of the distribution of optimal disparity ratios; these cases are also close to the median and 90-percent confidence limits for crime-reduction effectiveness. The curves are quite similar: All ascend quickly but begin to level off as the disparity ratio approaches the high end of the relevant range. Even though the optimal policy is out of reach, then, very modest levels of the disparity ratio will obtain most of the crime-reduction benefits. A ratio of 10.0, one-third the optimal value, would reduce crime by 76 to 82 percent of the maximum possible amount; even a ratio of 5.0 would obtain 56 to 62 percent of the maximum possible reduction. Higher disparity may be better, but—as with sentencing—a little disparity goes a long way.

This is particularly heartening, because it would be difficult to measure the disparity ratio associated with an operating selective program. The problem is

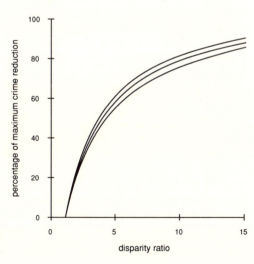

FIGURE 7.11. Moderately disparate police/prosecution program almost as effective as optimum.

that it is impossible to know for sure what would have happened to the target offenders had they not been targeted. Thus it is impossible to measure the increase in risks that any given individual runs. An aggregate result could be obtained through use of an experimental design; as suggested above, a carefully monitored quasi-experimental analysis could probably provide useful estimates. In any case, evaluating the disparity ratio for police and prosecutor programs is bound to be more difficult than for sentencing programs, so it is fortunate that small deviations do not seem to matter very much.

Of course, more offenders must be targeted to compensate should the risks to each target be reduced below the optimum. Although the optimal selection rate is relatively sensitive to small changes in the disparity ratio, small deviations from the optimum are pratically unimportant. For example, consider the most likely combination of population and criminal justice system parameters. If the disparity ratio were somehow constrained to be 10.0 (this is the most dramatic resource reallocation the police and prosecutor can muster), the best selection rate would be .08; if *dr* were now constrained to be only 5.0 (the prosecutor drops out the program, perhaps), *sr* should increase to .125. Nevertheless, if *sr* remained at .08, the crime-reduction benefits would be 95 percent as high as the optimum benefits. Again, this is a difference that makes no difference.

Selection Rate

Figure 7.12 shows the effects of constraining selection rate on the potential effectiveness of the selective program. The curves are similar in form to those of Figure 7.7 (and to those of Figures 7.6 and 7.11, for that matter): Although a

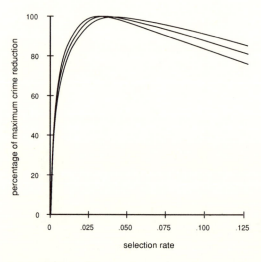

FIGURE 7.12. Narrowly focused police/prosecution program almost as effective as optimum.

selective program that chose a very small value would be clearly suboptimal, a selection rate as low as 1 percent of the offenders known to the police can still obtain 78 to 85 percent of the potential crime-reduction benefits. This works out to a 3.5 to 5.5 percent reduction in the aggregate crime rate—a sizable reduction despite the narrow focus of the program. On the other hand, achieving a disparity ratio of 30 for even so limited a group would appear to require something like 36 percent of the police and prosecutor's street-crime resources, so this is still an enormous program.

More Perspective

The philosophical problems that formed the core of the constraint problem for sentencing are not really at issue when considering programs that only manipulate the risks of incarceration. On the other hand, the constraints of knowledge and internal politics suggested above can be very important, particularly in the short run. To estimate the degree to which such constraints may be binding, and to inject at least a modicum of reality into this abstract discussion, let us consider the utility of current selective police and prosecution programs.

Although police have explicitly focused on frequent and dangerous offenders at least since the 1970s, comprehensive evaluations of their efforts have been rare. Two important exceptions were conducted by the Police Foundation, one in 1976, the other 10 years later. Although neither evaluation explicitly considered disparity ratios or selection rates, both provided information that can be converted to these forms.

The first study was conducted on two tactics employed by the Tactical Squad of the Kansas City Police Department—stakeouts and surveillance (Pate, Bowers, & Parks, 1976). In the stakeout, or "location-oriented-patrol" strategy, tactical officers were assigned to watch a specific location at which serious crimes had been committed in the past, or at which there was some other good reason to believe that a serious crime would be committed while the officers were at the scene. The surveillance, or "perpetrated-oriented-patrol" strategy was more directly focused on particular offenders: officers were directed to follow suspects around, in order to gather information that might help to build a case against them, or in hopes of catching them in the act of committing a crime. Although the stakeout tactics appeared to be oriented to locations rather than offenders, officers felt that geographic crime patterns resulted from the actions of especially frequent offenders who continued to attack the same neighborhood. Both tactics were evaluated partly on their success at arresting and convicting offenders identified as particularly dangerous by the department's Criminal Information Center (CIC).

Little information is provided in the evaluation as to the number of offenders identified as frequent and dangerous by the CIC, or the department's success in arresting them and obtaining their conviction. The evaluation notes, however, that the surveillance squad began its program with a list of 107 targets, all adults. As target offenders were arrested, or were found to have died, moved out of town, or quit committing crimes, they were replaced on the list by other offenders. If all targets were replaced as soon as they were disposed of, then the effective selection rate for this squad is equal to 107 divided by the number of street offenders active at any given time in Kansas City in the mid-1970s. As a rough cut at this, let us suppose the following: According to the FBI, 40,000 crimes were reported to the police in Kansas City in 1975; about 30 percent of all index crimes were reported to the police; about two-thirds of index crimes were committed by adults during the mid-1970s; the average index offense rate was about 7.5; and between 1.3 and 1.6 offenders participate in the average crime. If the system is in steady state, then 7,400 to 9,100 adults were responsible for Kansas City's crimes in 1975, and about 47 percent of these people—3,500 to 4,300—were known to police. Thus the (momentary) selection rate for the surveillance program would be between .025 and .031 of active adults.

The evidence on disparity ratios requires fewer cavalier assumptions. The evaluators collected the number of felony arrests, indictments, and convictions, and the number of hours spent obtaining these results, for both the stakeout and surveillance squads, and for a control group of rank-and-file patrol officers. A rough estimate of the disparity ratio can be obtained by dividing the results obtained through each tactic by the number of officer-years (providing a measure of each tactic's efficiency) and then dividing the efficiency figures for each of the offender-based tactics by the figures for the control group. The results of these calculations are shown in the first two columns of Table 7.12.

Similar methods may be applied to data collected as part of the second evaluation, of the Washington, DC, Police Department's Repeat Offender Project (ROP, pronounced "rope"). The ROP unit uses a variety of tactics to arrest predicted frequent offenders, but most are some adaptation of surveillance and warrant service. During 6 months in 1983, ROP worked a total of 289 target

TABLE 7.12

Disparity Ratios and Selection Rates Obtained by Police Repeat Offender Programs

Parameter	Kansas City		Washington, DC	
	Stakeouts	Surveillance	Surveillance	Stakeouts
dr(arrest)	11.942	6.702	7.833	6.111
dr(conviction)	7.385	4.077	na	na
Selection rate	.014 to .036		.015 to .038	

Sources. Kansas City: Pate, Bowers, & Parks, 1976. Washington: Martin & Sherman, 1985.

offenders (Martin, 1985). Targets were worked for 3 months, on average, before they were either arrested or replaced; thus some 145 offenders were selected at any given time. Some 52,000 index crimes were reported in Washington during 1983; using the same assumptions described above leads to a selection rate between .026 and .032—the same as the Kansas City surveillance squad.

Information about the disparity ratio obtained by the ROP unit is probably more accurate than that collected by the Kansas City evaluators because it was obtained using an experimental design (Martin, 1985, p. 5–4). The disparity ratio in this case is simply the arrest rate for the experimental group (which received the ROP "treatment") divided by the arrest rate for the control group. The evaluators provide arrest rates for two groups of offenders—ROP targets (most of whom were arrested when they were caught committing a crime while under surveillance) and warrant targets (who only needed to be located, since they were already wanted on an arrest or bench warrant). Results are provided in the last two columns of Table 7.12.

So much for selective police action. A thorough evaluation of selective prosecution was conducted by the Mitre Corporation in 1976; the evaluators considered career criminal programs operating in four urban counties: Franklin County (Columbus), Ohio; Kalamazoo, Michigan; Orleans Parish (New Orleans), Louisiana; and San Diego, California (Chelimsky & Dahmann, 1981). Their evaluation compared the number and outcomes of cases processed by the usual methods with those processed by a special career criminal unit. The special unit was expected to increase the likelihood of incarceration by devoting more attention to each target case, by assigning one prosecutor to handle each case throughout the judicial process, by restricting the scope of plea bargaining, and by working with the police department to ensure that the evidence was as strong as possible.

Data are available for both before and after periods for target offenders; thus the disparity ratio (for incarceration given arrest) may be calculated directly, using formula (7.2). Although it is tempting to estimate the selection rate as the proportion of all arrests that were selected for prosecution through the career criminal unit, this ignores the fact that frequent offenders are more likely to be arrested than others. A quick calculation provides a more accurate answer: As shown earlier in this chapter, the ratio of offense rates for predicted frequent offenders to rates of predicted infrequent offenders depends only upon the accuracy of the estimate and the skewness of the distribution of offense rates, and not on the selection rate. If $r^2 = .35$, it is reasonable to estimate that $\lambda_D = 2.6\lambda_N$, where D refers to dangerous offenders and N to nondangerous offenders. Simplifying somewhat the results of Chapter 5, we find that $q_j = k\lambda_j^{\beta q}$, where the most likely value of β_Q is $-.40$. Thus the ratio of arrest likelihoods for predicted dangerous offenders relative to the others is

$$AR(D/N) = (\lambda_D \, q_D)/(\lambda_N \, q_N),$$
$$= [3\lambda_N \, k(3\lambda_N)^{-.4}] \, / \, (\lambda_N k\lambda N^{-.4})$$
$$= 1.774. \tag{7.11}$$

Because cases involving predicted dangerous offenders were 1.774 times as likely to be presented to the prosecutor as those involving other offenders, the true selection rate was the apparent selection rate (that is, the proportion of all cases presented that were handled by the career criminal unit) divided by 1.774. Results of these rather arcane calculations are shown in Table 7.13.

Incidentally, these results suggest that one of the assumptions made above—that focusing on repeat offenders will reduce considerably the ability of the police and the prosecutor to work other cases—may not be correct. For example, if $\beta_P = 1.00$ (linear returns to scale), then from (7.6a) the Washington, DC, ROP unit must have used

$$[.03 \, (10)] \, / \, [.97 + .03 \, (10)] = .24$$

of the total resources of the department devoted to crime control. For any $\beta_P < 1.0$, ROP would use up more resources. And from (7.5), the total arrest rate must have decreased from q_0 to

$$[(1 - .03 \, (10)] \, q_0/ \, .97 = .722 \, q_0.$$

For any $\beta_P < 1.0$, the arrest rate would drop by more than that. Neither of these things happened. The Washington ROP unit employed 63 officers at the time of the evaluation cited above, about 1 percent of all sworn staff (Gay, 1985). Even assuming that the vast majority of patrol officers focus on order maintenance and public service, nowhere near 24 percent of the crime-control resources were sapped by ROP. Further, although ROP officers made fewer misdemeanor arrests while with the ROP unit than they had in their previous assignments (Martin,

TABLE 7.13
Disparity Ratios and Selection Rates
Obtained by Prosecution Career Criminal Units

City	pr(incarceration)	Selection rate
Columbus, Ohio	1.047	.012 to .021
Kalamazoo, Michigan	.955	.017 to .030
New Orleans, Louisiana	1.659	.024 to .042
San Diego, California	1.133	.007 to .013

Source. Chelimsky & Dahmann, 1981.

1985), they made just as many felony arrests, and the aggregate felony arrest rate for the Metropolitan Police remained stable. So the returns to scale appear to be increasing, rather than decreasing. In plain terms, it appears to be more efficient for police and prosecutors to work offenders than to work cases (see also Eck, 1983).

This suggests two things. First, relatively few resources need to be shifted from regular, case-driven crime control to repeat offenders to gain the results shown above. From the agency's viewpoint, repeat offender programs are cheaper than (implicitly) assumed above. Second, the results of these programs will be better than estimated above, because increasing the risks to frequent offenders will not require reducing the risks to the others by as much as assumed. Thus crime rates will be reduced by more than 6 percent for the optimal program, and suboptimal programs will look better, too.

Still, Tables 7.12 and 7.13 suggest that the selection rates and disparity ratios of these "known technology" programs are lower than those associated with an optimal program. To estimate the effectiveness of programs that may be mounted using known methods, let us consider a sample program that is representative of the best results obtained so far. Suppose the police and the prosecutor decided jointly to focus on the worst 3 percent of offenders; they will rely upon a selection device that is accurate with $.20 < r^2 < .50$; by applying additional resources to arresting and convicting these offenders, they will achieve a total disparity ratio, dr_T,

$$\begin{aligned} dr_T &= dr_P \, dr_{DA} \\ &= 8.0 \, (1.25) = 10, \end{aligned}$$

where dr_P and dr_{DA} are the disparity ratios of the police and the prosecutor working separately. How much of an effect can we expect such a program to have on the aggregate crime rate?

The answer depends upon the characteristics of the offending population. When this program is applied to our sample of 558 representative cases, the incapacitation model indicates that the crime rate could be reduced by about 3 percent; it is very unlikely that the reduction would be less than 1.8 percent, or greater than 4.7 percent. The effects of this (not too unreasonable) police and prosecution program are compared to the optimal program in Figure 7.13. As with sentencing programs, a feasible police and prosecutor program would be about half as effective as the optimum.

Selective Risks and Prison Construction

Like selective sentencing, selective police and prosecution programs and policies would make collective incapacitation more attractive. Recall that one of the barriers to natural filtering in the current criminal justice system is offender

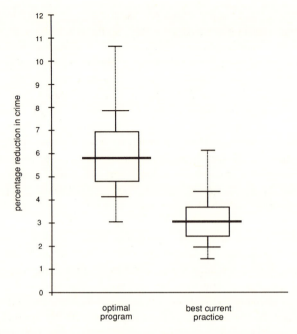

FIGURE 7.13. Best current practice about half as effective as optimal police/prosecution program.

learning: Because the most frequent offenders learn to avoid getting caught, they spend less time in jail and prison. They also come before the courts and parole boards less often, inhibiting selective sentencing efforts.

Table 7.14 shows the distribution of breakeven indirect benefit ratios associated with the current system, the best of the recent police and prosecution repeat offender programs, and the optimal selective-risk program. Again, if the indirect benefits of crime reduction are 2.6 times the direct benefits, it makes sense to add more prison space to the current criminal justice system. If the jurisdiction in question had first implemented selective-risk programs like Washington's and San Diego's, the indirect benefits would only need to be 2.2 to justify additional space; if it could increase the risks by a factor of 30 for the worst 4 percent of offenders, the indirect benefits ratio need be only 1.85 before prison construction made economic sense. If we knew the true ratio to be 2.5, we could be 42 percent sure that more prisons made sense; but we could be 75 percent certain under realistic selective-risk programs, and 90 percent certain under the best program.

Return on investment calculations provide similar answers. Assuming an indirect benefits ratio of 2.5, a 1-percent increase in prison space nationwide would most likely return -2.5 percent on our investment now; but it would return

TABLE 7.14
Distribution of Breakeven Indirect Benefits Ratios for Three Police/Prosecution Policies

	Current policy	Best current practice	Optimum program
Maximum	4.316	3.729	3.132
90th percentile	3.566	2.910	2.492
75th	3.028	2.497	2.111
Median	2.582	2.180	1.854
25th	2.320	1.931	1.625
10th	1.943	1.632	1.375
Minimum	1.762	1.338	1.083
Mean IBR	2.679	2.237	1.903
Standard deviation	(0.562)	(0.470)	(0.414)
Mean elasticity	0.156	0.177	0.197
Standard deviation	(0.023)	(0.025)	(0.027)

10.3 percent under the DC/San Diego program and 23.1 percent under the most effective selective-risk program. The increases in return for selective-risk programs are larger than for selective sentencing, which only makes sense. If the primary barrier to a selective system is offender learning, it seems more effective to deal with it directly rather than patch together an ad hoc response.

As with sentencing, it would be absurd to claim that these would in fact be the results if such a program were adopted. Too many untested assumptions are required; too many things can go wrong. Again, however, the size of the reductions is probably about right. By themselves, selective police and prosecutor programs will not solve the crime problem; but they will reduce it by 2 to 4 percent. The most likely reduction is about 1.5 million crimes per year. Evaluating each crime at $1,275—the direct costs to victims—produces a benefit of almost $2 billion, a substantial reduction in public suffering. And, barring egregious abuses of discretion, the ethical concerns that prompt many to object to selective sentencing are much less binding on these programs.

If police and prosecutors knew how, they should focus most of their criminal investigation and prosecution resources on about 4 percent of offenders, to increase the probability of incarceration given a crime by a factor of 30. No one knows how to achieve such a result, but repeat offender programs that represent the best of current practice may reduce crime by 2 to nearly 5 percent at no additional cost. Such a program would increase the attractiveness of collective incapacitation strategies, but it remains unclear whether prison construction would be cost-effective.

Changing both Risks and Sentences

Of the two policies examined above, the benefits of selective-risk programs appear to be about twice the benefits of selective sentencing. Over the long run, the disparity between the two is likely to become greater: The effectiveness of selective sentencing is primarily constrained by ethical concerns, whereas the primary constraints on police and prosecution programs are those of knowledge. As police and prosecutors become more adept at identifying frequent offenders and allocating their resources, disparity ratios will presumably become closer to their optimal values. So if we could choose only one of the two, we would probably prefer to choose selective police and prosecution programs.

Of course, there is no particular need for us to choose between them. True, one might reasonably argue that research funds are limited and that the advantages of concentrating research and evaluation resources on one kind of policy outweigh the benefits of examining them both. And it is probably true that bureaucracies exhibit a limited capacity for change. But changes in risks and sentences require alterations in the procedures of systematically different agencies, and the current enthusiasm for selective programs and policies suggests that few policymakers are waiting for definitive research results before they begin experimentation (see, e.g., McDonald, 1987; Spelman, 1990). So there seems little to be lost by pursuing both strategies simultaneously—if one is convinced that the benefits of each policy are sufficiently greater than the costs.

This is particularly true if the programs complement one another—if the benefits of the two taken together are greater than the sum of the benefits of each taken separately. In this case, there would be an extra bonus associated with joint adoption of selective policies and an added incentive for all criminal justice agencies to adopt.

The opposite is true if the programs are substitutes. In this case, the marginal value of adding (say) a selective sentencing program to a criminal justice system that was already selectively allocating its risks would be less than the value of selective sentencing otherwise. And there are short-term costs associated with any change in bureaucratic policies—procedures must be defined, personnel must be trained, supervision and monitoring costs must increase, and so on. So there may be an incentive for criminal justice agencies to pass the burden of selective action off onto other agencies. Because the startup costs are probably systematically higher for the judiciary than for the police and prosecutor, all else equal this would argue against selective sentencing policies.

These questions may be examined directly, by adapting the incapacitation model to account for simultaneous changes in both risks and sentences. The adaptation requires no new assumptions, so it is no less (but, of course, no more) reliable than previous estimates. Consider three possibilities: (1) a "modified just-deserts" selective sentencing proposal; (2) a "not-unreasonable" selective-risk proposal, modeled after already implemented programs; and (3) both.

Results are shown in Figure 7.14. The two shaded box plots show the estimated effects of adopting only a selective sentencing or a selective-risk program. The two unshaded box plots show the expected and estimated effects of adopting each, given that the other has been implemented already. If the two types of programs were neither complements nor substitutes, the unshaded plots would be identical. Instead, it is clear that each program enhances the effectiveness of the other. The estimated effects of adopting both programs is about 6 percent. So there is a premium associated with adopting both programs, averaging about 1 percent of all crimes.

Any crime reduction would be a welcome relief to a public accustomed to increasing (or at least nondecreasing) crime rates and the persistent failure of criminal justice innovations to have much effect on crime. An increase as large as 6 percent and one that required neither additional research, nor undue concessions to utilitarian concerns, nor increases in the social resources devoted to crime control, would be very pleasant, indeed. No jurisdiction has adopted such

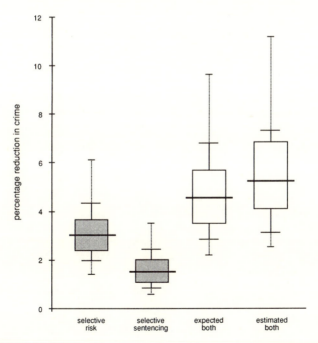

FIGURE 7.14. Selective risk and sentencing policies are complementary strategies.

a program to date, but it does not seem too unreasonable to suspect that one could do so.

This compares very favorably with the costs and benefits of collective incapacitation. If frequent offender programs of this kind could be implemented nationwide, it would prevent something like 3 million crimes per year, providing direct benefits to would-be victims of almost $4 billion. Indirect benefits could conceivably multiply these gains by a factor of 3 or 4. To achieve the same benefits through collective incapacitation, the prison population would have to be increased by about 40 percent, by about 350,000 beds, at a (direct) cost of $14 billion per year. If the indirect benefits are large enough, such an orgy of prison construction may be worth the cost. But if the same benefits can be achieved for free, it seems foolish to focus our attention on collective incapacitation.

If all criminal justice agencies in a jurisdiction adopted a constrained optimal program, they would cut aggregate crime rates by 4 to 8 percent. Thus selective-risk and selective sentencing programs complement and enhance one another. Although similar results could be achieved through collective incapacitation, it would cost several billion dollars.

8

Conclusions

Collective incapacitation is a gamble. The direct benefits are much less than the direct costs, but if crime reduction produces significant indirect benefits—reductions in anxiety, avoidance, protection, and insurance—it may pay off.

Selective incapacitation is a relatively sure thing. Police and prosecution programs that are known technologies, and modified just-deserts sentencing practices that most would find unobjectionable, both appear to work well under a wide variety of assumptions about the criminal population and require no additional criminal justice resources. If implemented, they also increase the likelihood that collective incapacitation policies will pay off (but by no means do they make it a certainty). Some 50 million serious crimes are committed each year; if this analysis is correct, these policies would reduce crime by 4 to 8 percent—a reduction of 2 to 4 million crimes per year. This would eliminate a considerable amount of pain, suffering, and financial loss.

How reasonable are these characterizations? Like any model, the incapacitation model developed here is no better than the assumptions on which it relies. With regard to the criminal population and constraints on resources, knowledge, and ethics, the model makes few assumptions that cannot be backed up with empirical evidence (albeit sometimes rather unpersuasive evidence). With regard to other factors, however, the assumptions needed do not square so well with available data or common sense. In this final section, let us consider how a more complete and accurate model could be developed, and what that model would be likely to show.

As described above, three principal assumptions were required:

- The criminal justice system is about the same in all jurisdictions throughout the United States.
- If the selective policies and programs described above were implemented, this would not affect the characteristics of the offender population.
- The only alternative to incapacitating an offender is to do nothing.

All three assumptions were made for the sake of convenience, rather than out of any conviction that they were even approximately correct. As shown below, they are not even close, and this may affect the results in important but unpredictable ways.

Heterogeneous Criminal Justice System

For simplicity's sake, all the results derived above assume that all criminal justice systems are very nearly the same. Specifically, incarceration rates per serious crime are everywhere between 1.0 and 1.65 percent, and the average time served given incarceration is about 1.4 years; frequent offenders are moderately adept at avoiding arrest, and current sentencing schemes do little to compensate. In an analysis as complex as this one, such simplifying assumptions could not be avoided. But a casual glance at the time served, the number of prisoners per capita, and even the crime rate for different localities suggests that they are all different. In particular, some may already be focusing their efforts on frequent and dangerous offenders: A growing number of police agencies have implemented repeat offender units, and many prosecutors have experimented with career criminal units and policies (Spelman, 1990); some states have made special provision for giving predicted recidivists longer sentences (McDonald, 1987). As shown earlier in this chapter, most of the benefits of targeting can be achieved through relatively undramatic methods. So some localities may have already gained most of the benefits of selective action.

As suggested by the results shown on Tables 7.12 and 7.13, however, police and prosecutor programs, at least, are still suboptimal. They select too few offenders for special treatment, and the treatment they provide does not increase the risks of incarceration sufficiently. Although current sentencing schemes were not examined above, a recent review of repeat offender laws supports the view that these schemes have similar flaws—they focus on too few offenders, and (with some notable exceptions) do not mete out sufficiently long sentences to those they select (McDonald, 1987, pp. 14–24). So even jurisdictions that are already focusing their efforts have work to do.

How much they have to do, of course, depends in part upon what they have already done. The optimal program characteristics derived above differ little within the range of average criminal justice system characteristics, but this tells us little about the best program for a jurisdiction that is working far outside that range. For example, we may know that the best selective police and prosecution program is about the same for jurisdictions that incarcerate offenders in 1.0 to 1.65 percent of the cases; but this need not be true for an extraordinarily effective jurisdiction that has achieved an incarceration rate of 3.0 percent.

At the risk of generalizing beyond the data available (a temptation to which policy analysts are particularly likely to succumb), some extrapolations beyond this range may be helpful. Drawing upon the results presented in Tables 6.4, 7.5, and 7.10, we might expect the following:

- On differences in average values: If the average probability of incarceration, given a crime, is higher than about 1.65 percent, or if the average sentence served is longer than 1.4 years, a greater proportion of offenders are already behind bars. Thus more will be gained by a fixed percentage increase in incapacitation, and collective incapacitation strategies are more likely to pay off. Further, the optimal selective program should spread its resources more thinly over more offenders. That is, the optimal selection rates would be higher, but the disparity ratios would be lower than those suggested above. If the average incarceration probability is lower than 1 percent or the average time served is less than 1.4 years, the opposite would be true.

- On differences in values among offenders: A criminal justice system that is already adept at learning who the frequent offenders are—that is, a system for which the correlation between offense rate and incarceration probability is close to zero, or even positive, and for which sentences already depend to large degree on predictions of future offense rates—need not implement a program with selection rates and disparity ratios as large as those recommended here. But because the worst offenders are more likely to filter through to incarceration, collective incapacitation strategies are more effective than estimated here. If, on the other hand, offenders are particularly adept at avoiding punishment in a particular jurisdiction, a larger program will be needed.

Thus the average value of the risks faced by criminal offenders can be expected to influence the tradeoff between selection rate and disparity ratio, whereas differences among offenders as to the risks they face influence the intensity of the program. Both also affect the cost-effectiveness of prison construction.

To obtain a better answer than this, it would be necessary to conduct an even larger study than that presented here. Data would have to be collected as to the distribution of incarceration probabilities and sentences from one jurisdiction to the next, and from one offender to the next within each jurisdiction. Although it was difficult enough to establish these parameters for the few locations considered above, there are good reasons to suppose that it could be done more easily in the future. For one, the self-report survey methods needed to estimate the relationship between offense rates and arrest probabilities have recently been demonstrated to be reasonably valid for a sample of recently adjudicated offenders (Chaiken & Chaiken, 1987), and for true incoming cohorts to incarceration (Horney & Marshall, 1991b; Mande & English, 1988). This suggests that such surveys could be administered, perhaps on a routine basis, by criminal justice agencies in many jurisdictions. Second, criminal justice recordkeeping systems are becoming more reliable and sophisticated, and better integrated among agencies (Perez, 1990; Spelman, 1988a). Thus information about individual arrest rates, the likelihood of conviction and incarceration given an arrest, and the sentence served given incarceration, are all becoming easier to collect.

The primary questions that such a study must answer are parallel to those considered here: What are the size, shape, and probable effectiveness of the optimal selective program? Still, such an analysis would have to be considerably more complex than this one, because interactions between characteristics of the offending population and of the criminal justice system must be considered.

Effect on Offender Population Characteristics

It is reasonable to suspect (but very difficult to prove) that offenders respond to the activities of the criminal justice system by changing their behavior. Any responses to the current system will already be included in parameters of the criminal population; so these responses will not affect estimates of the incapacitation effectiveness of the present system. But the results presented above as to the effectiveness of selective programs are not even roughly correct unless either offender adaptations to these policies are minor, or else the changes in risks and sentences are so small that they would go largely unnoticed.

If offenders do adapt, it should be reflected in their offense rates. Offenders facing higher risks or longer sentences—a higher "price" of crime—would reduce their offense rates. They would choose their crimes more carefully and reduce their reliance on illegitimate sources of income. They may even quit committing crimes entirely. On the other hand, offenders facing a lower "price" would take advantage of the change and commit crimes at higher rates. If the high-rate offenders that are the target of selective policies reduce their offending by more than the low- and medium-rate offenders increase their offending, the incapacitation model will underestimate the crime-control benefits of these policies; if the opposite is true, the model will produce overestimates.

Figure 8.1 shows how the long-term price of crime would change, if all criminal justice agencies in a jurisdiction adopted the feasible programs described above. The horizontal axis shows the cumulative percentage of offenders, ranging from least frequent to most frequent; the vertical axis shows the proportion of an offender's career he or she spends out on the street, able to commit crimes. The two curves correspond to "street-time" estimates before and after implementation of the feasible selective policies outlined above. Under the selective policy, street time would increase for low- and moderate-rate criminals by up to 10 percent; but it would be reduced by a similar margin for the most frequent offenders.

Philip Cook (1986) has considered the effects of selective incapacitation policies with deterrence in mind. He replicated Peter Greenwood's incapacitation model—a model similar to that used in chapters 6 and 7—but with the added element that each offender's offense rate responds to changes in his expected value of punishment given a crime. Cook used the following procedure:

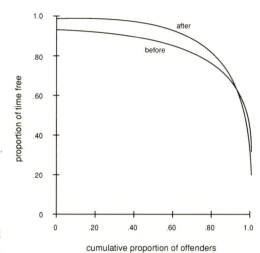

FIGURE 8.1. Selective policies will change the long-run price of crime.

1. Estimate the deterrence elasticity, ξ. ξ is defined as the percentage change in offense rate associated with a 1-percent change in expected sanctions per crime committed. (Cook used ξs of $-.3$ and -1.0.)
2. Estimate the effect of the selective incapacitation policy on the expected sanctions for offenders in each of several homogeneous offending groups.
3. Adjust the offense rates of members of each of these groups by ξ, and estimate the new crime rate on the basis of the new offense rates.

Cook found that deterrence effects offset the crime-control benefits of selective incapacitation. For high ξs (that is, when offense rates were assumed to be very sensitive to sanction levels), he found that the deterrence losses overwhelmed the incapacitation benefits.

These findings are confirmed when his procedure is applied to the incapacitation model and optimum feasible selective policies developed above. Figure 8.2 compares the net effectiveness of three selective policies before and after taking deterrent effects into account. If offenders have perfect information as to their risks and penalties, discount sentence lengths at an interest rate of .25 and adjust their offense rates by an ξ of $-.30$ (Cook, 1986), the effectiveness of the selective police and prosecution policy is reduced to essentially zero; 75 percent of the benefits of selective sentencing are eliminated; if both risks and sentences are made to be more selective, the model now predicts a 1-percent increase in crime. The results are even more dismal for $\xi = -1.0$. If this procedure is a reasonable map of reality, selective action may in fact do more harm than good.

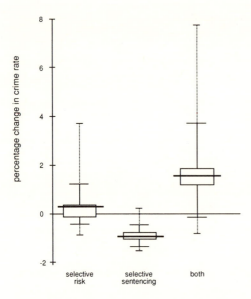

FIGURE 8.2. Deterrence losses may overwhelm incapacitation benefits.

   This analysis is certainly clever, and the basic result—that deterrence losses would offset incapacitation gains—is probably true. On the other hand, this procedure requires that a variety of asssumptions be made about how offenders obtain, evaluate, and respond to information about criminal sanctions; these assumptions affect the size (and perhaps the direction) of the results. A detailed review of these assumptions would be out of place here, but a short discussion suggests that deterrence is probably much less important than the results of Figure 8.2 suggest. Consider first how offenders obtain information about risks and penalties.

Obtaining Information

   If any change in punishment schedules is to have a deterrent effect on offense rates, offenders must first perceive that a change has occurred. Offenders may obtain their information about the change from three sources: personal experience; the experiences of friends and acquaintances who are involved with crime; and information obtained through third parties, such as the criminal grapevine and the mass media. Because arrest and conviction rates are fairly low, and because sentences depend upon a number of factors unrelated to offense rates (in most places, at least), the information obtained through these channels is liable to be highly imperfect. Thus even when an objective change in risks and penalties is rather large, it may go unnoticed or be incorrectly perceived after it has filtered through these channels; this is particularly true of low-rate offenders.

Consider personal experience first. It can be shown that the distribution of interincarceration times among street offenders is roughly Gompertz-distributed (Spelman, 1988b). This means that for any combination of offense rate, probable career length, and risk of incarceration given an offense, some lucky offenders will never be incarcerated while they are adults. The proportion is

$$p(\text{never}) = \exp -[1 - \exp(-\lambda q)]\ T\}. \tag{8.1}$$

If some selective program is implemented, then q, the probability of incarceration given a crime, will change; thus there will also be a change in the probability that an offender with given offense rate λ and career length T will never be incarcerated. Because selective police and prosecution programs shift risks from infrequent to frequent offenders, this probability should increase for the least frequent offenders. As shown in Figure 8.3, however, it cannot increase by very much, because it is very high to begin with. Assuming the most likely combination of offender population characteristics, for over 80 percent of the offenders the probability is less than .50 that they will ever serve a sentence in jail or prison. (This is equally true after implementation of an optimum feasible selective-risk program.) Because most offenders never do time, it is impossible that these offenders could ever identify a difference in their risk of doing time on the basis of personal experience. Although this result may seem startling, note

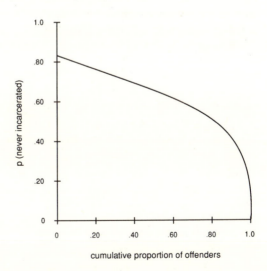

FIGURE 8.3. Most low-rate offenders never do time in jail or prison.

that many of these offenders are arrested, but are only fined or given suspended sentences or probation terms.

For the minority of offenders who spend some time in jails and prisons (estimated in Chapter 6 to be about 25 percent), it is possible that their personal experience could reveal changes in risks or penalties. But offenders will not generally recognize these changes immediately; each crime and incarceration experience will tell them something about their risks, and offender information will improve as they become more experienced. Even for those offenders who are convicted and incarcerated for their crimes, then, it may be years before they can make an informed estimate as to their risks.

A realistic assessment of the information-gathering and assessment process would be very complex and is well beyond the scope of this work. To illustrate the time requirements, however, consider the following (admittedly contrived) thought experiment. Two offenders have just embarked on an adult, criminal career. Lola commits about 14 serious crimes per year and receives no special attention from the police or the prosecutor. Heidi commits about 40 crimes per year and receives special attention according to the optimal, feasible program suggested above. Both have perfect information as to the average risk of incarceration per crime committed, and as to the nature and effectiveness of the selective program. Neither Lola nor Heidi has any idea whether they are targets; further, the only data available to them about their risks are their own experiences. How much time would have to elapse before the two offenders could be reasonably certain as to their own, personal incarceration rates?

Assume for simplicity that Lola and Heidi are both perfect Bayesians and that both crimes and incarcerations occur according to a Poisson process. Then each offender's assessment of her chances of being a target offender, given some previous number of incarcerations i during t years of street time, will be

$$p(H|i,t) = p_H \, p(i|H,t) \, / \, [p_H \, p(i|H,t) + (1 - p_H) \, p(i|L,t)], \qquad (8.2)$$

where p_H is the prior probability of being labeled a high-rate offender and receiving special attention—that is, the selection rate. The likelihood that this offender would have racked up i incarcerations in t years, given that she were considered a high-rate offender, is

$$p(i|H,t) = (\lambda qt)^i \, e^{-\lambda qt}/i! \qquad (8.3)$$

Plugging (8.3) into (8.2) and simplifying,

$$p(H|i,t) = [sr \, dr^i \, (e^{-\lambda qt})^{dr}] \, / \, [sr \, dr^i \, (e^{\ \lambda qt})^{dr} + (1 - sr) \, e^{\ \lambda qt}]. \quad (8.4)$$

Each offender's best guess at her likelihood of being a target offender at time t is the sum of (8.4) for all i, weighted by the true likelihood that she will obtain i incarcerations in t years. That is,

$$p(H|t) = \Sigma_i \ p(H|i,t) \ p(i|K), \tag{8.5}$$

where K is her true status. Finally, each offender will estimate her own risks of incarceration per crime committed to be

$$E(q|t) = dr \ q_L \ p(H|t) + q_L \ [1 - p(H|t)], \tag{8.6}$$

where $(dr \ q_L)$ and q_L are the true probabilities of incarceration for predicted high- and low-rate offenders, respectively.

Figure 8.4 shows results of this calculation for both offenders, for career lengths up to 10 years. At the start, neither offender has any information about her own risks, and her best guess is the average for all offenders. Over time, Heidi begins to recognize that she runs higher risks than average, and her expectation of the likelihood of incarceration increases steadily. For Lola, just the opposite is true. So personal experiences do provide useful information. But note how slowly this information is obtained: Even after committing crimes for 10 years, Heidi cannot be more than 60 percent certain that she is in fact the target of special police and prosecution efforts.

Most offender careers end long before 10 years have passed; aggregating the expected risks over all possible career lengths, we find that the average low-rate

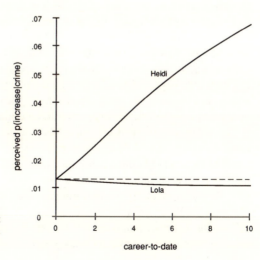

FIGURE 8.4. Offenders learn about their risks slowly, if personal experience is the only guide.

offender will perceive her risks to be about .0123 (some 14 percent higher than the true probability of .0108), and the typical high-rate offender will perceive her risks to be about .0486 (less than half the true probability of .1078). So the perceived risks will regress, rather dramatically, to the mean. We can expect that expected sentences will regress to the mean in a similar way.

We may reasonably conclude that, if the only information available to an offender about risks and penalties is personal experience, much of the change caused by selective programs will never be noticed.

All this assumes that criminal justice agencies will not inform the offender of her status. This is almost certainly an unrealistic assumption, but it stands in for a more reasonable assumption: Whether an offender is targeted or not is less at issue than the expected risks and penalties, and offenders will learn about the true effects of targeting on risks and penalties through experience. In the limiting case, selective programs and policies would have no effect on risks and penalties, and offenders would be entirely justified in snickering upon being told of their status.

The more important assumption is that personal experience is the only source of information about risks and penalties. It may be that offenders glean most of their data by observing the experiences of their colleagues. If an offender's reference group is large enough, it is certainly reasonable to believe that he or she will have ample information about levels of punishment. So we can expect that changes in policies that apply to all offenders—collective incapacitation policies, for instance—might be perceived correctly.

The problem is, much of the information offenders receive about selective policies may not apply to them. In fact, it will only be directly applicable if all the offenders in their reference group commit similar crimes at similar rates. But if a given offender commits crimes at low rates, then it is reasonable to suspect that many of the members of his or her reference group will commit crimes at higher rates and be more likely to suffer higher risks and penalties. For offenders who commit crimes at high rates, the bulk of their colleagues will suffer lower risks and penalties. Even if all offenders account for these differences in assessing their own expected risks and penalties, they will probably underestimate the differences between themselves and others. Most offenders simply will not know how often their colleagues have committed crime over the years; even when they do, their own experiences will probably "anchor" their estimates, resulting in an insufficient adjustment (Tversky & Kahneman, 1974). Thus their assessments of both the expected likelihood of punishment and the probable severity of punishment are liable to regress to the mean.

This is particularly likely if much of the offenders' information comes from the mass media or the underworld rumor mill. Here, the reference group is more or less the entire population of offenders in the neighborhood or metropolitan area. Because frequent offenders account for a disproportionate share of incarcerations and because their experiences are more newsworthy, low-rate offenders are more likely to hear about the experiences of their dangerous colleagues than of those more like themselves. It is not hard to imagine how unsophisticated, low-rate criminals could believe (wrongly) that an increase in risks and penalties aimed at high-rate offenders applies to them. It may even be possible for the system to use this to its advantage (Johnson & Payne, 1986).

Much depends upon the nature of the policy itself: If the policy is easily comprehensible or if offenders receive personal notification that they will receive special treatment, this will reduce much of the uncertainty and increase the accuracy of perceptions. This is particularly true of selective sentencing, which is most effective when controlled by fairly strict sentencing or parole guidelines. Nevertheless, for discretionary selective sentencing policies and especially for more fluid selective police and prosecution programs, it seems likely that offenders who must rely on vicarious experiences for their information will find it difficult to perceive the effects of selective policies accurately, and that they will find it even more difficult to apply their findings to themselves. All this is likely to water down the deterrent effects of selective policies considerably.

Evaluation

Raw data about arrests and penalties must be processed and evaluated before offenders can use them to guide their criminal decision making. Deterrence theories suggest that offenders make their decisions on the basis of expected levels of punishment, or crime "prices." Due to systematic biases in the evaluation process, however, offenders will probably underestimate differences in these prices among offenders and changes over time—even if they have obtained accurate information about their likelihood of incarceration and probable penalties.

The most familiar model for examining decisions under uncertainty is the subjectively expected utility or SEU model. For this model, the price of crime is the disutility of incarceration, multiplied by the subjective probability of incarceration given a crime. That is,

$$\text{Price} = q\, U(S),$$

where q is the probability of incarceration and $U(S)$ is the disutility of the expected sentence (or, more accurately, the expected disutility of the sentence, averaged over all likely sentences). This is the model used in calculating the effects shown in Figure 8.2.

Although the SEU model seems reasonable on its face, people appear to make systematically different decisions than the model would predict (Kahneman, Slovic, & Tversky, 1982). For our purposes, two differences are particularly important (Kahneman & Tversky, 1979):

- The likelihood of uncertain events appears to be evaluated on the basis of "risk weights" that do not obey the laws of probability.
- The benefits and costs of these events are best described by a "value function" that differs from the economic utility function in systematic ways.

This "prospect-theory" model suggests that offenders will discount many of the differences they perceive in incarceration probability and in expected penalties.

Offenders are liable to discount differences in incarceration probability because the risk-weighting function exhibits regression to the mean. For example, a probability of .60 would receive a higher risk weight than one of .30, but the risk weight would not be twice as large. This is particularly pronounced for low-probability events (less than about .10), suggesting that even large changes in small probabilities of incarceration will not be fully reflected in an offender's assessment of the price of crime (Lattimore & Witte, 1986).

Similarly, offenders will probably discount differences in expected sentences because of the shape of the value function. In the classic formulation, the utility function measures the utility associated with some level of wealth; additional increments of wealth are given ever-lower marginal utilities. The value function, on the other hand, measures the utility associated with some change in the level of wealth from the current level. Like the utility function, successive positive increments are valued at marginally decreasing rates; but successive negative increments are valued at marginally increasing rates. In the jargon of classical microeconomics, the value function is risk-averse with respect to gains in wealth and risk-seeking with respect to losses; the point of inflection is (most likely) the current endowment point.

Because time spent behind bars is a certain loss, prospect theory suggests that offenders will discount additional increments to expected jail and prison terms. For example, offenders will feel that a 10-year prison term is much worse than a 1-year jail term; but it will be nowhere near 10 times as bad. Thus a large increase in sentences for frequent offenders and a concurrent reduction for infrequent offenders should (if accurately perceived) change the evaluated price for members of both groups; but the change in price will not be nearly proportional to the change in penalties.

Although the current endowment is an obvious dividing line between risk-averse and risk-seeking evaluations, some people are willing to gamble in order to achieve a particular increase in wealth. This increase, called the "level of aspiration," is the inflection point for these individuals (Siegel, 1957). Because these individuals are already (by definition) willing to take risks in order to attain this level, their activities should be relatively resistant to changes in risks.

This reduces the importance of deterrent effects in two ways. First, it is most reasonable to believe that those offenders who aspire to attain some level of sophistication, competence, or cash flow through offending are predominantly low-rate or novice offenders. If this is the case, then their resistance to changes in risks will reduce the counterdeterrent impact of selective policies.

Second, levels of aspiration for low-rate offenders may themselves be affected by the experiences of high-rate offenders. If minor thieves see their full-time colleagues as more successful and professional than themselves, they may be tempted to emulate them. When confronted with the knowledge that high-rate offenders face greater punishments, it is reasonable to suppose that they will reduce their aspirations somewhat. Similarly, potential offenders who are not yet active may be deterred from starting if it becomes clear that criminality is (eventually) a dead end.

The deterrent effects shown in Figure 8.2 discount jail and prison terms at an interest rate of .25, so they account for the risk-seeking nature of the value function; but they do not account for regression to the mean in the risk-weighting function and do not account for any level of aspiration effects. Thus, on the basis of evaluation alone, these effects probably overstate the deterrent effects of police/prosecution and combined programs; they may overstate or understate the deterrent effects of sentencing programs, depending on the importance of aspiration levels and the appropriateness of a .25 interest rate.

Response

Once offenders have perceived and evaluated changes in the risks and penalties of criminal behavior, they will presumably respond by changing their levels of activity. The degree of responsiveness—the ξ—may vary from one offender to the next and may vary systematically among offenders of different offense rates, ages, and preferred crime types.

Unfortunately, virtually nothing is known about the size of even the aggregate elasticity. Literally dozens of ξs have been calculated on the basis of econometric analysis, but the prevailing opinion is that none of these estimates are persuasive: Reported crime and sanction data are unreliable; the level of aggregation (usually the state) is too large to be meaningful; because levels of punishment depend upon crime rates, as well as the other way around, crime and punishment are determined by a simultaneous system that is difficult to estimate and may not be in equilibrium at any given time. Daniel Nagin (1978), in reviewing the work completed during the 1960s and 1970s, found that

despite the intensity of the research effort, the empirical evidence is still not sufficient
for providing a rigorous confirmation of the existence of a deterrent effect. Perhaps
more important, the evidence is woefully inadequate for providing a good estimate of
the magnitude of whatever effect may exist. . . . There is still considerable uncertainty over whether that effect is trivial (even if statistically detectable) or profound. (pp.
135–136)

Deterrence effects doubtless exist for law-abiding citizens, and they may be
important for even the most dangerous offenders; but aggregate-based, econometric approaches have been unable to measure these effects with much validity.
More recent reviews (Brier & Fienberg, 1980; Schmidt & Witte, 1984) indicate
that the situation has not changed since 1978.

Common sense suggests a few, gross bounds on the aggregate value. The
aggregate elasticity must be less than zero, because a higher price should reduce,
rather than increase an individual's offense rate. It should also be greater than
negative 1, because otherwise society could reduce offense rates to virtually zero
by meting out very long sentences; this does not necessarily conflict with empirical data, but it makes little theoretical sense.

Criminal decision making is sufficiently different from most economic behavior that an examination of price elasticities for other goods is unlikely to be
helpful. Nevertheless, it is reasonable to suspect that values of ξ should differ
among offenders in predictable ways. For economic goods, price elasticities
depend upon two factors: the availability of substitutes and the effect of the price
change on total income. ξ should be large (that is, the response to a change in
price should be large) when substitutes are easily available and when the change
has a big effect on total income (Boulding, 1966). Let us consider each of these
effects, starting with the substitution effect.

Expressed in the terms of criminal decision making, we may consider
substitutes to include alternative sources of income that are unaffected by the
selective policies. Frequent offenders whose criminal activities were primarily
motivated by the need for cash, for example, might respond to an increase in
expected punishment by taking jobs as cab drivers or cooks; they might also
increase their rates of forgery, fraud, or drug dealing, if these offenses were not
covered by the selective policies. So offenders who are capable of obtaining and
holding legitimate jobs, or those who can learn and use new (and presumably less
dangerous) criminal skills should reduce their offense rates by the greatest
amounts.

By and large, the substitution factor argues in favor of larger ξs for infrequent, less-dangerous offenders. Their low offense rates suggest that many are
already holding down legitimate jobs or perhaps nontargeted criminal activities;
they could thus respond more easily to a higher price than offenders for whom
burglary and robbery are a major source of income and a full-time occupation.
Due to limitations of time, it is also reasonable to suspect that they could respond

more easily to a lower price. An increase of 20 percent in burglary rates is easier to envision for an offender who commits 10 burglaries per year than for one who commits 100 or 200, for example.

Total income (both monetary and nonmonetary) depends more or less directly on the amount of time an offender spends out of jail and prison, so we may consider the percentage of time spent free as a measure of this factor. All else equal, then, ξ should be greatest for those offenders whose street time will be most affected by the selective policies.

The total income factor argues in favor of a larger response to a given stimulus among high-rate offenders. This is because high-rate offenders spend much less of their criminal careers on the street, and much more behind bars. For example, under current policies a frequent offender who commits crimes in the 95th percentile can expect to spend about 60 percent of his or her active career on the street; if the amount of punishment administered to offenders like this were increased by 25 percent as a result of selective policies, their street time would be reduced to 50 percent of their active careers. Thus a 25-percent increase in punishment would lead to a 17 percent reduction in the offender's expected income. Now consider the case of the median offenders, who now spend some 87 percent of their careers under incarceration; even if they were never punished, the resulting increase in income would be only 15 percent. So four times as much punishment would have a smaller income effect.

The relative importance of substitution and income effects is complex for all goods, and crime is no exception. It is plausible to suppose that moderately good substitutes are available for many offenders, so that ξs are high, especially for the least dangerous; thus deterrence losses would offset incapacitation gains. It seems equally plausible to suppose that minimal income effects among infrequent offenders limit significant ξs to the most dangerous; thus deterrence benefits supplement, rather than offset the benefits of selective incapacitation. Given current information, there is simply no way to tell.

When perception, evaluation, and response effects are all considered together, it is hard to know what to expect. The bulk of the evidence suggests that deterrent effects will reduce the utility of selective policies somewhat. But it is seems unlikely that these effects will be as large as suggested by Figure 8.2; it is even possible that deterrence will increase the benefits of selective policies.

Much depends upon the information available to offenders. It would be beneficial to provide frequent offenders with relatively good information as to their (now-increased) risks, because we want to deter them as well as incapacitate them. This argues in favor of simple policies that offenders will find easy to understand. The deterrence effects for infrequent offenders are a pure loss, however; here, we would like to increase their uncertainty as to whether they are target offenders or not. This argues for more complicated targeting procedures.

A compromise policy has been adopted by police and prosecutors in several jurisdictions (Gay, 1985; Spelman, 1990). Targeting procedures and outcomes are kept a secret until offenders have been arrested; then the offenders are informed of their status and warned that they will continue to be a target offender until they die or move out of state. In theory, this maintains maximum deterrent effects on the most frequent offenders while maintaining it for the others. On the other hand, all offenders eventually quit offending or reduce their levels of offending as they age, so such policies raise the specter of harassment and unfair disparities in punishment. It is also possible that the criminal justice system ultimately spends most of its selective resources on once-frequent but now-burnt-out offenders. This is particularly likely to be true for sentencing statutes that provide for very long (25-year) sentences for those who commit even minor crimes, if they have three prior convictions for serious felonies (McDonald, 1987). Thus maintaining the deterrent effects may force the system to water-down or even lose the incapacitation effects. On balance, it probably makes more sense from a deterrence standpoint to keep selection policies mysterious, but the tradeoffs are by no means obvious.

Deterrence effects may well prove to be important, but it is unlikely that they are so important that they would overwhelm the benefits of selective policies. Further research will be helpful if it clarifies how offenders gather, process, and evaluate information about risks and penalties, and how they use this information to guide their decision making. In the meantime, however, our uncertainty about deterrence is simply too great for the concept to be very helpful in the development of selective criminal justice policies.

An analysis should be conducted of the sensitivity of the results described above to differences in criminal justice system characteristics. As more is learned about the nature of deterrence, these findings should be incorporated into the analysis, as well. These adjustments will change the expected utility of selective policies and the nature of the optimal policy, but it is difficult to predict how.

Intermediate Sanctions and Partial Incapacitation

As discussed in Chapter 1, one reason for the political acceptance of prison construction is its simplicity: Criminals behind bars cannot get at the rest of us. No doubt there is something especially reassuring about the notion of 24-hour-per-day protection, and failures of complete incapacitation—escapes, or crimes committed by temporarily furloughed offenders—seem particularly frightening. On the other hand, incapacitation works, not by changing the motivations of offenders, but by separating them from opportunities to commit crime. In theory, less-drastic means could be used to separate offenders from opportunities: They may be exiled; they may be required to spend their free time in locations that are secure (halfway houses) or that have few or no potential victims (house arrest); they may be restrained from staying out late, or from seeing former colleagues, former victims, or others who might tempt them to commit further crimes. Such methods will probably not prevent all the crimes in which these offenders would otherwise have taken part, but—depending upon how much they cost—they may prevent enough of these crimes to be worth the trouble for some offenders.

Most methods of "partial incapacitation" fall within the category of intermediate sanctions: intensive supervision probation, house arrest with or without electronic monitoring, day reporting centers, and the like (McCarthy, 1987). They are considerably cheaper than imprisonment. Few require expensive, secure structures; guards, food, utilities, and other round-the-clock expenses are much reduced, if not eliminated; because the offenders remain on the street, they may continue to hold down jobs, support their families, and contribute to the social life of their community. So we can anticipate far lower costs than the $40,000 per year we estimated for imprisonment.

Unfortunately, because intermediate sanctions incapacitate only partially (if at all), the benefits are also lower. In fact, one may reasonably argue that the crime-reduction benefits are zero. The marginal offender commits few crimes per year—no more than 20—and it is unlikely that restrictions in the time available to commit a crime would by themselves be sufficient to reduce this by much. It simply does not take very long to commit 20 crimes.

One counterargument is that many criminals do not actively seek opportunities and would presumably commit no crimes at all if they never came into contact with a particularly tempting target. By reducing the frequency of contact with tempting targets, we reduce the chances that passive offenders will be lured into recidivism. Whether the counterargument is persuasive depends primarily on one's stance regarding opportunity theories of crime. A second counterargument turns the debate from incapacitation to deterrence and rehabilitation: If intermediate sanctions succeed, it is because offenders get the social services they need to stay away from crime (drug treatment, job training), or else because they are afraid of getting sent to prison. If this argument is correct, it may be misleading to refer to intermediate sanctions as partial incapacitation; probation and parole managers should emphasize service provision rather than surveillance. But the effect on the benefits of the program is the same: Intermediate sanctions would prevent some, but not all, of the crimes that would have been committed had we done nothing to punish the offender.

A more persuasive argument against intermediate sanctions is that they do not appear to work. Although initial evaluations suggested that they were much more effective at preventing recidivism than regular probation or imprisonment (Erwin, 1986; Pearson, 1988), the control groups for these evaluations were not selected at random, and there is reason to believe the results are biased. A randomized experiment conducted in California in 1988 suggested no difference in recidivism between intensive supervision probation and other intermediate sanctions on the one hand, and regular probation on the other. That is, the number and timing of arrests and incarcerations was similar for both types of sanctions (Petersilia & Turner, 1990).

Although these results appear to be definitive, the California experiments were not very powerful. The difference in felony rearrest rates between ISP and regular probation was only statistically significant in one site (perhaps not coincidentally, the site with the most intensive program). Still, 90-percent confidence intervals for the "effect sizes" of the programs are quite wide. If we define "ISP effects" as the percentage change in felony arrest rate associated with assignment to ISP, then in Contra Costa County, $-28\% <$ ISP effects $< +73\%$; in Los Angeles County, $-42\% <$ ISP effects $< +61\%$; and in Ventura County: $-73\% <$ ISP effects $< -16\%$. If all three sites are aggregated, we can be 90 percent certain that $-38\% <$ ISP effects $< +7\%$, with a most likely ISP effect of -15%. So it is by no means inconceivable that ISP reduced true arrest rates by a moderate amount in every site. Except for the exceptionally intensive program in Ventura County, sample sizes are simply too small to allow for definitive statements.

At 28 contacts per month, the successful Ventura County program is among the most intensive in the nation (Byrne, 1986; Petersilia & Turner, 1990). Further research may well reveal that, for the range of intensities typical of most intermediate sanction programs, the effect size is zero and the arrest rate remains unchanged. But there are at least two ways in which arrest rates could understate the effectiveness of intermediate sanctions. The first is often offered in response to the indefinite findings of other rehabilitation programs: There are a variety of sanctions and a variety of individuals; it may be that some sanctions work very well for some individuals, but these successes are obscured by all the null effects produced by the wrong people in the wrong programs. Careful examination of successful programs suggests that this may in fact be a large part of the problem with rehabilitation programs (Gendreau & Ross, 1979, 1987).

The second reason for suspecting a bias in arrest rates was offered by Joan Petersilia and Susan Turner (1990) as a caveat to their experimental findings. The arrest rate is defined as the offense rate multiplied by the probability of arrest per crime (λq, in the notation used throughout this book). If λq does not change over time, it may be that both λ and q have stayed the same; but it is also possible that q has increased and λ decreased by a proportionate amount (or vice versa). In fact, if we could be fairly certain that q has increased, we could measure the probable reduction in λ.

It is difficult to be sure, but available evidence suggests that q may well be higher for offenders receiving intermediate sanctions than others. Law enforcement contacts were an important part of ISP in two of the three jurisdictions studied; each month, police in these jurisdictions checked on ISP offenders between 4 and 12 times as often as they checked on the control group of regular probationers. Probation officers also appeared to be watching the ISP group more carefully: The rate of technical violations was as much as 50 percent higher for the intermediate sanction group as for the regular probation group (Petersilia & Turner, 1990). This does not by any means prove that q increased or that λ decreased for the intermediate sanction group in any of the three jurisdictions. But it shows that "no-effect" findings are consistent with potentially large reductions in λ.

All this suggests that intermediate sanctions may well succeed in reducing λ, although the effects may not be very large—perhaps 20 or 30 percent. Despite this modest degree of effectiveness, a back-of-the-envelope analysis shows that intermediate sanctions are worthy of further exploration, and further that in many states intermediate sanctions may be the least-cost alternative for dealing with many offenders now sentenced to jail and prison.

Least Cost Alternative

Let us suppose for the sake of argument that some intermediate sanctions may reduce offense rates for some offenders. Denote the effectiveness of these sanctions—the proportion by which they reduce the offense rate—by γ (gamma). γ may vary from zero (no incapacitation, deterrence, or rehabilitative effect) to 1 (offenders commit no crimes while under intermediate sanctions). Assume that γ equals 0 for regular probation and parole, and that it is 1.0 for jail and prison.

For simplicity, let us lump all intermediate sanctions together. The most expensive of these, electronic monitoring, costs about $10 per day, including operational, administrative, and hardware costs (Arrigona, 1991); let us round this off to $3,500 per year for all intermediate sanctions. Because the offender remains in the community, unemployment, welfare, and family costs are not a factor. For comparison, the costs of imprisonment are about $40,000 per year. Although regular probation is not costless, the average costs are much less than for prison or any intermediate sanction. Perhaps more important, the marginal cost is nearly zero, because what happens in practice is that the additional offender is simply tacked onto a caseload of 200 or more. To simplify the math, assume the marginal costs of regular probation are in fact zero.

As described in Chapter 6, the average crime costs the victim $1,275, and it costs the rest of us some proportion of $1,275 between 0 and 4 (the indirect benefits ratio, or *IBR*); the benefits of crime reduction are simply the cost savings if these crimes are never committed. Thus the costs of putting an individual offender i under any of three sanctions can be expressed as follows:

Regular probation: $C = 1275 \, (IBR + 1) \, \lambda_i$.
Intermediate sanction: $C = 1275 \, (IBR + 1) \, \lambda_i \, \gamma + 3500$.
Prison: $C = 40000$.

Given some offender i, the (utilitarian) judge's job is to identify the means of punishment that costs society the least.

Now suppose the judge is faced with the marginal offender under the current system—the least frequent and dangerous offender now being sent to prison. If the least-cost alternative is in fact to send the marginal offender to prison, we need more prison cells to hold offenders like this one who are not now being sent to prison due to lack of space. If the least-cost alternative is to send the marginal offender to regular probation, we need fewer prisons; if an intermediate sanction is the best choice, we need both fewer prisons and (probably) more intermediate sanctions.

As shown in Chapter 6, the number of crimes prevented by incapacitating the marginal offender under the current system is about 8.8; it is 90 percent certain to be between 6.5 and 11.2. To narrow the range further would require collecting more information about the criminal population. The cost equations above show that, given λ, the best choice depends upon IBR and γ. The higher the IBR, the more costly the average crime and the more beneficial full incapacitation policies will be; the higher the value of γ, the more effective are intermediate sanctions and the more likely it is that their cheaper cost will overwhelm the increased effectiveness of prison. By costing-out all reasonable combinations of IBR and γ for the relevant range of λ, we can identify those combinations that favor each of the three alternatives.

Results of such a calculation are shown in Figure 8.5. The combinations of

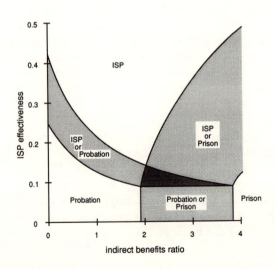

FIGURE 8.5. Best choice for marginal offender may be regular probation, intensive supervision, or prison.

IBR and γ have been divided into seven regions—three regions where it is 95 percent or more certain that one of the alternatives is best; three regions where we can eliminate one but not two of the alternatives; and one region (the triangular section in the center) where the three alternatives are about equally costly and none is definitely better than the others.

The figure speaks for itself, but a few comments may make it easier to hear. First, note that unless γ > .0875, intermediate sanctions cannot be cost-effective. This threshold of effectiveness is set by the ratio of prison costs to intermediate sanction costs (40,000/3,500 = .0875). In general, if the ratio of effectiveness to cost for intermediate sanctions (here, .0875/3500) is not greater than the ratio for prison (1/40,000), the intermediate sanction will not be worth the costs. If this is the case, the choice is identical to the breakeven analysis conducted in Chapter 6: prison is certainly best if *IBR* > 3.8; regular probation is certainly best if *IBR* < 1.8; for values between these two extremes, we cannot be sure which is best without more information about the criminal population.

Next, note that prison is only certain to be the best policy for a very limited range of values of *IBR* and γ. Even if *IBR* were as large as 3.8 (it probably is not—the highest estimate thus far is 3.5), we could be certain that prison is the best policy for the marginal offender only if intermediate sanctions were utterly ineffective. If γ is greater than .30, intermediate sanctions are probably the best choice, even if *IBR* is as high as 3.8. (γ > .30 is hardly unrealistic. For the Ventura County ISP program mentioned above, the most likely value of γ was .45, even assuming no change in *q*. Petersilia & Turner, 1990, p. 146.) So this casts further doubt as to the need for more prison cells.

Finally, note that it may be cheaper to do nothing than to put an offender on an intermediate sanction, even if the sanction is moderately effective. Unless *IBR* is large, for example, sentencing low-rate offenders to intensive supervision or electronic monitoring—"widening the net"—may well be a waste of money.

These are estimates associated with the current system. If the criminal justice system becomes more selective, the marginal offender becomes more frequent and dangerous, and more worthy of imprisonment. In Chapter 7, it was shown that, for integrated selective police, prosecution, and sentencing policies relying on known technology, incapacitating the marginal offender would prevent 8 to 14 crimes, with a best guess of 11. Figure 8.6 shows the least-cost alternative calculations for this selective system. Although prison is somewhat more likely to be the best alternative and regular probation somewhat less—the whole graph has shifted to the left—for the most reasonable combinations of *IBR* and γ there remains considerable uncertainty.

Intermediate sanctions are relatively new, and little is known about their effectiveness. Thus γ could be anywhere from 0 to .50, or even greater. Similarly, virtually nothing is known about the indirect benefits of crime reduction, other than that they exist. Finally, there is considerable uncertainty as to the

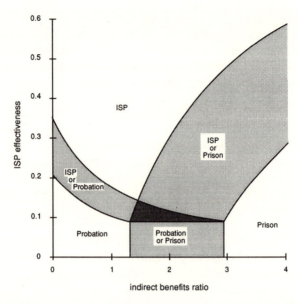

FIGURE 8.6. Selective programs increase attractiveness of prison, intensive supervision, but best choice still uncertain.

offense rate of the marginal, imprisoned offender, too. Thus our current position could be literally anywhere on Figure 8.5; our position given implementation of selective policies could be anywhere on Figure 8.6.

On the other hand, note the need for cheap sanctions, even if they do not work very well. Intensive supervision, day reporting centers, or electronic monitoring may be only slightly better than regular probation (or doing nothing), but this difference may well be enough to justify a fairly dramatic shift in prison construction policies. And because they involve few fixed costs, intermediate sanctions are likely to prove more flexible should conditions change. Thus if further research reveals that some intermediate sanctions are even slightly effective at reducing crime, further development of these sanctions is probably the least cost alternative.

Even if they are not very effective, intermediate sanctions may be the least cost alternative for the marginal imprisoned offender because they are much cheaper than prison. Whether now-imprisoned offenders should be released to intermediate sanctions or regular probation depends upon much that is not yet known, but if research shows that intermediate sanctions are even slightly effective, they are likely to be a better alternative than prison construction.

Policy Prescription

The results presented above are very uncertain. Every jurisdiction is different. Deterrent effects may enhance, offset, or even overwhelm the incapacitative effects of selective activity. Intermediate sanctions may be much more (or much less) cost-effective than full incapacitation. Even for those parts of the analysis in which our uncertainty has been taken explicitly into account—the characteristics of the offending population—there is no guarantee that these characteristics will apply to all jurisdictions. Further research may even show some of them to be simply wrong. So it would be inappropriate to consider these figures to be revealed truths.

On the other hand, so what? As suggested in Chapter 1, the appropriate standard is not truth, but utility. The criminal justice system—like any human institution—must make decisions on the basis of the best available information. Flawed though it may prove to be, I believe that the results of this analysis represent the best that can be done given available knowledge.

Do we need more prison beds? Unless it can be shown that the indirect benefits of a marginal reduction in crime are substantial, and at least twice the direct benefits, it is hard to justify further jail and prison construction. Although more prisons make better sense if the criminal justice system becomes more selective, even an optimally selective system (currently out of reach due to constraints on knowledge and ethics) cannot justify additional beds without recourse to significant indirect benefits. Even the most careful and comprehensive study will not resolve this issue to everyone's satisfaction, but current evidence is not convincing by anyone's standards.

Would selective criminal justice policies be beneficial? A 4- to 8-point reduction in aggregate crime rates may not be overwhelming, but it would certainly be a good thing. Deterrent effects may reduce these benefits somewhat, but they are unlikely to eliminate them entirely. And, although few may prefer selective policies on ethical grounds, most find it acceptable. Selective police and prosecutor programs have passed all of their court tests; some programs even have the (tacit) approval of the American Civil Liberties Union (E. Spurlock, personal communication, January 14, 1987). Although some would consider the modified just-deserts sentencing scheme described above to be unfair, they are outnumbered.

This hardly suggests that we know all we need to know about selective policies. As shown above, the benefits of selective policies depend greatly on the accuracy of selection methods; they also depend on characteristics of the criminal population and of the current criminal justice system. Although better information about the offending population and the activities of the current system will probably not affect the optimal policies by much, it may help a great deal in estimating the probable benefits of selection. This, in turn, will enable society to make more intelligent tradeoffs between crime control and ethical concerns, and between incapacitation on the one hand and deterrence, rehabilitation, and social reform on the other.

Finally, it is appropriate to restate (as if anyone could have missed it) that incapacitation cannot, by itself, solve the crime problem. Under the most favorable conditions considered in Chapters 6 and 7, no more than 22 percent of potential crimes can be prevented through incapacitation. Even the most-favorable selective policy would reduce crime by no more than 7 percent. Criminal justice policies that deter and rehabilitate individual offenders, broader-based policies aimed at ameliorating continuing social problems such as chronic poverty and unemployment, teenage pregnancy and child abuse, and the like, and entirely different approaches aimed at reducing the number of criminal opportunities rather than just the number of criminals, all deserve continued attention. Society will continue to incapacitate criminals, and selective policies can help to make incapacitation more effective; but the crime problem can never be substantially reduced through incapacitation alone.

References

Abell, R. B. (1989). Beyond Willie Horton: The battle of the prison bulge. *Policy Review, 47*, 32–35.

Aitchison, J., & Brown, J. A. C. (1962). *The lognormal distribution.* Cambridge, UK: Cambridge University Press.

Aitchison, J., & Brown, J. A. C. (1954). On criteria for descriptions of income distribution. *Metroeconomica, 6*, 88–107.

Allport, F. H. (1934). The J-curve hypothesis of conforming behavior. *Journal of Social Psychology, 5*, 141–183.

Arrigona, N. (1991). *Texas correctional costs, 1989–1990: Uniform system cost project: Cost per day for criminal justice services.* Austin, TX: Criminal Justice Policy Council.

Avi-Itzhak, B., & Shinnar, R. (1973). Quantitative models in crime control. *Journal of Criminal Justice, 1*, 185–217.

Beard, R. E. (1948). Some experiments in the use of the incomplete gamma function for the approximate calculation of actuarial functions. *Proceedings of the Centennial Assembly, Institute of Actuaries, 2*, 89–107.

Beck, A. J. (1991). *Profile of jail inmates, 1989* (Bureau of Justice Statistics Special Report). Washington, DC: Bureau of Justice Statistics.

Becker, H. S. (1963). *Outsiders: Studies in the sociology of deviance.* New York: Free Press.

Billington, R., & Allan, R.N. (1983). *Reliability evaluation of engineering systems: Concepts and techniques.* New York: Plenum Press.

Binny, J. (1967). Thieves and swindlers. In H. Mayhew (Ed.), *London labour and the London poor,* vol. 4, *Those that will not work.* London, UK: Frank Cass and Company. (Original work published 1862)

Birnbaum, Z. W. & Saunders, S. C. (1958). A statistical model for life-length of materials. *Journal of the American Statistical Association, 53*, 151–160.

Black, D. J. (1970). Production of crime rates. *American Sociological Review, 35*, 733–748.

Bliss, C. I. (1934). The method of probits. *Science, 79*, 38–39.

Blumstein, A., & Cohen, J. (1979). Estimation of individual crime rates from arrest records. *Journal of Criminal Law and Criminology, 70*, 561–585.

Blumstein, A., Cohen, J., & Hsieh, P. (1982). *The duration of adult criminal careers* (Final report to the National Institute of Justice). Pittsburgh: Carnegie-Mellon University, School of Urban and Public Affairs.

Blumstein, A., Cohen, J., & Nagin, D. (Eds.). (1978). *Deterrence and incapacitation: Estimating the effects of criminal sanctions on crime rates* (Report of the Panel on Research on Deterrent and Incapacitative Effects). Washington, DC: National Academy of Sciences.

Blumstein, A., Cohen, J., Roth, J. A., & Visher, C. A. (1986). *Criminal careers and "career criminals"* (Vol. 1). Washington, DC: National Academy of Sciences.

Blumstein, A., Farrington, D. P., & Moitra, S. (1985). Delinquency careers: Innocents, amateurs, and persisters. In M. Tonry & N. Morris (Eds.), *Crime and justice: An annual review of research* (Vol. 6, pp. 187–219). Chicago: University of Chicago Press.

Blumstein, A., & Graddy, E. (1982). Prevalence and recidivism in index arrests: A feedback model. *Law and Society Review, 16*, 265–290.

Boissevain, C. H. (1939). Distribution of abilities depending upon two or more independent factors. *Metroeconomica, 13*, 49–58.

Boland, B., & Wilson, J. Q. (1978). Age, crime and punishment. *The Public Interest, 51*, 22–34.

Boland, B., Brady, E., Tyson, H., & Bassler, J. (1983). *The prosecution of felony arrests, 1979.* Washington, DC: U.S. Bureau of Justice Statistics.

Boulding, K. E. (1966). *Economic analysis: Microeconomics* (Vol. 1). New York: Harper & Row.

Box, G. E. P. & Behnken, D. W. (1960). Some new three level designs for the study of quantitative variables. *Technometrics, 2*, 455–476.

Box, G. E. P., Hunter, W. G. & Hunter, J. S. (1978). *Statistics for experimenters: An introduction to design, data analysis, and model building.* New York: John Wiley & Sons.

Boydstun, J. E., Mekemson, R. L., Minton, M. C., & Keesling, W. (1981). *Evaluation of the San Diego Police Department's career criminal program.* San Diego: Systems Development Corporation.

Bradburn, N. M. (1974). *Response effects in surveys: A review and synthesis.* Chicago: Aldine.

Brier, S. S., & Fienberg, S. E. (1980). Recent econometric modeling of crime and punishment: Support for the deterrence hypothesis? *Evaluation Review, 4*, 147–191.

Brosi, K. B. (1979). *A cross-city comparison of felony case processing.* Washington, DC: Institute for Law and Social Research.

Brown, E. J., Flanagan, T. J., & McLeod, M. (Eds.). (1984). *Sourcebook of criminal justice statistics, 1983.* Washington, DC: U.S. Government Printing Office.

Bruce, A. A. (1968). The history and development of the parole system in Illinois. In A. A. Bruce, Harno, A. J., Burgess, E. W., & Landesco, J. (Eds.), *The workings of the indeterminate-sentence law and the parole system in Illinois* (pp. 1–63). Montclair, NJ: Patterson Smith. (Original published in 1928)

Bugliosi, V. (1978). *Till death us do part: A true murder mystery.* New York: Norton.

Bureau of Justice Statistics. (1991a). *Criminal victimization in the United States*, annual. Washington, DC: U.S. Government Printing Office.

Bureau of Justice Statistics. (1991b). *Correctional populations in the United States, 1989.* Washington, DC: U.S. Government Printing Office.

Burt, C. (1943). Ability and income. *British Journal of Educational Psychology, 13*, 83–98.

Byrne, J. M. (1986). The control controversy: A preliminary examination of intensive probation supervision programs in the United States. *Federal Probation, 50*, 4–16.

Byrne, J. M., Lurigio, A., & Baird, C. (1989). The effectiveness of the new intensive supervision programs. *Research in Corrections, 2*, 1–48.

Capote, T. (1965). *In cold blood: A true account of a multiple murder and its consequences.* New York: Random House.

Caulkins, J. P. (1990). *The distribution and consumption of illicit drugs: Mathematical models and their policy implications.* Unpublished doctoral dissertation, Massachusetts Institute of Technology, Cambridge.

Cavanagh, D. P. (1990). *A cost benefit analysis of prison cell construction and alternative sanctions.* Cambridge: BOTEC Analysis Corp.

Chaiken, J. M. (1981). Models used for estimating crime rates. In M. A. Peterson, H. B. Braiker, & S. M. Polich (Eds.), *Who commits crimes: A survey of prison inmates* (pp. 224–252). Cambridge: Oelgeschlager, Gunn & Hain.

Chaiken, J. M. (1984, November). *Methods for estimating and predicting crime rates of high-rate offenders.* Paper presented at the meeting of the American Society of Criminology, Cincinnati.

Chaiken, J. M., & Chaiken, M. R. (1982). *Varieties of criminal behavior.* Santa Monica: Rand.

Chaiken, M. R., & Chaiken, J. M. (1987). *Selecting "career criminals" for priority prosecution.* Waltham: Brandeis University, Florence Heller Graduate School.

Chaiken, J. M., & Rolph, J. E. (1987). *Identifying high-rate serious criminal offenders.* Santa Monica: Rand.

Champernowne, D. G. (1953). A model of income distribution. *Economic Journal, 63,* 318–351.

Chang, S. K., Simms, W. H., Makres, C. M., & Bodnar, A. (1979). *Crime analysis system support: Descriptive report of manual and automated crime analysis functions.* Gaithersburg, MD: International Association of Chiefs of Police.

Chelimsky, E., & Dahmann, J. (1981). *Career criminal program national evaluation: Final report.* Washington, DC: U.S. Government Printing Office.

Christensen, L. R., Jorgenson, D. W. & Lau, L. J. (1971). Conjugate duality and the transcendental logarithmic production function. *Econometrica, 39,* 255–256.

Church, T., Jr., Carlson, A., Lee, J., & Tan, T. (1978). *Justice delayed: The pace of litigation in urban trial courts.* Williamsburg: National Center for State Courts.

Clark, J. P., & Tifft, L. L. (1966). Polygraph and interview validation of self-reported delinquent behavior. *American Sociological Review, 31,* 516–523.

Claster, D. (1967). Comparison of risk perception between delinquents and non-delinquents. *Journal of Criminal Law, Criminology, and Police Science, 58,* 80–86.

Clinard, M. B., & Quinney, R. (1973). *Criminal behavior systems: A typology.* New York: Holt, Rinehart & Winston.

Cohen, J. (1978). The incapacitative effect of imprisonment: A critical review of the literature. In A. Blumstein, J. Cohen, & D. Nagin (Eds.), *Deterrence and incapacitation: Estimating the effects of criminal sanctions on crime rates* (pp. 187–243). Washington, DC: National Academy of Sciences.

Cohen, J. (1983). Incapacitation as a strategy for crime control: Possibilities and pitfalls. In M. Tonry & N. Morris (Eds.), *Crime and justice: An annual review of research* (Vol. 5, pp. 1–84). Chicago: University of Chicago Press.

Cohen, J. (1986). Research on criminal careers: Individual frequency rates and offense seriousness. In A. Blumstein, J. Cohen, J. A. Roth, & C. A. Visher (Eds.), *Criminal careers and "career criminals"* (Vol. 1, pp. 292–418). Washington, DC: National Academy Press.

Cohen, L. E., & Felson, M. (1979). Social change and crime rate trends: A routine activity approach. *American Sociological Review, 44,* 588–608.

Cohen, M. A. (1988). Pain, suffering, and jury awards: A study of the cost of crime to victims. *Law and Society Review, 22,* 537–555.

Cohen, R. (1991). *Prisoners in 1990* (Bureau of Justice Statistics Bulletin). Washington, DC: Bureau of Justice Statistics.

Conklin, J. E. (1975). *The impact of crime.* New York: Macmillan.

Conklin, J. E. (1972). *Robbery and the criminal justice system.* Philadelphia: J. B. Lippincott.

Cook, F. J. (1971). There's always a crime wave. In D. R. Cressey (Ed.), *Crime and criminal justice* (pp. 23–37). Chicago: Quadrangle.

Cook, P. J. (1980). Research in criminal deterrence: Laying the groundwork for the second decade. In N. Morris & M. Tonry (Eds.), *Crime and justice: An annual review of research* (Vol. 2, pp. 211–268). Chicago: University of Chicago Press.

Cook, P. J. (1986). Criminal incapacitation effects considered in an adaptive choice framework. In D. B. Cornish & R. V. Clarke (Eds.), *The reasoning criminal: Rational choice perspectives on offending* (pp. 202–216). New York: Springer-Verlag.

Cornish, D. B., & Clarke, R. V. (Eds.). (1986). *The reasoning criminal: Rational choice perspectives on offending.* New York: Springer-Verlag.

Cory, B., & Gettinger, S. (1984). *1984, Time to build? The realities of prison construction.* New York: Edna McConnell Clark Foundation.

Cowell, F. A. (1977). *Measuring inequality: Techniques for the social sciences.* New York: John Wiley & Sons.

Cox, D. R. (1962). *Renewal theory.* London: Methuen.

Derman, C., Gleser, L. J., & Olkin, I. (1973). *A guide to probability theory and its application.* New York: Holt, Rinehart & Winston.

DiIulio, J. J., Jr. (1990). *Crime and punishment in Wisconsin* (Wisconsin Policy Research Institute report, Vol. 3, No. 7). Milwaukee: Wisconsin Policy Research Institute.

DuBow, F., McCabe, E., & Kaplan, G. (1979). *Reactions to crime: A critical review of the literature.* Washington, DC: U.S. Government Printing Office.

Dunford, F. W. & Elliott, D. S. (1984). Identifying career offenders using self-reported data. *Journal of Research in Crime and Delinquency, 21,* 57–87.

Eck, J. E. (1979). *Managing case assignments: The burglary investigation decision model replication.* Washington, DC: Police Executive Research Forum.

Eck, J. E. (1983). *Solving crimes: The investigation of burglary and robbery.* Washington, DC: Police Executive Research Forum.

Eck, J. E., & Spelman, W. (1987). *Problem solving: Problem-oriented policing in Newport News.* Washington, DC: Police Executive Research Forum.

Eck, J. E., & Spelman, W. (1983). *Solving crimes: Technical appendixes.* Unpublished manuscript. Police Executive Research Forum, Washington, DC.

Edgington, E. S. (1972). An additive method for combining probability values from independent experiments. *Journal of Psychology, 80,* 351–363.

Einstadter, W. J. (1969). The social organization of armed robbery. *Social Problems, 17,* 64–83.

Eisenstein, J., & Jacob, H. (1977). *Felony justice: An organizational analysis of criminal courts.* Boston: Little, Brown.

Elliott, D., Huizinga, D., & Ageton, S. S. (1985). *Explaining delinquency and drug use.* Beverly Hills: Sage.

English, K. (1990, November). *Measuring crime rates in Colorado: 1988–1989.* Paper presented to the American Society of Criminology, Baltimore.

Erwin, B. S. (1986). Turning up the heat on probationers in Georgia. *Federal Probation, 50,* 17–24.

Eysenck, H. J. (1960). Learning theory and behaviour therapy. In H. J. Eysenck (Ed.), *Behaviour therapy and the neuroses* (pp. 4–21). Oxford: Pergamon.

Farah, B. G., & Vale, E. (1985). Crime: A tale of two cities. *Public Opinion, 8* (4), 57–58.

Farrington, D. P. (1983). Offending from 10 to 25 years of age. In K. T. Van Dusen & S. A. Mednick (Eds.), *Prospective studies of crime and delinquency* (pp. 17–37). Hingham, MA: Kluwer-Nijhoff.

Farrington, P. (1973). Self-reports of deviant behavior: Predictive and stable? *Journal of Criminal Law and Criminology, 64,* 99–110.

Federal Bureau of Investigation (Annual). *Crime in the United States: The uniform crime reports.* Washington, DC: U.S. Government Printing Office.

Feeney, F., Dill, F., & Weir, A. (1983). *Arrests without conviction: How often they occur and why.* Washington, DC: National Institute of Justice.

Feinberg, J. (1970). *Doing and deserving: Essays in the theory of responsibility.* Princeton: Princeton University Press.

Fischer, D. R. (1984). *Risk assessment: Sentencing based on probabilities.* Des Moines: Iowa Office for Planning and Programming, Statistical Analysis Center.

Flanagan, T. J., & Maguire, K. (Eds.). (1990). *Sourcebook of criminal justice statistics—1989.* Washington, DC: U.S. Government Printing Office.

Fletcher, G. (1982). The recidivist premium. *Criminal Justice Ethics, 2,* 54–59.

Frum, H. F. (1958). Adult criminal offense trends following juvenile delinquency. *Journal of Criminal Law, Criminology, and Police Science, 7,* 29–49.

Gallup crime audit: One household in four victim of crime; public backs local crime-watch patrols. (1982). *The Gallup Report, 200,* 17–25.

Gallup, G., Jr. (1989). *The Gallup Report* (Report No. 285). Princeton: The Gallup Poll.

Gay, W. G. (1985). *Targeting law enforcement resources: The career criminal focus.* Washington, DC: U.S. Government Printing Office.

Gay, W. G., Beall, T. M., & Bowers, R. A. (1984). *A four-site assessment of the integrated criminal apprehension program.* Washington, DC: University City Science Center.

Gay, W. G., Schell, T. H., & Schack, S. (1977). *Prescriptive package: Improving patrol productivity: Routine patrol* (Vol. 1). Washington, DC: U.S. Government Printing Office.

Geis, G. (1967). White collar crime: The heavy electrical equipment antitrust cases of 1961. In M. B. Clinard & R. Quinney (Eds.), *Criminal behavior systems: A typology* (pp. 139–151). New York: Holt, Rinehart & Winston.

Gendreau, P., & Ross, R. R. (1979). Effective correctional therapy: Bibliotherapy for cynics. *Crime and Delinquency, 25,* 463–489.

Gendreau, P., & Ross, R. R. (1987). Revivification of rehabilitation: Evidence from the 1980s. *Justice Quarterly, 4,* 349–407.

Gibbons, D. C. (1968). *Society, crime, and criminal careers.* Englewood Cliffs, NJ: Prentice-Hall.

Goldstein, H. (1990). *Problem-oriented policing.* Philadelphia: Temple University Press.

Gottfredson, D. M., Hoffman, P. B., Sigler, M. H., & Wilkins, L.T. (1975). Making paroling policy explicit. *Crime and Delinquency, 21,* 34–44.

Gottfredson, M. R., & Hirschi, T. (1986). The true value of lambda would appear to be zero: An essay on career criminals, criminal careers, selective incapacitation, cohort studies, and related topics. *Criminology, 24,* 213–233.

Gottfredson, M. R., & Hirschi, T. (1990). *A general theory of crime.* Stanford: Stanford University Press.

Gottfredson, S. D. (1984). Institutional responses to prison crowding. *New York University Review of Law and Social Change, 12,* 259–273.

Gottfredson, S. D., & Gottfredson, D. M. (1986). Accuracy of prediction models. In A. Blumstein, J. Cohen, J. A. Roth, & C. A. Visher (Eds.), *Criminal careers and "career criminals"* (Vol. 2, pp. 212–290). Washington, DC: National Academy of Sciences.

Green, E. (1961). *Judicial attitudes in sentencing: A study of the factors underlying the sentencing practices of the criminal court of Philadelphia.* London: Macmillan.

Greenberg, D. (1975). The incapacitative effect of punishment: Some estimates. *Law and Society Review, 2,* 541–580.

Greene, J. R. & Mastrofski, S. D. (Eds.). (1988). *Community policing: Rhetoric or reality?* New York: Praeger.

Greenwood, P. W. (1982). *Selective incapacitaion.* Santa Monica: Rand.

Greenwood, P. W., Chaiken, J. M., Petersilia, J., & Prusoff, L. (1975). *The criminal investigations process: Observations and analysis* (Vol. 3). Santa Monica: Rand.

Greenwood, P. W., Petersilia, J., & Chaiken, J. (1977). *The criminal investigative process.* Lexington, MA: Lexington.

Greenwood, P. W. & Turner, S. (1987). *Selective incapacitation revisited: Why the high-rate offenders are hard to predict.* Santa Monica: Rand.

Greer, W. W. (1984). What is the cost of rising crime? *New York Affairs, 8,* 6–16.

Guilkey, D. C., Lovell, A. K., & Sickles, R. C. (1983). A comparison of the performance of three flexible functional forms. *International Economic Review, 4,* 591–616.

Gundy, P. M. (1951). The expected frequencies in a sample of an animal population in which the abundance of species are log-normally distributed, Part I. *Biometrika, 38,* 427–434.

Guttman, L. A. (1945). A basis for analyzing test-retest reliability. *Psychometrika, 10,* 225–282.

Haldane, J. B. S. (1942). Moments of the distribution of powers and products of normal variates. *Biometrika, 32*, 226–242.

Harris, C. M. (1968). The Pareto distribution as a queue service discipline. *Operations Research, 16*, 307–313.

Heady, E. O. (1961). *Agricultural production functions.* Ames: Iowa State University Press.

Hellman, D. A., & Naroff, J. L. (1979). The impact of crime on urban residential property values. *Urban Studies, 16*, 105–112.

Herdan, G. (1958). The relation between the dictionary distribution and the occurrence distribution of word length and its importance for the study of quantitative linguistics. *Biometrika, 45*, 222–228.

Hicks, J. (1946). *Value and capital.* New York: Oxford University Press.

Hill, W.F. (1963). *Learning: A survey of psychological interpretation.* Scranton, PA: Chandler.

Hirschi, T. (1969). *Causes of delinquency.* Berkeley: University of California Press.

Hirschi, T., Hindelang, M. J., & Weis, J. G. (1980). The status of self-report measures. In M. W. Klein & K. S. Teilmann (Eds.), *Handbook of criminal justice evaluation* (pp. 473–488). Beverly Hills: Sage.

Hoffman, P. B., & Beck, J. L. (1984). Burnout: Age at release from prison and recidivism. *Journal of Criminal Justice, 12*, 617–623.

Hoffman, P. B., & Stone-Meierhoefer, B. (1979). Post release arrest experiences of federal prisoners: A six-year follow-up. *Journal of Criminal Justice, 7*, 193–216.

Hood, R., & Sparks, R. (1970). *Key issues in criminology.* New York: McGraw-Hill.

Horney, J., & Marshall, I. (1991a). *An experimental comparison of two self-report methods for measuring lambda.* Unpublished manuscript. Omaha: University of Nebraska at Omaha, Department of Criminal Justice.

Horney, J., & Marshall, I. (1991b). Measuring lambda through self-reports. *Criminology, 29*, 401–425.

Hunter, J. E., Schmidt, F. L., & Jackson, G. B. (1982). *Meta-analysis: Combining research findings across studies.* Beverly Hills: Sage.

Inciardi, J. (1975). *Careers in crime.* Chicago: Rand McNally.

Institute for Law and Social Research. (1977). *Curbing the repeat offender: A strategy for prosecutors.* Washington, DC: U.S. Government Printing Office.

Irwin, J. O. (1968). The generalized Waring distribution applied to accident theory. *Journal of the Royal Statistical Society, Series A, 131*, 205–225.

Irwin, J. (1970). *The felon.* Englewood Cliffs, NJ: Prentice-Hall.

Johnson, E., & Payne, J. (1986). The decision to commit a crime: An information-processing analysis. In D. B. Cornish & R. V. Clarke (Eds.), *The reasoning criminal.* New York: Springer-Verlag.

Johnson, N. L. & Kotz, S. (1967). *Continuous univariate distributions.* New York: Houghton-Mifflin.

Johnston, B. L., Miller, N. P., Schoenberg, R., & Weatherly, L. R. (1973). Discretion in felony sentencing: A study of influencing factors. *Washington Law Review, 48*, 857–880.

Kahn, R. L., & Cannell, C. F. (1957). *The dynamics of interviewing.* New York: John Wiley & Sons.

Kahneman, D., & Tversky, A. (1979). Prospect theory: An analysis of decision under risk. *Econometrica, 47*, 263–291.

Kahneman, D., Slovic, P., & Tversky, A. (Eds.). (1982). *Judgment under uncertainty: Heuristics and biases.* New York: Cambridge University Press.

Kansas City Police Department. (1977). *Response time analysis: Executive summary.* Kansas City, MO: Board of Police Commissioners.

Kapteyn, J. C. (1903). *Skew frequency curves in biology and statistics.* Groningen, Germany: Nordhoff.

Kelling, G. L., Pate, T., Dieckman, D., & Brown, C. E. (1974). *The Kansas City preventive patrol experiment: A technical report.* Washington, DC: Police Foundation.

Kleiman, M. A. R. (1992). *Against excess: Drug policy for results.* New York: Basic Books.

Kmenta, J. (1972). *Elements of econometrics.* New York: Macmillan.

Kotz, S., & Neumann, J. (1963). On the distribution of precipitation amounts for periods of increasing length. *Journal of Geophysical Research, 68,* 3635–3640.

Krohm, G. (1973). The pecuniary incentives of property crime. In S. Rotenberg (Ed.), *The economics of crime and punishment* (pp. 31–34). Washington, DC: American Enterprise Institute for Public Policy Research.

Ladd, E. C. (1988). Problems or voting issues. *Public Opinion, 11*(2), 33–36.

Langan, P. A. (1985). *The prevalence of imprisonment* (Bureau of Justice Statistics Special Report). Washington, DC: Bureau of Justice Statistics.

Langan, P. A., & Dawson, J. M. (1990). *Felony sentences in state courts, 1988* (Bureau of Justice Statistics Bulletin). Washington, DC: Bureau of Justice Statistics.

Lanne, W. F. (1935). Parole prediction as science. *Journal of Criminal Law and Criminology, 26,* 377–400.

Larsen, C. R. (1983). *Costs of incarceration and alternatives.* Phoenix: Arizona State University Center for the Study of Justice.

Larson, R. C., & Odoni, A. R. (1981). *Urban operations research.* Englewood Cliffs, NJ: Prentice-Hall.

Lattimore, P., & Witte, A. (1986). Models of decision making under uncertainty: The criminal choice. In D. B. Cornish & R. V. Clarke (Eds.), *The reasoning criminal* (pp. 129–155). New York: Springer-Verlag.

Lebergott, S. (1959). The shape of the income distribution. *American Economic Review, 49,* 328–347.

Lemert, E. M. (1958). The behavior system of the systematic check forger. *Social Problems, 6,* 141–149.

Lemert, E. M. (1967). *Human deviance, social problems, and social control.* Englewood Cliffs, NJ: Prentice-Hall.

Lindgren, S. A. (1988). The cost of justice. In Bureau of Justice Statistics (Ed.), *Report to the nation on crime and justice* (pp. 113–127, second ed.). Washington, DC: Bureau of Justice Statistics.

Loeber, R., & Dishion, T. (1983). Early predictors of male delinquency: A review. *Psychological Bulletin, 94*(10), 68–99.

Maltz, M. (1984). *Recidivism.* New York: Academic.

Mande, M. J., & English, K. (1988). *Individual crime rates of Colorado prisoners: Final report, 1988.* (Denver: Colorado Division of Criminal Justice, Research Unit.)

Marquis, K. (1981). *Quality of prisoner self-reports, arrest and conviction response errors.* Santa Monica: Rand.

Martin, S. E. (1985). *Catching career criminals: A study of the repeat offender project: Technical report.* Washington, DC: Police Foundation.

Mason, R. L., Gunst, R. F., & Hess, J. L. (1989). *Statistical design and analysis of experiments with applications to engineering and science.* New York: John Wiley & Sons.

Mayer, T. (1960). The distribution of ability and of earnings. *Review of Economics and Statistics, 42*(5), 189–195.

McCarthy, B. (Ed.). (1987). *Intermediate punishments: Intensive supervision, home confinement and electronic surveillance.* Monsey, NY: Criminal Justice Press.

McDonald, W. F. (1987). *Repeat offender laws in the United States: Their form, use, and perceived value.* Washington, DC: U.S. Government Printing Office.

Meisenhelder, T. (1977). An exploratory study of exiting from criminal careers. *Criminology, 15,* 319–344.

Moder, J. J., & Elmaghraby, S. E. (Eds.). (1978). *Handbook of operations research: Models and applications.* New York: Van Nostrand Reinhold.

Monahan, J. (1982). The case for prediction in the modified desert model of criminal sentencing. *International Journal of Law and Psychiatry, 5,* 103–113.

Moore, M. H. (1986). Purblind justice: Normative issues in the use of predictive or discriminating tests in the criminal justice system. In A. Blumstein, J. Cohen, J. A. Roth, & C. A. Visher (Eds.), *Criminal careers and "career criminals"* (Vol. 2, pp. 314–355). Washington, DC: National Academy Press.

Moore, M. H., Estrich, S. R., McGillis, D. & Spelman, W. (1984). *Dangerous offenders: The elusive target of justice.* Cambridge: Harvard University Press.

Morris, N. (1982). *Madness and the criminal law.* Chicago: University of Chicago Press.

Moser, C. A. & Kalton, G. (1972). *Survey methods in social investigation.* New York: Basic.

Mosteller, F. & Tukey, J. W. (1977). *Data analysis and regression: A second course in statistics.* Reading, MA: Addison-Wesley.

Nagin, D. (1978). General deterrence: A review of the empirical evidence. In A. Blumstein, J. Cohen, & D. Nagin (Eds.), *Deterrence and incapacitation: Estimating the effects of criminal sanctions on crime rates* (pp. 95–139). Washington, DC: National Academy of Sciences.

Normandeau, A. (1972). Violence and robbery: A case study. *Acta Criminologica, 5,* 77.

Ohlin, L. E. (1951). *Selection for parole: A manual for parole prediction.* New York: Russell Sage Foundation.

Pareto, V. (1972). *Manual of political economy.* London: Macmillan. (Original published 1897)

Pate, T., Bowers, R. A., & Parks, R. (1976). *Three approaches to criminal apprehension in Kansas City: An evaluation report.* Washington, DC: Police Foundation.

Pearson, F. S. (1988). Evaluation of New Jersey's intensive supervision program. *Crime and Delinquency, 34,* 437–448.

Pen, J. (1974). *Income distribution.* Hammondsworth: Penguin.

Perez, J. (1990). *Tracking offenders, 1987* (Bureau of Justice Statistics Bulletin). Washington, DC: Bureau of Justice Statistics.

Petersilia, J. (1980). Criminal career research: A review of recent evidence. In N. Morris & M. Tonry, *Crime and justice: An annual review of research* (Vol. 2, pp. 321–379). Chicago: University of Chicago Press.

Petersilia, J., & Turner, S. (1990). *Intensive supervision for high-risk probationers: Findings from three California experiments.* Santa Monica: Rand.

Petersilia, J., Greenwood, P. W., & Lavin, M. (1978). *Criminal careers of habitual felons.* Santa Monica: Rand.

Peterson, M. A., Braiker, H. B., & Polich, S. M. (1980). *Doing crime: A survey of California prison inmates.* Santa Monica: Rand.

Peterson, M., Chaiken, J., Ebener, P., & Honig, P. (1981). *Survey of prison and jail inmates: Background and method.* Santa Monica: Rand.

Peterson, R. A., Pittman, D. J., & O'Neal, P. (1962). Stabilities in deviance: A study of assaultive and non-assaultive offenders. *Journal of Criminal Law, Criminology, and Police Science, 53,* 44–49.

Pigou, A. C. (1932). *The economics of welfare.* London: Macmillan.

Pittman, D. J., & Handy, W. (1964). Patterns in criminal aggravated assault. *Journal of Criminal Law, Criminology, and Police Science, 55,* 462–470.

Public backs wholesale prison reform. (1982). *The Gallup Report, 200* (May), 3–16.

Quandt, R. E. (1966). Old and new methods of estimation and the Pareto distribution. *Metrika, 10,* 55–82.

Reaves, B. A. (1992). *Pretrial release of felony defendants, 1990* (Bureau of Justice Statistics Bulletin). Washington, DC: Bureau of Justice Statistics.

Reiss, A. J., Jr. (1980). Understanding changes in crime rates. In S. E. Fienberg & A. J. Reiss, Jr. (Eds.), *Indicators of crime and criminal justice: Quantitative studies* (pp. 11–17). Washington, DC: U.S. Government Printing Office.

Rhodes, W. M. & Conly, C. (1981). Crime and mobility: An empirical study. In P. J. Brantingham & P. L. Brantingham (Eds.), *Environmental criminology* (pp. 167–188). Beverly Hills: Sage.

Rhodes, W. M., Tyson, H., Weekly, J., Conly, C., & Powell, G. (1982). *Developing criteria for identifying career criminals*. Washington, DC: Institute for Law and Social Research.

Riccio, L. J. (1974). Direct deterrence: An analysis of the effectiveness of police patrol and other crime prevention strategies. *Journal of Criminal Justice, 2*, 207–217.

Robinson, W. S. (1950). Ecological correlations and the behavior of individuals. *American Sociological Review, 15*, 351–357.

Roebuck, J. B. (1967). *Criminal typology: The legalistic, physical-constitutional-hereditary, psychological-psychiatric, and sociological approaches*. Springfield: Charles C. Thomas.

Rolph, J. E., & Chaiken, J. M. (1987). *Identifying high-rate serious criminals from official records*. Santa Monica: Rand.

Rolph, J. E., Chaiken, J. M., & Houchens, R. L. (1981). *Methods for estimating the crime rates of individuals*. Santa Monica: Rand.

Rosenthal, R. (1978). Combining results of independent studies. *Psychological Bulletin, 85*, 185–193.

Rossi, P. H., Berk, R. A., & Lenihan, K. J. (1980). *Money, work and crime: Experimental evidence*. New York: Academic.

Roy, A. D. (1950). The distribution of earnings and of individual output. *Economic Journal, 60*, 489–505.

Rutherford, R. S. G. (1955). Income distributions: A new model. *Econometrics, 23*, 277–294.

Saerndal, C. (1964). Estimation of the parameters of the gamma distribution by sample quantiles. *Technometrics, 6*, 405–414.

Schack, S., Schell, T. H., & Gay, W. G. (1977). *Prescriptive package: Improiving patrol productivity: Specialized patrol* (Vol. 2). Washington, DC: U.S. Government Printing Office.

Schmideberg, M. (1960). The offender's attitude toward punishment. *Journal of Criminal Law, Criminology, and Police Science, 51*, 328–334.

Schmidt, P., & Witte, A. D. (1984). *An economic analysis of crime and justice*. New York: Academic.

Schnelle, J., Kirchner, R., Casey, J., Uselton, P., & McNees, M. (1977). Patrol evaluation research: A multiple-baseline analysis of saturation police patrolling during day and night hours. *Journal of Applied Behavioral Analysis, 10*, 33–40.

Schur, E. M. (1969). *Our criminal society: The social and legal sources of crime in America*. Englewood Cliffs, NJ: Prentice-Hall.

Sechrest, L. B., White, S. O., & Brown, E. D. (1979). *The rehabilitation of criminal offenders: Problems and prospects*. Washington, DC: National Academy of Sciences.

Seidman, D., & Couzens, M. (1974). Getting the crime rate down: Political pressure and crime reporting. *Law and Society Review, 8*, 457–493.

Sellin, T., & Wolfgang, M. E. (1964). *The measurement of delinquency*. New York: John Wiley & Sons.

Shane-DuBow, S., Brown, A. P., & Olsen, E. (1985). *Sentencing reform in the United States: History, content, and effect*. Washington, DC: U.S. Government Printing Office.

Shannon, L. W. (1982). Assessing the relationship of adult criminal careers to juvenile careers. Washington, DC: Office of Juvenile Justice and Delinquency Prevention.

Shelton v. Tucker, 364 U. S. 494 (1960).

Shenk, J. F., & Klaus, P. A. (1984). *The economic cost of crime to victims* (Bureau of Justice Statistics Special Report). Washington, DC: U.S. Bureau of Justice Statistics.

Sherman, L. W., & Glick, B. D. (1984). *The quality of police arrest statistics* (Police Foundation reports). Washington, DC: Police Foundation.

Shinnar, S., & Shinnar, R. (1975). The effects of the criminal justice system on the control of crime: A quantitative approach. *Law and Society Review, 9*, 581–611.

Shover, N. (1973). The social organization of burglary. *Social Problems, 20*, 499–514.

Shover, N. (1985). *Aging criminals*. Beverly Hills: Sage.

Siegel, S. (1957). Level of aspiration and decision making. *Psychological Review, 64*, 253–262.

Silberman, C. E. (1977). *Criminal violence, criminal justice*. New York: Random House.

Simon, H. A. (1957). The compensation of executives. *Sociometry, 20*, 32–35.

Simon, H. A., & Bonini, C. P. (1958). The size distribution of business firms. *American Economic Review, 48*, 607–617.

Singer, R. G. (1979). *Just deserts: Sentencing based on equality and desert*. Cambridge, MA: Ballinger.

Snell, T. L., & Morton, D. C. (1992). *Prisoners in 1991* (Bureau of Justice Statistics Bulletin). Washington, DC: Bureau of Justice Statistics.

Snyder, H. N. (1989). *Juvenile court statistics, 1986*. Washington, DC: U.S. Government Printing Office.

Spelman, W. (1983). The crime control effectiveness of selective criminal justice policies. In D. McGillis, M. H. Moore, S. R. Estrich, & W. Spelman (Eds.), *Dealing with dangerous offenders: Selected papers* (Vol. 2, Sec. 8, pp.1–75). Cambridge: Harvard University, John F. Kennedy School of Government.

Spelman, W. (1986). *The depth of a dangerous temptation: Another look at selective incapacitation*. Cambridge: Harvard Law School.

Spelman, W. (1988a). *Beyond bean counting: New approaches for managing crime data*. Washington, DC: Police Executive Research Forum.

Spelman, W. (1988b). *The incapacitation benefits of selective criminal justice policies*. Unpublished doctoral dissertation, Harvard University, Cambridge.

Spelman, W. (1990). *Repeat offender programs for law enforcement*. Washington, DC: Police Executive Research Forum.

Spelman, W., & Brown, D. K. (1984). *Calling the police: Citizen reporting of serious crime*. Washington, DC: U.S. Government Printing Office.

Spelman, W., Oshima, M., & Kelling, G. L. (1986). *On the competitive nature of ferreting out crime* (Final report to the Florence V. Burden Foundation). Cambridge: Harvard University, John F. Kennedy School of Government.

Staehle, H. (1943). Ability, wages, and income. *Review of Economics and Statistics, 25*, 77–87.

Stocking, C. B. (1978). *The Marlowe-Crowne scale in survey data*. Unpublished doctoral dissertation, University of Chicago, Chicago.

Sutherland, E. H. (1937). *The professional thief*. Chicago: University of Chicago Press.

Sutherland, E. H. (1947). *Principles of criminology*. Philadelphia: J. B. Lippincott.

Sutherland, E. H., & Cressey, D. R. (1970). *Criminology*. Philadelphia: J. B. Lippincott.

Takacs, L. (1969). On Erlang's formula. *Annals of Mathematical Statistics, 40*, 71–78.

Taub, R. D., Taylor, G., & Dunham, J. (1984). *Patterns of neighborhood change: Race and crime in urban America*. Chicago: University of Chicago Press.

Thaler, R. (1978). A note on the value of crime control: Evidence from the property market. *Journal of urban economics, 5*, 137–145.

Tillman, R. (1987). The size of the "criminal population': The prevalence and incidence of adult arrest. *Criminology, 25*, 561–579.

Tversky, A., & Kahneman, D. (1974). Judgment under uncertainty: Heuristics and biases. *Science, 185*, 1124–1131.

U. S. Bureau of the Census. (Annual). *Statistical Abstract of the United States*, annual. Washington, DC: U.S. Government Printing Office.

U. S. Sentencing Commission. (1987). *Revised draft: Sentencing guidelines*. Washington, DC: author.

van Dine, S. W., Conrad, J. P., & Dinitz, S. (1979). *Restraining the wicked*. Lexington, MA: Lexington.

Visher, C. A. (1986). The Rand second inmate survey: A reanalysis. In A. Blumstein, J. Cohen, J. A. Roth, & C. A. Visher (Eds.), *Criminal careers and "career criminals"* (Vol. 2, pp. 161–211). Washington, DC: National Academy of Sciences.

Visher, C. A., & Roth, J. A. (1986). Participation in criminal careers. In A. Blumstein, J. Cohen, J. A. Roth, & C. A. Visher (Eds.), *Criminal careers and "career criminals"* (Vol. 1, pp. 211–291). Washington, DC: National Academy Press.

von Hirsch, A. (1976). *Doing justice: Report of the Committee for the Study of Incarceration*. New York: Hill & Wang.

von Hirsch, A. (1985). *Past and future crimes: Deservedness and dangerousness in the sentencing of criminals*. New Brunswick, NJ: Rutgers University Press.

von Hirsch, A., & Gottfredson, D. M. (1983). Selective incapacitation: Some queries about research design and equity. *New York University Review of Law and Social Change*, *12*, 11–51.

Ward, P. (1970). Careers in crime: The FBI story. *Journal of Research in Crime and Delinquency*, *7*, 207–218.

Willmer, M. A. P. (1970). *Crime and information theory*. Edinburgh: Edinburgh University Press.

Wilson, J. Q. (1984). *Thinking about crime*. New York: Basic.

Wilson, J. Q., & Boland, B. (1976). Crime. In W. Gorham & N. Glazer (Eds.), *The urban predicament*. Washington, DC: Urban Institute.

Wilson, J. Q., & Herrnstein, R. J. (1985). *Crime and human nature*. New York: Simon & Schuster.

Wilson, J. Q., & Kelling, G. L. (1982, March). Broken windows: The police and neighborhood safety. *The Atlantic*, 29–36.

Wilson, J. Q., & Kelling, G. L. (1989). Making neighborhoods safe. *The Atlantic*, *263*, 46–52.

Witte, A. D., & Schmidt, P. (1977). An analysis of recidivism using the truncated lognormal distribution. *Applied Statistics*, *26*, 302–311.

Wolfgang, M. E. (1958). *Patterns in criminal homicide*. Philadelphia: University of Pennsylvania Press.

Wolfgang, M. E., & Tracy, P. E. (1983). The 1945 and 1958 birth cohorts: A comparison of the prevalence, incidence, and severity of delinquent behavior. In D. McGillis, M. H. Moore, S. R. Estrich & W. Spelman (Eds.), *Dealing with dangerous offenders: Selected papers* (Vol. 2, Sec. 1, pp. 1–56). Cambridge: Harvard University, John F. Kennedy School of Government.

Wolfgang, M. E., Figlio, R. M., & Sellin, T. (1972). *Delinquency in a birth cohort*. Chicago: University of Chicago Press.

Wolfgang, M. E., Figlio, R. M., Tracy, P. E., & Singer, S. I. (1985). *The national survey of crime severity*. Washington, DC: U.S. Government Printing Office.

Yule, G. U., & Kendall, M. G. (1950). *An introduction to the theory of statistics*. London: Charles Griffin & Company.

Zedlewski, E. W. (1987). *Making confinement decisions* (NIJ Research in Brief). Washington, DC: National Institute of Justice.

Zedlewski, E. W. (1989). New mathematics of imprisonment: A reply to Zimring and Hawkins. *Crime and Delinquency*, *35*, 169–173.

Zimring, F. E., & Hawkins, G. (1988). The new mathematics of imprisonment. *Crime and Delinquency*, *34*, 425–436.

Index

Active offenders, 167
  arrests of, 172, 175
  collective incapacitation of, 207, 215, 217, 220
  criminal career of, 132, 134, 143–144, 145, 148, 158, 163
  defined, 24
  offense rates for, 55, 74–76, 91, 116, 163
  selective incapacitation of, 239
  weighted samples of, 23–25, 29, 30, 41, 42
Adult offenders
  arrests of, 172
  collective incapacitation of, 199, 211–213, 215, 218–219
  criminal career of, 130
  offense rates for, 59–60, 73
Age, 17, 304
  arrests and, 18
  criminal career and, 19, 128, 141, 142–156, 161, 163–164
  offense rates and, 66–67, 92–93, 94, 163–164
  selective incapacitation and, 258
  in weighted samples, 28–30, 40
  See also Adult offenders; Juvenile offenders
Alaska, 221
American Civil Liberties Union, 311
Analytical models, 12, 19
  of collective incapacitation, 199
  of criminal career, 150
  of offense rates, 56, 80, 109–110, 124
  of selective incapacitation, 250
Antitrust violations, 238
Anxiety about arrests, 193
Apprenticeship model, 102
Arkansas, 221

Armed robbery
  arrests for, 175
  offense rates for, 84, 85
Arrestee population
  criminal career in, 134
  offense rates in, 70, 71–73
  See also Offender population
Arrest records, 7, 169, 170, 171, 176–177, 185, 195
  on collective incapacitation, 213
  criminal career estimated from, 129, 130, 132, 134–135, 141, 145, 146, 150
  offense rates estimated from, 70, 71–72, 73
  recidivism estimated from, 73
  on specialists, 103
  validity of, 49–52
  in weighted samples, 35
Arrests, 17, 18, 19, 21, 167–195, 294, 296
  anxiety about, 193
  average probability of, 167–172
  collective incapacitation and, 199, 200, 201, 203, 209, 212, 213, 220–221
  criminal career and, 129, 142–148, 149, 157
  defined, 168
  empirical estimates of, 169–172, 183
  filtering estimates of, 177–178
  indicators of probability of, 187–195
  offender evaluation of, 299
  offense rates and, 44, 72, 73, 81–84, 167, 192, 193, 249, 291
  partial incapacitation and, 306, 309
  recidivism and, 73
  selective incapacitation and, 191, 194–195, 230, 232, 234, 235, 239, 240, 241,

325

Arrests (*Cont.*)
  selective incapacitation and (*Cont.*)
    242, 244, 245, 246, 249, 269, 271,
    281–283
  sentences and, 37, 38
  skewed distributions of, 49–50, 81–84,
    181, 200
  tactics used for, 173–176
  validity of estimates of, 47–52
  weighted samples on, 26, 30, 33–35, 171
  See also Arrestee population; Arrest records
Arrest-switch matrixes, 102–104
Assault, 18
  arrests for, 35, 49, 169, 170, 171, 172,
    185, 193
  collective incapacitation for, 198, 210
  costs of, 223
  criminal career in, 127, 135
  generalists and, 106, 107
  incarceration probability for, 36
  offense rates for, 60, 80, 96, 100, 101, 106,
    107, 109
  sentences for, 38, 39
  specialists and, 109
  weighted samples on, 35, 36, 38, 39
Auto theft
  arrests for, 35, 49, 171
  collective incapacitation for, 210
  costs of, 223
  criminal career in, 135
  generalists and, 106
  incarceration probability for, 36
  offense rates for, 60, 101, 106, 107, 111
  sentences for, 38, 39
  specialists in, 107
  weighted samples on, 35, 36, 38, 39
Avi-Itzhak/Shinnar model, 12, 19, 110
  collective incapacitation in, 200, 207, 208,
    212
  selective incapacitation in, 248

Baby-boom offenders, 131, 149
Back-end selective programs: *see* Selective
  sentences
Backward-looking scales, 230, 231, 246
Bail, 167, 245
Bathtub-shaped functions, 150, 152, 209
Bayesian processes, 296
Benefit-cost ratios, 10, 11–12
  of crime control, 224–225, 227

Benefit-cost ratios (*Cont.*)
  imperfect information and, 8, 9
  offense rates as, 56–62, 67, 68, 79
  perfect information and, 6
  of prison expansion, 13, 14–15, 224–225,
    227, 229
Benefits
  of crime control, 222–224, 307
  of prison expansion, 222–224
  of selective incapacitation, 233, 234
  See also Benefit-cost ratios; Direct benefits;
    Indirect benefits
Bias
  in arrest rate estimates, 49–50, 178, 179,
    184, 186, 194, 306
  in criminal career estimates, 131, 134, 135–
    136, 148, 149, 155, 156, 161
  in offense rate estimates, 70, 72–73, 109, 110
  in partial incapacitation studies, 305
  weighted sample introduction of, 30
  See also Sample bias
Bivariate distributions, of offense rates, 119,
    120–124
Blacks, 45, 102, 194
Bliss point, 4, 6, 229
Box-and-whisker plots, 81–82, 84–85
Box-Behnken design, 217, 249, 266
Box plots, 172, 287
Breakeven analysis, 224–227, 264, 265, 309
Burgess method, 244
Burglary, 18, 302, 303
  arrests for, 35, 49, 169, 170, 171
  collective incapacitation for, 205, 210
  costs of, 223
  criminal career in, 126, 135, 164–165
  generalists and, 105, 106
  incarceration probability for, 36
  offense rates for, 33, 34, 44, 57, 60, 80,
    90, 100, 101, 105, 106, 107, 108, 111,
    164–165
  selective incapacitation for, 238, 241, 242
  sentences for, 38, 39
  specialists in, 107, 108
  weighted samples on, 33, 34, 35, 36, 38,
    39
Burnout, 131, 155, 156, 304
  mathematical model of, 150–152, 153, 154
Business robbery
  arrests for, 35, 49
  offense rates for, 101

California, 30
    arrests in, 35, 170, 171, 177, 190, 213
    collective incapacitation in, 210, 213, 215
    criminal career in, 39, 137, 139, 162, 163, 164
    incarceration probability in, 36
    incoming cohort in, 41, 42
    offense rates in, 12, 67, 74, 75, 77, 78, 85, 96, 105, 117, 118, 119, 120, 122, 163, 164
    partial incapacitation in, 305–306
    selective incapacitation in, 281, 284, 285
    selective sentences in, 15
    sentences in, 39, 210
    specialization in, 105, 122
Career criminals, 10, 154, 290
    arrests of, 193
    as generalists, 105
    offense rates of, 69
    selective incapacitation of, 281
Careers in Crime program, 130–131
Categorical incapacitation, 10
Central composite design, 249
Child abuse, 238
Chronic recidivists, 81, 82
Civil cases, 64, 222
Civil libertarians, 10, 11
Clearance rates, 168, 170, 174, 193
Collective incapacitation, 19, 48, 55, 98, 109, 197–227, 288, 289, 291
    crime elasticity and, 220–221
    defined, 9
    direct benefits of, 289
    direct costs of, 289
    effectiveness of, 216–227
        limitations on, 211–216
        modeling of, 198–211
    offender information on, 298
    prison expansion and, 221–227, 283–284
Colorado, 43, 45, 77
Commercial robbery: *see* Business robbery
Community service programs, 239
Community treatment centers, 244
Community watch programs, 195
Complete information: *see* Perfect information
Compromise optimal selective policies, 271, 272, 274, 275
Computer simulation models: *see* Simulation models
Con artists, 101, 171

Constraints, 237–247
    on control parameters, 274–285
    on selective scales, 256–258, 259, 271–272
    See also Ethical constraints; Knowledge constraints; Resource constraints
Contra Costa County, California, 306
Control parameters, constraints on, 274–285
Conventional criminals, 127
Conviction records, 7
Convictions, 21, 36, 291, 294
    collective incapacitation and, 199, 201, 209, 214
    number of arrests leading to, 177, 191
    offense rates and, 78
    recidivism and, 73–74
    selective incapacitation and, 230, 234, 235, 239, 240, 242, 244, 245, 246, 271, 273
    self-reports of, 47–49
Cost-effectiveness
    of intermediate sanctions, 309
    of prison expansion, 19, 291
    of selective incapacitation, 101
Costs
    of crime, 2–4, 8, 64–65, 222–224, 285, 307
    of crime control, 2–4, 221–222, 225–226, 233, 307–308
    fixed, 276
    of incarceration, 8, 250
    of partial incapacitation, 305, 307–310
    of prison expansion, 55, 70, 101, 221–222, 225–226
    of selective incapacitation, 233, 246–247, 288
    variable, 276
    See also Benefit-cost ratios; Cost effectiveness; Direct costs; Indirect costs
Crime analysis, 174, 175, 276
Crime control, 108, 311
    arrests and, 167
    benefit-cost ratios of, 224–225, 227
    benefits of, 222–224, 307
    collective incapacitation and, 221–227, 289
    costs of, 2–4, 221–222, 225–226, 233, 307–308
    direct benefits of, 225, 288, 289
    direct costs of, 224–225, 289
    indirect benefits of, 224–227, 284–285, 288, 289, 307–308, 309, 311

Crime control (*Cont.*)
  partial incapacitation and, 305, 309
  production of, 4–10
  selective incapacitation and, 233, 234, 240,
    248, 250, 251, 252–253, 254–256,
    257–258, 259, 260, 263–264, 265,
    266, 267–268, 270, 271, 272, 274,
    277–278, 279, 283, 284–285, 287–
    288, 289
Crime costs, 2–4, 8, 64–65, 222–224, 285,
  307
Crime elasticity, 220–221, 250
Criminal career, 12, 14–16, 19, 21, 125, 125–
  165
  average length of, 128, 129–140
  burnout in: *see* Burnout
  collective incapacitation and, 200, 203,
    206–209, 212, 213, 214, 217
  distribution of, 128, 141–165
  dropout in: *see* Dropout
  incarceration risks and, 295, 297–298
  offense rates and, 19, 66, 72, 91, 92, 125,
    128, 141, 156–165, 208–209, 214,
    249
  selective incapacitation and, 125, 140, 147,
    154, 156–157, 249, 271
  selective sentences and, 15–16, 142, 156
  sentences and, 37, 38, 125, 138–140, 141,
    154, 156
  weighted samples on, 23, 29, 30, 39, 41,
    135–136, 138
Criminal justice system
  collective incapacitation and, 209–211
  heterogeneous model of, 290–292
Criminal records
  arrests and, 187, 188, 192
  selective incapacitation and, 230
  sentences and, 37–38
  See also Arrest records; Official records
Cross-sectional explanations, 88–91

Dangerous offenders, 290
  arrests of, 191
  criminal career of, 125
  generalists as, 105–107
  imperfect information on, 7–10
  offense rates for, 13
  perfect information on, 6
  selective incapacitation of, 219, 231–232,

Dangerous offenders (*Cont.*)
  selective incapacitation of (*Cont.*)
    234, 238, 242–243, 244, 252, 261,
    262, 273, 275, 276, 279–280, 282
  See also Violent offenders
Day reporting centers, 310
Death Row, 21–22
Decision making under uncertainty, 299–300
Decoy operations, 173, 174, 242
DeKalb County, Georgia, 241
Demographic characteristics
  arrests and, 186, 187, 192, 194
  criminal career and, 145–146, 161
Depression, The, 149
Descriptive scales: *see* Backward-looking
  scales
Deterrence, 5, 6, 22, 23, 25, 55, 307, 312
  of active offenders, 25
  collective incapacitation and, 200
  offender evaluation and, 299, 301
  offender responsiveness and, 302, 303, 304
  offense rates and, 58, 64, 101
  partial incapacitation and, 305
  selective incapacitation and, 239, 264, 271,
    292–294, 311
  See also Special deterrence
Deterrence elasticity, 293
Detroit riots, 102
Dichotomous outputs, 235–237
Direct benefits
  of collective incapacitation, 289
  of crime control, 225, 288, 289
  of prison expansion, 264
Direct costs
  of collective incapacitation, 289
  of crime, 64, 65, 222, 285
  of crime control, 224–225, 289
  of prison expansion, 224–225
Directed patrol tactics, 173, 174, 175
Disparity ratios, 235–236, 248, 249, 250,
    257, 266, 286
  constraints on, 242, 243, 246, 247, 258–
    260, 261–264, 275, 276, 277–278,
    279, 280, 281
  incarceration production function and, 273–
    274
  optimal selective policies and, 253, 254–
    255, 256, 268, 269, 270, 271, 283,
    291

Distributions
  of criminal career, 128, 141–165
  of offense rates, 56, 79–100, 248
  See also Bivariate distributions; Exponential
    distributions; Gamma distributions;
    LogNormal distributions; Normal distri-
    butions; Pareto distributions; Poisson
    distributions; Skewed distributions;
    Univariate distributions; Weibull distri-
    butions
Domestic crimes, 238
Dropout, 131, 136–137, 138, 139, 140
  age and, 142–156
  collective incapacitation and, 201–202,
    206–209
  mathematical models of, 150–154
  offense rates and, 156–165
Drug abuse, 17, 23
  arrests and, 186
  criminal career and, 156
  offense rates for, 94, 99
Drug abuse history, 7, 93
Drug dealing, 57, 302
  arrests for, 35
  incarceration probability for, 36
  offense rates for, 63–64, 106
  recruitment-replacement hypothesis and,
    58
  selective incapacitation for, 238
  sentences for, 38, 39
  weighted samples on, 23, 35, 36, 38, 39
Drug treatment programs, 194
Dual-bias hypothesis, 43, 49–52

Ecological fallacy, 104
Economic changes, 145–146
Economic crimes, 164
Economic models of incapacitation, 2–10
Education, 45, 188
Elasticity statistics, 247, 264–265
Electronic monitoring, 4, 244, 305, 307, 309,
    310
Embezzlement, 90, 238
Empirical estimates, of arrest rates, 169–172,
    183
Employment, 7, 17, 302, 305
  arrests and, 185, 188, 193, 194
  collective incapacitation and, 221
  criminal career and, 131, 156, 164

Employment (*Cont.*)
  offense rates and, 61, 88–89, 93, 94, 99,
    101, 164
Enabling factors, 90–91
England, 67, 68
Erlang distributions, 112, 113
Erlang's Loss Formula, 28
Ethical constraints, 237, 245–246, 247, 258–
    259, 264, 286, 289, 311
  on control parameters, 274–275
  on optimal selective policies, 253, 271
  on selective scales, 256–257
Execution, 4, 61
Exponential distributions, of criminal career,
    131, 133, 139, 141, 147, 154–156,
    208
External reliability, of offense rates, 45, 47–49

Federal Bureau of Investigation (FBI), 280
  on arrests, 72, 168
  on criminal career, 129, 130–131, 132, 144,
    146
  index crimes of: *see* Index crimes
Felonies, 304
  arrests for, 168, 176
  criminal career and, 157
  partial incapacitation and, 306
  selective incapacitation for, 283
Filtering estimates
  of arrest selectivity, 177–178
  of collective incapacitation, 213–216
Fines, 296
Fingerprints, 174, 176
First-time offenders, 71, 73, 134, 259
Fixed costs, 276
Flashers, 107
Florida, 36, 241
Follow-up investigations, 173, 174–175, 176
Forgery, 12, 18, 302
  arrests for, 35, 49, 171, 172, 193
  costs of, 223
  generalists and, 106
  incarceration probability for, 36
  offense rates for, 63, 64, 75, 100, 106, 111
  sentences for, 38, 39
  weighted samples on, 35, 36, 38, 39
Forward-looking scales, 230–231, 232, 233,
    246
Franklin County, Ohio, 281

Fraud, 12, 18, 302
  arrests for, 35, 49, 170, 171, 172
  collective incapacitation for, 210
  costs of, 223
  generalists and, 106
  incarceration probability for, 36
  offense rates for, 63, 64, 75, 100, 106, 111
  sentences for, 38, 39
  weighted samples on, 35, 36, 38, 39
Frequent offenders: *see* High-rate offenders
Front-end selective programs, 271, 272
Full factorial designs, 217
Furloughs, 304

Gamma distributions, of offense rates, 52, 53,
    80, 111, 112, 113, 114, 115, 117–118,
    119, 120, 124
Generalists
  arrests of, 193
  collective incapacitation of, 205
  dangerousness of, 105–107
  offense rates of, 101, 104, 105–107, 108–
    109, 120, 121–123
Georgia, 241
Gompertz distributions, 295
Greenwood model, 80, 98–100, 128, 138,
    154, 292
Group offending: *see* Multiple offender crimes

Habitual offenders, 167, 176
Halfway houses, 305
Heterogeneous criminal justice system, 290–
    292
Heterogeneous offense rates, 200, 203–206,
    216, 220
Heteroskedastic measurement errors, 53
High-rate offenders, 21, 42, 290, 291, 292
  arrests of, 17, 18, 175, 177, 179, 187, 191–
    192
  collective incapacitation of, 198, 199, 203,
    208, 209, 211, 212
  criminal career of, 125, 138–140, 142, 154,
    157–158, 161, 163, 164, 165
  generalists as, 105
  information evaluation by, 300, 301
  information sources of, 295, 296, 298–299
  offense rates of, 13, 44, 46–47, 69, 86–87,
    91, 92–93, 97, 98, 99, 105, 109, 111–
    112, 116, 163, 164, 165
  responsiveness of, 303, 304

High-rate offenders (*Cont.*)
  selective incapacitation of, 219, 229, 232,
    234, 235, 238, 239, 240, 256, 260,
    261, 262, 263, 265, 276, 279–280,
    283, 286, 288
  selective sentences for, 15
  specialists as, 109
Hispanics, 188, 194
Homicide, 222
  arrests for, 193
  collective incapacitation for, 212
  criminal career in, 126, 127, 135
  offense rates for, 64
Homogeneous crime model, 108–109
  collective incapacitation and, 200, 205, 213
  selective incapacitation and, 240, 241, 243,
    293
House arrest, 61, 305

IBR: *see* Indirect benefits ratio
Imperfect information
  in offender population, 294–295
  optimal selective policies under, 269–271
  production under, 7–10
Incapacitation policies, 12–18
Incarceration costs, 8, 250
Incarceration length, 197, 247, 248–265
Incarceration probability, 299
  collective incapacitation and, 209–210
  offender evaluation of, 300
  selective incapacitation and, 197, 247
  sentences and, 37, 38
  weighted samples on, 26, 30, 35–37
Incarceration production functions, 266, 268,
    269, 270, 271
  constraints and, 275
  effects of changes in, 272–274
Incarceration rates, 290–292
Incarceration risks, 295, 296–298
  selective incapacitation and, 265–286
Incivilities, 223
Income, 114, 303
  iron law of, 111
  offense rates and, 88–89
  from wages, 89, 194
Incoming cohorts, 291
  collective incapacitation and, 215
  offense rates of, 63, 70, 74, 76–77, 79
  weighted samples of, 22, 23, 24, 25–30,
    39–40, 41, 42

Indeterminate sentences, 262
Index crimes, 41, 42
  collective incapacitation for, 209, 215
  criminal career and, 134
  offense rates for, 12, 57, 63–64, 65, 67, 73,
      75, 116, 162
  recidivism and, 73
  selective incapacitation for, 280, 281
Indifference curves, 4, 8
Indirect benefit multipliers, 225
Indirect benefits
  breakeven analysis of: *see* Breakeven analy-
      sis
  of collective incapacitation, 289
  of crime control, 224–227, 284–285, 288,
      289, 307–308, 309, 311
  of prison expansion, 224–227, 264–265,
      284–285
  of selective incapacitation, 264, 265
Indirect benefits ratio (IBR), of crime control,
      307–308
Indirect costs, of crime, 64, 222–224
Informants, 7
  arrests caused by, 174, 175, 176, 195
  selective incapacitation and, 241, 244, 266
Infrequent offenders: *see* Low-rate offenders
INSLAW prosecution scale, 231, 232, 257,
      258, 272
Insurance fraud, 90
Intensive offenders, 84
Intensive supervision probation (ISP), 244,
      305, 306–307, 310
Interception patrol, 173, 176
Intermediate sanctions, 304–310, 311
Intermittent offenders, 84
Internal quality, of offense rate surveys, 45–
      47
International Association of Chiefs of Police,
      102
Investigations: *see* Follow-up investigations
Iowa Assessment Scale, 231, 232
Iron law of income, 111
ISP: *see* Intensive supervision probation

Jacksonville, Florida, 36
Jobs: *see* Employment
Joyriders, 25
Judges, 195
  criminal career and, 139
  least cost alternative and, 308

Judges *(Cont.)*
  selective incapacitation and, 230, 233, 234,
      235, 236, 239, 262, 264, 266, 270
Jury awards, 106, 222
Just-deserts model, 11, 55
  offense rates and, 101
  selective incapacitation and, 231, 259, 261–
      262
  See also Modified just-deserts model
Juvenile offenders, 23, 57
  arrests of, 48, 178–179
  collective incapacitation of, 199, 200, 211,
      213, 216
  convictions of, 48
  criminal career of, 39, 130, 136
  offense rates for, 59–60, 67, 68, 102

Kalamazoo, Michigan, 281
Kansas City Police Department, 279–280, 281
Knowledge constraints, 237, 244–245, 246,
      247, 252, 264, 286, 289, 311
  on control parameters, 275–277, 279
  on optimal selective policies, 253, 271
  on selective scales, 256

Lambda: *see* Offense rate
Larceny, 18
  arrests for, 49, 171
  collective incapacitation for, 210
  cost of, 223
  incarceration probability for, 36
  offense rates for, 60, 80, 105, 111
  sentences for, 38, 39
  weighted samples on, 36, 38, 39
Law of Proportionate Effect, 89
Least cost alternative, 307–310
Least restrictive alternative, 10
Level of aspiration, 300–301
Limited information: *see* Imperfect information
Lineups, 174
Location-oriented patrol: *see* Stakeouts
LogNormal distributions
  of arrest rates, 181, 184
  of criminal career, 159–160, 162
  of offense rates, 80, 91, 92, 111, 113–114,
      115, 117, 118, 119, 120, 121, 123–
      124, 159–160, 162, 204, 205, 212,
      213, 218
Lorenz curve of offense rates, 82–83, 84, 86,
      87, 109, 121

Lorenz curve of offense rates (*Cont.*)
  collective incapacitation and, 204, 205
  selective incapacitation and, 218
Los Angeles County, California, 306
Louisiana, 281
Low-rate offenders, 23, 292
  arrests of, 17, 18, 175, 189, 191, 192
  collective incapacitation of, 208, 209, 212
  criminal career of, 130, 154, 157, 158, 161,
    163, 164, 165
  information evaluation by, 300, 301
  information sources of, 295, 296–297, 299
  offense rates of, 55, 86–87, 91, 92–93, 97,
    98, 99, 105, 116, 163, 164, 165
  responsiveness of, 302–303
  selective incapacitation of, 232, 235, 236,
    239, 246, 260, 262, 263, 265
  specialization by, 105

Making Confinement Decisions (Zedlewski),
    12
MAPE: *see* Mean absolute percent error
Marginal offenders, 13, 14
Marital status, 93, 94
Markov processes, 103
Matching moments method, 52, 53
Mathematical models
  of collective incapacitation, 216
  of dropout rates, 150–154
  of offender and police learning, 180–183
  of offense rates, 109–124
Maximum likelihood methods, 53
Mean absolute percent error (MAPE), 213,
    214
Mean cost rating, 231
Medium-rate offenders, 292, 303
  collective incapacitation of, 208, 209, 212
  criminal career of, 154, 157, 158, 161, 163,
    164–165
  offense rates of, 93, 97, 98, 99, 116, 163,
    164–165
  selective incapacitation of, 232, 260
Method of operations (M.O.), 102, 176, 266
Michigan, 30
  arrests in, 35, 177
  criminal career in, 39, 137, 162, 163, 164
  incarceration probability in, 36, 37
  offense rates in, 12, 74, 77, 85, 105, 110,
    117, 118, 119, 120, 122, 163, 164
  selective incapacitation in, 281

Michigan (*Cont.*)
  specialization in, 105, 122
Military service, 65, 188, 194
Misdemeanor arrests, 282
Mitre Corporation survey, 281
M.O.: *see* Method of operations
Moderate-rate offenders: *see* Medium-rate
    offenders
Modified just-deserts model, 259, 263, 264,
    265, 286–287, 289, 311
Monte Carlo experiments, 115–116
Motive, 87, 90, 91, 92, 100
Mug books, 174
Multiple offender crimes
  collective incapacitation for, 199, 220–221,
    224
  offense rates for, 59–61, 62
Multiple regressions, 187, 245
Murder: *see* Homicide

National Crime Survey, 59, 60
Nebraska, 46–47, 77
Negative binomial distributions, of offense
    rates, 112
New Orleans, Louisiana, 281
Newton-Raphson method, 115
New York City, 71, 224
Nonrandom response errors, in arrest rate esti-
    mates, 186
Normal distributions
  of arrest rates, 181
  of offense rates, 52, 53, 88, 89, 90, 113,
    114, 123–124, 204

Occasional property offenders, 127
Occupational and corporate offenders, 127
Offender learning
  arrests and, 175–192, 193, 195
    prior research on, 176–180
    tests of, 180–187
  selective incapacitation and, 218, 219, 283–
    284, 285
Offender multipliers, 180
Offender population, 66–68, 69–79, 292–304
  critical importance of, 69–70
  information evaluation by, 299–301
  information sources of, 294–299
  responsiveness of, 301–304
  selective incapacitation of, 250–252, 268,
    269, 283, 292–294, 311

Offender population (*Cont.*)
  See also Arrestee population
Offense rates, 55–124, 292, 294
  arrests and, 44, 72, 73, 81–84, 167, 192, 193, 249, 291
  average value of, 69–79
  as benefit-cost ratio, 56–62, 67, 68, 79
  collective incapacitation and, 48, 55, 98, 109, 200, 201, 202, 204–205, 208–209, 210–211, 212, 213, 214, 215, 217, 220–221
  criminal career and, 19, 66, 72, 91, 92, 125, 128, 141, 208–209, 214, 249
    dropout in, 156–165
  distribution of: *see* Distributions
  of generalists, 101, 104, 105–107, 108–109, 120, 121–123
  heterogeneous, 200, 203–206, 216, 220
  incarceration risks and, 295
  mathematical models of, 109–124
  as measure of risk, 62
  measuring of, 63–68
  partial incapacitation and, 307, 308, 310
  reanalysis of, 12–13
  selective incapacitation and, 48, 53, 55, 83, 86, 87, 96–97, 98, 99–101, 105, 106–107, 108–109, 111, 116, 218, 231, 232, 248, 249, 262–263, 269, 281, 293
  selective sentences and, 15, 98, 109
  sentences and, 37, 38, 76, 78, 81, 93, 210–211
  of specialists, 100–109, 120, 121–123
  unadjusted, 59
  uncertainty about, 17, 18
  validity of, 18, 42–53, 65, 67
  weighted samples on, 23, 26, 30, 31–33, 34, 41, 74, 111–112, 215
Official records
  on offense rates, 47–49, 65, 70, 74
  on recidivism, 74
  validity of, 21, 47–49
  in weighted samples, 30
  See also Arrest records; Victim reports
Ohio, 281
Opportunity, 87–88, 90, 91, 92, 100
Optimal selective policies, 247, 252–256, 265, 273–274, 283, 290, 291, 292, 311
  compromise, 271, 272, 274, 275
  control parameter constraints and, 277

Optimal selective policies (*Cont.*)
  identification of, 268–271
  offender information on, 295–296
  sensitivity of, 271

Pareto distributions, of offense rates, 80, 111, 113, 114–116, 117, 118–119, 120, 124
Parole, 307
  crime reduction and, 167
  criminal career and, 157
  offense rates and, 78
  selective incapacitation and, 199, 245
Parole boards, 195
  criminal career and, 125, 139, 157
  offense rates and, 81
  selective incapacitation and, 230, 233, 234, 235, 236, 264, 266
Parole Commission scales, 232
Parole officers, 305
Partial incapacitation, 244, 304–310
Partial likelihood method, 245
Pattern analysis, 258
Pattern recognition methods, 245
Perfect information
  in offender population, 296
  optimal selective policies under, 253–255
  production under, 4–6, 7, 8
  selective incapacitation and, 99–100, 262–263, 293
Perpetrator-oriented patrol: *see* Surveillance
Persisters, 158–160, 161
  collective incapacitation of, 198, 211
  offense rates of, 84
  selective incapacitation of, 229, 231, 238
Personal crimes
  arrests for, 50, 169, 170, 171, 172, 186, 187, 188, 189, 190, 192–193
  collective incapacitation for, 209, 210
  criminal career and, 129, 135, 137, 139, 162, 163
  offense rates for, 53, 56, 59, 60, 79, 80, 86, 89, 96, 97, 100–109, 110, 113, 116, 117, 118–119, 120, 121–123, 163
  specialization in, 100–109, 120, 121–123
Personal robbery
  arrests for, 49
  offense rates in, 101

Philadelphia
  collective incapacitation in, 215
  offense rates in, 55, 67, 68, 71, 81, 82
Philadelphia cohort study, 55, 82
Physical evidence, 173, 176, 276
Pimping, 63
Plea bargaining, 244, 281
Poisson distributions, 296
  of offense rates, 112, 123–124
  in weighted samples, 26, 28
Police, 10, 44, 167, 168, 192–193, 194, 290,
      301, 303–304
  costs of, 3
  imperfect information and, 8
  specialization and, 102
  tactics used by, 173–175
  See also Police learning; Selective police ac-
      tion
Police Foundation study, 279
Police learning, 175–192, 193, 195
  prior research on, 176–180
  tests of, 180–187
Police multipliers, 180
Predictive scales: see Forward-looking scales
Preventive patrol: see Random preventive pa-
      trol
Price fixing, 126
Prison expansion, 311
  benefit-cost ratios of, 13, 14–15, 224–225,
      227, 229
  benefits of, 222–224
  collective incapacitation and, 221–227,
      283–284
  cost-effectiveness of, 19, 291
  costs of, 55, 70, 101, 221–222, 225–226
  direct benefits of, 264
  direct costs of, 224–225
  effectiveness of, 12–13, 14–15
  indirect benefits of, 224–227, 264–265,
      284–285
  offense rates and, 61
  selective incapacitation and, 229, 264–265,
      283–285
Probation, 13, 239, 296, 305, 310
  costs of, 308, 309
  criminal career and, 138
  intensive supervision, 244, 305, 306–307,
      310
Probation officers, 305, 307

Production
  of crime control, 4–10
  under imperfect information, 7–10
  under perfect information, 4–6, 7, 8
Production functions, 2, 239, 240–242, 246,
      250; see also Incarceration production
      functions
Production possibilities frontier, 4, 6, 8, 9,
      198–199, 218, 219–220, 229
Professional criminals, 127
PROMIS recordkeeping system, 37
Property crimes, 18
  arrests for, 49, 50, 169, 170, 171, 172,
      185–186, 187, 188, 189, 190, 193–
      194
  collective incapacitation for, 209, 210
  criminal career and, 129, 135, 137, 138,
      139, 162, 163, 164
  offense rates for, 53, 56, 59, 60, 75, 77,
      79, 80, 86, 89, 96, 100–109, 110,
      111, 113, 116, 118–119, 120–123,
      163, 164
  specialization in, 100–109, 120–123, 193
  See also Specialists
Proportionate random error hypothesis, 51
Prosecutors, 3, 8–9, 10, 290, 301, 303–304;
      see also Selective prosecution
Prospect-theory model, 300
Prostitution, 58
Pseudonyms, 71
Purse-snatches, 104

Quitters, 158–160

Race, 17, 18, 246, 257
Racine, Wisconsin, 67, 68
Random errors, in arrest rate estimates, 179,
      180, 183
Random measurement errors
  in arrest rate estimates, 186
  in offense rate estimates, 51, 53
Random noise, 73
Random preventive patrol, 173–174, 175,
      239, 242
Random proportionate change hypothesis, 93
Random sampling errors
  in offense rate estimates, 162
  in selective methods, 231

Rand survey, 12, 17, 18, 19, 216, 220
  on arrest rates, 129, 170, 171, 172, 175,
      177, 179, 180, 183, 185, 187
  on criminal career, 129, 132, 134,
      135–138, 142, 148–150, 152, 160–
      161, 162–164
  on offense rates, 42–44, 56, 65, 67, 69,
      75–76, 78, 160–161, 162–164, 211,
      215
    distribution of, 79, 81, 84, 88, 93, 100
    internal quality of, 45–47
    mathematical modeling of, 110, 111–113
    specialization and, 104, 105, 106, 107
  reanalysis of, 32, 44, 46, 56, 106, 136, 197
  on selective incapacitation, 231, 232
  weighted samples in, 18, 22–42, 111–112,
      135–136, 138, 171, 200, 215; see also
      Weighted samples
Rand 1 survey, 30, 31, 44, 47
Rand 2 survey, 30, 31, 32, 42, 44, 46, 47
Rape
  arrests for, 34
  collective incapacitation and, 198
  criminal career in, 135
  offense rates for, 60, 64
Rapid response, 173, 176
Reanalysis
  of dual-bias hypothesis, 49–52
  of incapacitation policies, 12–16
  of National Crime Survey, 59
  of Rand survey, 32, 44, 46, 56, 106, 136,
      197
Recidivism, 290
  chronic, 81, 82
  criminal career and, 72, 157
  offense rates and, 68, 72, 73–74, 81, 98
  partial incapacitation and, 305–306
  selective incapacitation and, 232
Recidivism scales, 98
Recruitment-replacement hypothesis, 57–59,
      64
Regression analysis, 37, 266
Rehabilitation, 1, 5, 6, 22, 25, 55, 307, 312
  collective incapacitation and, 200, 222
  criminal career and, 125, 151
  partial incapacitation and, 305
  selective incapacitation and, 239, 264
Relative-improvement-over-chance statistic,
      231

Reliability
  of arrest estimates, 185, 186, 187, 189–190
  of offense rate estimates, 45, 47–49
Renewal theory, 142
Repeat Offender Project (ROP), 280–281,
      282–283
Resource allocation, 62
  in selective incapacitation, 10, 229, 230,
      233–237, 268, 278, 286
Resource constraints, 237–244, 247, 264, 289
  on control parameters, 275–276
  on optimal selective policies, 252, 253
Resource levels, 9
Restitution, 239
Retributivism: see Just-deserts model
Risk-averse evaluations, 300
Risk-seeking evaluations, 300, 301
Risk-weighting functions, 300, 301
Robbery, 18, 302
  armed: see Armed robbery
  arrests for, 169, 170, 171, 172, 177, 185,
      193
  business: see Business robbery
  collective incapacitation for, 205, 210
  costs of, 223
  criminal career in, 135, 164–165
  generalists and, 105, 106, 107
  incarceration probability for, 36
  offense rates for, 33, 34, 57, 58–59, 60, 80,
      90, 96, 100, 104, 105, 106, 107, 108,
      109, 164–165
  personal: see Personal robbery
  selective incapacitation for, 238, 241, 242
  selective sentences for, 15, 16
  sentences for, 38, 39
  specialization in, 104, 108, 109
  street, 35
  weighted samples on, 33, 34, 36, 38, 39
Robust methods, 52, 113, 114, 118
ROP: see Repeat Offender Project

St. Petersburg, Florida, 241
Salaries: see Wages
Salient Factor Scores, 157, 258, 272
Sample bias, 21–22, 134, 135–136; see also
      Weighted samples
Sample frames, 22–30
Sample quantiles, 114
Sanction ratios, 235

San Diego, California, 36, 281, 284, 285
Selection methods, 230–232, 236, 246, 249,
    257, 311
Selection rates, 236, 246, 247, 248, 257, 296
    constraints on, 242, 259–264, 275, 276–
        277, 278–279, 280, 281, 282
    defined, 235
    incarceration length and, 249, 250
    incarceration production function and, 273–
        274
    incarceration risks and, 266
    optimal selective policies and, 253, 254–
        255, 256, 268, 269, 270, 271, 283,
        291
Selective deinstitutionalization, 260
Selective incapacitation, 2, 19, 79–80, 191,
    194–195, 198, 199, 229–288, 289,
    292–294
    arrests and: *see* Arrests
    crime elasticity and, 250
    criminal career and, 125, 140, 147, 154,
        156–157, 249, 271
    in current system, 218–220
    defined, 10
    effectiveness of, 248
    incarceration length and, 197, 247, 248–265
    incarceration probability and, 197, 247
    incarceration risks and, 265–286
    offender evaluation of, 301
    offender information on, 295–299
    offender responsiveness to, 302, 303
    offense rates and, 48, 53, 55, 83, 86, 87,
        96–97, 98, 99–101, 105, 106–107,
        108–109, 111, 116, 218, 231, 232,
        248, 249, 262–263, 269, 281, 293
    policy prescription for, 311–312
    uncertainty about, 16–18
    See also Constraints; Optimal selective poli-
        cies; Selective police action; Selective
        prosecution; Selective scales; Selective
        sentences
Selective Incapacitation (Greenwood), 12
Selective police action, 19, 286–288, 289, 311
    constraints on, 238, 239–240, 241–242,
        243, 245, 246, 247, 286
    incarceration length and, 250
    incarceration risks and, 265–285
    least cost alternative in, 309
    offender information on, 295, 296, 297, 299

Selective police action (*Cont.*)
    resource allocation in, 230, 233, 235, 236,
        268, 278
Selective prosecution, 19, 286–288, 289, 311
    arrests and, 191
    constraints on, 239, 240, 241, 243, 245,
        246, 247, 286
    crime control and, 167
    incarceration length and, 250
    incarceration risks and, 265–285
    least cost alternative in, 309
    offender information on, 295, 296, 297, 299
    resource allocation in, 230, 233, 235, 236,
        268
Selective scales, 244–245
    constraints on, 256–258, 259, 271–272
    incarceration length and, 250
Selective sentences, 19, 210, 245, 248, 265–
        266, 267–268, 283, 289, 293
    arrests and, 191, 195
    changes in, 286–288
    control parameter constraints on, 274, 276,
        278, 279
    criminal career and, 15–16, 142, 156
    effectiveness of, 11, 15–16
    ethical constraints on, 246
    incarceration length and, 251
    least cost alternative in, 309
    offender information on, 299
    offender learning and, 284, 285
    offense rates and, 15, 98, 109
    optimal selective policies and, 269–270,
        271
    resource allocation and, 233–235
    selective scales and, 271–272
Self-reports
    on arrests, 35, 47–52, 170, 171, 178–180,
        185
    on collective incapacitation, 213, 232
    on criminal career, 39, 134, 148, 149, 150
    on offense rates, 13, 42–43, 45, 47–49, 53,
        63, 65, 70, 74, 87, 232, 291
    validity of, 21–22, 42–43, 45, 47–49
Sellin-Wolfgang seriousness index, 64
Sensitivity analysis, 162
Sentences, 239, 290, 292, 294, 301
    average length of, 14
    collective incapacitation and, 201, 205, 209,
        210–211, 291

Sentences (*Cont.*)
  crime control and, 167
  criminal career and, 37, 38, 125, 138–140,
    141, 154, 156
  indeterminate, 281
  offender evaluation of, 300
  offender responsiveness to, 302, 304
  offense rates and, 37, 38, 76, 78, 81, 93,
    210–211
  selective incapacitation and: *see* Selective
    sentences
  suspended, 296
  weighted samples on, 28, 29, 30, 37–38
Sentencing Commission, U.S., 233
Serial murderers, 23
SEU model: *see* Subjectively expected utility
    model
Shoplifters, 25
Simpson's Rule, 204
Simulation models, 12, 56, 80, 108, 124
Skewed distributions
  of arrest rates, 49–50, 81–84, 181, 200
  of crime-control rates, 254
  of criminal career, 155, 200
  of offense rates, 56, 69, 79–80, 81–97,
    100, 113, 200, 204, 205, 212, 217,
    218, 220
    reasons for, 87–97
    selective incapacitation and, 232, 262–
      263, 269, 281
Social preference functions, 202–203
Special deterrence
  arrests and, 190–191
  collective incapacitation and, 200
  criminal career and, 165
Specialists, 17, 175
  arrests of, 193, 194
  collective incapacitation of, 205
  offense rates of, 100–109, 120, 121–123
Stakeouts, 173, 174, 175, 176, 241
  selective incapacitation and, 244, 279–280
Standard error of coefficients, for offense
    rates, 96
Standard error of estimates, for offense rates,
    94–96
Steady-state, of criminal career, 131, 132–133,
    134, 141, 145
Street crimes
  collective incapacitation for, 212

Street crimes (*Cont.*)
  offense rates for, 57–58
  selective incapacitation for, 237–238, 275,
    279
Street robbery, 35
Street time, 292, 296, 303
  arrests and, 191
  offense rates and, 31–32, 33, 44, 89
Subjectively expected utility (SEU) model,
    299–300
Sudden stresses, 151–152, 153
Surveillance, 10, 173, 174, 175, 176
  selective incapacitation and, 242, 244, 279–
    280
Survival analysis, 258
Suspended sentences, 296

Tax evasion, 90
Temporarily inactive offenders, 65–66
Tetrachoric r^2, 231, 232
Texas, 30
  arrests in, 35, 177, 190
  criminal career in, 39, 137, 162, 163,
    164
  incarceration probability in, 36, 37
  incoming cohort in, 42
  offense rates in, 12, 74, 77, 85, 96, 104–
    105, 117, 118, 119, 120, 122, 163,
    164
  sentences in, 39
  specialization in, 104–105, 122
Theft
  arrests for, 35, 170
  generalists and, 105, 106
  offense rates for, 64, 100, 101, 105,
    106
  specialization in, 101
  See also Auto theft
Time-scale factors, in offense rates, 63, 65–66
Time-series analysis
  of arrests, 143, 144
  of crime control, 226
  of offense rates, 91–97
Translog functions, 250, 266
2-Year window
  arrests in, 183, 191
  offense rates in, 88, 93, 116, 124
  See also Window 1; Window 2; Window 3
Type-2 errors, 97

Unadjusted offense rates, 59
Uncertainty
    about selective incapacitation, 16–18
    decision making under, 299–300
Unemployment, 246, 258, 307
Univariate distributions, of offense rates, 113,
        116–119, 120, 123–124
Unweighted samples, 39, 40–42, 111–112

Validity, 21–53
    of offense rates, 18, 42–53, 65, 67
    See also Weighted samples
Value functions, 300, 301
Vandalism, 63
Variable costs, 276
Ventura County, California, 306, 309
Vertical prosecution, 244, 275
Vicarious victimization, 223
Victimless crimes, 63
Victim reports, 59–60, 64, 169, 211, 222
Victims, 305
    arrests caused by, 174, 175, 176
    costs to, 2–3, 222, 285
    selective incapacitation and, 276, 285, 288
Violent offenders, 18
    collective incapacitation of, 211
    generalists as, 105–106
    offense rates of, 59, 64, 75, 77
    women as, 19
    See also Dangerous offenders
Violent personal criminals, 127

Wages, 89, 194
Warrant service, 280, 281
Washington, D.C.
    arrests in, 129, 168, 170, 171
    collective incapacitation in, 215
    criminal career in, 129, 135, 136, 138, 142,
        144, 153–154
    offense rates in, 71, 72

Washington, D.C. (*Cont.*)
    selective incapacitation in, 280–281, 282–
        283, 284
Watts riots, 102
Weed-out function, 150–152, 153, 155, 156
Weibull distributions
    of collective incapacitation, 214
    of criminal career, 152, 153, 154, 208
Weighted samples, 18, 22–42, 200
    on arrests, 26, 30, 33–35, 171
    on criminal career, 23, 29, 30, 39, 41, 135–
        136, 138
    data for, 30–39
    deriving sample weights in, 39–42
    on offense rates, 23, 26, 30, 31–33, 34, 41,
        74, 111–112, 215
    sample frame in, 22–30
Weighted scales, 230
Welfare payments, 61, 101, 221, 307
White-collar crimes, 238
Whites, 194
Wichita, Kansas, 241
Wife-beating, 126, 238
Window 1
    arrests in, 34, 187
    criminal career in, 160–161, 162–163
    offense rates in, 45, 94, 162–163
Window 2
    arrests in, 34, 186, 188
    criminal career in, 160–161, 162–163
    offense rates in, 45, 94, 162–163
Window 3
    arrests in, 34, 187, 188
    criminal career in, 160, 161, 162, 163
    offense rates in, 31, 32, 45, 94, 162, 163
Winsorizing, 52, 75–76, 77, 78
Wire taps, 275
Wisconsin, 67, 68, 78
Witnesses, 173, 174, 175, 176, 241, 276
Women, 19